Study Guide
to accompany

FINANCIAL ACCOUNTING
TOOLS FOR BUSINESS DECISION-MAKING

Fifth Canadian Edition

Paul D. Kimmel Ph.D., CPA
University of Wisconsin–Milwaukee, Wisconsin

Jerry K. Weygandt Ph.D., CPA
University of Wisconsin–Madison, Wisconsin

Donald E. Kieso Ph.D., CPA
Northern Illinois University, DeKalb, Illinois

Barbara Trenholm MBA, FCA
University of New Brunswick, Fredericton, New Brunswick

Wayne Irvine BComm, CFA, CA
University of Calgary, Alberta

PREPARED BY:

Michelle Lum MBA, CA
Wilfrid Laurier University, Waterloo, Ontario

John Wiley & Sons Canada, Ltd.

Copyright © 2012 John Wiley & Sons Canada, Ltd.

All rights reserved. No part of this work covered by the copyrights herein may be reproduced, transmitted, or used in any form or by any means—graphic, electronic, or mechanical—without the prior written permission of the publisher.

Any request for photocopying, recording, taping, or inclusion in information storage and retrieval systems of any part of this book shall be directed to the Canadian copyright licensing agency, Access Copyright. For an Access Copyright licence, visit www.accesscopyright.ca or call toll-free, 1-800-893-5777.

Care has been taken to trace ownership of copyright material contained in this text. The publishers will gladly receive any information that will enable them to rectify any erroneous reference or credit line in subsequent editions.

Library and Archives Canada Cataloguing in Publication

Lum, Michelle
 Study guide to accompany Financial accounting, tools for business decision-making, fifth Canadian edition / Michelle Lum.

Supplement to: Financial accounting.
ISBN 978-1-11802-450-8

 1. Accounting—Problems, exercises, etc.   I. Title.   II. Title: Financial accounting, tools for business decision-making, fifth Canadian edition.

HF5635.F44 2011 Suppl.   657'.044   C2011-903646-0

Production Credits
Acquisitions Editor: Zoë Craig
Vice President and Publisher: Veronica Visentin
Senior Marketing Manager: Aida Krneta
Editorial Manager: Karen Staudinger
Production Manager: Tegan Wallace
Developmental Editor: Sara Tinteri
Design: Laserwords Private Limited, Chennai, India
Typesetting: Thomson Digital
Cover Design: Tegan Wallace
Cover Photo: © Michael Christopher Brown/Corbis
Printing: Friesens

Printed and bound in Canada
1 2 3 4 5 FP 16 15 14 13 12

John Wiley & Sons Canada, Ltd.
6045 Freemont Blvd.
Mississauga, Ontario L5R 4J3

Contents

Chapter 1	The Purpose and Use of Financial Statements	1
Chapter 2	A Further Look at Financial Statements	15
Chapter 3	The Accounting Information System	33
Chapter 4	Accrual Accounting Concepts	51
Chapter 5	Merchandising Operations	71
Chapter 6	Reporting and Analyzing Inventory	95
Chapter 7	Internal Control and Cash	115
Chapter 8	Reporting and Analyzing Receivables	131
Chapter 9	Reporting and Analyzing Long-Lived Assets	151
Chapter 10	Reporting and Analyzing Liabilities	177
Chapter 11	Reporting and Analyzing Shareholders' Equity	203
Chapter 12	Reporting and Analyzing Investments	225
Chapter 13	Statement of Cash Flows	247
Chapter 14	Performance Measurement	265

APPENDICES

Appendix A	Financial Statements of HMV Group plc	283
Appendix B	Financial Statements of WHSmith PLC	300

chapter 1

The Purpose and Use of Financial Statements

Chapter Overview

Chapter 1 introduces you to a variety of financial accounting topics. You will learn about users and uses of accounting information, and the importance of ethical behaviour in the preparation of accounting information. You will then learn about the primary forms of business organization, the three main types of business activity, and the basic financial statements that are used to communicate accounting information to users.

Review of Specific Study Objectives

Users and Uses of Financial Statements

Accounting is the information system that identifies and records the economic events of an organization, and then communicates them to a wide variety of interested users. Efficient operation of the world's economic systems requires highly transparent, relevant, and reliable reporting of accounting and financial information for use by users in making their business decisions.

study objective 1
Identify the users and uses of accounting.

Two broad types of users are internal users and external users:

- **Internal users** are the people who work for the company, including managers who plan, organize, and run the company. Accounting information helps answer

2 Study Guide to Accompany Financial Accounting: Tools for Business Decision-Making, Fifth Canadian Edition

questions such as, "Does the company have enough resources to build a new manufacturing plant?" Internal reports help provide the information required to make an informed decision.

- **External users** work outside of the company and include investors (who use accounting information to decide whether to buy, hold, or sell shares in the company); lenders and other creditors (who use accounting information to evaluate the risk of lending to the company); tax authorities (who use accounting information to review the company's compliance with tax laws); regulators (who use accounting information to review the company's compliance with prescribed rules); customers; labour unions; and economic planners.

In order for accounting and financial information to be useful to both internal and external users, the information must be prepared by individuals with high standards of ethical behaviour.

Accountants and other financial professionals adhere to extensive rules of ethical conduct to guide their behaviour and preparation of accounting and financial information. Ethics in accounting is of utmost importance because users require credible accounting information in order to make informed business decisions. An external user, for example, may use accounting information to decide whether or not to invest in the company and an internal user may use accounting information to decide whether or not to expand the company.

Forms of Business Organization

study objective 2
Describe the primary forms of business organization.

There are three different forms of business organization. They are as follows:

- A **proprietorship** is a business owned by one person. It is simple to set up, and the owner has control over the business. Because they are so simple to organize, there are many thousands of proprietorships operating in the business world.

- A **partnership** is a business owned by more than one person. It provides strength in numbers: each partner may bring economic resources or unique talents or skills to the business.

- A **corporation** is a separate legal entity owned by shareholders who have shares in the corporation. Because a corporation is a separate legal entity, its shareholders have limited liability (its shareholders are not responsible for the corporation's debts unless they have personally guaranteed them). The corporation may issue and sell more of the corporation's shares to raise additional funds for the company.

  - The shares of a **public corporation** or **publicly traded corporation** are traded (bought or sold) on an organized, public stock exchange.
  - The shares of a **private corporation** are not traded on an organized, public stock exchange, and are not available for purchase by the general public.
  - In Canada, public corporations must apply **International Financial Reporting Standards (IFRS)** in preparing their financial statements, whereas private corporations have a choice between applying **IFRS** or **Accounting Standards for Private Enterprises (ASPE)** in preparing their financial statements.

CHAPTER 1   The Purpose and Use of Financial Statements   3

Types of Business Activity

There are **three types of business activity** that the accounting information system tracks: financing, investing, and operating.

> **study objective 3**
>
> Explain the three main types of business activity.

- **Financing activities** relate to raising funds for the corporation from sources external to the corporation. The **two primary external sources of funds** are borrowing money and issuing shares.

  - A company may **borrow money** by taking out a loan at a bank or by borrowing money from other lenders (for example, bondholders who have purchased the corporation's bonds). A **creditor** is a person or entity to whom the company owes money. A **liability** is a debt or other obligation, and represents a creditor's claim on the company. A creditor has a legal right to be paid at an agreed-upon time, whereas a shareholder has no legal right to the corporation's resources until all of its creditors are paid. There are **short-term liabilities** such as bank indebtedness and short-term loans (notes) payable, which may result from direct borrowing or purchasing on credit. There are also **long-term liabilities** such as notes payable, mortgages payable, finance lease obligations, and bonds payable, which are borrowed for longer periods of time.
  - A corporation may also **issue shares** to investors. Share capital represents the total amount paid into the corporation by shareholders for shares issued or sold. Common shares and preferred shares are two types or classes of shares that a corporation can issue. A shareholder is an owner of the corporation and may receive payments in the form of dividends. Some corporations, however, do not pay any dividends to shareholders as they are not legally required to do so. As noted above, shareholder claims are secondary to creditor claims.
  - Companies can also use cash for financing activities, such as repaying debt or repurchasing shares from investors.

- **Investing activities** involve the purchase (or sale) of long-lived resources, called **assets**, which a company needs in order to operate. Examples of assets are long-term investments and property, plant, and equipment, such as land, buildings, and vehicles. Cash is another example of an asset that is often used for financing and investing activities.

- **Operating activities** relate to sales of products or services in the normal course of business. Different companies have different operating activities. A paper company produces and sells paper; a dairy company produces and sells milk; and an accounting firm provides accounting, audit, tax, and business advisory services. As a company operates, it earns revenues.

  - **Revenues** are increases in economic resources—normally increases in assets, but sometimes decreases in liabilities—that result from the company's operating activities.
  - **Expenses** are the costs of assets consumed, or services used, in the process of generating revenues.
  - If revenues exceed expenses, a company reports a **profit** (also called net income or net earnings). If expenses exceed revenues, a company reports a **loss** (also called net loss).

4 Study Guide to Accompany Financial Accounting: Tools for Business Decision-Making, Fifth Canadian Edition

Content and Purpose of Financial Statements

study objective 4

Describe the content and purpose of each of the financial statements.

Users of financial information are interested in a company's assets, liabilities, owners' equity (shareholders' equity for a corporation), revenues, and expenses. This financial **information is provided in the form of financial statements**, which form the backbone of financial accounting. There are four basic financial statements: the income statement (also called the statement of earnings), the statement of changes in equity, the statement of financial position (also called the balance sheet), and the statement of cash flows.

- The **income statement** reports revenues and expenses to show how successfully the company has performed during a period of time. Only **revenues and expenses**—and the difference between revenues and expenses (profit or loss)—appear on the income statement. Note that the "Cash" account does not belong on the income statement because cash is an asset (a resource owned by the company). Also note that **issuance of shares and distribution of dividends do not affect the company's profit**.

- The **statement of changes in equity** shows the amounts and causes of changes in total shareholders' equity for the period, as well as the changes in each component of shareholders' equity (including share capital and retained earnings) during the period.

  - The column in the statement of changes in equity that shows the **change in share capital** will show the beginning balance of share capital, plus any increase in share capital due to new shares issued, less any decrease in share capital due to shares repurchased by the company, to arrive at ending share capital.
  - The column in the statement of changes in equity that shows the **change in retained earnings** will show profit (loss) added to (deducted from) beginning retained earnings, and deduction of dividends, to arrive at ending retained earnings. (Remember that a company will have either a profit or a loss; it cannot have both at the same time.) The retained earnings balance at any balance sheet date represents cumulative profit that has been earned by the company and not paid out in the form of dividends.

Private companies following ASPE prepare a statement of retained earnings rather than a statement of changes in equity. The statement of retained earnings summarizes only the change in retained earnings during the period.

- The **statement of financial position** reports assets and claims to those assets at a specific point in time. There are **two types of claims**: claims of creditors (liabilities) and claims of shareholders. The statement of financial position is an expanded expression of the **basic accounting equation**, which is as follows:

$$\text{Assets} = \text{Liabilities} + \text{Shareholders' Equity}$$

Please note that this is a mathematical equation and must be in balance at all times. It can be used to answer questions such as: If assets total $100 and liabilities total $20, what is total shareholders' equity? (Answer: $80, because $20 plus something must equal $100, and that something must be $80.)

- The **statement of cash flows** provides financial information about a company's cash receipts and cash payments for a specific period of time. Here, a user will find information about the company's financing, investing, and operating activities.

- Note the **interrelationships between statements**:

  1. Profit or loss from the income statement appears on the statement of changes in equity.

CHAPTER 1 The Purpose and Use of Financial Statements   5

2. The ending balances of share capital and retained earnings on the statement of changes in equity are the same numbers reported in the shareholders' equity section of the statement of financial position for share capital and retained earnings.
3. The ending balance of cash on the statement of cash flows is the same number reported on the statement of financial position for cash.

Because of the interrelationships between the financial statements, financial statements must be prepared in a certain order: (1) income statement, (2) statement of changes in equity, (3) statement of financial position, and (4) statement of cash flows.

- Companies usually present **comparative financial statements**, which show financial statements for more than one period, normally two years.

- Please be aware of the following when you **prepare financial statements**:
  1. All statements **must have a heading**. The company name appears on the first line, the name of the financial statement appears on the second line, and the date appears on the third line. With respect to **dates**, the **statement of financial position date** is at a point in time (such as June 30, 2012, or December 31, 2012), while the **date on the income statement, statement of changes in equity, and statement of cash flows** is for a period of time (such as "Month ended June 30, 2012" or "Year ended December 31, 2012").
  2. The number at the top of a column in a financial statement should be shown with a dollar sign to indicate that it is the first number in the column. The final number in a financial statement, such as Profit or Total Assets, should also be shown with a dollar sign and should be double-underlined to indicate that it is a final total. If there is a negative number, such as a Loss, then it should be presented in parentheses or brackets. These are conventions applied by preparers of financial statements and understood by users of financial statements.
  3. Numbers are often reported in thousands (or millions) of dollars and, as a result, the last three (or six) digits are often omitted from the financial statement amounts that are presented.

- Recall that in Canada, public corporations must apply **IFRS** in preparing their financial statements, whereas private corporations have a choice between applying **IFRS** or **ASPE** in preparing their financial statements. Below is a comparison of IFRS and ASPE, for key topics discussed in Chapter 1:

comparing
IFRS and ASPE

Key Differences	International Financial Reporting Standards (IFRS)	Accounting Standards for Private Enterprises (ASPE)
Accounting standards	Publicly traded corporations must use IFRS; private corporations can choose to use IFRS or ASPE.	Private corporations can choose to use IFRS or ASPE. Once the choice is made, it must be applied consistently
Terminology	The balance sheet is more commonly known as the statement of fi nancial position and net income as profi t under IFRS.	The statement of fi nancial position is more commonly known as the balance sheet and profi t as net income under ASPE.
Statement of changes in equity vs. statement of retained earnings	A statement of changes in equity must be pre-sented that shows the changes in all components of shareholders' equity (e.g., share capital and retained earnings).	A statement of retained earnings is pre-sented that shows the change in only one component—retained earnings—of share-holders' equity.

Study Guide to Accompany Financial Accounting: Tools for Business Decision-Making, Fifth Canadian Edition

Chapter Self-Test

As you work through questions and problems, remember to use the **Decision Toolkit** discussed and used in the text:

1. *Decision Checkpoints*: Ask a question relevant to the decision being made.
2. *Info Needed for Decision*: Make a choice regarding the information needed to answer the question.
3. *Tools to Use for Decision*: Review what the information identified in step 2 does for the decision-making process.
4. *How to Evaluate Results*: Identify specifically how the information identified in step 2 should be evaluated to answer the question relevant to the decision being made.

Note: The notation "(SO 1)" means that the question relates to study objective 1.

Multiple Choice

Please circle the correct answer.

(SO 1)
1. Which of the following would not be considered an internal user of accounting data for a particular company?
   a. Marketing manager
   b. Investor
   c. Accounting clerk
   d. Engineering supervisor

(SO 1)
2. Which one of the following groups uses accounting information to determine whether the company's profit will result in a share price increase?
   a. Investors
   b. Auditors
   c. Creditors
   d. Production managers

(SO 1)
3. For financial statements to be useful to users, preparers of financial statements must have high standards of ethical behaviour. Which of the following steps should be considered when analyzing ethical situations?
   a. Recognize the ethical situation and the ethical issues involved.
   b. Identify and analyze the main elements in the situation, including the stakeholders involved.
   c. Identify the alternatives, weigh the impact of each alternative on various stakeholders, and select the most ethical alternative.
   d. All of the above.

(SO 2)
4. Which of the following statements is correct?
   a. A proprietor has no personal liability for debts of his or her business.
   b. There are far more corporations than there are proprietorships and partnerships.
   c. Revenue produced by corporations is generally greater than that produced by proprietorships and partnerships.
   d. It is very difficult for a corporation to raise capital.

CHAPTER 1   The Purpose and Use of Financial Statements   7

5. A business organized as a corporation   (SO 2)
   a.   is not a separate legal entity in most provinces.
   b.   requires that shareholders be personally liable for the debts of the
         business.
   c.   is not owned by its shareholders.
   d.   has an indefinite life.

6. Sale of a delivery truck previously used in the company's operations is an   (SO 3)
   example of a(n)
   a.   financing activity.
   b.   delivering activity.
   c.   operating activity.
   d.   investing activity.

7. Which of the following activities involves raising the necessary funds to support   (SO 3)
   the company?
   a.   Operating
   b.   Investing
   c.   Financing
   d.   Delivering

8. Which of the following activities involves putting company resources into action   (SO 3)
   to generate a profit?
   a.   Delivering
   b.   Financing
   c.   Investing
   d.   Operating

9. Use of funds generated from the company's operations to repay debt is an   (SO 3)
   example of a(n)
   a.   operating activity.
   b.   investing activity.
   c.   financing activity.
   d.   income activity.

10. A company's earning of revenues is an example of a(n)   (SO 3)
    a.   operating activity.
    b.   investing activity.
    c.   financing activity.
    d.   statement of financial position activity.

11. Payment of accounts payable (amounts owed to suppliers for materials and   (SO 3)
    supplies purchased on credit) is an example of a(n)
    a.   operating activity.
    b.   investing activity.
    c.   financing activity.
    d.   statement of financial position activity.

8   Study Guide to Accompany Financial Accounting: Tools for Business Decision-Making, Fifth Canadian Edition

(SO 4)   12.   Which of the following accounts would be found on an income statement?
a.   Revenues, salary expense, and dividends
b.   Revenues and salary expense
c.   Revenues, salary expense, and cash
d.   Salary expense, dividends, and cash

(SO 4)   13.   If revenues are $20,000 and expenses are $5,000, then the company
a.   had a loss of $25,000.
b.   had a profit of $20,000.
c.   had a profit of $15,000.
d.   had a loss of $15,000.

(SO 4)   14.   If beginning retained earnings is $10,000, the loss is $3,000, and dividends are $1,000, then ending retained earnings shown on the statement of changes in equity and statement of financial position is
a. $14,000.
b. $12,000.
c. $8,000.
d. $6,000.

(SO 4)   15.   Which of the following is an appropriate date for a statement of financial position?
a.   December 31, 2012
b.   Month ending December 31, 2012
c.   Quarter ending December 31, 2012
d.   Year ending December 31, 2012

(SO 4)   16.   Which of the following is the correct expression of the basic accounting equation?
a.   Liabilities = Assets + Shareholders' Equity
b.   Shareholders' Equity = Assets + Liabilities
c.   Assets = Liabilities + Shareholders' Equity
d.   Assets = Liabilities − Shareholders' Equity

(SO 4)   17.   Assets total $20,000, common shares total $9,000, and retained earnings total $6,000. What is the dollar amount of liabilities?
a. $23,000
b. $17,000
c. $11,000
d. $5,000

(SO 4)   18.   The statement that shows the operating, investing, and financing activities of a company is the
a.   statement of changes in equity.
b.   statement of cash flows.
c.   income statement.
d.   statement of financial position.

(SO 4)   19.   At the end of 2011, a company had total assets of $100,000 and total shareholders' equity of $60,000. During 2012, the same company had profit of $15,000, and at

CHAPTER 1   The Purpose and Use of Financial Statements   9

the end of 2012 the company had total assets of $120,000. Assuming no dividends
were paid in 2012, total liabilities at the end of 2012
   a.   increased by $5,000.
   b.   had a balance of $60,000.
   c.   decreased by $15,000.
   d.   had a balance of $75,000.

20.   Payment of a $7,000 dividend   (SO 4)
      a.   decreases profit by $7,000.
      b.   increases net cash used by investing activities by $7,000.
      c.   decreases retained earnings and total shareholders' equity by $7,000.
      d.   decreases share capital and total shareholders' equity by $7,000.

Problems

1.   Classify each of the following items first as a financing, investing, or   (SO 3)
      operating activity, and then indicate whether the transaction increases or
      decreases cash.

      a.   Inventory is purchased for cash.
      b.   A company sells services for cash.
      c.   A company buys equipment for cash.
      d.   Dividends are paid to shareholders.
      e.   A company sells equipment for cash.
      f.   Employees are paid.
      g.   A company borrows money from the bank.
      h.   A company issues shares.
      i.   A company repays a loan.

2.   Using the accounts given below, prepare a statement of financial position for   (SO 4)
      Jerome Corporation on September 30, 2012:

Common shares	$15,000
Bank loan payable	5,000
Accounts receivable	7,000
Unearned revenue	6,000
Retained earnings	24,000
Supplies	2,000
Prepaid insurance	3,000
Office equipment	17,000
Accounts payable	1,000
Cash	22,000

3.   Use the following accounts and information to prepare, in good form,   (SO 4)
      an income statement, a statement of changes in equity, and a statement

10 **Study Guide to Accompany Financial Accounting: Tools for Business Decision-Making, Fifth Canadian Edition**

of financial position for Azro Corporation for the month ended September 30, 2012.

Maintenance expense	$ 2,400
Accounts receivable	1,400
Office buildings	60,000
Supplies	400
Revenues	16,100
Common shares	52,000
Retained earnings (beginning)	18,900
Dividends	1,000
Insurance expense	2,200
Cash	15,600
Notes payable	3,300
Accounts payable	3,100
Salaries expense	10,000
Income tax expense	400

(SO 4) 4. Refer to the HMV and WHSmith financial statements found in the appendices at the end of this study guide for information in answering the following questions. Do not forget to use the **Decision Toolkit** approach for help in answering the questions.

 a. For HMV and WHSmith, what is the total amount of each company's classes of assets in 2010?

 b. For HMV and WHSmith, which class of liabilities has the largest total dollar amount in 2010?

 c. Were the companies profitable in 2010? What has been the trend of each company's profit over the two years shown?

 d. What was the biggest expense in 2010 for each of the companies?

Solutions to Self-Test

Multiple Choice

1. b The investor would not be considered an internal user.

2. a Accounting information is the major source of information that investors use to assess whether the company's profits will result in a share price increase.

3. d Identification and analysis of the ethical situation and selection of the most ethical alternative are key steps used in analyzing ethical situations.

4. c Proprietors are liable for debts of their businesses, there are more proprietorships and partnerships than there are corporations, and corporations can raise capital through selling of shares and bonds.

5. d Corporations are legal entities, corporations do not require shareholders to be personally responsible for debts of the business, and corporations are owned by their shareholders.

6. d Sale of a long-lived asset, such as a delivery truck, is an investing activity.

CHAPTER 1   The Purpose and Use of Financial Statements   11

7. c   Raising of funds is a financing activity.

8. d   The day-to-day operations that put company resources into action to generate a profit are called operating activities.

9. c   Use of cash to repay debt is a financing activity.

10. a   Generating revenues (and incurring expenses related to those revenues) in the normal course of business is considered an operating activity.

11. a   Payment of accounts payable is an operating activity.

12. b   Dividends appear on the statement of changes in equity, and cash is an asset on the statement of financial position.

13. c $20,000 - $5,000 = $15,000

14. d $10,000 - $3,000 - $1,000 = $6,000

15. a   The statement of financial position shows balances at a specific point in time, not for a period of time.

16. c   Answer c is the correct expression of the basic accounting equation.

17. d   Assets = Liabilities + Shareholders' Equity

Total Shareholders' Equity = Common Shares + Retained Earnings. ($9,000 + $6,000 = $15,000). Therefore, Assets − Shareholders' Equity = Liabilities ($20,000 − $15,000 = $5,000).

18. b   The statement of changes in equity shows changes in share capital and retained earnings during the period, the income statement summarizes revenue and expense activity during the period, and the statement of financial position shows assets, liabilities, and shareholders' equity items at a specific point in time.

19. a   Using the accounting equation A = L + SE, at the end of 2011, A of $100,000 − SE of $60,000 = L of $40,000. During 2012, profit would increase SE from $60,000 to $75,000 because profit would increase retained earnings, which is a component of SE. At the end of 2012, A of $120,000 − SE of $75,000 = L of $45,000. Therefore liabilities increased from $40,000 at the end of 2011 to $45,000 at the end of 2012, representing a $5,000 increase.

20. c   Payment of dividends does not affect the income statement. On the statement of cash flows under ASPE, payment of dividends is considered a financing activity. Under IFRS, payment of dividends is considered an operating or financing activity. Payment of dividends decreases retained earnings as reported on the statement of changes in equity. Ending retained earnings is included in and reported with total shareholders' equity on the statement of changes in equity and statement of financial position.

Problems

1.

a.   Operating activity; cash is decreased.
b.   Operating activity; cash is increased.
c.   Investing activity; cash is decreased.
d.   Financing activity under ASPE and operating or financing activity under IFRS; cash is decreased.

12   **Study Guide to Accompany Financial Accounting: Tools for Business Decision-Making, Fifth Canadian Edition**

    e.   Investing activity; cash is increased.
    f.   Operating activity; cash is decreased.
    g.   Financing activity; cash is increased.
    h.   Financing activity; cash is increased.
    i.   Financing activity; cash is decreased.

2.

JEROME CORPORATION
Statement of Financial Position
September 30, 2012
Assets

Cash		$22,000
Accounts receivable		7,000
Supplies		2,000
Prepaid insurance		3,000
Office equipment		17,000
Total assets		$51,000

Liabilities and Shareholders' Equity

Liabilities		
Accounts payable	$ 1,000	
Unearned revenue	6,000	
Bank loan payable	5,000	
Total liabilities		$12,000
Shareholders' equity		
Common shares	$15,000	
Retained earnings	24,000	
Total shareholders' equity		39,000
Total liabilities and shareholders' equity		$51,000

3.

AZRO CORPORATION
Income Statement
Month Ended September 30, 2012

Revenues		
Revenues		$16,100
Expenses		
Salaries expense	$10,000	
Maintenance expense	2,400	
Insurance expense	2,200	
Total expenses		14,600
Profit before income tax		1,500
Income tax expense		400
Profit		$ 1,100

CHAPTER 1 The Purpose and Use of Financial Statements   13

AZRO CORPORATION
Statement of Changes in Equity
Month Ended September 30, 2012

	Common Shares	Retained Earnings	Total Equity
Balance, September 1	$52,000	$18,900	$70,900
Profit		1,100	1,100
Dividends		(1,000)	(1,000)
Balance, September 30	$52,000	$19,000	$71,000

AZRO CORPORATION
Statement of Financial Position
September 30, 2012

Assets

Cash	$15,600
Accounts receivable	1,400
Supplies	400
Office buildings	60,000
Total assets	$77,400

Liabilities and Shareholders' Equity

Liabilities

Accounts payable	$ 3,100	
Notes payable	3,300	
Total liabilities		$ 6,400

Shareholders' equity

Common shares	$52,000	
Retained earnings	19,000	
Total shareholders' equity		71,000
Total liabilities and shareholders' equity		$77,400

4. Please note that the amounts shown for HMV and WHSmith are stated in pounds (£) millions.

a.

	HMV	WHSmith
Current assets	£360.1	£285
Non-current assets	345.3	228
Total assets	£705.4	£513

b. Current liabilities was the largest class of liabilities for each company, in the amounts of £551.5 for HMV and £300 for WHSmith.

c. HMV was profitable in 2010. It earned profit of £49.2 in 2010, which compares with profit of £44.2 in 2009. WHSmith was profitable in 2010. It earned profit of £69 in 2010, which compares with profit of £63 in 2009.

d. Cost of sales was the largest expense for both companies: £1,855.6 for HMV and £650 for WHSmith.

chapter 2

A Further Look at Financial Statements

Chapter Overview

Chapter 2 takes a further look at the statement of financial position and discusses ratio analysis using financial statements. The conceptual framework for the preparation and presentation of financial statements is also discussed.

Review of Specific Study Objectives

The Classified Statement of Financial Position (Balance Sheet)

- The **statement of financial position** (also called **balance sheet**) presents a snapshot of the company's financial position at a point in time. The **classified statement of financial position** groups asset, liability, and equity items into standard classifications. The classified statement of financial position provides readers with classification totals, which are very helpful in evaluating the company's financial position at the statement date, and performing related ratio analysis.

> **study objective 1**
>
> Identify the sections of a classified statement of financial position.

- Common asset classifications are as follows:

  1. **Current assets** are assets that are expected to be converted into cash, sold, or used within one year of the company's financial statement date or its operating cycle, whichever is longer. A merchandising company's operating cycle is the average time between purchasing of inventory and receiving of cash from the sale of inventory

to customers. Current assets may be listed in order of liquidity (commonly done by North American companies), or in reverse order of liquidity. A highly liquid asset is one that can be converted into cash very quickly; a listing of current assets in order of liquidity would list cash first, whereas a listing of current assets in reverse order of liquidity would list cash last. Current assets include **cash, short-term investments, accounts receivable, inventory, supplies, and prepaid expenses.**

2. **Non-current assets** are assets that are not expected to be converted into cash, sold, or completely used up within one year of the company's financial statement date or its operating cycle. Non-current assets include **long-term investments; property, plant, and equipment; intangible assets and goodwill; and other assets.**

a. **Long-term investments** include investments in shares and debt securities of other corporations that the company's management intends to hold for many years.

b. **Property, plant, and equipment** are tangible assets (assets with physical substance) that have relatively long useful lives and are currently being used in operating the business. Examples include **land, buildings, equipment,** and **furniture.** Most long-lived assets have limited useful lives during which they are expected to help generate revenues (except for land, which is considered to have an unlimited useful life). In a process called **depreciation**, the cost of each limited-life property, plant, and equipment asset is allocated to the future periods that represent the asset's estimated useful life. This process of depreciation requires recording each period's allocated cost of property, plant, and equipment as depreciation expense, which is a deduction from revenues in calculating profit. Therefore, each period, the process of depreciation matches the cost of property, plant, and equipment to the revenues they help earn. Accumulated depreciation is the cumulative amount of depreciation that has been recorded to date for a particular asset. A typical statement of financial position may show total cost and total accumulated depreciation for each asset group (e.g., buildings and improvements, fixtures and equipment, and leasehold improvements). Because accumulated depreciation represents cumulative consumption of each asset group, it is subtracted from the cost of the related asset group to arrive at the **carrying amount** (also called net book value or book value) of the asset group. Because accumulated depreciation is subtracted from the asset amount to arrive at the carrying amount, accumulated depreciation is considered a **contra asset** account.

c. **Intangible assets and goodwill** are assets that have no physical substance. **Intangible assets** represent a privilege or right granted to, or held by, a company. Examples of intangible assets include **patents, copyrights, franchises, trademarks, trade names, and licences** that give the company exclusive right of use for a specified period of time. Intangible assets with limited useful lives are amortized over their useful lives in a process called amortization, which is similar to the process of depreciation of property, plant, and equipment. **Goodwill** results from acquisition of another company for a price higher than the fair value of the purchased company's net identifiable assets. Goodwill is not amortized and is reported separately from other intangible assets. Companies using ASPE rather than IFRS tend to use one term— amortization—for both depreciation of property, plant, and equipment and amortization of intangible assets.

d. **Other assets** are assets that do not fit into any of the above asset categories, and include items such as non-current receivables, deferred income tax assets, and property held for sale.

CHAPTER 2 A Further Look at Financial Statements   17

- **Common liability classifications are as follows:**
  1. **Current liabilities** are obligations that are to be paid or settled within one year of the company's financial statement date or its operating cycle, whichever is longer. Current liabilities include **bank indebtedness, accounts payable, accrued liabilities** (such as salaries payable, interest payable, and income tax payable), **notes payable** (including bank loans payable), and **current maturities of non-current debt**. Current liabilities may be listed in the order in which they are expected to be paid (commonly done by North American companies), in reverse order of expected payment date, or in an alternative order according to company norm.
  2. **Non-current liabilities** are obligations that are expected to be paid beyond one year from the statement of financial position date. For example, if the statement of financial position date is December 31, 2010, and an obligation is due on January 31, 2012, the obligation is considered a non-current liability as at December 31, 2010. Non-current liabilities include **notes payable** (including bank loans payable, mortgages payable, and bonds payable), **lease obligations, pension and benefit obligations, and deferred income tax liabilities**.

- **Shareholders' equity** consists of at least two components: share capital and retained earnings. **Share capital** is capital invested in or contributed to the company by its shareholders; for example, common shares. **Retained earnings** is the cumulative profit that has been retained for use in the company. (Recall from Chapter 1 that retained earnings represents cumulative profit that has been earned by the company and not paid out in the form of dividends.) Shareholders' equity may contain other components, such as accumulated other comprehensive income, which will be discussed in later chapters.

- Companies that present their classified statement of financial position **in order of liquidity** will show current assets first (with assets listed in order of liquidity within the current assets category), followed by non-current assets, current liabilities (with liabilities listed in the order they are expected to be paid within the current liabilities category), non-current liabilities, and shareholders' equity. Companies that present their classified statement of financial position **in reverse order of liquidity** will show non-current assets first, followed by current assets (with assets listed in reverse order of liquidity within the current assets category), followed by shareholders' equity, non-current liabilities, and current liabilities (with liabilities listed in reverse order of expected payment date within the current liabilities category).

Using the Statement of Financial Position

- Financial statements are used to assess a company's financial health and performance. To make the numbers in financial statements more useful and meaningful, users conduct **ratio analysis**, which expresses the relationships between selected items of financial statement data.

- One ratio calculation by itself does not convey very much information. For more meaningful analysis, the ratio should be compared with benchmarks (e.g., ratios from prior years for the same company, ratios of a competitor in the same industry, or industry average ratios for particular industries).

> **study objective 2**
>
> Identify and calculate ratios for analyzing a company's liquidity, solvency, and profitability.

- **Liquidity** refers to a company's ability to pay obligations that are expected to become due within the next year.

  - One measure of liquidity is **working capital**, which is the difference between current assets and current liabilities. If current assets are $300 and current liabilities are $100, then working capital is $200. A company with a larger positive working capital has a greater likelihood of being able to pay upcoming liabilities. A company with a negative working capital may need to borrow money in order to pay upcoming liabilities.
  - Another measure of liquidity is **current ratio**, which is calculated by dividing current assets by current liabilities. If current assets are $300 and current liabilities are $100, then current ratio is 3:1, meaning that the company has $3 of current assets for every $1 of current liabilities. As mentioned earlier, a ratio by itself does not convey very much information. A company with a current ratio of 3:1 may still have difficulty paying upcoming liabilities if, for example, its current assets contain significant uncollectible accounts receivable or slow-moving inventory. When assessing a company's liquidity, additional ratios should be calculated and supplemented with deeper analysis of the composition of current assets and current liabilities. This will be discussed further in later chapters.

- **Solvency** refers to a company's ability to survive over a long period of time, to pay interest as it becomes due, and to repay the face value of debt at maturity.

  - The **debt to total assets ratio** is one source of information about a company's solvency. It measures the percentage of assets financed by lenders and other creditors rather than by shareholders. It is calculated by dividing total liabilities (both current and non-current) by total assets. In general, a higher debt to total assets ratio means there is a greater risk that the company will not be able to pay its debts as they mature. If total liabilities are $3 million and total assets are $5 million, then the debt to total assets ratio is 60%, meaning that for every dollar invested in company assets, creditors and other lenders have provided $0.60.

Using the Income Statement

- **Profitability ratios** measure a company's operating success (or failure) for a specific period of time. Two such ratios are **earnings per share** and **price-earnings ratio**.

- **Earnings per share** measures the profit earned per common share. It is calculated by dividing profit available to common shareholders by the weighted average number of common shares.

  - Note that under IFRS, earnings per share must be reported in the financial statements, but that under ASPE, earnings per share does not need to be reported in financial statements.

- The **price-earnings ratio** measures the market price per share relative to earnings per share. It is calculated by dividing market price per share by earnings per share. The price-earnings ratio will be higher if investors think that current profit levels will continue or increase (their expectations would be reflected in a higher market price per share).

CHAPTER 2 A Further Look at Financial Statements 19

Conceptual Framework for Financial Reporting

- The **conceptual framework** for financial reporting guides decisions about what to present in financial statements, alternative ways of reporting economic events, and appropriate ways of communicating this information. The conceptual framework for financial reporting has five main sections:

  1. Objective of financial reporting
  2. Qualitative characteristics of useful financial information
  3. Underlying assumption
  4. Elements of financial statements
  5. Measurement of the elements of financial statements

1. The **objective of financial reporting** is to provide financial information about a company that is useful to existing and potential investors, lenders, and other creditors in making decisions about providing resources to the company.

2. **Qualitative characteristics of useful financial information** are divided into **fundamental qualitative characteristics** and **enhancing qualitative characteristics**.

   a. **Fundamental qualitative characteristics** are essential qualitative characteristics that must be present in accounting information in order for the information to be useful for decision-making purposes. The two fundamental qualitative characteristics of accounting information are **relevance** and **faithful representation**.

      - Accounting information that is **relevant** will make a difference in users' decisions. Relevant information may have **predictive value** (in helping users make predictions about future events), **confirmatory or feedback value** (in helping users confirm or correct their previous predictions or expectations), or both. Accounting information is **material** if its omission or misstatement could influence the decisions of users. Therefore, materiality should be considered when determining the relevance of a piece of accounting information.

        It is important to note that an item that is material for one company may be immaterial for another company. For example, assume companies A and B each have a $1,000 error in their financial statements, and Company A's profit is $10,000, while company B's profit is $100,000. The $1,000 error is most likely material for Company A because the error is equivalent to 10% of its profit, while the $1,000 error is most likely immaterial for Company B because it is equivalent to only 1% of its profit.

      - Accounting information that is **faithfully represented** reflects the underlying economic reality of what really exists or happened, and is **complete**, **neutral** (not biased toward one stakeholder or another), and **free from material error**.

   b. **Enhancing qualitative characteristics** are characteristics that improve the usefulness of accounting information. The four enhancing qualitative characteristics of accounting information are **comparability**, **verifiability**, **timeliness**, and **understandability**.

> **study objective 3**
>
> Describe the framework for the preparation and presentation of financial statements.

- Accounting information that is **comparable** enables users to identify and understand similarities and differences among financial statement items both between companies (intercompany) and across years for the same company (intracompany). Accounting information that is **verifiable** is information that different knowledgeable and independent users would agree is faithfully represented. Accounting information that is **timely** is available to decision makers before it loses its ability to influence decisions. Accounting information that is **understandable** is classified, characterized, presented clearly and concisely, and understood by a reasonably informed user.

c. The **cost constraint** provides that the benefits of financial reporting information should justify the costs of providing and using it.

3. The **going concern assumption** is the underlying assumption in financial reporting, and assumes that a company will continue in operation for the foreseeable future. If a company is not assumed to be a going concern (and the company is not expected to continue in operation for the foreseeable future), then different assumptions would influence the preparation of financial statements. For example, certain assets may be reported at fair value or liquidation value.

4. **Elements of financial statements** are the items used to convey accounting information in financial statements. Elements of financial statements include **assets, liabilities, equity, income** (including revenue and gains), and **expenses** (including losses).

- An **asset** is a resource controlled by the company as a result of past events and from which future economic benefits are expected to flow to the company.
- A **liability** is a present obligation of the company arising from past events, the settlement of which is expected to result in an outflow from the company of resources embodying economic benefits.
- **Equity** is the residual interest in the company's assets after deducting all its liabilities.
- **Income** includes both revenue and gains. Revenue arises in the course of the company's ordinary activities while gains may or may not arise from ordinary activities.
- **Expenses** include both losses and expenses that arise from ordinary company activities. Losses may or may not arise from ordinary activities.

5. Two key **measurement principles of financial statement elements** include historical cost and fair value.

- The **historical cost basis of accounting** states that assets and liabilities should be recorded at their cost at the time of acquisition, and should remain reported at cost during the time that the asset or liability is held. In general, most assets are recorded at historical cost because the fair value of assets may not always be reliably determinable or faithfully representative.
- The **fair value basis of accounting** states that certain assets and liabilities should be recorded and reported at fair value (e.g., the price that would be received if an asset were sold today). Usually, fair value basis of accounting is applied to assets only if they have fair values that are easily verifiable and neutral. For example, assets that are actively traded, such as certain investment securities, are measured under the fair value basis of accounting.

CHAPTER 2 A Further Look at Financial Statements 21

The conceptual framework for financial reporting is summarized below:

Objective of Financial Reporting		

Qualitative Characteristics of Useful Financial Information		
Fundamental Qualitative Characteristics	Enhancing Qualitative Characteristics	Constraint

1. Relevance
  • Predictive value
  • Confirmatory value
  • Material
2. Faithful representation
  • Complete
  • Neutral
  • Free from material error
	1. Comparability
	2. Verifiability
	3. Timeliness
	4. Understandability
		1. Cost

Underlying Assumption—Going Concern	

Elements	Measurement of the Elements
1. Assets 2. Liabilities 3. Equity 4. Revenue 5. Expenses	1. Historical cost 2. Fair value

Recall that in Canada, public corporations must apply **IFRS** in preparing their financial statements, whereas private corporations have a choice between applying **IFRS** or **ASPE** in preparing their financial statements. Below is a comparison of IFRS and ASPE, for key topics discussed in Chapter 2:

comparing
IFRS and ASPE

Key Differences	International Financial Reporting Standards (IFRS)	Accounting Standards for Private Enterprises (ASPE)
Terminology	The term *depreciation* refers to the allocation of the cost of depreciable tangible assets over their useful lives. The term *amortization* refers to the allocation of the cost of certain kinds of intangible assets over their useful lives.	The term *amortization* is used for the allocation of the cost of both depreciable tangible assets and certain kinds of intangible assets over their useful lives.
Earnings per share	Required to present in financial statements	Not required to present in financial statements
Conceptual framework for financial reporting	Still under development	Same general framework currently under development by international and U.S. standard setters anticipated to be applied to private enterprises when complete

22 **Study Guide to Accompany Financial Accounting: Tools for Business Decision-Making, Fifth Canadian Edition**

Chapter Self-Test

As you work through questions and problems, remember to use the **Decision Toolkit** discussed and used in the text:

1. *Decision Checkpoints*: Ask a question relevant to the decision being made.
2. *Info Needed for Decision*: Make a choice regarding the information needed to answer the question.
3. *Tools to Use for Decision*: Review what the information identified in step 2 does for the decision-making process.
4. *How to Evaluate Results*: Identify specifically how the information identified in step 2 should be evaluated to answer the question relevant to the decision being made.

Note: The notation "(SO 1)" means that the question relates to study objective 1.

Multiple Choice

Please circle the correct answer.

(SO 1)   1. Which of the following statements reports the ending balance of the retained earnings account?
   a. Statement of changes in equity and statement of financial position
   b. Statement of changes in equity only
   c. Statement of financial position only
   d. Statement of cash flows only

(SO 1)   2. Which of the following is considered a current asset on a classified statement of financial position?
   a. Marketable securities
   b. Notes receivable, due in three years
   c. Building
   d. Patent

(SO 1)   3. Which of the following is included in property, plant, and equipment on a classified statement of financial position?
   a. Supplies
   b. Investment in Intel Corporation shares
   c. Land
   d. Depreciation expense

(SO 1)   4. Current liabilities are $10,000, non-current liabilities are $20,000, common shares are $50,000, and retained earnings are $70,000. Total shareholders' equity is
   a. $150,000.
   b. $140,000.
   c. $120,000.
   d. $70,000.

(SO 2)   5. Profit before income tax is $72,000, income tax expense is $18,000, and weighted average number of common shares during the year is 50,000. There are no preferred shares. Earnings per share is
   a. $1.80.
   b. $1.44.

CHAPTER 2   A Further Look at Financial Statements   23

    c. $1.08.

    d. $0.93.

6. Profit available to common shareholders is $140,000 and weighted average   (SO 2)
number of common shares during the year is 80,000. The market price of each
common share is $8.75. The price-earnings ratio is

    a.   5.

    b.   4.

    c.   4.375.

    d.   16.

7. The ability to pay obligations that are expected to become due within the next   (SO 2)
year is called

    a.   working capital.

    b.   profitability.

    c.   solvency.

    d.   liquidity.

8. Non-current assets are $120,000, total assets are $180,000, non-current liabilities   (SO 2)
are $100,000, and shareholders' equity is $50,000. The current ratio is

    a.   2:1.

    b.   1.2:1.

    c.   0.5:1.

    d.   0.3:1.

9. Which ratio measures the percentage of assets financed by creditors rather than   (SO 2)
by shareholders?

    a.   Current ratio

    b.   Debt to total assets ratio

    c.   Free cash flow ratio

    d.   Price-earnings ratio

10. A company with a debt to total assets ratio of 42.5%, operating in an industry   (SO 2)
with an average debt to total assets ratio of 57.0%, is

    a.   more liquid compared with its competitors in the industry.

    b.   less liquid compared with its competitors in the industry.

    c.   less likely to be able to pay its debts as they come due, compared with its
competitors in the industry.

    d.   more likely to be able to pay its debts as they come due, compared with its
competitors in the industry.

11. Company A has a price-earnings ratio of 12 times, and Company B has a   (SO 2)
price-earnings ratio of 16 times, therefore

    a.   Company A must have higher earnings per share than Company B.

    b.   Company B must have higher earnings per share than Company A.

    c.   investors are more confident in Company B's future profitability than
Company A's future profitability.

    d.   investors are more confident in Company A's future profitability than
Company B's future profitability.

24   Study Guide to Accompany Financial Accounting: Tools for Business Decision-Making, Fifth Canadian Edition

(SO 2)   12.   Profit is $7,500, total assets are $500,000, weighted average number of common shares is 5,000, market price per share is $20, sales are $100,000, and total liabilities are $357,140. Based on this information, the price-earnings ratio is
a.   1.4.
b.   13.3.
c.   1.0.
d.   10.0.

(SO 3)   13.   If accounting information has predictive value, it is useful in making predictions about
a.   future government audits.
b.   new accounting principles.
c.   foreign currency exchange rates.
d.   the future events of a company.

(SO 3)   14.   Accounting information should be neutral in order to be
a.   a faithful representation of what really exists or happened.
b.   complete.
c.   relevant.
d.   understandable.

(SO 3)   15.   Accounting information is _____ if it makes a difference in a user's decision.
a.   faithfully representative
b.   relevant
c.   comparable
d.   understandable

(SO 3)   16.   _____ results when users can identify and understand similarities in, and differences among, financial statement items.
a.   Relevance
b.   Understandability
c.   Comparability
d.   Reliability

(SO 3)   17.   Which of the following is not an enhancing qualitative characteristic of useful information?
a.   Comparability
b.   Completeness
c.   Verifiability
d.   Timeliness

(SO 3)   18.   The objective of financial reporting is to
a.   prepare financial statements using the accrual basis of accounting.
b.   prepare financial statements that have all the fundamental and enhancing qualitative characteristics of useful financial information.
c.   include all material information in the financial statements.
d.   provide financial information about a company that is useful to existing and potential investors, lenders, and other creditors in making decisions about providing resources to the company.

CHAPTER 2   A Further Look at Financial Statements   25

19. The going concern assumption   (SO 3)
   a. assumes that some companies will eventually fail.
   b. does not have important implications in accounting.
   c. assumes that a company will continue in operation for the foreseeable future.
   d. is an underlying assumption, and should always be applied.

20. In the conceptual framework for financial reporting, the income element of   (SO 3)
   financial statements
   a. includes both revenue and gains.
   b. includes revenue only.
   c. represents the company's profit.
   d. is the residual interest in the company's assets after deducting all liabilities.

21. In the conceptual framework for financial reporting, the expenses element of   (SO 3)
   financial statements includes
   a. only expenses that arise from the company's ordinary activities.
   b. losses as well as expenses that arise from ordinary company activities.
   c. only losses that arise from ordinary activities.
   d. only losses that do not arise from ordinary activities.

22. The _____ basis of accounting states that assets and liabilities should   (SO 3)
   be recorded at their historical cost at the time of acquisition.
   a. fair value
   b. cost
   c. relevance
   d. reliability

23. In determining which measurement principle to use, the factual nature of   (SO 3)
   the _____ figures must be weighted against the relevance of the
   _____ figures.
   a. fair value, historical cost
   b. historical cost, fair value
   c. faithfully representative, material
   d. faithfully representative, predictive

24. The constraint that says, "Make sure the information is worth it," is the   (SO 3)
   a. cost constraint.
   b. materiality constraint.
   c. relevance constraint.
   d. reliability constraint.

Problems

1. The following presents December 31, 2012, year-end balances for the Variety   (SO 1)
   Corporation:

Cash	$ 5,900
Accounts payable	3,300

26   Study Guide to Accompany Financial Accounting: Tools for Business Decision-Making, Fifth Canadian Edition

Accumulated depreciation—equipment	$13,500
Prepaid insurance	1,400
Common shares	25,000
Intangible assets	5,500
Accounts receivable	13,600
Retained earnings	49,300
Equipment	63,000
Land	10,500
Inventory	14,400
Long-term notes payable	20,000
Salaries payable	3,200

a.   Prepare a classified statement of financial position in order of liquidity.
b.   Prepare a classified statement of financial position in reverse order of liquidity.

2.   Consider the following data from Meadows Corporation: (SO 2)

	2012	2011
Current assets	$ 61,000	$ 50,000
Total assets	108,000	85,000
Current liabilities	47,000	39,000
Total liabilities	80,000	62,000
Net sales	200,000	180,000
Profit available to common shareholders	30,000	20,000
Market price per common share	$9.00	$6.40
Weighted average number of common shares	30,000	25,000

Calculate the following and explain what the results mean:
a.   Working capital for 2012 and 2011
b.   Current ratio for 2012 and 2011
c.   Debt to total assets for 2012 and 2011
d.   Earnings per share for 2012 and 2011
e.   Price-earnings ratio for 2012 and 2011

3.   Selected components of the conceptual framework are shown below.   (SO 3)

1.   Going concern

2.   Predictive value

3.   Neutrality

4.   Understandability

5.   Verifiability

CHAPTER 2   A Further Look at Financial Statements   27

6. Timeliness

7. Faithful representation

8. Comparability

9. Confirmatory value

10. Cost constraint

11. Materiality

Match each of the following statements with one of the items on the above list.

_____ a.   Information has this quality if different knowledgeable and independent users can reach consensus that the information is faithfully represented.

_____ b.   Accounting information cannot be biased toward one set of users over another.

_____ c.   Information that is presented must portray what really exists or happened.

_____ d.   Information has this quality if it is classified, characterized, and presented clearly and concisely.

_____ e.   Relevant information helps users make predictions about future events.

_____ f.   Accounting information must be available to decision makers before it loses its ability to influence their decisions.

_____ g.   The company will remain in operation for the foreseeable future.

_____ h.   Information has this quality if users can identify and understand similarities in, and differences among, items.

_____ i.   Information has this quality if it provides users with feedback regarding their previous predictions or expectations.

_____ j.   The value of the information provided in financial reporting information should justify the cost of providing it.

_____ k.   This is an important component of relevance, which requires accountants to consider whether omission or misstatement of the information could influence the decisions of users.

4.   Refer to the HMV and WHSmith financial statements found in the appendices at the end of this study guide for information in answering the following questions. Do not forget to use the **Decision Toolkit** approach for help in answering the questions.   (SO 1)

a.   The statement of financial position for HMV shows property, plant, and equipment of £167.3 million at the end of 2010. What does this amount represent?

b.   Can WHSmith meet its near-term obligations in 2009 and 2010? Comment on the trend that you see.

c.   Calculate the debt to total assets ratio for both companies for 2010.

28 Study Guide to Accompany Financial Accounting: Tools for Business Decision-Making, Fifth Canadian Edition

Solutions to Self-Test

Multiple Choice

1. a The statement of changes in equity reports the ending balance of the retained earnings account, as does the statement of financial position (in its shareholders' equity section).

2. a Notes receivable due in three years, building, and patent are all non-current assets.

3. c Supplies is a current asset; investment in Intel Corporation shares is not a property, plant, or equipment item; and depreciation expense is an expense on the income statement.

4. c $50,000 + $70,000 = $120,000.

5. c ($72,000 − $18,000) ÷ 50,000 common shares = $1.08.

6. a Earnings per share = $140,000 ÷ 80,000 common shares = $1.75.
   Price-earnings ratio = $8.75 ÷ $1.75 = 5.

7. d Working capital is the difference between current assets and current liabilities. Profitability refers to a company's operating success during a specified period of time. Solvency is a company's ability to pay interest as it comes due and to repay the face value of the debt at maturity.

8. a Current assets = $180,000 − $120,000 = $60,000. Current liabilities = $180,000 − $100,000 − $50,000 = $30,000. Current ratio = $60,000 ÷ $30,000 = 2:1.

9. b The debt to total assets ratio is the percentage of assets financed by creditors rather than by shareholders.

10. d The debt to total assets ratio is not a measure of liquidity. A lower debt to total assets ratio suggests favourable solvency and better ability to pay debts as they come due.

11. c Price-earnings ratio = market price per share ÷ earnings per share. A higher price-earnings ratio means that investors are more confident that current profit levels will continue or increase in the future.

12. b EPS = $7,500 ÷ 5,000 = $1.50.
   P-E Ratio = $20 ÷ $1.50 = 13.3 times.

13. d Financial information has predictive value if it helps users make predictions about the future events of a company.

14. a For accounting information to be a faithful representation of what really exists or happened, the information must be complete, neutral, and free from material error.

15. b Accounting information is relevant if it makes a difference in a user's decision.

16. c Comparability results when users can identify and understand similarities in, and differences among, financial statement items.

CHAPTER 2   A Further Look at Financial Statements   29

17. b   The four enhancing qualitative characteristics of useful information are comparability, verifiability, timeliness, and understandability.

18. d   The objective of financial reporting is to provide financial information about a company that is useful to existing and potential investors, lenders, and other creditors in making decisions about providing resources to the company. The accrual basis of accounting, qualitative characteristics of useful information, and the concept of materiality guide the preparation of useful financial information.

19. c   The going concern assumption assumes that a company will continue in operation for the foreseeable future. If a company is not assumed to be a going concern, then different assumptions would influence the preparation of financial statements.

20. a   In the conceptual framework for financial reporting, the income element of financial statements includes both revenue and gains; profit is not an element classification. Equity is the residual interest in the company's assets after deducting all its liabilities.

21. b   In the conceptual framework for financial reporting, the losses element of financial statements includes losses as well as those expenses that arise from the company's ordinary activities, where losses may or may not arise from ordinary activities.

22. b   The cost basis of accounting states that assets and liabilities should be recorded at their cost at the time of acquisition. The fair value basis of accounting states that certain assets and liabilities should be recorded and reported at fair value (e.g., the price that would be received if an asset is sold).

23. b   In determining which measurement principle to use, the factual nature of the historical cost figures must be weighed against the relevance of the fair value figures.

24. a   The cost constraint ensures that the value of the information provided in financial reporting is greater than the cost of providing it.

Problems

1.   a.

VARIETY CORPORATION
Statement of Financial Position
December 31, 2012

Assets

Current assets

Cash	$ 5,900
Accounts receivable	13,600
Inventory	14,400

30   Study Guide to Accompany Financial Accounting: Tools for Business Decision-Making, Fifth Canadian Edition

Prepaid insurance		1,400	
Total current assets			$ 35,300

Non-current assets

Property, plant, and equipment

Land		$10,500	
Equipment	$63,000		
Less: accumulated depreciation—equipment	13,500	49,500	
Total property, plant, and equipment			60,000
Intangible assets			5,500
Total assets			$100,800

Liabilities and Shareholders' Equity

Current liabilities

Accounts payable	$ 3,300		
Salaries payable	3,200		
Total current liabilities		$ 6,500	

Non-current liabilities

Notes payable	20,000		
Total non-current liabilities		20,000	
Total liabilities			$26,500

Shareholders' equity

Common shares		$25,000	
Retained earnings		49,300	
Total shareholders' equity			74,300
Total liabilities and shareholders' equity			$100,800

b.

VARIETY CORPORATION
Statement of Financial Position
December 31, 2012

Assets

Non-current assets

Intangible assets			$ 5,500

Property, plant, and equipment

Land		$10,500	
Equipment	$63,000		

CHAPTER 2   A Further Look at Financial Statements   31

Less: accumulated depreciation—equipment	13,500	49,500	
Total property, plant, and equipment			60,000
Total non-current assets			65,500

Current assets

Prepaid insurance	$ 1,400	
Inventory	14,400	
Accounts receivable	13,600	
Cash	5,900	
Total current assets		35,300
Total assets		$100,800

Shareholders' Equity and Liabilities

Shareholders' equity

Common shares	$ 25,000	
Retained earnings	49,300	
Total shareholders' equity		$ 74,300

Liabilities

Non-current liabilities

Notes payable	$ 20,000	
Total non-current liabilities		$ 20,000

Current liabilities

Salaries payable	$ 3,200	
Accounts payable	3,300	
Total current liabilities		6,500
Total liabilities		26,500
Total shareholders' equity and liabilities		$100,800

2.

a. Working Capital = Current Assets − Current Liabilities
2012: $61,000 − $47,000 = $14,000
2011: $50,000 − $39,000 = $11,000
Working capital is a measure of liquidity. Since this company's working capital is positive, there is a greater likelihood that it will be able to pay its current liabilities.

b. Current Ratio = Current Assets ÷ Current Liabilities
2012: $61,000 ÷ $47,000 = 1.30:1
2011: $50,000 ÷ $39,000 = 1.28:1
The current ratio is another measure of liquidity. In 2012, the company had $1.30 of current assets for every dollar of current liabilities. In 2011, it had $1.28 of current assets for every dollar of current liabilities; therefore, the company's current ratio improved slightly.

c. Debt to Total Assets = Total Debt ÷ Total Assets
2012: $80,000 ÷ $108,000 = 74%
2011: $62,000 ÷ $85,000 = 73%

32   **Study Guide to Accompany Financial Accounting: Tools for Business Decision-Making, Fifth Canadian Edition**

This ratio measures the percentage of assets that is financed by creditors rather than by shareholders. In 2012, $0.74 of every dollar invested in assets was provided by creditors. In 2011, $0.73 of every dollar invested in assets was provided by creditors. In general, a higher percentage of debt to total assets means there is greater risk that the company will be unable to pay its debts as they come due.

d. Earnings per Share = Profit Available to Common Shareholders ÷ Weighted Average Number of Common Shares
2012: $30,000 ÷ 30,000 = $1.00
2011: $20,000 ÷ 25,000 = $0.80
This ratio is a measure of profitability. It measures the profit earned for each common share, and provides a useful perspective of shareholder investment return.

e. Price-Earnings Ratio = Market Price per Share ÷ Earnings per Share
2012: $9.00 ÷ $1.00 = 9 times
2011: $6.40 ÷ $0.80 = 8 times
This ratio reflects investors' assessment of the company's future profitability. This ratio will be higher if investors think that the company's current profit level will persist or increase in the future.

3.

a.	5	g.	1
b.	3	h.	8
c.	7	i.	9
d.	4	j.	10
e.	2	k.	11
f.	6		

4.   Please note that the amounts shown for HMV and WHSmith are stated in pounds (£) millions.

a. The £167.3 million represents the carrying amount of HMV's property, plant, and equipment. The notes to HMV's financial statements would include a detailed breakdown of this amount.

b. WHSmith's working capital (current assets less current liabilities) is £285 − £300 = (£15) in 2010 and £262 − £281 = (£19) in 2009. WHSmith may require additional financing to meet its near-term obligations in 2010 and 2009. The trend shows that working capital has increased slightly from 2009 to 2010.
The current ratio also showed a small increase in 2010 as follows: for 2010 it was £285 ÷ £300 = 0.95:1, and for 2009 it was £262 ÷ £281 = 0.93:1.

c.

HMV:

Debt to total assets: $\dfrac{£605.0}{£705.4} = 85.8\%$

WHSmith:

Debt to total assets: $\dfrac{£327}{£513} = 63.7\%$

chapter 3

The Accounting Information System

Chapter Overview

Chapter 3 discusses analysis and recording of accounting transactions, and the accounting information system. You will learn about accounts, debits, and credits, and the basic steps in the recording process: journalizing, posting transactions to the general ledger, and preparing a trial balance.

Review of Specific Study Objectives

Accounting Transactions

- The **accounting information system** is the system of collecting and processing transaction data and communicating financial information to decision makers.

- An accounting information system begins with determining what relevant transaction data should be collected and processed.

- An **accounting** transaction occurs when assets, liabilities, or shareholders' equity items change as a result of some economic event.

  The accounting equation is as follows:

$$\text{Assets} = \text{Liabilities} + \text{Shareholders' Equity}$$

study objective 1

Analyze the effects of transactions on the accounting equation.

34   Study Guide to Accompany Financial Accounting: Tools for Business Decision-Making, Fifth Canadian Edition

- Different transactions will affect the components of the accounting equation in different ways, and it is important to remember that the **accounting equation** must **always be in balance** after each transaction is recorded. The accounting equation is a mathematical equation. For example, if an asset is increased, there must be a corresponding decrease in another asset, or an increase in a liability or shareholders' equity item. It is also possible for two or more items to be affected. For example, supplies may be purchased and paid for partially by cash with a promise to pay the remaining the balance at a future date. In that case, supplies, an asset account, would increase; cash, another asset account, would decrease; and accounts payable, a liability account, would increase by the balance to be paid at a future date.

- With respect to specific aspects of the accounting equation:

  1. If a company receives cash for work to be performed in the future, the company should not record this cash as revenue. The company should record an increase in cash on the left side of the equation (because cash is an asset), and an increase in unearned revenue (a liability account) on the right side of the equation. The amount is considered unearned revenue, and not earned revenue, because the company is obligated to provide the related good or service at a future date.
  2. Revenues increase shareholders' equity.
  3. Expenses decrease shareholders' equity.
  4. Some events are not transactions or economic events, and are not recorded. For example, the hiring of an employee or the beginning of an employees' strike are events that would not be recorded in the accounting system because no asset, liability, or shareholders' equity account is immediately affected by these events.

- The accounting information system uses accounts. An **account** is an individual accounting record of increases and decreases in a specific asset, liability, or shareholders' equity item.

- The simplest form of an account is the **T account**, so named because of its shape. A T account has an **account** title, a left side (called the debit side), and a right side (called the credit side).

- **Debit (DR) means left, while credit (CR) means right.** These terms are simply directional signals. A debit or credit does not necessarily mean good or bad, and does not necessarily mean increase or decrease. However, if a debit causes a particular account to increase, a credit would cause the same account to decrease; and if a credit causes a particular account to increase, a debit would cause the same account to decrease.

Debits and Credits

study objective 2

Define debits and credits and explain how they are used to record transactions.

- **To debit an account** means to enter an amount on the left side of the account. **To credit an account** means to enter an amount on the right side of the account. If an account has $300 on the debit side and $100 on the credit side, then the account has an overall debit balance of $200. If an account has $500 on the credit side and $200 on the debit side, then the account has an overall credit balance of $300. To calculate the **balance** of an account containing many amounts on both sides of the account, add all of its debit amounts to arrive at total debits, and add all of its credit amounts to arrive at total credits, then subtract total credits from total debits to arrive at the account balance. If total debits exceed total credits, then the account has a debit balance. If total credits exceed total debits, then the account has a credit balance.

CHAPTER 3 The Accounting Information System 35

- In each and every transaction recorded, the **total amount of debits recorded must equal the total amount of credits recorded.** The equality of debits and credits is the basis for the **double-entry accounting system and it keeps the accounting equation in balance.**

- The following is a **summary of the debit/credit rules** by account type ("+" means increase, while "−" means decrease). For example, to increase an asset account by $100, the asset account should be debited by $100 (or to decrease an asset account by $100, the asset account should be credited by $100).

	Debit	Credit
Assets	+	−
Dividends	+	−
Expenses	+	−
Liabilities	−	+
Shareholders' Equity	−	+
Revenues	−	+

- The **normal balance** of an account is its increase (plus) side. For example, an asset account normally has a debit balance. The dividend account is increased by a debit, so its normal balance is a debit. Revenue accounts are increased by credits, so the normal balance of a revenue account is a credit. Sometimes, an account may have a balance other than its normal balance. For example, the cash account (an asset account) may have a credit balance in the company's books if it is overdrawn at the bank.

- Remember that **shareholders' equity has two components: common shares** (or share capital if there is more than one class of shares) **and retained earnings.** Both follow the debit/credit rules for shareholders' equity accounts (indicated above).

- **Retained earnings** can be further divided into three components: revenues and expenses (which determine profit), and dividends. **Dividends and expenses both reduce shareholders' equity;** therefore, they follow debit/credit rules contrary to shareholders' equity debit/credit rules. **Common shares, retained earnings, and revenues all increase shareholders' equity;** therefore, they follow shareholders' equity debit/credit rules.

- Since assets are on the left side of the accounting equation and liabilities and shareholders' equity are on the right side of the accounting equation, the debit/credit rules for assets are contrary to the debit/credit rules for liabilities and shareholders' equity items.

The Recording Process

- The recording process begins with a **source document.**

- Each **transaction** is analyzed and recorded in the form of a **journal entry**, which is entered in a **general journal**. The information entered in the general journal is then **transferred to** the appropriate accounts in the **general ledger** (a book of accounts).

- The **general journal** may be recorded on paper or stored as an electronic file on a computer.

> **study objective 3**
>
> Identify the basic steps in the recording process.

36   Study Guide to Accompany Financial Accounting: Tools for Business Decision-Making, Fifth Canadian Edition

- **Journalizing** is the process of entering transaction data in the general journal. Transactions entered in the general journal are listed in **chronological order**. A **complete journal entry** consists of the following:

    1. The date of the transaction.
    2. The accounts and amounts to be debited and credited.
    3. An explanation of the transaction.

- A typical journal entry has the following format:

		Debit	Credit
May 12	Supplies	500	
	Cash		500
	(Purchased supplies for cash)		

    Note that the title of the account to be credited is **indented**. This decreases the possibility of switching the debit and credit accounts or amounts, and makes it easier to see that the cash account is the account that should be credited.

- The **general ledger** contains all the asset, liability, shareholders' equity, revenue, and expense accounts maintained by the company, and all the information about the changes in each account.

- The **general ledger** may be recorded on paper or may be stored as an electronic file on a computer.

- The **chart of accounts** is the framework for the accounting database. It lists the accounts and account numbers that identify where the accounts are in the general ledger. Account numbers will usually start with assets first, followed by liabilities and shareholders' equity accounts.

- **Posting** is the process of transferring general journal entries to general ledger accounts. Posting accumulates the effects of journalized transactions in individual accounts in the general ledger.

- Consider the journal entry above in which supplies was debited and cash was credited for $500 on May 12. To post the journal entry to the general ledger, the date would be recorded and $500 would be written in the debit column under the general ledger account Supplies. The date would be recorded again and $500 would be written in the credit column under the general ledger account Cash.

The Trial Balance

study objective 4

Prepare a trial balance.

- A **trial balance** is a list of general ledger accounts and their balances at a specific time. A trial balance is usually prepared at the end of an accounting period. Accounts are listed in the order in which they appear in the general ledger, with each account balance listed in the appropriate debit or credit column. The **total dollar amount of the debits must equal the total dollar amount of the credits**; otherwise, there is an error that must be corrected. The **primary purpose** of a trial balance is to prove the mathematical equality of debits and credits in the general ledger. It also helps uncover errors from journalizing and posting and is useful in the preparation of financial statements.

- Even if **a trial balance has total debits equal to total credits, mistakes may still be present.** For example, if a particular journal entry has not been posted, then an

CHAPTER 3 The Accounting Information System   37

error has occurred, but the trial balance will still be in balance. Or, if a journal entry is posted twice, the same is true. If a journal entry was posted to the general ledger for $500 instead of $5,000 on both the debit and the credit sides, then an error has occurred, but once again, the trial balance will still be in balance. If a $200 debit is posted to cash instead of to another asset account, then an error has occurred, but the trial balance will still be in balance.

comparing
IFRS and ASPE

Key Differences	International Financial Reporting Standards (IFRS)	Accounting Standards for Private Enterprises (ASPE)
No significant differences		

Chapter Self-Test

As you work through questions and problems, remember to use the **Decision Toolkit** discussed and used in the text:

1. *Decision Checkpoints*: Ask a question relevant to the decision being made.
2. *Info Needed for Decision*: Make a choice regarding the information needed to answer the question.
3. *Tools to Use for Decision*: Review what the information identified in step 2 does for the decision-making process.
4. *How to Evaluate Results*: Identify specifically how the information identified in step 2 should be evaluated to answer the question relevant to the decision being made.

Note: The notation "(SO 1)" means that the question relates to study objective 1.

Multiple Choice

Please circle the correct answer.

1. If a company receives cash from a customer before performing services for the customer, then   (SO 1)
   a. assets increase, and liabilities decrease.
   b. assets increase, and shareholders' equity increases.
   c. assets decrease, and liabilities increase.
   d. assets increase, and liabilities increase.

2. If a company performs services for a customer and receives cash for the services, then   (SO 1)
   a. assets increase, and liabilities decrease.
   b. assets increase, and shareholders' equity increases.
   c. assets decrease, and liabilities increase.
   d. assets increase, and liabilities increase.

38   Study Guide to Accompany Financial Accounting: Tools for Business Decision-Making, Fifth Canadian Edition

(SO 1)   3. When collection is made on an accounts receivable balance, then
    a.   total assets will remain the same.
    b.   total assets will decrease.
    c.   total assets will increase.
    d.   shareholders' equity will increase.

(SO 1)   4. Which of the following items has no effect on retained earnings?
    a.   Expense
    b.   Dividends
    c.   Common Shares
    d.   Revenue

(SO 1)   5. A partial payment of an account payable will
    a.   not affect total assets.
    b.   increase liabilities.
    c.   not affect shareholders' equity.
    d.   decrease profit.

(SO 2)   6. An accountant has debited an asset account for $1,000 and credited a liability account for $400. Which of the following might be done to complete the recording of the transaction?
    a.   Credit a different asset account for $400.
    b.   Debit a shareholders' equity account for $400.
    c.   Debit a different asset account for $600.
    d.   Credit a different asset account for $600.

(SO 2)   7. An account has $600 on the debit side and $400 on the credit side. The overall balance in the account is a
    a.   debit of $200.
    b.   credit of $200.
    c.   debit of $600.
    d.   credit of $400.

(SO 2)   8. Which of the following statements is correct?
    a.   A debit decreases an asset account.
    b.   A credit decreases a liability account.
    c.   A debit increases an expense account.
    d.   A credit decreases a revenue account.

(SO 2)   9. Which of the following statements is incorrect?
    a.   A debit increases the Dividends account.
    b.   A debit increases an expense account.
    c.   A credit increases a revenue account.
    d.   A credit increases the Dividends account.

(SO 3)   10. Which of the following is the correct sequence of events in the accounting cycle?
    a.   Analyze a transaction; post it in the general ledger; record it in the general journal.

CHAPTER 3 The Accounting Information System 39

b. Analyze a transaction; record it in the general journal; post it in the general ledger.

c. Record a transaction in the general journal; analyze the transaction; post it in the general ledger.

d. None of the above is in the correct sequence.

11. Transactions are initially recorded in chronological order in a _____ (SO 3) before they are transferred to the individual accounts.

    a. general journal

    b. general register

    c. general ledger

    d. T account

12. To record equipment depreciation expense of $500 on December 31, the correct (SO 3) journal entry would be

    a.

Dec. 31	Equipment	500	
	Accumulated Depreciation—Equipment		500
	(To record equipment depreciation expense)		

    b.

Dec. 31	Accumulated Depreciation—Equipment	500	
	Depreciation Expense		500
	(To record equipment depreciation expense)		

    c.

Dec. 31	Depreciation Expense	500	
	Accumulated Depreciation—Equipment		500
	(To record equipment depreciation expense)		

    d.

Dec. 31	Depreciation Expense	500	
	Equipment		500
	(To record equipment depreciation expense)		

13. If a corporation borrows money and issues a three-month note in exchange, then (SO 3) the journal entry requires a

    a. debit to Notes Payable and a credit to Cash.

    b. debit to Notes Payable and a credit to Unearned Revenue.

    c. debit to Cash and a credit to Notes Payable.

    d. debit to Cash and a credit to Unearned Revenue.

14. If a company pays its employees their weekly salaries, then the journal entry (SO 3) requires a

    a. debit to Unearned Revenue and a credit to Cash.

    b. debit to Retained Earnings and a credit to Cash.

    c. debit to Cash and a credit to Salaries Expense.

    d. debit to Salaries Expense and a credit to Cash.

40 Study Guide to Accompany Financial Accounting: Tools for Business Decision-Making, Fifth Canadian Edition

(SO 3)   15. A general ledger of a company contains
    a.   only Asset and Liability accounts.
    b.   all Asset, Liability, and Shareholders' Equity accounts.
    c.   only Shareholders' Equity accounts.
    d.   only Asset and Shareholders' Equity accounts.

(SO 3)   16. The entire group of accounts maintained by a company is referred to collectively as the
    a.   general ledger.
    b.   general journal.
    c.   general register.
    d.   T accounts.

(SO 3)   17. If an accountant wants to know the balance in the company's cash account, he/she would look in
    a.   the general journal.
    b.   the general ledger.
    c.   both the general journal and the general ledger.
    d.   neither the general journal nor the general ledger.

(SO 3)   18. When an accountant posts, he/she is transferring amounts from
    a.   the general ledger to the general journal.
    b.   T accounts to the general ledger.
    c.   the general journal to the general ledger.
    d.   the general ledger to T accounts.

(SO 3)   19. If an account is debited in a journal entry, then
    a.   that account will be debited in the general ledger.
    b.   that account will be credited in the general ledger.
    c.   that account will be both debited and credited in the general ledger.
    d.   none of the above is correct.

(SO 4)   20. Which of the following is the correct sequence of events in the accounting cycle?
    a.   Prepare a trial balance; journalize; post.
    b.   Journalize; post; prepare a trial balance.
    c.   Post; journalize; prepare a trial balance.
    d.   Prepare a trial balance; post; journalize.

(SO 4)   21. The primary purpose of a trial balance is to
    a.   get a total of all accounts with a debit balance.
    b.   get a total of all accounts with a credit balance.
    c.   prove the mathematical equality of debits and credits after posting.
    d.   get a list of all accounts used by a company.

(SO 4)   22. Which of the following errors, each considered individually, would cause the trial balance to be out of balance?
    a.   A payment of $75 to a creditor was posted as a debit to Accounts Payable and a debit of $75 to Cash.

CHAPTER 3 The Accounting Information System 41

b. Cash received from a customer on account was posted as a debit of $350 to Cash and as a credit of $350 to Revenue.

c. A payment of $59 for supplies was posted as a debit of $95 to Supplies and a credit of $95 to Cash.

d. A transaction was not posted.

23. If total debits and total credits of a trial balance are not equal, it could be due to   (SO 4)

a. failure to record or post a transaction.

b. recording of the same erroneous amount for both the debit and the credit parts of a transaction.

c. an error in calculating the account balances.

d. recording of a transaction more than once.

Problems

1. On June 1, 2012, a new company began performing repairs on small engines; it had the following transactions in June: (SO 1, 2)

June 1	The company issued common shares for cash.
2	Paid cash for a one-year insurance policy.
3	Paid landlord for June rent.
4	Purchased office equipment, paying cash for part of the amount due and signing a note for the remainder.
5	Paid for advertising used during June.
6	Purchased office supplies on account.
7	Completed repair services for a customer who paid in cash.
8	Purchased repair supplies on account. These supplies will be used during June.
9	Billed customer for repair services done.
10	Received cash from a customer for repair services to be performed next month.
19	Paid for office supplies purchased on June 6.
22	Paid employee salaries.
23	Paid for repair supplies purchased on June 8.
25	Received payment from customer for repair services billed on June 9.
26	Paid dividends.

Examine the above transactions in an answer sheet like the one shown below:

a. Name the accounts affected in each transaction.

b. Categorize the accounts that you named in (a) above as one of Assets (A), Liabilities (L), Common Shares (CS), Revenue (Rev), Expense (Exp), or Dividends (Div). To do this step, use the accounts in the expanded accounting equation where Shareholders' Equity is divided into Common Shares

42 **Study Guide to Accompany Financial Accounting: Tools for Business Decision-Making, Fifth Canadian Edition**

and Retained Earnings, and Retained Earnings is further divided into Revenues, Expenses, and Dividends as shown below:

Assets = Liabilities + Shareholders' Equity

Common Shares + Retained Earnings

+ Revenues − Expenses − Dividends

c. Identify whether the accounts increase or decrease.
d. Signify the increase or decrease with a debit (Dr) or credit (Cr).

The first one has been done for you as an example.

Date	a. Account Names	b. Category of Account	c. Increase or Decrease	d. Dr or Cr
June 1	Common Shares	CS	Increase	Cr
	Cash	A	Increase	Dr

(SO 1, 2) 2. For each of the following accounts, indicate whether the account is an Asset, Liability, or Shareholders' Equity account and whether the account normally possesses a debit (Dr) or credit (Cr) balance.

	Type of Account: Asset, Liability, or Shareholders' Equity	Normal Balance: Debit or Credit
a. Cash		
b. Accounts payable		

c. Unearned revenue		
d. Land		
e. Service revenue		
f. Accounts receivable		
g. Rent expense		
h. Common shares		
i. Loan payable		
j. Dividends		
k. Prepaid rent		
l. Notes payable		

3. Journalize the following business transactions. Identify each transaction by letter. (SO 3)
    You may omit explanations for the transactions.

    a. Shareholders invest $40,000 in cash to start an interior decorating
        business.
    b. Purchased office equipment for $5,500, paying $2,000 in cash, and signed a
        30-day, $3,500 note payable.
    c. Purchased $350 of office supplies on account.
    d. Billed $3,000 to clients for services provided during the past month.
    e. Paid $750 in cash for the current month's rent.
    f. Paid $225 cash on account for office supplies purchased in transaction (c).
    g. Received a bill for $500 for advertising for the current month.
    h. Paid $2,300 cash for office salaries.
    i. Paid $1,000 cash dividends to shareholders.
    j. Received a cheque for $2,000 from a client in payment of their outstanding
        account from transaction (d).

4. The following is an alphabetical listing of accounts for Davis Corporation. (SO 4)
    Prepare a trial balance on September 30, 2012, assuming that all accounts have
    their normal balance.

Accounts payable	$ 4,000
Advertising expense	5,000
Cash	35,000
Common shares	20,000
Dividends	2,000
Equipment	15,000
Prepaid insurance	3,000
Rent expense	6,000
Retained earnings	30,000
Salaries expense	8,000
Service revenue	15,000
Unearned revenue	5,000

44   **Study Guide to Accompany Financial Accounting: Tools for Business Decision-Making, Fifth Canadian Edition**

(SO 2)   5.   Refer to the HMV and WHSmith financial statements found in the appendices at the end of this study guide for information in answering the following questions. Do not forget to use the **Decision Toolkit** approach for help in answering the questions.

a.   Did the companies pay dividends in 2010? What were the amounts for each company, and where do you find this information?

b.   What were total assets, liabilities, and shareholders' equity for WHSmith in 2010?

Solutions to Self-Test

Multiple Choice

1.   d   Cash (an asset) increases, and Unearned Revenue (a liability) increases.

2.   b   Cash (an asset) increases, and shareholders' equity increases because one of its components, revenue, increases.

3.   a   Cash (an asset) increases, and Accounts Receivable (an asset) decreases; therefore, total assets will remain the same.

4.   c   Common Shares is a component of shareholders' equity and has no effect on retained earnings.

5.   c   The asset Cash is decreased, the liability Accounts Payable is decreased, and shareholders' equity is not affected.

6.   d   An example would be:

Office Supplies	1,000	
Accounts Payable		400
Cash		600

7.   a $600 DR $-$ $400 CR $=$ $200 DR.

8.   c   A debit increases an asset account and an expense account. A credit increases a liability account and a revenue account.

9.   d   A debit increases the Dividends account.

10.   b   The first three steps in the accounting cycle are analyze a transaction, record it in the general journal, and post it in the general ledger.

11.   a   The general ledger is a collection of accounts, and a T account is a form of account.

12.   c   Depreciation Expense (an expense) increases, and Accumulated Depreciation—Equipment (a contra asset) increases.

13.   c   The company receives an asset (Cash increases with a debit to Cash), and its liabilities increase (Notes Payable increases with a credit to Notes Payable).

14.   d   Expenses increase with a debit, and Cash decreases with a credit to Cash.

15.   b   All asset, liability, and shareholders' equity accounts are included in the general ledger.

CHAPTER 3 The Accounting Information System 45

16. a   The general journal is the book of original entry, and T accounts are simply a form of account.

17. b   The easiest way to find the balance in an account is to look in the general ledger. Using the general journal, all debit and credit entries to cash would have to be added and subtracted to determine the balance in the account, which would be very time-consuming.

18. c   Posting involves transferring information from the general journal to the general ledger.

19. a   Whatever is done to an account in the journal entry is done to that account in the general ledger.

20. b   The first four steps in the accounting cycle are analyze business transactions, journalize the transactions, post to general ledger accounts, and prepare a trial balance.

21. c   While the trial balance may give a list of all accounts (although an account with a zero balance may not be listed), and lists debit and credit balances, these are not the primary purposes of the trial balance.

22. a   Two debits will cause the trial balance to be out of balance.

23. c   Answers a, b, and d reflect errors that would not cause the trial balance to be out of balance.

Problems

1.

Date	a. Account Names	b. Category of Account	c. Increase or Decrease	d. Dr. or Cr.
June 1	Common Shares	CS	Increase	Cr
	Cash	A	Increase	Dr

Common Shares is a component of Shareholders' Equity (SE) and the account increases because the company has issued shares.

June 2	Prepaid Insurance	A	Increase	Dr
	Cash	A	Decrease	Cr

The insurance policy will last one year; therefore, it is an asset because it has value beyond the month of June. The common name for this account is Prepaid Insurance.

June 3	Rent Expense	Exp	Increase	Dr
	Cash	A	Decrease	Cr

This rent will be used up in June; therefore, it is an expense incurred for the purpose of generating revenues in June. Rent Expense is part of Retained Earnings, which is part of Shareholders' Equity. Management would assign the account name "Rent Expense" in the chart of accounts where all of the accounts anticipated to be used by the business would be identified. These accounts would be listed in order of the

46 Study Guide to Accompany Financial Accounting: Tools for Business Decision-Making, Fifth Canadian Edition

accounting equation, with assets listed first, followed by liabilities, then shareholders' equity items.

June 4	Equipment	A	Increase	Dr
	Cash	A	Decrease	Cr
	Note Payable	L	Increase	Cr

Three accounts are affected. The account name "Equipment" is assigned by management in the chart of accounts, as explained in the June 3 note. Management could have assigned the account name "Office Equipment" instead. The key point is that this item is an asset. When the name of the account is not provided, as in this example, you are free to use a name that describes the nature of the item as long as you recognize that the item is, in this case, an asset. Note Payable is used when there is a formal agreement that money is owed (in this case, the transaction states that a note was signed).

June 5	Advertising Expense	Exp	Increase	Dr
	Cash	A	Decrease	Cr

Advertising is used in the current month for the purpose of generating revenues, which makes it an expense in the current month.

June 6	Office Supplies	A	Increase	Dr
	Accounts Payable	L	Increase	Cr

There is no indication that the office supplies were used up in June; therefore, they have future value, which makes the item an asset. The account name "Supplies" could have been used, as opposed to "Office Supplies." The key point is that this item is an asset. Accounts Payable is the account used to reflect amounts owed to suppliers.

June 7	Cash	A	Increase	Dr
	Repair Revenue	Rev	Increase	Cr

The company has performed work, so it has earned revenue. The account name "Repair Revenue" is used to describe the type of revenue that was earned. Other account names, such as "Revenue" or "Service Revenue," could have been used as well. The key point is that this is a revenue account. Revenue is part of Retained Earnings, which is part of Shareholders' Equity.

June 8	Repair Supplies Expense	Exp	Increase	Dr
	Accounts Payable	L	Increase	Cr

The repair supplies are expensed because they will be used in the current month for the purpose of generating revenues. The account name "Repair Supplies Expense" is used to reflect the nature of supplies used and to differentiate these supplies from office supplies. These supplies were purchased on account, meaning that the company has a liability and will pay cash in the future.

June 9	Accounts Receivable	A	Increase	Dr
	Repair Revenue	Rev	Increase	Cr

The company has billed the customer for repair work done; therefore, it has earned revenue regardless of the fact that the customer has not yet paid for the work done.

CHAPTER 3   The Accounting Information System   47

As a result, the customer owes money to the company. Accounts Receivable is the asset account used to reflect amounts due from customers for goods or services provided. The account name "Repair Revenue" was explained in the June 7 transaction. It should also be noted that once the name of the revenue account has been decided upon, it must be used for all subsequent similar revenue transactions. For example, if the account had been named "Service Revenue" in the June 7 transaction, then "Service Revenue" would have been used in this transaction as well.

| June 10 | Cash | A | Increase | Dr |
| | Unearned Repair Revenue | L | Increase | Cr |

The company has received cash for repair work to be done in the future. This transaction must be recorded even though the work has not yet been done, because cash has been received. The company owes the customer repair work (to be done next month), so the company must recognize a liability because it is obligated to provide the repair service next month. As previously explained, there is flexibility in deciding on the name for this account. For example, the account name "Unearned Revenue" could have been used instead of "Unearned Repair Revenue."

| June 19 | Accounts Payable | L | Decrease | Dr |
| | Cash | A | Decrease | Cr |

The company is now paying cash for the office supplies that it purchased on June 6. It is therefore discharging or eliminating the liability. Accordingly, Accounts Payable is decreased.

| June 22 | Salary Expense | Exp | Increase | Dr |
| | Cash | A | Decrease | Cr |

Employees are being for paid for work done in June. It is an expense incurred for the purpose of generating revenues.

| June 23 | Accounts Payable | L | Decrease | Dr |
| | Cash | A | Decrease | Cr |

The company is now paying cash for the repair supplies that it purchased on June 8. It is therefore discharging or eliminating the liability. Accordingly, Accounts Payable is decreased.

| June 25 | Accounts Receivable | A | Decrease | Cr |
| | Cash | A | Increase | Dr |

The company is now receiving cash for the work done for a customer and billed on June 9. The customer has now paid the amount owing to the company; therefore, the Accounts Receivable account must be decreased. You should note that the revenue was already recognized on June 9 and it should not be recognized again in this transaction.

| June 26 | Dividends | Div | Increase | Dr |
| | Cash | A | Decrease | Cr |

Dividends are a distribution of retained earnings and not an expense—they are not incurred to generate revenues.

2.

	Type of Account: Asset, Liability, or Shareholders' Equity	Normal Balance: Debit or Credit
a. Cash	Asset	Debit
b. Accounts payable	Liability	Credit
c. Unearned revenue	Liability	Credit
d. Land	Asset	Debit
e. Service revenue	Shareholders' Equity	Credit
f. Accounts receivable	Asset	Debit
g. Rent expense	Shareholders' Equity	Debit
h. Common shares	Shareholders' Equity	Credit
i. Loan payable	Liability	Credit
j. Dividends	Shareholders' Equity	Debit
k. Prepaid rent	Asset	Debit
l. Notes payable	Liability	Credit

3.

		Debit	Credit
a.	Cash	40,000	
	Common Shares		40,000
b.	Office Equipment	5,500	
	Cash		2,000
	Notes Payable		3,500
c.	Office Supplies	350	
	Accounts Payable		350
d.	Accounts Receivable	3,000	
	Decorating Revenue		3,000
e.	Rent Expense	750	
	Cash		750
f.	Accounts Payable	225	
	Cash		225
g.	Advertising Expense	500	
	Accounts Payable		500
h.	Office Salaries Expense	2,300	
	Cash		2,300
i.	Dividends	1,000	
	Cash		1,000
j.	Cash	2,000	
	Accounts Receivable		2,000

CHAPTER 3 The Accounting Information System 49

4.

DAVIS CORPORATION
Trial Balance
September 30, 2012

	Debit	Credit
Cash	$35,000	
Prepaid insurance	3,000	
Equipment	15,000	
Accounts payable		$ 4,000
Unearned revenue		5,000
Common shares		20,000
Retained earnings		30,000
Dividends	2,000	
Service revenue		15,000
Advertising expense	5,000	
Salaries expense	8,000	
Rent expense	6,000	
	$ 74,000	$ 74,000

5. Please note that the amounts shown for HMV and WHSmith are stated in pounds (£) millions.

   a. HMV paid dividends of £31.2 in 2010, and WHSmith paid dividends of £26 in 2010. This information was found in the Retained Earnings section of the Statement of Changes in Equity. We will learn more about this statement in chapter 11.

   b. Total assets were £513, total liabilities were £327, and total shareholders' equity was £186. Total liabilities plus total shareholders' equity equals £513, which equals total assets.

chapter 4

Accrual Accounting Concepts

Chapter Overview

Chapter 4 discusses revenue and expense recognition, and key steps in the accrual accounting process, including recording adjusting entries prior to preparation of an adjusted trial balance and recording closing entries prior to preparation of a post-closing trial balance.

Review of Specific Study Objectives

Timing Issues

- In accounting, the **periodicity assumption** (or time period assumption) assumes that **the economic life of a business can be divided into artificial time periods**. As a result, it is assumed that a company's financial statements can be prepared and reported on a periodic basis. An accounting time period may be one month, one quarter, or one year. Some business transactions affect more than one accounting period; for such transactions, it is important to consider the impact on all affected periods.

- In general, **revenue is recognized** (recorded in the form of a journal entry) in the accounting period when all three of the following criteria are met:

  1. The sales or performance effort is substantially complete.

> **study objective 1**
>
> Explain when revenues and expenses are recognized and how this forms the basis for accrual accounting.

52   **Study Guide to Accompany Financial Accounting: Tools for Business Decision-Making, Fifth Canadian Edition**

2. The amount of revenue is determinable (measurable).
3. Collection of the revenue is reasonably assured.

- The first criterion for revenue recognition states that the sales or performance effort must be substantially complete, or that the revenue must be earned before it is recorded. For a service firm, revenue is considered earned at the time the service is performed, which may or may not be at the time when cash is received. For example, a company may perform a service for a client and in return receive the client's promise to pay in the future. In this case, when the service is performed, the company would record the related revenue, and increase accounts receivable (an asset account) to reflect the client's promise to pay in the future.

- **Expenses are recognized** when, due to an ordinary activity, there is a decrease in future economic benefits related to a decrease in an asset or an increase in a liability and the change can be measured reliably. Expense recognition will often coincide with revenue recognition; for example, if a company performs services and records revenue in an accounting period, then any expenses that the company incurred to earn the related revenue are generally recorded in that same accounting period. However, some expenses are recorded in the period they are incurred, due to uncertainty about whether they will eventually contribute to revenue. For example, research expenditures, which are typically incurred with the expectation that a new product or service will be developed for sale in future periods, are recorded as an expense in the period in which they are incurred, due to uncertainty about whether the research will eventually lead to a saleable product or service.

- Under **accrual basis accounting**, transactions affecting a company's financial statements are recorded in the periods in which the events occur, rather than in the periods in which the company actually receives or pays cash.

- Under **cash basis accounting**, revenue is recorded only when cash is received, and an expense is recorded only when cash is paid. Financial statements prepared under cash basis accounting are often misleading because revenues will not necessarily be recognized when earned, and expenses will not necessarily be recognized when there is a decrease in future economic benefits related to a decrease in an asset or an increase in a liability.

The Basics of Adjusting Entries

study objective 2
Describe the types of adjusting entries and when they are recorded and prepare adjusting entries for prepayments.

- At the end of each accounting period, prior to the preparation of financial statements, **adjusting (journal) entries** are recorded in order to account for such things as revenues that have been earned but not yet recorded and expenses that have been incurred but not yet recorded.

- Before adjusting entries are recorded, some accounts may have incorrect balances because some events are not recorded daily, some costs expire with the passage of time and are not recorded during the accounting period, and some items may simply be unrecorded for a variety of reasons.

- There are **two broad groups of adjusting entries: prepayments and accruals.** **Prepayments** include prepaid expenses (expenses paid for in cash, but not yet used or consumed, and therefore recorded as assets) and unearned revenues (cash received for revenues not yet earned, and therefore recorded as liabilities). **Accruals** include

CHAPTER 4   Accrual Accounting Concepts   53

accrued revenues (revenues earned but not yet received in cash or recorded) and accrued expenses (expenses incurred but not yet paid in cash or recorded).

- There are **two important items** to note before we look at the specifics of adjusting entries:

  1. Adjusting entries will usually affect one income statement account and one statement of financial position account. For example, if an adjusting entry requires a debit to an income statement account, then the credit must be to a statement of financial position account. Or, if an adjusting entry requires a debit to a statement of financial position account, then the credit must be to an income statement account.
  2. Adjusting entries will never affect the Cash account. If the Cash account is affected, then the entry is simply recording a transaction, not an adjustment to the accounts.

Prepayments

- **Prepaid expenses** (or prepayments) are costs that are paid for in cash before they are used or consumed. They are initially recorded as assets and expire either with the passage of time or through use. An adjusting entry for a prepaid expense results in an increase (a debit) to an expense account and a decrease (a credit) to an asset account. A good general rule is that as an asset is used or consumed, its cost becomes an expense.

- **Supplies** are one example of a prepaid expense. For example, if a company purchases $800 of supplies at the beginning of the accounting period, and at the end of the accounting period, a physical count shows that only $200 of supplies remain, $600 of supplies were used in the accounting period. However, at the end of the account-ing period, the Supplies asset account may still show an $800 balance (as a result of the original purchase of supplies at the beginning of the accounting period). If $800 of supplies is recorded on the statement of financial position as at the end of the accounting period, the statement of financial position would not be faithfully representative, because only $200 of supplies remain on hand as at that date. The statement of financial position must reflect the general ledger balances of statement of financial position accounts; therefore, an adjusting entry to adjust the Supplies account by $600 ($800 − $200) is required:

Supplies Expense	600	
Supplies		600
(To record supplies used)		

After the adjusting entry is recorded and posted, the Supplies account will show the correct balance of $200 ($800 − $600), which will also be shown on the statement of financial position. **If the adjusting entry is not recorded**, expenses would be understated, profit would be overstated, assets would be overstated, and shareholders' equity would be overstated, by $600.

- **Insurance** and **rent** are two more examples of prepaid expenses. For example, if a company pays six months' rent ($2,400) at the beginning of March and wants to prepare financial statements as at the end of March, the company should reflect in those financial statements that one month ($400) of the six months' rent has been consumed, and that only five months' rent ($2,000) remains prepaid as at the end of March. However, before adjustment, the Prepaid Rent asset account may still

54   **Study Guide to Accompany Financial Accounting: Tools for Business Decision-Making, Fifth Canadian Edition**

show the full $2,400 balance (for six months' rent paid at the beginning of March). Therefore, an adjusting entry is required for the amount of $400 ($2,400 − $2,000) to adjust the Prepaid Rent account to its correct balance:

Rent Expense	400	
Prepaid Rent		400
(To record expired rent)		

After the entry is recorded and posted, the Prepaid Rent account will show the correct balance of $2,000 ($2,400 − $400), which will be shown on the statement of financial position. **If the adjusting entry is not recorded**, expenses would be understated, profit would be overstated, assets would be overstated, and shareholders' equity would be overstated, by $400.

- The adjusting entry for **depreciation** is another example of a prepayment adjusting entry. Long-lived assets, such as vehicles, equipment, and buildings, are recorded as assets in the year they are acquired, because they are expected to provide economic benefits in future periods. Therefore, acquisition of these assets is essentially a long-term prepayment for services, and throughout the useful life of these long-lived assets, part of the acquisition cost should be recorded as an expense each period. **Depreciation** is the process of allocating the acquisition cost of a long-lived or non-current asset to expense over its useful life, in a rational and systematic manner. It is important to remember that **depreciation is an allocation concept, and not a valuation concept**. Depreciation is not an attempt to reflect the actual change in the value of the asset.

A common practice for calculating depreciation expense is to divide the asset's cost by its estimated useful life. This is known as the **straight-line method of depreciation**. For example, if a vehicle costs $18,000 and has an estimated useful life of five years, depreciation expense for the vehicle is $3,600 per year, or $300 per month. The following entry records one month of depreciation:

Depreciation Expense	300	
Accumulated Depreciation—Vehicle		300
(To record monthly depreciation)		

Accumulated Depreciation is a contra asset account, which is offset against, or subtracted from, the Vehicle asset account on the statement of financial position. A contra asset account's normal balance is a credit. Accumulating depreciation expense in a contra asset account on the statement of financial position allows the financial statement user to see the original cost of the asset as well as the portion of the asset cost that has been depreciated to date. The statement of financial position presentation for this vehicle after adjustment is:

Vehicle	$18,000
Less: Accumulated depreciation—Vehicle	300
Carrying amount	17,700

The asset's **carrying amount**, or book value, is $17,700. The carrying amount is calculated by subtracting the accumulated depreciation from the cost of the asset.

CHAPTER 4 Accrual Accounting Concepts 55

Depreciation is also commonly known as *amortization* and the carrying amount is also commonly known as *book value.*

As was true with Supplies and Prepaid Rent, **if the adjusting entry is not recorded**, expenses would be understated, profit would be overstated, assets would be overstated, and shareholders' equity would be overstated, by $300.

- **Unearned revenues** arise when cash is received before revenue is earned. Unearned revenues are the opposite of prepaid expenses (unearned revenue on one company's books is a prepaid expense on the payer company's books). Magazine subscriptions and rent are two examples of transactions that can give rise to unearned revenues. For example, if company A pays company B $6,000 for six months' rent in advance, company A will record Prepaid Rent of $6,000, and company B will record Unearned Rent Revenue of $6,000. After one month of the six months' rent has been consumed, company B will record the following adjusting entry to show that it has earned one month of rent revenue ($6,000 ÷ 6 = $1,000):

Unearned Rent Revenue	1,000	
Rent Revenue		1,000
(To record revenue earned)		

The adjusting entry requires a decrease (debit) to the Unearned Rent Revenue liability account and an increase (credit) to the Rent Revenue account. **If the adjusting entry is not recorded**, revenue, profit, and shareholders' equity would be understated by $1,000, and liabilities would be overstated by $1,000. Most liabilities are satisfied or settled by payment of cash. However, **unearned revenue is settled by delivery of goods or performance of a service**.

Accruals

- Adjusting entries for **accruals** record **accrued revenues** (revenues earned but not yet received in cash or recorded at the financial statement date), and **accrued expenses** (expenses incurred but not yet paid or recorded at the financial statement date).

  An adjusting entry for an accrual will **increase** both a **statement of financial position** and an **income statement** account.

- **Accrued revenues** are revenues earned but not yet received in cash or recorded at the financial statement date. Examples include interest revenue, rent revenue, and service revenue. Accrued revenues may be earned as time passes (e.g., interest revenue and rent revenue) or they may be earned from goods delivered or services performed that have not been billed or collected yet (e.g., service revenue). The adjusting entry to record accrued revenue requires an **increase in a receivable (debit) and an increase in a revenue (credit)**. For example, if a company has earned $300 in interest revenue, which has not been collected in cash or recorded at the financial statement date, the company would record an adjusting entry to recognize the revenue as of the financial statement date:

Interest Receivable	300	
Interest Revenue		300
(To record interest revenue)		

If the adjusting entry is not recorded, assets and shareholders' equity would be understated, and revenues and profit would be understated, by $300. When the

---

study objective 3

Prepare adjusting entries for accruals and describe how adjusting entries affect the income statement and the statement of financial position.

56 Study Guide to Accompany Financial Accounting: Tools for Business Decision-Making, Fifth Canadian Edition

company collects the interest revenue in cash, it will record a debit to Cash and a credit to Interest Receivable (not Interest Revenue).

- **Accrued expenses** are expenses incurred but not yet paid or recorded at the financial statement date. Examples include interest expense, rent expense, tax expense, and salaries expense. The adjusting entry to record an accrued expense requires an **increase (debit) to an expense account and an increase (credit) to a liability account**.

  For example, assume that on November 1, a company borrows $12,000 at 6% interest for six months, and that the principal and all interest are due on May 1. If the company prepares financial statements as at December 31, then the company must record an adjusting entry for the interest owed but not yet paid or recorded as at December 31. Interest owed is calculated by multiplying the note's face value by the interest rate, which is expressed as an annual rate. The company's accrued interest expense amounts to $12,000 \times 0.06 \times {}^2/_{12}$ or $120; therefore, the company would record an adjusting entry to recognize the accrued interest expense as at the financial statement date:

Interest Expense	120	
Interest Payable		120
(To record accrued interest)		

  It is important to note that the Notes Payable account is not affected in the adjusting entry. Notes Payable would have been credited when the principal of $12,000 was borrowed, and will be debited when the principal of $12,000 is repaid. **If the adjusting entry for accrued interest expense is not recorded**, liabilities and interest expense would be understated, and profit and shareholders' equity would be overstated, by $120.

- For accounting purposes, corporate income taxes must be recorded as an accrued expense, based on the current year's estimated profit. Corporations pay corporate income tax payments throughout the year in the form of monthly instalments; however, these instalments are normally based on the income tax that was actually payable in the preceding year. If there was no preceding year (if this is the company's first year of operations) or if there was no tax payable in the preceding year, then no income tax instalments are required to be paid. However, **income tax expense** must still be accrued based on the current year's estimated profit. The following adjusting entry would be recorded to accrue $500 of estimated corporate taxes owing:

Income Tax Expense	500	
Income Tax Payable		500
(To record income tax expense)		

- In summary, the **accrual basis of accounting** requires that transactions affecting a company's financial statements are recorded in the periods in which the events occur, rather than when the company actually receives or pays cash. This gives rise to the need for adjusting entries, which record any events that occurred in the period that are not yet recorded as at the financial statement date. Adjusting entries bring the accounts up to date as at the financial statement date, and allow for preparation of financial statements in accordance with the accrual basis of accounting.

- Public companies must record adjusting entries at least quarterly, while private companies must record adjusting entries at least annually. More frequent adjustments (e.g., monthly) are also common for both types of companies.

CHAPTER 4 Accrual Accounting Concepts 57

The Adjusted Trial Balance and Financial Statements

- An **adjusted trial balance** is prepared after adjusting entries have been journalized and posted. The purpose of an adjusted trial balance is to prove the equality of total debit balances and total credit balances in the general ledger, after all adjusting entries have been journalized and posted.

- Since the adjusted trial balance reflects account balances that have been brought up to date as at the financial statement date, the adjusted trial balance can be used to prepare the financial statements. The **income statement** is prepared using revenue and expense accounts. The **statement of changes in equity** is prepared using shareholders' equity accounts, including retained earnings. (A statement of retained earnings is prepared by private companies using ASPE.) The **statement of financial position** is prepared using asset, liability, and shareholders' equity accounts (with retained earnings equal to ending retained earnings as reported on the statement of changes in equity).

> **study objective 4**
>
> Describe the nature and purpose of the adjusted trial balance, and prepare one.

Closing the Books

- **Temporary accounts** are accounts that relate to only a particular accounting period (e.g., revenues, expenses, and dividends). In contrast, **permanent accounts** are accounts with balances that carry forward to future accounting periods (e.g., statement of financial position accounts such as assets, liabilities, and shareholders' equity).

- At the end of the accounting period, **temporary account balances are closed or zeroed out, and transferred to the permanent shareholders' equity account, Retained Earnings. Closing entries** formally record in the general ledger the transfer of the balances in the revenue, expense, and dividends accounts to the Retained Earnings account. Closing entries transfer revenues and expenses to another temporary account, Income Summary, and then transfer the resulting profit or loss in Income Summary to Retained Earnings.

- **Closing entries accomplish two things.** They update the Retained Earnings account, and they eliminate the balance in each temporary account, making each temporary account ready to accumulate data in the next accounting period.

- A **post-closing trial balance** is prepared after closing entries have been journalized and posted. The purpose of the post-closing trial balance is to prove the equality of total debit balances and total credit balances in the general ledger, after all closing entries have been journalized and posted. The post-closing trial balance also helps to confirm that all temporary accounts have a zero balance going into the next accounting period. Only permanent accounts should appear on the post-closing trial balance. If, for example, a post-closing trial balance shows a balance of $5,000 in Salaries Expense, then the Salaries Expense temporary account was incorrectly excluded when closing entries were recorded.

- A company under IFRS may record amounts in **Other Comprehensive Income** accounts throughout the year. Other Comprehensive Income accounts are temporary accounts, and are closed out to related shareholders' equity accounts at the end of each accounting period. The related shareholders' equity accounts may be totalled and classified in a single **Accumulated Other Comprehensive Income** account in shareholders' equity.

> **study objective 5**
>
> Prepare closing entries and a post-closing trial balance.

58 Study Guide to Accompany Financial Accounting: Tools for Business Decision-Making, Fifth Canadian Edition

- The accounting cycle was introduced in Chapter 3. The cycle begins with analysis of business transactions and ends with the preparation of a post-closing trial balance. The steps are done in sequence and are repeated in each accounting period.

  Steps 1–3 may be done on a daily basis in the accounting period.

  Steps 4–7 may be done periodically, such as monthly, quarterly, or annually.

  Steps 8 and 9 are usually done only at the end of a company's annual accounting period.

  The steps in the **accounting cycle** are as follows:

  1. Analyze business transactions.
  2. Journalize the transactions.
  3. Post to general ledger accounts.
  4. Prepare a trial balance.
  5. Journalize and post adjusting entries: prepayments/accruals.
  6. Prepare an adjusted trial balance.
  7. Prepare financial statements: Income statement, Statement of changes in equity, Statement of financial position, Statement of cash flows.
  8. Journalize and post closing entries.
  9. Prepare a post-closing trial balance.

  Below is a comparison of IFRS and ASPE, for key topics discussed in Chapter 4:

comparing
IFRS and ASPE

Key Differences	International Financial Reporting Standards (IFRS)	Accounting Standards for Private Enterprises (ASPE)
Frequency of adjusting entries	Public companies must release quarterly financial statements so adjusting entries have to be made at least quarterly, although many will record adjusting entries every month.	Private companies usually release financial statements to their banker, and shareholder(s), along with certain financial information to the Canada Revenue Agency on an annual basis so adjusting entries may be done only at year end, although many will record adjusting entries more frequently.
Terminology	The term *depreciation* refers to the allocation of the cost of depreciable tangible assets over their useful lives. The term *amortization* refers to the allocation of the cost of certain kinds of intangible assets over their useful lives.	The term *amortization* is used for the allocation of the cost of both depreciable tangible assets and certain kinds of intangible assets over their useful lives.
Closing entries	Other comprehensive income components are closed into accumulated other comprehensive income components.	Comprehensive income is not reported.

CHAPTER 4 Accrual Accounting Concepts 59

Chapter Self-Test

As you work through the questions and problems, remember to use the **Decision Toolkit** discussed and used in the text:

1. *Decision Checkpoints:* Ask a question relevant to the decision being made.
2. *Info Needed for Decision:* Make a choice regarding the information needed to answer the question.
3. *Tools to Use for Decision:* Review what the information identified in Step 2 does for the decision-making process.
4. *How to Evaluate Results:* Identify specifically how the information identified in Step 2 should be evaluated to answer the question relevant to the decision being made.

Note: The notation "(SO 1)" means that the question relates to study objective 1.

Multiple Choice

Please circle the correct answer.

1. A company that sells appliances should normally recognize revenue when   (SO 1)
    a.   a customer places an order for an appliance.
    b.   a customer pays for an appliance before receiving delivery of it.
    c.   a customer receives delivery of an appliance.
    d.   a customer pays for an appliance after receiving delivery of it.

2. In 2012, the Abbott Corporation pays expenses of $3,000, and bills a customer   (SO 1)
   $10,000 for work performed in 2012. The customer pays Abbott in 2013. If
   Abbott uses the cash basis of accounting, Abbott will report
    a.   revenue of $10,000 in 2012.
    b.   revenue of $10,000 in 2013.
    c.   expenses of $3,000 in 2013.
    d.   profit of $7,000 in 2012.

3. In 2012, the Abbott Corporation pays expenses of $3,000, and bills a customer   (SO 1)
   $10,000 for work performed in 2012. The customer pays Abbott in 2013.
   If Abbott uses the accrual basis of accounting, Abbott will report
    a.   revenue of $10,000 in 2012.
    b.   revenue of $10,000 in 2013.
    c.   expenses of $3,000 in 2013.
    d.   profit of $7,000 in 2013.

4. Adjusting journal entries must be prepared   (SO 2)
    a.   at the end of every calendar year.
    b.   at the end of every month.
    c.   when the accountant has time to write them.
    d.   whenever financial statements are to be prepared.

5. A company has the following results for the year ended December 31, 2012:   (SO 2)

Revenues	$160,000
Depreciation expense	50,000

60   **Study Guide to Accompany Financial Accounting: Tools for Business Decision-Making, Fifth Canadian Edition**

Rent expense	10,000
Wages expense	25,000
Advertising expense	30,000
Dividends	10,000
Utilities expense	15,000

The corporate income tax rate is 40%, and no instalment payments were made during 2012. The corporate income taxes for 2012 will be paid on March 31, 2013. What adjusting entry, if any, is required on December 31, 2012, with respect to corporate income tax?

a. Income Tax Expense   8,000

   Income Tax Payable   8,000

b. Income Tax Expense   12,000

   Income Tax Payable   12,000

c. Income Tax Payable   8,000

   Income Tax Expense   8,000

d. No entry is required.

(SO 2)   6. Cash received and recorded as a liability before revenue is earned is called
  a.   an accrued revenue.
  b.   an unearned revenue.
  c.   an unrecorded revenue.
  d.   none of the above.

(SO 2)   7. On October 1, a company paid $6,000 for a one-year insurance policy, and debited Prepaid Insurance and credited Cash. The adjusting entry on December 31 will require a
  a.   debit to Insurance Expense for $1,500.
  b.   debit to Insurance Expense for $4,500.
  c.   credit to Prepaid Insurance for $4,500.
  d.   credit to Cash for $1,500.

(SO 2)   8. At the beginning of an accounting period, a company purchased $800 of supplies, and debited Supplies and credited Cash. At the end of the accounting period, a physical count of supplies shows that only $100 of supplies are still on hand. The adjusting entry will require a
  a.   credit to Supplies Expense for $700.
  b.   debit to Supplies Expense for $100.
  c.   debit to Supplies for $700.
  d.   credit to Supplies for $700.

(SO 2)   9. Little Corporation received $5,000 from a customer for work to be done in the future, and debited Cash and credited Unearned Revenue. At the end of the accounting period, Little has earned $2,000 of the revenue. The adjusting entry will require a
  a.   debit to Cash for $2,000.
  b.   debit to Service Revenue for $2,000.
  c.   credit to Service Revenue for $2,000.
  d.   credit to Service Revenue for $3,000.

CHAPTER 4 Accrual Accounting Concepts   61

10. Interest expense on a note payable is normally recognized   (SO 3)
    a.   on the date the note payable is signed.
    b.   on a daily basis throughout the life of the note payable.
    c.   periodically throughout the life of the note payable; for example, prior to
         financial statement preparation and/or at the time the payment of interest.
    d.   at the time of payment of interest.

11. At the end of the accounting period, Cherry Corporation has not billed a   (SO 3)
    customer for $400 of rent. The adjusting entry will require a
    a.   debit to Cash for $400.
    b.   credit to Accounts Receivable for $400.
    c.   credit to Unearned Revenue for $400.
    d.   credit to Rent Revenue for $400.

12. If the adjusting entry for an accrued expense is not recorded, then   (SO 3)
    a.   liabilities and expenses will be understated.
    b.   liabilities and expenses will be overstated.
    c.   profit will be understated.
    d.   liabilities and shareholders' equity will be overstated.

13. Hirani Corporation pays its employees $1,000 per five-day (Monday-Friday)   (SO 3)
    week. The last day of the month falls on a Thursday, and financial statements will
    be prepared as at that date. The adjusting entry for salaries will require a
    a.   debit to Salaries Payable for $200.
    b.   credit to Salaries Expense for $200.
    c.   debit to Salaries Expense for $200.
    d.   debit to Salaries Expense for $800.

14. Failure to record accrued interest expense at the end of an accounting period (SO 3)
    would cause
    a.   profit to be understated.
    b.   an overstatement of assets and an overstatement of liabilities.
    c.   an understatement of expenses and an understatement of liabilities.
    d.   an overstatement of expenses and an overstatement of liabilities.

15. Failure to record accrued revenue at the end of an accounting period would cause (SO 3)
    a.   profit to be overstated.
    b.   an understatement of assets and an understatement of revenues.
    c.   an understatement of revenues and an understatement of liabilities.
    d.   an understatement of revenues and an overstatement of liabilities.

16. Which of the statements below is not true?   (SO 4)
    a.   An adjusted trial balance should show general ledger account balances.
    b.   An adjusted trial balance can be used to prepare financial statements.
    c.   An adjusted trial balance proves the mathematical equality of total debit
         balances and total credit balances in the general ledger after all adjustments
         have been made.
    d.   An adjusted trial balance is prepared before all transactions have been
         journalized.

62   Study Guide to Accompany Financial Accounting: Tools for Business Decision-Making, Fifth Canadian Edition

(SO 5)   17.   Financial statements can be prepared directly from the
- a.   trial balance.
- b.   adjusted trial balance.
- c.   post-closing trial balance.
- d.   reversing trial balance.

(SO 5)   18.   Which of the following is a temporary account?
- a.   The dividends account
- b.   An asset account
- c.   A liability account
- d.   A shareholders' equity account

(SO 5)   19.   Other Comprehensive Income accounts are
- a.   temporary accounts.
- b.   permanent accounts.
- c.   shareholders' equity accounts.
- d.   closed out to Retained Earnings at the end of each accounting period.

(SO 5)   20.   Which of the following correctly describes the closing process?
- a.   Profit or loss is transferred to the Cash account.
- b.   Profit or loss is transferred to the Accumulated Other Comprehensive Income account.
- c.   Permanent accounts become ready to accumulate data in the next accounting period.
- d.   Each revenue account and each expense account is closed to Income Summary, which is in turn closed to Retained Earnings.

(SO 5)   21.   Which is the correct order of selected steps in the accounting cycle?
- a.   Post to general ledger accounts, journalize transactions, prepare a trial balance, prepare financial statements.
- b.   Journalize transactions, post to general ledger accounts, journalize and post closing entries, journalize and post adjusting entries.
- c.   Journalize transactions, post to general ledger accounts, journalize and post adjusting entries, journalize and post closing entries.
- d.   Prepare financial statements, journalize and post adjusting entries, journalize and post closing entries, prepare a post-closing trial balance.

Problems

(SO 2, 3)   1.   The following are transactions for Cassie Corporation, for the month of June:

1. The Supplies account shows a balance of $1,500, but a physical count on June 30 shows only $300 of supplies on hand.
2. Cassie purchased a one-year insurance policy for $3,600 on May 1. Cassie debited Prepaid Insurance.
3. On June 1, Cassie received $1,200 from another corporation, which is renting a small building from Cassie for six months beginning on June 1. Cassie credited Unearned Rent Revenue.
4. Cassie performed services for a client totalling $900, but has not yet billed the client or recorded the transaction.
5. Cassie pays employees $2,000 per five-day (Monday - Friday) week and June 30 falls on a Wednesday.

CHAPTER 4 Accrual Accounting Concepts 63

6. Cassie owns a van that cost $18,000 and has a useful life of six years. The van was purchased in early April of this year, and no depreciation has been recorded for the van so far this year.

a. Prepare the adjusting entries.

Date	Account Titles	Debit	Credit

b. What type of account is the account that was credited in (6) above? Show how the van would be reflected on Cassie's statement of financial position, after the adjusting entry in (6) is recorded.

2. For each of the following, identify whether assets, liabilities, shareholders' equity (SO 2, 3) (SE), or profit were overstated (O), understated (U), or not affected (NA). Assume that the company's year end is June 30.

a. The company did not record an adjusting entry for a June utility bill received in July.

b. During June, $700 of supplies were purchased and debited to the Supplies account. At the end of June, an inventory count showed that only $300 of supplies was left on hand.

The following adjusting entry was made:

Supplies Expense   300
    Supplies   300

c. The company completed work for a customer on June 30, but a bill for the work was not prepared until July.

d. The company did not record an adjusting entry for equipment depreciation.

e. At the beginning of June, Unearned Revenue had a balance of $1,000. During the month of June, $700 of that unearned revenue was earned, but no adjusting entry was recorded.

64   **Study Guide to Accompany Financial Accounting: Tools for Business Decision-Making, Fifth Canadian Edition**

(SO 2, 3)   3.   The Upshaw Park Corporation prepares monthly financial statements. Presented below is an income statement for the month of June:

UPSHAW PARK CORPORATION
Income Statement
Month Ended June 30

Revenues		
Admission revenues		$30,000
Expenses		
Insurance expense	$4,200	
Salary expense	4,000	
Depreciation expense	2,200	
Advertising expense	700	
Total expenses		11,100
Profit before income tax		18,900
Income tax expense		0
Profit		$18,900

Additional data: When the income statement was prepared, the following information was not taken into consideration:

1. An electricity bill for $1,500 was received on the last day of the month for electricity used in the month of June.
2. An advance payment of $1,000 was received in June for park space to be rented in July. The amount was included in admission revenues for June.
3. Supplies on hand at the beginning of the month were $2,000. Upshaw purchased additional supplies during June for $1,500 in cash. At June 30, $1,100 of supplies was on hand.
4. At the beginning of the month, Upshaw purchased a new truck, with an estimated useful life of eight years, for $38,400 cash. Truck depreciation was not included in depreciation expense for June.
5. Salaries owed to employees as at the end of the month totalled $4,400. The salaries were paid on July 3.
6. Income tax expense not yet paid is estimated to be at the rate of 40% of profit before income tax.

Prepare a corrected income statement.

(SO 2, 3)   4.   Refer to the HMV and WHSmith financial statements found in the appendices at the end of this study guide for information in answering the following questions. Do not forget to use the **Decision Toolkit** approach for help in answering the questions.

a.   Using HMV's statement of financial position and income statement, identify items that may result in adjusting entries for prepayments.

b.   Using WHSmith's statement of financial position and income statement, identify accounts that may be involved in adjusting entries for accruals.

CHAPTER 4 Accrual Accounting Concepts 65

Solutions to Self-Test

Multiple Choice

1. c In general, revenue recognition occurs when the sales or performance effort is substantially complete, the amount is determinable (measurable), and collection is reasonably assured. Assuming that collection is reasonably assured, the company should normally record revenue when a customer receives delivery of an appliance.

2. b Under the cash basis of accounting, revenue would not be reported in 2012 because Abbott was not paid in 2012. However, Abbott would report the expenses because they were paid in 2012. Therefore, Abbott would report a loss of $3,000 (the expenses paid) in 2012.

3. a Under the accrual basis of accounting, revenue would be reported in 2012 because Abbott performed the work in 2012. The expenses would also be reported in 2012. Therefore, Abbott would report a profit of $7,000 in 2012, not 2013.

4. d Adjusting entries are prepared whenever financial statements are to be prepared.

5. b Profit before income tax = $30,000; therefore, income tax expense = $30,000 × 40% = $12,000. Remember that Dividends is not an expense and does not enter into the calculation of profit before (or after) income tax.

6. b An accrued revenue is a revenue that has been earned but not yet received in cash or recorded. *Unrecorded revenue* is an accounting term, but it is not appropriate in this instance.

7. a The adjusting entry is:

Insurance Expense	1,500	
Prepaid Insurance		1,500

$6,000 × $^3/_{12}$ = $1,500

8. d The adjusting journal entry is:

Supplies Expense	700	
Supplies		700

9. c The adjusting entry is:

Unearned Revenue	2,000	
Service Revenue		2,000

10 c Expenses are recognized when, due to an ordinary activity, there is a decrease in future economic benefits related to a decrease in an asset or an increase in a liability and this change can be measured reliably. Interest expense is incurred as time passes; however, interest expense would not normally be recognized on a daily basis. Interest expense on a note payable is normally recognized periodically throughout the life of the note payable; for example, prior to financial statement preparation and/or at the time payment of interest.

66 Study Guide to Accompany Financial Accounting: Tools for Business Decision-Making, Fifth Canadian Edition

11. d   The adjusting entry is:

Accounts Receivable	400	
Rent Revenue		400

12. a   The adjusting entry would debit an expense and credit a liability, thereby increasing both accounts. If an expense is not recorded, profit will be overstated (as will shareholders' equity) and, if a liability is not recorded, liabilities will be understated.

13. d   The adjusting entry is:

Salaries Expense	800	
Salaries Payable		800

14. c   An adjusting entry for an accrued expense would increase an expense account and increase a liability account. Failure to record such an entry would result in an understatement of expenses, an overstatement of profit, and understatement of a liability.

15. b   An adjusting entry for accrued revenue would increase a revenue account and increase an asset account. Failure to record such an entry would result in an understatement of revenue, an understatement of profit, and understatement of an asset.

16. d   The adjusted trial balance is prepared after all adjusting entries have been journalized and posted. It shows the adjusted balance of each account at the end of the accounting period. The purpose of the adjusted trial balance is to prove the equality of total debit balances and total credit balances in the general ledger after all adjustments have been made.

17. b   The trial balance does not include the effects of adjusting entries, the post-closing trial balance excludes all temporary accounts, and there is no such thing as a reversing trial balance.

18. a   Asset, liability, and shareholders' equity accounts are all permanent accounts.

19. a   Other Comprehensive Income accounts are temporary accounts, and are closed out to related shareholders' equity accounts at the end of each accounting period.

20. d   Profit or loss is not transferred to the Cash or AOCI account, permanent accounts are not closed, and revenue and expense accounts are closed to Income Summary (which is then closed to Retained Earnings).

21. c   All of the other answers are incorrect.

Problems

1.   a

1. Supplies Expense	1,200	
Supplies		1,200
(To record supplies used, $1,500 − $300)		

CHAPTER 4   Accrual Accounting Concepts   67

2. Insurance Expense	600	
Prepaid Insurance		600
(To record insurance expired)		

$3,600 \div 12$ months $=$ $300 per month

$300 per month $\times$ 2 months $=$ $600

3. Unearned Rent Revenue	200	
Rent Revenue		200
(To record rent earned)		

$1,200 $\div$ 6 months $=$ $200 per month

4. Accounts Receivable	900	
Service Revenue		900
(To record revenue earned)		

5. Salaries Expense	1,200	
Salaries Payable		1,200
(To record accrued salaries)		

$2,000 $\div$ 5 days $=$ $400 per day

$400 per day $\times$ 3 days $=$ $1,200

6. Depreciation Expense	750	
Accumulated Depreciation—vehicles		750
(To record depreciation)		

$18,000 $\div$ 6 years $=$ $3,000 per year $\times {}^{3}/_{12}$

b. Accumulated Depreciation is a contra asset account, which is offset against, or subtracted from, the related asset account on the statement of financial position. After the adjusting entry is recorded, the van would be reflected on Cassie's statement of financial position as follows:

Vehicles	$18,000
Less: Accumulated depreciation—vehicles	750
Carrying amount	17,250

The $17,250 is the carrying amount of the asset and has no relationship to the fair value of the asset. Depreciation is an allocation concept, not a valuation concept.

2.

Item	Assets	Liabilities	Profit	SE	Reason
a.	NA	U	O	O	The utility expense was incurred in June. Profit affects shareholders' equity; if profit was overstated, SE was also overstated.

b.	O	NA	O	O	The adjusting entry should have been:

Supplies Expense   400

    Supplies   400

Therefore, Supplies Expense was understated and Supplies was overstated.

c.	U	NA	U	U	The work was done in June so revenue should have been recognized in June with the following adjusting entry:

Accounts Receivable

    Revenue

d.	O	NA	O	O	The adjusting entry should have been:

Depreciation Expense

    Accumulated Depreciation

      —Equipment

Accumulated depreciation is a contra asset account; therefore, it would reduce assets.

e.	NA	O	U	U	The adjusting entry should have been:

Unearned Revenue   700

    Revenue   700

3.

UPSHAW PARK CORPORATION

Income Statement

Month Ended June 30

Revenues		
Admission revenues ($30,000 − $1,000)		$29,000
Expenses		
Salary expense ($4,000 + $4,400)	$8,400	
Insurance expense	4,200	
Depreciation expense ($2,200 + $400)	2,600	
Supplies expense ($2,000 + $1,500 − $1,100)	2,400	
Utilities expense	1,500	
Advertising expense	700	
Total expenses		19,800
Profit before income tax		9,200
Income tax expense ($9,200 × 40%)		3,680
Profit		$ 5,520

(*Note:* Depreciation on new truck is $38,400 ÷ 8 years = $4,800 per year; $4,800 per year ÷ 12 months = $400 per month)

CHAPTER 4 Accrual Accounting Concepts 69

4.

a. Examples of prepayments found on HMV's statement of financial position include property, plant, and equipment and intangible assets. According to HMV's notes to financial statements, depreciation and amortization expense (related to long-term prepayment of property, plant, and equipment and intangible assets, respectively), were deducted in arriving at operating profit on the income statement.

b. Examples of accruals found on WHSmith's statement of financial position include trade and other receivables, trade and other payables, and provisions. Trade and other receivables includes trade accounts receivable, which records revenue earned but not yet collected. Trade and other payables includes trade accounts payable, which records accruals for amounts owing to trade suppliers. Provisions are liabilities of uncertain timing or amount, which are accrued to faithfully represent WHSmith's obligations. In addition, some of the finance revenue (investment income) reported on the income statement likely relate to accrued interest income earned on bank deposits, and some of the finance costs reported on the income statement likely relate to accrued finance costs related to provisions.

chapter 5

Merchandising Operations

Chapter Overview

Chapter 5 discusses the differences between service companies and merchandising companies, and key accounting concepts related to merchandising operations.
You will learn how to prepare journal entries for purchases and sales under a perpetual inventory system, and how to prepare and analyze the income statement of a merchandising company.

Review of Specific Study Objectives

Merchandising vs. Service Companies

- The **operating cycle** of a merchandising company is usually longer than the operating cycle of a service company, because a merchandising company will purchase merchandise for cash or on account first, before it can sell the merchandise for cash or on account.

- A merchandising company's primary source of revenue is the sale of merchandise, called **sales revenue**. Expenses are divided into two categories: cost of goods sold (the total cost of the merchandise that was sold during the period) and operating expenses. Profit (or loss) is determined as follows:

> study objective 1
>
> Identify the differences between service and merchandising companies.

72   Study Guide to Accompany Financial Accounting: Tools for Business Decision-Making, Fifth Canadian Edition

	Sales revenue
−	Cost of goods sold
=	Gross profit
−	Operating expenses
=	Profit (loss) before income tax
−	Income tax expense
=	Profit (loss)

- A merchandising company will use one of two kinds of systems to account for inventory and cost of goods sold: the **perpetual inventory system** or the **periodic inventory system**.

  In a perpetual system, detailed records are maintained of the cost of each product that is purchased and sold. Because detailed records are maintained perpetually (or continuously), at all times throughout the accounting period, these records show the quantity and cost of inventory purchased, sold, and on hand. Each time a sale occurs, cost of the goods sold is determined, and transferred from the Merchandise Inventory asset account to the Cost of Goods Sold expense account. Implementation of calculator systems, bar codes, and optical scanners makes such a detailed system practicable.

  In a periodic system, detailed inventory records are not maintained throughout the period. Cost of Goods Sold is **determined only at the end of the accounting period** when a physical count of goods is conducted. The physical count of goods at the end of the accounting period determines ending inventory. Calculation of Cost of Goods Sold in a periodic system is as follows:

	Beginning inventory
+	Cost of goods purchased
=	Cost of goods available for sale
−	Ending inventory
=	Cost of goods sold

- A perpetual system provides better inventory control. Goods on hand can be counted at any time, and quantities on hand can be compared with perpetual inventory records. Any shortages can be investigated immediately. The quantity of inventory can be managed so that neither too much nor too little inventory is on hand at a given time.

Perpetual Inventory System—Purchases

study objective 2

Prepare entries for purchases under a perpetual inventory system.

- **Purchases**, either for cash or on account (credit), are normally recorded when goods are transferred from the seller (supplier) to the buyer (merchandiser). A business document (e.g., a cancelled cheque or a cash register receipt for a cash purchase, or a purchase invoice for a credit purchase) will provide written evidence of the purchase.

- A purchase is recorded with a debit to Merchandise Inventory and a credit to Cash or Accounts Payable. The Merchandise Inventory account is used only for purchases of goods that will be resold. If the company buys a different type of asset (e.g., supplies for internal use and not for resale), then the debit will be to a separate account (e.g., Supplies).

CHAPTER 5 Merchandising Operations 73

- Freight terms are normally indicated on the purchase invoice. Freight terms determine whether the seller or buyer must pay the cost of transporting the goods to the buyer's place of business, and whether the seller or buyer is responsible for the risk of damage to the merchandise during transit. Freight terms are often expressed as **FOB shipping point** or **FOB destination**. FOB means "free on board."

  FOB shipping point means that the buyer (merchandiser) must pay the freight cost of transporting the goods from the shipping point (usually the seller's place of business) to the destination (usually the buyer's place of business), and that the buyer is responsible for the risk of damage to the merchandise during transit. The buyer would include the freight cost in its cost of purchasing the inventory. The buyer would record the freight cost with a debit to Merchandise Inventory and a credit to Cash or Accounts Payable.

  FOB destination means that the seller (supplier) must pay the freight cost of transporting the goods from the shipping point to the destination, and that the seller is responsible for the risk of damage to the merchandise during transit. However, the seller's cost of transporting the goods is not considered a cost of its inventory. The seller would record the transport cost with a debit to Freight Out or Delivery Expense and a credit to Cash or Accounts Payable, where Freight Out or Delivery Expense is an operating expense account.

- Purchased goods may be unsuitable due to damage, defect, or inferior quality, or they may not meet the buyer's specifications. A **purchase return** is recorded when goods are returned to the seller. A **purchase allowance** is recorded when the purchaser keeps the merchandise but is granted an allowance (deduction) by the seller. A purchase return or allowance is recorded by debiting Cash or Accounts Payable and crediting Merchandise Inventory.

- Purchase terms may include a **quantity discount** for a bulk purchase. Quantity discounts are not recorded or accounted for separately. If a quantity discount is applied, the net amount of the invoice is recorded as the purchase cost.

- Credit terms may include a **purchase discount** to encourage buyers to pay the amount owed early. Purchase credit terms are noted on the purchase invoice, and specify the amount of the discount and the time period during which it is offered. For example, credit terms of 1/10, n/30 means that the purchaser will receive a 1% cash discount on the invoice price (net of any purchase returns or allowances) if the invoice is paid within 10 days; otherwise, the full net amount of the invoice is due within 30 days. For example, assume that on May 1, a buyer purchases $5,000 of merchandise on account with credit terms of 2/10, n/30:

Merchandise Inventory	5,000	
Accounts Payable		5,000
(To record purchase on account)		

If the invoice is paid by May 11, then the following entry is required:

Accounts Payable	5,000	
Cash ($5,000 − $100)		4,900
Merchandise Inventory ($5,000 × 2%)		100
(To record payment—with discount on credit terms 2/10, n/30)		

74   Study Guide to Accompany Financial Accounting: Tools for Business Decision-Making, Fifth Canadian Edition

If the buyer pays after May 11, then the following entry is required:

Accounts Payable	5,000	
Cash		5,000
(To record payment—no discount)		

It is usually advantageous for the buyer to take all purchase discounts. Passing up a 2/10, n/30 discount is the equivalent of paying an annual interest rate of 36.5% (2% $\times$ 365 $\div$ 20)! Some companies even borrow money at a lower interest rate in order to pay within the purchase discount period, and avoid higher annual interest rates.

Perpetual Inventory System—Sales

---

study objective 3

Prepare entries for sales under a perpetual inventory system.

- Sales revenues are recorded when earned, and for a merchandising company, revenue is typically earned when ownership of the merchandise transfers from the seller (merchandiser) to the buyer (customer). Sales may be for cash or on account (credit) and should be supported by a business document (a cash register tape for cash sales and a sales invoice for credit sales).

- Two entries are made for each sale in a perpetual inventory system: one entry to record the sale and another entry to record the cost of the merchandise sold. If goods that were purchased at a cost of $200 are sold for cash of $400, the following entries are required:

Cash	400	
Sales		400
(To record a cash sale)		
Cost of Goods Sold	200	
Merchandise Inventory		200
(To record the cost of merchandise sold)		

The selling price of the goods is used for the amount recorded in the first entry, while the purchase cost of the goods is used for the amount recorded in the second entry. If the goods were sold on account, the entries above would have been the same, except for the debit in the first entry, which would have been a debit to Accounts Receivable instead of Cash.

- When a company collects sales taxes from selling a product or service, the sales taxes collected are not recorded as sales revenue. Sales taxes collected are recorded separately with a credit to a liability account (e.g., Sales Taxes Payable). When the sales taxes are remitted to the government, the payment is recorded with a debit to the related liability account.

- The **Sales** account is used only for sale of merchandise inventory. If an asset is sold, the credit is recorded in the related asset account. A company may choose to have several Sales accounts, with each one dedicated to a different product line or type. Tracking sales by product line or type would give management information needed to manage its inventory. However, often only one total sales figure is reported on the income statement.

- If goods sold are later returned to the merchandiser, two entries are required. If the goods that were sold in the entry above are all returned to the merchandiser in good working order, the required entries are:

CHAPTER 5   Merchandising Operations   75

Sales Returns and Allowances	400	
Cash		400
(To record return of goods)		
Merchandise Inventory	200	
Cost of Goods Sold		200
(To record cost of goods returned)		

Once again, note that the selling price of the goods is used for the amount recorded in the first entry, while the purchase cost of the goods is used for the amount recorded in the second entry.

- Sales Returns and Allowances is a **contra revenue account** to Sales. If a debit to record the return of goods is recorded in the Sales account, the return would be hidden in the Sales account. Instead, the Sales Returns and Allowances contra revenue account is used to provide management with the information necessary to monitor the amount of goods returned and correct any consistent problems. For example, high Sales Returns and Allowances may suggest that the goods the company is selling are poor quality, or that the company itself is making errors in delivery or shipment of goods, and that management should take steps to deal with the problem(s).

- Similar to a purchase discount, the merchandiser may offer the customer a **sales discount** to encourage early payment of the amount owed. For example, assume that on May 1, a merchandiser purchases $5,000 of merchandise on account, and that the merchandiser sells this merchandise to a customer on account for $6,000 with credit terms of 2/10, n/30. The entries to record the sale on the books of the merchandiser are as follows:

Accounts Receivable	6,000	
Sales		6,000
(To record sales on account)		
Cost of Goods Sold	5,000	
Merchandise Inventory		5,000
(To record the cost of merchandise sold)		

If the merchandiser's customer pays for the goods by May 11 (within the 10-day discount period), the entry to record collection is as follows:

Cash ($6,000 − $120)	5,880	
Sales Discounts ($6,000 × 2%)	120	
Accounts Receivable		6,000
(To record collection within the 2/10, n/30 discount period)		

If the merchandiser's customer pays for the goods after May 11, the entry to record collection is as follows:

Cash	6,000	
Accounts Receivable		6,000
(To record collection—no discount taken)		

Sales Discounts is another contra revenue account to Sales.

76   Study Guide to Accompany Financial Accounting: Tools for Business Decision-Making, Fifth Canadian Edition

- Below is a summary of typical revenue and contra revenue accounts used by merchandising companies:

Account Name	Account Type	Normal Balance
Sales	Revenue	Credit
Sales Returns and Allowances	Contra Revenue	Debit
Sales Discounts	Contra Revenue	Debit

Income Statement

study objective 4

Prepare a single-step and a multiple-step income statement.

- In a **single-step income statement**, total expenses are subtracted from total revenues to determine profit (or loss) before income tax. This income statement is called a single-step income statement because only one subtraction is required to arrive at profit (or loss) before income tax. However, on a single-step income statement, income tax expense is normally shown separately, and subtracted from profit (or loss) before income tax to arrive at profit (or loss).

- In a **multiple-step income statement**, several steps are shown in determining profit (or loss), in order to provide financial statement users with additional useful information. The multiple-step income statement shows five main steps:

  1. Net sales: Sales returns and allowances and sales discounts are subtracted from gross sales to determine net sales.
  2. Gross profit: cost of goods sold is subtracted from net sales to determine gross profit.
  3. Profit from operations: operating expenses are deducted from gross profit to determine profit from operations.
  4. Non-operating activities: the results of activities that are not related to operations are added (as other revenues and gains) or subtracted (as other expenses and losses) to determine profit before income tax.
  5. Profit: income tax expense is subtracted from profit before income tax to determine profit (or loss).

- Private companies under ASPE do not have to list their expenses in any particular order. However, companies following IFRS must present their expenses either by nature of expense or function of expense. Presentation of **expenses by nature** focuses on the natural classification and type of each expense (e.g., change in inventories of finished goods and work in process, salaries expense, depreciation expense), whereas presentation of **expenses by function** focuses on the business function of each expense (e.g., cost of goods sold, selling expense, administrative expense).

- Profit from operations is considered sustainable and long-term, while profit from non-operating activities is considered nonrecurring and short-term. It is important for a company to derive the bulk of its profit from its main line of operations, and not from peripheral activities, such as sale of assets.

- If there are no non-operating activities, the multiple-step income statement appears as follows:

CHAPTER 5 Merchandising Operations   77

```
    Sales revenue
 −  Cost of goods sold
 =  Gross profit
 −  Operating expenses
 =  Profit before income tax
 −  Income tax expense
 =  Profit (loss)
```

- If there are non-operating activities, the multiple-step income statement appears as follows:

```
    Sales revenue
 −  Cost of goods sold
 =  Gross profit
 −  Operating expenses
 =  Profit from operations
 +  Other revenues and gains
 −  Other expenses and losses
 =  Profit before income taxes
 −  Income tax expense
 =  Profit (loss)
```

Profitability

- A company's **gross profit margin** is calculated by dividing gross profit by net sales. Gross profit margin should be closely monitored. A decline in gross profit margin may result from decreasing selling prices due to increased competition, or from increasing costs of merchandise that are not passed on to customers. High-volume businesses usually have low gross profit margins, while low-volume businesses usually have high gross profit margins.

> **study objective 5**
>
> Calculate the gross profit margin and profit margin.

- A company's **profit margin** is the percentage of each dollar of sales that results in profit. Profit margin is calculated by dividing profit by net sales for the period.

Periodic Inventory System

- A **periodic inventory system** differs from a perpetual inventory system in various ways. In a periodic inventory system, cost of goods sold is calculated only at the end of an accounting period; in a perpetual inventory system, cost of goods sold is affected each time inventory is sold.

> **study objective 6**
>
> Prepare entries for purchases and sales under a periodic inventory system and calculate cost of goods sold (Appendix 5A).

- In a periodic inventory system, a physical count of inventory is taken at the end of the accounting period to determine the cost of inventory on hand. This cost of ending inventory is then subtracted from the cost of goods available for sale during the period, to calculate the cost of goods sold during the period. In a periodic inventory system, purchases of inventory are recorded in the Purchases account, not in the Merchandise Inventory account, and there are separate accounts for Purchase Returns and Allowances, Purchase Discounts, and Freight In.

- For example, on April 4, Orion Corporation purchased $5,000 of inventory on account with credit terms of 2/10, n/30. Orion paid shipping costs of $200 on

78 Study Guide to Accompany Financial Accounting: Tools for Business Decision-Making, Fifth Canadian Edition

April 5, and returned $500 of merchandise on April 7. Orion paid the amount due on April 13. The journal entries for these transactions are as follows:

April 4	Purchases	5,000	
	Accounts Payable		5,000
	(To record purchases on account)		
5	Freight In	200	
	Cash		200
	(To record freight payment)		
7	Accounts Payable	500	
	Purchase Returns and Allowances		500
	(To record return of merchandise)		
13	Accounts Payable ($5,000 − $500)	4,500	
	Purchase Discounts ($4,500 × 2%)		90
	Cash ($4,500 − $90)		4,410
	(To record payment within discount period)		

Note the following:

1. Purchases is a temporary expense account reported on the income statement. Its normal balance is a debit.
2. Purchase Returns and Allowances and Purchase Discounts are temporary contra expense accounts, with normal credit balances.
3. Purchase discounts are not applied to freight in charges. Freight in is part of the cost of goods purchased, and is a temporary expense account with a normal debit balance.

- Sale of merchandise is recorded in the same way it is recorded in a perpetual inventory system.

- Under a periodic inventory system, **cost of goods sold is calculated at the end of the accounting period**, as follows:

Cost of goods sold:			
Inventory, January 1			$ 30,000
Purchases		$90,000	
Less: Purchase returns and allowances	$15,000		
Purchase discounts	5,000	20,000	
Net purchases		70,000	
Add: Freight in		10,000	
Cost of goods purchased			80,000
Cost of goods available for sale			110,000
Inventory, December 31			70,000
Cost of goods sold			$ 40,000

Below is a comparison of IFRS and ASPE, for key topics discussed in Chapter 5:

CHAPTER 5 Merchandising Operations 79

comparing
IFRS and ASPE

Key Differences	International Financial Reporting Standards (IFRS)	Accounting Standards for Private Enterprises (ASPE)
Income statement	Expenses must be classified by nature or by function.	Expenses can be classified in any manner the company finds useful.

Chapter Self-Test

As you work through the questions and problems, remember to use the **Decision Toolkit** discussed and used in the text:

1. *Decision Checkpoints:* Ask a question relevant to the decision being made.
2. *Info Needed for Decision:* Make a choice regarding the information needed to answer the question.
3. *Tools to Use for Decision:* Review what the information identified in Step 2 does for the decision-making process.
4. *How to Evaluate Results:* Identify specifically how the information identified in Step 2 should be evaluated to answer the question relevant to the decision being made.

Note: The notation "(SO 1)" means that the question relates to study objective 1. All questions marked with an asterisk (*) relate to material in Appendix 5A.

Multiple Choice

Please circle the correct answer.

1. The operating cycle of a merchandising company is ordinarily _____ that of a service company. (SO 1)
    a. the same as
    b. shorter than
    c. longer than
    d. four times as long as

2. Which of the following statements is correct? (SO 1)
    a. A periodic inventory system allows better control over inventory than does a perpetual inventory system.
    b. A perpetual inventory system allows better control over inventory than does a periodic inventory system.
    c. A periodic inventory system affects the Cost of Goods Sold account each time a sale occurs.
    d. A perpetual inventory system calculates cost of goods sold only at the end of the accounting period.

80   **Study Guide to Accompany Financial Accounting: Tools for Business Decision-Making, Fifth Canadian Edition**

(SO 2)   3. Pine Corporation, which uses a perpetual inventory system, purchased $3,000 of merchandise on account on June 4. What entry is required on June 8, when Pine returns $500 of the merchandise to the seller?

a.	Accounts Payable	500	
	Merchandise Inventory		500
b.	Merchandise Inventory	500	
	Accounts Payable		500
c.	Accounts Payable	500	
	Purchase Returns		500
d.	Cash	500	
	Merchandise Inventory		500

(SO 2)   4. Radchenko Corporation uses a perpetual inventory system, and purchased $2,000 of merchandise on account on July 5. Credit terms were 2/10, n/30. Radchenko returned $400 of the merchandise on July 9. When Radchenko pays the purchase invoice on July 11, the journal entry will require a
a.   debit to Accounts Payable for $2,000.
b.   debit to Accounts Payable for $1,600.
c.   credit to Cash for $1,600.
d.   debit to Merchandise Inventory for $32.

(SO 2)   5. Cosmos Corporation uses a perpetual inventory system, and purchased $2,000 of merchandise on account on July 5. Credit terms were 2/10, n/30. Cosmos returned $400 of the merchandise on July 9. When Cosmos pays the purchase invoice on July 21, the journal entry will require a
a.   debit to Accounts Payable for $2,000.
b.   credit to Accounts Payable for $1,600.
c.   credit to Cash for $1,600.
d.   debit to Cash for $1,600.

(SO 2)   6. Elizabeth Corporation uses a perpetual inventory system, and purchased merchandise on November 30, on which it must pay shipping charges. When Elizabeth pays the shipping charges of $200, the journal entry will require a debit to
a.   Delivery Expense.
b.   Cash.
c.   Freight In.
d.   Merchandise Inventory.

(SO 3)   7. Which of the following statements is correct?
a.   A company that uses a perpetual inventory system records only one journal entry when it sells merchandise.
b.   A company that uses a perpetual inventory system records two journal entries when it sells merchandise.
c.   A company that uses a perpetual inventory system debits Merchandise Inventory and credits Cost of Goods Sold when it sells merchandise.
d.   None of the above is correct.

CHAPTER 5 Merchandising Operations 81

8. Cynthia Corporation uses a perpetual inventory system, and received $500 of returned merchandise, which it had sold a week earlier for $750 on account. Assuming the merchandise is not damaged, Cynthia's journal entry to record the return will require a
    a. debit to Sales Returns and Allowances for $750.
    b. debit to Cost of Goods Sold for $500.
    c. debit to Accounts Receivable for $750.
    d. credit to Merchandise Inventory for $500.

(SO 3)

9. Sales Returns and Allowances and Sales Discounts are
    a. revenue accounts.
    b. expense accounts.
    c. contra revenue accounts.
    d. contra expense accounts.

(SO 3)

10. A company that uses a perpetual inventory system sold $400 of merchandise on July 23 with credit terms of 1/10, n/30. The buyer paid the amount due on July 30. Which journal entry will the selling company record on July 30?

(SO 3)

a.	Cash	400	
	Accounts Receivable		400
b.	Cash	400	
	Sales Discounts		4
	Accounts Receivable		396
c.	Accounts Receivable	400	
	Sales Discounts		4
	Cash		396
d.	Cash	396	
	Sales Discounts	4	
	Accounts Receivable		400

11. Sales revenues are $10,000, sales returns and allowances are $500, sales discounts are $1,000, and freight out is $250. What is the dollar amount of net sales?
    a. $11,500
    b. $10,500
    c. $8,500
    d. $8,250

(SO 4)

12. Which of the following is not an example of a function of expense classification?
    a. Administrative expense
    b. Selling expense
    c. Cost of goods sold
    d. Depreciation expense

(SO 4)

13. Gross profit is $50,000, operating expenses are $15,000, income tax expense is $9,000, and net sales are $75,000. Profit is
    a. $10,000.
    b. $25,000.
    c. $26,000.
    d. $35,000.

(SO 4)

82   Study Guide to Accompany Financial Accounting: Tools for Business Decision-Making, Fifth Canadian Edition

(SO 4)   14. Profit is $15,000, operating expenses are $20,000, income tax expense is $3,000, and net sales are $75,000. Gross profit is
    a. $35,000.
    b. $37,000.
    c. $38,000.
    d. $55,000.

(SO 4)   15. Profit is $15,000, operating expenses are $20,000, income tax expense is $3,000, and net sales are $75,000. Cost of goods sold is
    a. $35,000.
    b. $37,000.
    c. $38,000.
    d. $55,000.

(SO 4)   16. Which of the following is not true about a multiple-step income statement?
    a.   Operating expenses are deducted from gross profit to determine profit from operations.
    b.   There may be a section for non-operating activities.
    c.   There may be a section for operating assets.
    d.   Cost of goods sold is subtracted from net sales to determine gross profit.

(SO 5)   17. Profit is $15,000, operating expenses are $20,000, income tax expense is $3,000, and net sales are $75,000. Gross profit margin is
    a.   47%.
    b.   49%.
    c.   51%.
    d.   73%.

(SO 5)   18. After gross profit is calculated, operating expenses are deducted to determine
    a.   gross profit margin.
    b.   profit from operations.
    c.   cost of goods sold.
    d.   profit margin.

(SO 5)   19. A decline in a company's gross profit margin could be caused by all of the following, except
    a.   selling products with a lower markup.
    b.   clearance of discontinued inventory.
    c.   paying lower prices to suppliers.
    d.   increasing competition resulting in decreasing selling prices.

(SO 6)   *20. Frank Corporation has the following account balances:

Purchases	$28,000
Sales returns and allowances	4,000
Purchase discounts	2,500
Freight in	1,875
Freight out	2,500

CHAPTER 5   Merchandising Operations   83

The cost of goods purchased for the period is
a. $30,500.
b. $27,375.
c. $29,875.
d. $25,875.

*21.   Wales Corporation had beginning merchandise inventory of $15,000. During   (SO 6)
the period, purchases were $70,000, purchase returns were $2,000, and freight in
was $5,000. A physical count of inventory at the end of the period showed that
$10,000 of inventory was still on hand. Cost of goods available for sale was
a. $82,000.
b. $78,000.
c. $88,000.
d. $92,000.

*22.   Calculation of cost of goods sold under the periodic inventory system equals   (SO 6)
a.   beginning inventory + ending inventory − purchases.
b.   beginning inventory + ending inventory + purchases.
c.   beginning inventory + purchases − ending inventory.
d.   ending inventory + purchases − beginning inventory.

*23.   Under a periodic inventory system, an acquisition of merchandise is debited to the   (SO 6)
a.   Merchandise Inventory account.
b.   Cost of Goods Sold account.
c.   Purchases account.
d.   Accounts Payable account.

Problems

1.   Hiller Corporation is a merchandising company, and had the following transac-   (SO 2, 3, 6)
tions during the month of January.

Jan. 5   Purchased goods costing $10,000. The goods were shipped FOB
shipping point with terms 2/10, n/30.

7   Hiller paid freight costs of $100 on the January 5 purchase.

10   Hiller returned $2,000 of the goods purchased on January 5 to its
supplier. (Ignore freight on this return.)

12   Hiller sold $2,000 of merchandise to Ms. Jones with terms 2/10, n/30
and FOB destination. The cost of the goods sold was $1,600.

14   Hiller paid the amount due to its supplier.

16   Hiller paid $50 in freight costs on the goods sold and shipped them to
Ms. Jones.

20   Ms. Jones returned $100 of goods sold to her on January 12. The
returned goods originally cost Hiller $80 and were put back on Hiller's
store shelf for resale. (Ignore freight on this return.)

84   Study Guide to Accompany Financial Accounting: Tools for Business Decision-Making, Fifth Canadian Edition

Jan. 21   Ms. Jones paid her account in full.

25   Hiller purchased $500 of general office supplies on account.

a.   Record the above transactions for Hiller Corporation, assuming that Hiller uses a perpetual inventory system.

*b.   Record the above transactions for Hiller Corporation, assuming that Hiller uses a periodic inventory system.

(SO 2, 3)   2.   The following summarized information has been selected from the Merchandise Inventory account of a company from its two most recent years. The company uses a perpetual inventory system.

	Year 1	Year 2
Balance in account, beginning of period	$ 400	$ (d)
Purchases of merchandise	1,000	900
Returns of merchandise purchased	100	(e)
Net purchases	870	690
Purchase discounts on merchandise	(a)	60
Freight costs incurred on merchandise purchased	(b)	100
Cost of goods purchased	1,000	790
Cost of goods sold	750	(f)
Balance in account, end of period	(c)	400

From the above information, reconstruct the company's Merchandise Inventory account.

(SO 4)   3.   From the appropriate accounts below, prepare a multiple-step income statement for Book Corporation for the year ended January 31, 2012.

Cash	$ 13,000
Rental revenue	5,000
Interest revenue	1,000
Utilities expense	15,000
Cost of goods sold	24,000
Insurance expense	2,000
Accounts receivable	12,000
Sales returns and allowances	4,000
Advertising expense	7,000
Merchandise inventory	35,000
Depreciation expense	8,000
Sales	118,000
Freight out	3,000
Loss on sale of equipment	1,500

CHAPTER 5   Merchandising Operations   85

Sales discounts	5,000
Salaries expense	23,000
Rent expense	10,000
Interest expense	2,000
Income tax expense	7,800

*4.   Willis Merchandising Corporation uses a periodic inventory system and prepares   (SO 6)
monthly financial statements. All accounts have been adjusted except for merchandise inventory. A physical count of merchandise inventory on September 30,
2012, indicates that $3,300 of inventory is on hand. A partial listing of account
balances is as follows:

Accounts receivable	$ 5,000
Cash	9,000
Accounts payable	7,000
Merchandise inventory, September 1	2,500
Freight in	1,000
Purchase returns and allowances	900
Sales discounts	700
Purchases	26,000
Sales	49,000

Prepare an income statement through to gross profit for Willis Merchandising
Corporation for the month ended September 30, 2012.

*5.   The following table includes a company's cost of goods sold information from its   (SO 6)
two most recent years. The company uses a periodic inventory system.

	Year 1	Year 2
Beginning inventory	$ 400	$ (e)
Purchases	1,000	900
Purchase returns and allowances	100	(f)
Purchase discounts	(a)	60
Net purchases	870	690
Freight in	(b)	100
Cost of goods purchased	1,000	(g)
Cost of goods available for sale	(c)	(h)
Ending inventory	(d)	400
Cost of goods sold	750	(i)

Fill in the lettered blanks to complete the cost of goods sold sections.

6.   Refer to the HMV and WHSmith financial statements found in the appendices at   (SO 4, 5)
the end of this study guide for information in answering the following questions.
Do not forget to use the **Decision Toolkit** approach for help in answering the
questions.

86 Study Guide to Accompany Financial Accounting: Tools for Business Decision-Making, Fifth Canadian Edition

 a. Compare the gross profit and gross profit margin for both companies for 2010. Assume that the industry average for gross profit margin was 30.9% in 2010.

 b. What are the operating expenses and profit from operations for each company for 2010?

 c. Calculate and compare the profit margin for both companies for 2010. Assume that the industry average for profit margin was 2.4% in 2010.

Solutions to Self-Test

Multiple Choice

1. c A merchandising company purchases merchandise before it sells merchandise, which lengthens its operating cycle.

2. b Periodic inventory systems do not keep up-to-date, detailed records of inventory on hand, making control over inventory more difficult. In perpetual inventory systems, the Cost of Goods Sold account is affected each time a sale occurs.

3. a Since the purchase was on account, the entry to record the return requires a decrease in the Accounts Payable liability account. Since Pine uses a perpetual inventory system, all merchandise purchases are recorded in the Merchandise Inventory account. A decrease in merchandise purchases due to a return of merchandise requires a credit to the Merchandise Inventory account. If Pine had used a periodic inventory system, the return would have been recorded as a credit to Purchases Returns and Allowances.

4. b The journal entry is:

Accounts Payable	1,600	
Merchandise Inventory		32
Cash		1,568

5. c The journal entry is:

Accounts Payable	1,600	
Cash		1,600

6. d The journal entry is:

Merchandise Inventory	200	
Cash		200

7. b A perpetual inventory system requires two journal entries when merchandise is sold. The first journal entry records the sale (debit to Cash or Accounts Receivable and credit to Sales). The second journal entry records the cost of the sale (debit to Cost of Goods Sold and credit to Merchandise Inventory).

8. a The journal entries are:

Sales Returns and Allowances	750	
Accounts Receivable		750
Merchandise Inventory	500	
Cost of Goods Sold		500

CHAPTER 5 Merchandising Operations 87

9. c While these accounts have normal debit balances, they are not expense accounts, and they are not revenue accounts. They are subtracted from a revenue account, making them contra revenue accounts.

10. d The journal entry requires a debit to Cash, but not for $400, since the buyer receives a $4 discount for paying within 10 days. Accounts Receivable must be credited for $400, the full amount owed. The $4 difference between the amount owed and the amount of cash received is recorded as a debit to Sales Discounts.

11. c $10,000 − $500 − $1,000 = $8,500.

12. d Depreciation expense is an example of a nature of expense classification.

13. c $50,000 − $15,000 − $9,000 = $26,000.

14. c $15,000 + $3,000 + $20,000 = $38,000.

15. b $15,000 + $3,000 + $20,000 = $38,000 of gross profit; $75,000 − $38,000 = $37,000.

16. c Assets are not included in any income statement.

17. c $15,000 + $3,000 + $20,000 = $38,000 of gross profit; $38,000 ÷ $75,000 = 51% (rounded).

18. b Sales − cost of goods sold = gross profit; gross profit − operating expenses = profit from operations.

19. c Paying lower prices to suppliers would result in an increase in gross profit.

20. b $28,000 − $2,500 + $1,875 = $27,375.

21. c $15,000 + $70,000 − $2,000 + $5,000 = $88,000.

22. c Beginning inventory + purchases = cost of goods available for sale; cost of goods available for sale − ending inventory = cost of goods sold.

23. c Under a periodic inventory system, an acquisition of merchandise would be debited to the Purchases account.

Problems

1.

a. Jan. 5 Merchandise Inventory   10,000
                  Accounts Payable   10,000
          (To record purchase of goods, with terms 2/10, n/30, FOB shipping point)

      7 Merchandise Inventory   100
                  Cash   100
          (To record freight on purchase)
          [FOB shipping point means Hiller, the buyer, is responsible for picking up the goods from the supplier's warehouse or shipping point.]

Jan. 10	Accounts Payable	2,000	
	Merchandise Inventory		2,000
	(To record return of goods to supplier)		

12	Accounts Receivable	2,000	
	Sales		2,000
	(To record sale of goods, with terms 2/10, n/30, FOB destination)		
	Cost of Goods Sold	1,600	
	Merchandise Inventory		1,600
	(To record cost of goods sold)		

14	Accounts Payable	8,000	
	Merchandise Inventory		160
	Cash		7,840
	(To record payment, net of purchase return, within the discount period)		

Discount = ($10,000 − $2,000) × 0.02 = $160

[Discount does not apply to freight.]

16	Freight Out	50	
	Cash		50
	(To record freight on sale of goods)		

[FOB destination means that it is Hiller's responsibility to pay the freight.]

20	Sales Returns and Allowances	100	
	Accounts Receivable		100
	(To record return of goods by Ms. Jones)		
	Merchandise Inventory	80	
	Cost of Goods Sold		80
	(To record cost of the goods returned)		

21	Cash	1,862	
	Sales Discounts	38	
	Accounts Receivable		1,900
	(To record collection of account within the discount period)		

Discount = ($2,000 − $100) × 0.02 = $38

25	Office Supplies	500	
	Accounts Payable		500
	(To record purchase of office supplies)		

[Note that the amount is not debited to Merchandise Inventory because these supplies are not goods for resale.]

CHAPTER 5 Merchandising Operations 89

b. Jan. 5 Purchases   10,000
                    Accounts Payable   10,000
         (To record purchase of goods with terms 2/10, n/30, FOB shipping point)

       7 Freight In   100
                    Cash   100
         (To record freight on purchase)
         [FOB shipping point means that Hiller, the buyer, is responsible for
         picking up the goods from the supplier's warehouse or shipping point.]

      10 Accounts Payable   2,000
                    Purchase Returns and Allowances   2,000
         (To record return of goods to supplier)

      12 Accounts Receivable   2,000
                    Sales   2,000
         (To record sale of goods, with terms 2/10, n/30, FOB destination)

      14 Accounts Payable   8,000
                    Purchase Discounts   160
                    Cash   7,840
         (To record payment, net of purchase return, within the discount period)
         Discount = ($10,000 − $2,000) × 0.02 = $160
         [Discount does not apply to freight.]

      16 Freight Out   50
                    Cash   50
         (To record freight on sale of goods)
         [FOB destination means that it is Hiller's responsibility to pay the freight.]

      20 Sales Returns and Allowances   100
                    Accounts Receivable   100
         (To record return of goods by Ms. Jones)

      21 Cash   1,862
         Sales Discounts   38
                    Accounts Receivable   1,900
         (To record collection of account within the discount period)
         Discount = ($2,000 − $100) × 0.02 = $38

      25 Office Supplies   500
                    Accounts Payable   500
         (To record purchase of office supplies)
         [Note that the amount is not debited to the Purchases account because
         these supplies are not goods for resale.]

90   Study Guide to Accompany Financial Accounting: Tools for Business Decision-Making, Fifth Canadian Edition

2.

Merchandise Inventory

Beg. of Year 1	Bal.	400		
(Purchases)		1,000	100	(Purchase returns)
(Freight)		(b) 130	(a) 30	(Purchase discounts)
			750	(Cost of goods sold)
End of Year 1; Beg. of Year 2	Bal. (c), (d)	650		
(Purchases)		900		
			(e) 150	(Purchase returns)
(Freight)		100	60	(Purchase discounts)
			(f) 1,040	(Cost of goods sold)
End of Year 2	Bal.	400		

The missing data can be calculated as follows:

a. Purchases − purchase returns − purchase discounts = net purchases.
    $1,000 − $100 − purchase discounts = $870.
    Purchase discounts = $30.

b. Net purchases + freight = Cost of goods purchased.
    $870 + freight = $1,000.
           Freight = $130.

c. Ending inventory = $400 + $1,000 + $130 − $100 − $30 − $750
                     = $650.

d. Opening inventory Year 2 = ending inventory Year 1
                             = $650.

e. Purchases − purchase returns − purchase discounts = net purchases.
    $900 − purchase returns − $60 = $690.
    Purchase returns = $150.

f. Beginning inventory + cost of goods purchased − cost of goods sold =
    ending inventory.
    $650 + $790 − cost of goods sold = $400.
    Cost of goods sold = $650 + $790 − $400 = $1,040.
Note: Other calculations may arrive at the answers shown above.

3.

BOOK CORPORATION
Income Statement
Year Ended January 31, 2012

Sales revenue		
Sales		$118,000
Less: Sales returns and allowances	$ 4,000	

Sales discounts	5,000	9,000
Net sales		109,000
Cost of goods sold		24,000
Gross profit		85,000
Operating expenses		
Salaries expense	$23,000	
Utilities expense	15,000	
Rent expense	10,000	
Depreciation expense	8,000	
Advertising expense	7,000	
Freight out	3,000	
Insurance expense	2,000	
Loss on sale of equipment	1,500	
Total operating expenses		69,500
Profit from operations		15,500
Other revenues and gains		
Rental revenue	$ 5,000	
Interest revenue	1,000	
Total non-operating revenues	6,000	
Other expenses and losses		
Interest expense	2,000	
Net non-operating revenue		4,000
Profit before income tax		19,500
Income tax expense		7,800
Profit		$ 11,700

*4.

WILLIS MERCHANDISING CORPORATION
Income Statement
Month Ended September 30, 2012

Sales revenues		
Sales	$49,000	
Less: Sales discounts	700	
Net sales		$48,300
Cost of goods sold		
Merchandise inventory, September 1	$ 2,500	
Purchases	$26,000	
Less: Purchase returns and allowances	900	

Net purchases	25,100	
Add: Freight in	1,000	
Cost of goods purchased		26,100
Cost of goods available for sale		28,600
Merchandise inventory, September 30		3,300
Cost of goods sold		25,300
Gross profit		$23,000

*5.

    a. $30 ($1,000 − $100 − $870)
    b. $130 ($1,000 − $870)
    c. $1,400 ($400 + $1,000)
    d. $650 ($1,400 [from c] − $750)
    e. $650 (from d)
    f. $150 ($900 − $60 − $690)
    g. $790 ($690 + $100)
    h. $1,440 ($650 [from e] + $790 [from g])
    i. $1,040 ($1,440 [from h] − $400)

6.   Please note that the amounts shown for HMV and WHSmith are stated in pounds (£) millions.

    a.

	HMV	WHSmith
Net sales	£ 2,016.6	£1,312
Cost of sales	1,855.6	650
Gross profit	161.0	662
Gross profit margin	£ 161.0 = 8.0%	£ 662 = 50.5%
	£ 2,016.6	£1,312

WHSmith's gross profit margin is higher than both HMV's gross profit margin and industry average gross profit margin in 2010.

    b. Each of the companies uses slightly different terminology that has the same meaning as profit from operations, as follows:

		HMV	WHSmith
Gross profit (from above)		£161.0	£662
Less operating expenses:			
HMV: (£86.2 − £0.3)	=	85.9	
WHSmith: (£495 + £80 − £2)	=		573
Operating profit		£ 75.1	£ 89

c.

	HMV	**WHSmith**
HMV: £49.2 ÷ £2,016.6 =	2.4%	
WHSmith: £69 ÷ £1,312 =		5.3%

WHSmith's profit margin is higher than both HMV's profit margin and industry average profit margin in 2010.

chapter 6

Reporting and Analyzing Inventory

Chapter Overview

Chapter 6 explains how to determine inventory quantities and continues with a discussion of inventory cost determination methods, including the specific identification method and the first-in, first-out (FIFO) and average cost formulas. Chapter 6 also discusses the effects of inventory errors on the income statement and the statement of financial position, financial statement presentation of inventory, and analysis of inventory using financial statements.

Review of Specific Study Objectives

Determining Inventory Quantities

- All companies need to determine quantity of inventory at the end of each accounting period, whether they are using **a periodic inventory system or a perpetual inventory system**.

- If a company is using a **perpetual inventory system**, the company should take a physical count of inventory on hand at year end for two purposes:

  1. to check the accuracy of its perpetual inventory records, and
  2. to determine the amount of inventory lost due to shrinkage or theft.

> **study objective 1**
>
> Describe the steps in determining inventory quantities.

- If a company is using a **periodic inventory system**, it should take a physical count of inventory on hand at year end for two purposes:

  1. to determine ending inventory (inventory on hand on the statement of financial position date), and
  2. to determine the cost of goods sold for the period.

- Physically counting inventory involves actually counting, weighing, or measuring each item of inventory on hand. To minimize errors in counting inventory, a company should ensure that it has a good system of internal control in place. **Internal control** is a process designed to help an organization achieve reliable financial reporting, effective and efficient operations, and compliance with relevant laws and regulations. Some internal control procedures for counting inventory include the following:

  1. The counting should be done by employees who do not have responsibility for the custody or record-keeping of the inventory.
  2. Each counter should establish the validity of each inventory item. This includes checking that the items actually exist, checking the quantity of each item on hand, and checking the condition of the items.
  3. There should be a second count by another employee or auditor. Counting should take place in teams of two.
  4. Prenumbered inventory tags should be used to ensure that all inventory items are counted and that none are counted more than once.

- Before the counting process begins, ownership of goods must be determined to ensure that all goods included in the count actually belong to the company, and that the count includes all goods that are owned by the company on the date of the count.

- **Goods in transit should be included in the company's inventory count if the company has legal title to the goods on the date of the count.** The shipping terms of the inventory purchase usually determine the date of transfer of ownership of the goods, as follows:

  1. If shipping terms are **FOB (free on board) shipping point**, ownership of the goods transfers to the buyer at the point when the public carrier accepts the goods from the seller (at the shipping point).
  2. If shipping terms are **FOB destination**, ownership of the goods transfers to the buyer at the point when the goods arrive at the buyer's destination (at the destination point).

- In some lines of business, it is customary for a company to ship goods to a third party, and for the third party (consignee) to sell the goods on behalf of the shipper company (consignor) in exchange for a fee, without ever transferring legal title or ownership of the goods to the consignee. Goods shipped under this type of arrangement are called **consigned goods**, and are considered the inventory of the consignor until the consignee sells the inventory to a customer (even though the inventory is physically located on the consignee's premises until the time of sale to a customer). Because consigned goods are considered the inventory of the consignor until the consignee sells the inventory to a customer, these goods must be included in the inventory count of the consignor and not the consignee. For example, if Charlie ships goods from his inventory to Barb's place of business, and Barb agrees to try to sell the goods on Charlie's behalf in exchange for a commission or fee, Charlie

CHAPTER 6 Reporting and Analyzing Inventory 97

(the consignor) owns the goods at all times, until they are sold to a customer by Barb (the consignee). Even though the goods are physically located on Barb's business premises, legal title and ownership of the goods do not transfer to Barb at any point in this arrangement. Therefore, when Charlie takes a physical count of his inventory, he must remember to include any remaining consigned goods on Barb's business premises in his count of inventory.

- After the quantities of inventory units on hand have been determined, unit costs are applied to each type of inventory unit to determine the total cost of ending inventory on hand. However, the total cost of ending inventory on hand will depend on the method of cost determination (or method of applying unit costs) used with each type of inventory unit.

Inventory Cost Determination Methods and Their Effects

- The specific identification method of cost determination tracks the actual physical flow of goods in a perpetual inventory system. Under this method, each item in inventory is linked to its specific unit cost so that total cost of ending inventory on hand can be calculated as the sum of the costs of each item on hand. **Specific identification is appropriate and required for goods that are not ordinarily interchangeable, and for goods that are produced and segregated for specific projects.** This method is most often used if a company sells a limited number of uniquely identifiable and easily distinguishable items with high unit costs, such as cars or antiques. While specific identification works well if a company sells high unit-cost items that can be clearly identified from purchase through to sale, there are also disadvantages to using this method. For example, management may manipulate profit by choosing to sell units with higher or lower purchase costs, which would affect cost of goods sold and therefore profit.

> **study objective 2**
>
> Apply the methods of cost determination—specific identification, FIFO, and average—under a perpetual inventory system.

- Because the specific identification method is only suitable for certain kinds of inventories, other methods of cost determination (known as "cost formulas") are available, including:

  1. FIFO
  2. Average

  While specific identification is normally only used in a perpetual inventory system, FIFO and average can be used in both the perpetual and periodic inventory systems. We will begin by examining each formula under a perpetual inventory system.

- **First-in, first-out (FIFO)** assumes that the earliest (oldest) goods purchased are the first ones to be sold. This does not necessarily mean that the oldest units are in fact sold first, only that the costs of the oldest units are flowed to cost of goods sold first. Although a cost formula chosen by a company does not have to match the actual physical flow of goods, it should correspond as closely as possible. FIFO generally does match the actual physical flow of goods because it is good business practice to sell the oldest units first.

- **Average cost** recognizes that it is not possible to measure a specific physical flow of inventory when the goods available for sale are homogeneous or indistinguishable. Under average cost, the cost of inventory units sold is flowed to cost of goods sold based on the weighted average unit cost of the goods that are available for sale.

98 Study Guide to Accompany Financial Accounting: Tools for Business Decision-Making, Fifth Canadian Edition

- To illustrate how the FIFO and average cost formulas work in a perpetual inventory system, assume that the following purchases are made:

Oct. 10	100 units @ $2
Nov. 11	200 units @ $3
Dec. 15	300 units @ $4

If 400 units are sold on December 20, FIFO yields the following:

	Purchases			Cost of Goods Sold			Balance		
Date	Units	Cost	Total	Units	Cost	Total	Units	Cost	Total
Oct. 10	100	$2	$ 200				100	$2	$ 200
Nov. 11	200	$3	600				100 / 200	$2 / $3	} 800
Dec. 15	300	$4	1,200				100 / 200 / 300	$2 / $3 / $4	} 2,000
Dec. 20				100 / 200 / 100	$2 / $3 / $4	} $1,200	200	$4	800

Note that using FIFO always results in the same cost of goods sold and ending inventory amounts, whether a perpetual or periodic inventory system is used.

Under average cost in a perpetual inventory system, a new average cost is calculated after each purchase is made. Assume that the same purchases made under FIFO are also made in this example. When the 400 units are sold under the average cost formula, the following results:

	Purchases			Cost of Goods Sold			Balance		
Date	Units	Cost	Total	Units	Cost	Total	Units	Cost	Total
Oct. 10	100	$2	$ 200.00				100	$2.00	$ 200.00
Nov. 11	200	$3	600.00				300	$2.67[1]	800.00
Dec. 15	300	$4	1,200.00				600	$3.33[2]	2,000.00
Dec. 20				400	$3.33	$1,333.33	200	$3.33	666.67

[1]$800 ÷ 300 = $2.67
[2]$2,000 ÷ 600 = $3.33

In contrast to FIFO, average cost will result in different cost of goods sold and ending inventory amounts, depending on whether a perpetual or periodic inventory system is used.

---

study objective 3

Explain the financial statement effects of the inventory cost determination methods.

Effects of Cost Determination Methods

- If companies have goods that are not ordinarily interchangeable, or goods that have been produced and segregated for specific projects, they must use the specific identification method to determine the cost of their inventory. Otherwise, a company can choose to use either FIFO or average cost. A company that can make this choice should consider the following guidelines in making its choice:

CHAPTER 6   Reporting and Analyzing Inventory   99

1. Choose a method that corresponds as closely as possible to the physical flow of goods.
2. Report an inventory cost on the statement of financial position that is close to the inventory's recent cost.
3. Use the same method for all inventories having a similar nature and usage in the company.

- The amount of ending inventory affects both the statement of financial position and income statement, because ending inventory is included as a current asset on the statement of financial position and because the amount of ending inventory affects the amount of cost of goods sold, which is included on the income statement.

- The following table summarizes the financial statement effects of the three cost determination methods, assuming that cost per unit of inventory is rising:

	Specific Identification	FIFO	Average
Income statement			
Cost of goods sold	Variable	Lowest	Highest
Gross profit	Variable	Highest	Lowest
Profit	Variable	Highest	Lowest
Statement of financial position			
Cash (pre-tax)	Same	Same	Same
Ending inventory	Variable	Highest	Lowest
Retained earnings	Variable	Highest	Lowest

If cost per unit of inventory is declining, the financial statement effects will be the inverse of those summarized above. If cost per unit of inventory is stable or constant, the three methods will yield the same financial statement effects. The financial statement effects summarized above are the same whether a company uses a perpetual or periodic inventory system. Also, all three inventory cost determination methods will have the same cash flow effects, because sales and purchases are not affected.

Inventory Errors

- Errors in determining ending inventory affect cost of goods sold and profit in two successive accounting periods because ending inventory of one accounting period is beginning inventory of the next accounting period.

> study objective 4
>
> Identify the effects of inventory errors on the financial statements.

- An error in beginning inventory will have a reverse effect on profit of the same accounting period (if beginning inventory is understated, then cost of goods sold will be understated, and profit will be overstated). An error in ending inventory will have the same effect on profit of the same accounting period (if ending inventory is understated, then cost of goods sold will be overstated, and profit will be understated).

- An error in ending inventory of the current period will have the same effect on profit of the same accounting period, and the reverse effect on profit of the next accounting period, because the error in ending inventory of the current period will carry into beginning inventory of the next accounting period, if not found and corrected. Therefore, if the error in ending inventory of the current period is not found and corrected, total profit of the two accounting periods will be correct, because the

100   **Study Guide to Accompany Financial Accounting: Tools for Business Decision-Making, Fifth Canadian Edition**

error's effect on profit of the current period will be offset by a reverse effect on profit of the next accounting period.

- An error in beginning inventory does not result in a corresponding error in ending inventory for that same period, assuming that ending inventory is calculated correctly at the end of that same period.

- On the statement of financial position, if ending inventory is overstated, then both assets and shareholders' equity will be overstated. If ending inventory is understated, then both assets and shareholders' equity will be understated.

Presentation and Analysis of Inventory

study objective 5
Demonstrate the presentation and analysis of inventory.

- Appropriate financial statement presentation of inventory is important because inventory is often the largest current asset (merchandise inventory) on the statement of financial position, and because cost of goods sold is often the largest expense (cost of goods sold) on the income statement. Inventory on the statement of financial position should be presented at **lower of cost and net realizable value (LCNRV)**. For a merchandising company, **NRV** is the selling price of the inventory less any costs required to make the goods ready for sale.

- At the end of each accounting period, the **LCNRV** rule is applied as follows:
  1. Determine cost of the inventory (using the specific identification, FIFO, or average cost method).
  2. Determine NRV of the inventory.
  3. Compare the values determined in steps 1 and 2. Determine if NRV is lower than cost.
  4. If NRV is lower than cost, adjust and report inventory on the financial statements at NRV rather than cost.

  The LCNRV rule should be applied to individual inventory items, rather than total inventory, although in certain cases, it can be applied to groups of similar items.

- The adjusting journal entries to apply the LCNRV rule are as follows:

  Cost of Goods Sold

      Merchandise Inventory

  (To record decline in inventory value from original cost to NRV)

  If, after writedown of inventory, there is clear evidence of an increase in NRV because of changed economic circumstances, the amount of the writedown can be reversed, by an amount that does not exceed the lesser of the increase in NRV and the original writedown. The reversal would be recorded as follows:

  Merchandise Inventory

      Cost of Goods Sold

  (To reverse previous writedown of inventory)

  The reported cost of inventory may never exceed its original cost.

- The **inventory turnover ratio** measures the number of times, on average, that inventory is sold ("turned over") during the period. Inventory turnover is calculated by

CHAPTER 6   Reporting and Analyzing Inventory   101

dividing cost of goods sold by average inventory, where average inventory is the average of beginning and ending inventory. If a company's cost of goods sold is $50,000 and its average inventory is $16,000, then its inventory turnover is 3.1 times (rounded). A 3.1 inventory turnover ratio means that the company sold its entire inventory about three times in the accounting period.

● **Days in inventory** is calculated by dividing 365 days by inventory turnover. Using the same example as above, days in inventory = 365 days ÷ 3.1 = 118 days, which means that it takes the company about 118 days to sell inventory.

● **Both inventory turnover and days in inventory ratios must be compared with benchmarks to be meaningful.** They may be compared with the same company's ratios from prior periods, with a competitor's ratios, or with industry average ratios.

Inventory Cost Formulas in Periodic Systems

● Both FIFO and average cost, described earlier in the chapter for a perpetual inventory system, may also be used in a periodic inventory system.

● Using the following data, ending inventory and cost of goods sold will be calculated assuming a periodic inventory system. Under a periodic inventory system, we assume that the entire pool of inventory cost of goods available for sale will be allocated between cost of goods sold and ending inventory.

> **study objective 6**
>
> Apply the inventory cost formulas—FIFO and average—under a periodic inventory system (Appendix 6A).

Date	Units	Unit Cost	Total Cost
Feb. 1	300	$4	$ 1,200
Mar. 9	400	5	2,000
May 8	600	6	3,600
June 3	500	7	3,500
	1,800		$10,300

A physical count shows that there are 550 units in ending inventory. The February 1 units are beginning inventory, and total cost of goods available for sale is $10,300. To allocate cost of goods available for sale between ending inventory and cost of goods sold, ending inventory is calculated first, followed by cost of goods sold.

FIFO:

If there are 550 units remaining in ending inventory, 1,250 units were sold during the period (1,800 units available for sale − 550 units remaining on hand at the end of the period).

FIFO assumes that the earliest (oldest) goods purchased are the first ones sold; therefore, inventory on hand at the end of the period is assumed to be the inventory most recently purchased. To calculate the cost of 550 units, begin counting from the most recent (June 3) purchase:

June 3	500	×	$7	=	$3,500
May 8	50	×	6	=	300
	550				$3,800

Cost of goods sold is calculated by subtracting ending inventory from total cost of goods available for sale. (Total cost of goods available for sale minus ending inventory equals total cost of goods sold.) Cost of goods sold is calculated as follows:

Cost of goods available for sale	$10,300
Less: Ending inventory	3,800
Cost of goods sold	$ 6,500

Average cost:

To calculate average unit cost, divide total cost of goods available for sale ($10,300) by total units available for sale (1,800). The average unit cost is $5.72. Note that the company did not pay exactly $5.72 for any of the units purchased; $5.72 is simply the weighted average unit cost.

The weighted average unit cost is applied to ending inventory as follows:

Ending inventory: 550   × $5.72   = $3,147.22

(Note that unrounded numbers have been used for the weighted average in this calculation.)

Cost of goods sold is calculated as follows:

Cost of goods available for sale	$10,300.00
Less: Ending inventory	3,147.22
Cost of goods sold	$ 7,152.78

comparing
IFRS and ASPE

Key Differences	International Financial Reporting Standards (IFRS)	Accounting Standards for Private Enterprises (ASPE)
No significant differences		

Chapter Self-Test

As you work through the questions and problems, remember to use the **Decision Toolkit** discussed and used in the text:

1. *Decision Checkpoints:* Ask a question relevant to the decision being made.
2. *Info Needed for Decision:* Make a choice regarding the information needed to answer the question.
3. *Tools to Use for Decision:* Review what the information identified in step 2 does for the decision-making process.
4. *How to Evaluate Results:* Identify specifically how the information identified in step 2 should be evaluated to answer the question relevant to the decision being made.

Note: The notation "(SO 1)" means that the question relates to study objective 1. All questions marked with an asterisk (*) relate to material in Appendix 6A.

CHAPTER 6 Reporting and Analyzing Inventory

Multiple Choice

Please circle the correct answer.

1. A company that uses a perpetual inventory system must still take a physical inventory count at year end, for the following reasons: (SO 1)
   a. to check the accuracy of the perpetual inventory records and to determine the amount of inventory lost due to theft or shrinkage.
   b. to determine cost of goods sold.
   c. to determine the amount of inventory on hand.
   d. to determine ownership of the goods.

2. Consigned goods are (SO 1)
   a. never counted as part of the consignee's ending inventory.
   b. counted as part of the consignee's ending inventory until the goods are sold to a customer.
   c. held for sale on the consignor's premises.
   d. counted as part of the consignee's ending inventory, as well as the consignor's ending inventory, until the goods are sold to a customer.

3. If goods are shipped FOB destination, which of the following parties owns the goods while they are in transit (and would therefore include the goods in its inventory while they are in transit)? (SO 1)
   a. The public carrier delivering the goods
   b. The buyer
   c. The seller
   d. Both the buyer and the seller

4. Ceil ships goods on consignment to Jerry, who agrees to try to sell the goods in exchange for a 25% commission. At the end of the accounting period, which of the following parties should include the consigned goods in their inventory? (SO 1)
   a. Ceil
   b. Jerry
   c. Both Ceil and Jerry
   d. Neither Ceil nor Jerry

5. Which of the following methods of cost determination is most similar to actual physical flow of goods? (SO 1)
   a. NRV
   b. FIFO
   c. Average cost
   d. Specific identification

6. Under a perpetual inventory system, (SO 2)
   a. cost of items sold is allocated to cost of goods sold as each item is sold.
   b. inventory is physically counted at the end of the year to determine ending inventory, and therefore cost of goods sold.
   c. only the specific identification cost method may be used.
   d. using average cost formula, the weighted average unit cost is calculated based on the weighted average cost of all units available for sale in the period.

104   Study Guide to Accompany Financial Accounting: Tools for Business Decision-Making, Fifth Canadian Edition

(SO 2)   7. The results under _____ in a perpetual inventory system are the same
               as under a periodic inventory system.
               a.   average cost
               b.   FIFO
               c.   specific identification
               d.   none of the above

(SO 2)   8. Assume that a company uses a perpetual inventory system and the specific identi-
               fication method to determine the cost of its inventory. Assume that this company
               purchases the following inventory: a diamond necklace for $19,000, a diamond
               tiara for $14,000, diamond earrings for $8,000, and a diamond ring for $10,000.
               During June, the company sells the diamond tiara for $20,000 and the diamond
               necklace for $25,000. What is the company's cost of goods sold for June?
               a. $19,000
               b. $14,000
               c. $33,000
               d. $18,000

(SO 2)   9. Assume the same data used in question 8. What is the company's ending inven-
               tory at the end of June?
               a. $33,000
               b. $18,000
               c. $29,000
               d. $45,000

(SO 3)   10. Under a perpetual inventory system, a company can use either FIFO or aver-
               age cost, if its goods are ordinarily interchangeable. Which of the following is an
               objective that the company should consider in making a choice between FIFO
               and average cost?
               a.   Choose a method that corresponds as closely as possible to the physical flow
                    of goods.
               b.   Report an inventory cost on the statement of financial position that is close
                    to the inventory's earliest or oldest costs.
               c.   Always use the same inventory cost determination method, consistently
                    from one period to the next.
               d.   None of the above.

(SO 3)   11. Which cost determination method results in an amount of cost of goods sold on
               the income statement that is closest to the actual cost of goods sold?
               a.   FIFO
               b.   Specific identification
               c.   Average cost
               d.   All are equal.

(SO 5)   12. Net sales are $80,000, cost of goods sold is $30,000, and average inventory is
               $20,000. Inventory turnover is
               a.   4.0 times.
               b.   2.7 times.

CHAPTER 6   Reporting and Analyzing Inventory   105

c.   1.5 times.
d.   0.2 times.

13. If beginning inventory is overstated, then the current year's   (SO 4)
    a.   cost of goods sold is overstated.
    b.   cost of goods sold is understated.
    c.   ending inventory is overstated.
    d.   ending inventory is understated.

14. A company reports profit of $50,000 in 2012 and $75,000 in 2013. Later, it was   (SO 4)
    discovered that two errors were made: ending inventory in 2012 was understated
    by $10,000, and ending inventory in 2013 was overstated by $5,000. Corrected
    profit is
    a.   2012: $60,000; 2013: $60,000.
    b.   2012: $60,000; 2013: $80,000.
    c.   2012: $40,000; 2013: $80,000.
    d.   2012: $40,000; 2013: $60,000.

15. Assume the following information about a company's inventory: (SO 5)

Item	Cost	NRV	Quantity on hand
A	$12	$15	170
B	$ 8	$ 5	155
C	$15	$15	135

    After applying the LCNRV rule, what amount of inventory would the company
    report on its statement of financial position?
    a. $5,350
    b. $5,305
    c. $4,840
    d. $4,065

16. On January 1, a company had inventory of $14,000. On December 31 of the same   (SO 5)
    year, the company had inventory of $18,000. Sales for the year were $400,000,
    and the gross profit margin was 30%. What is the company's inventory turnover
    for the year?
    a.   7.5 times
    b.   20.0 times
    c.   17.5 times
    d.   15.6 times

17. Using the information in question 16 above, days in inventory (rounded to the   (SO 5)
    nearest day) is
    a.   18 days.
    b.   21 days.
    c.   23 days.
    d.   49 days.

106   Study Guide to Accompany Financial Accounting: Tools for Business Decision-Making, Fifth Canadian Edition

(SO 6)   *18.   The following data apply to Czepanski Company, which uses a periodic inventory system:

Date	Units	Unit Cost	Total Cost
Feb. 5	200	$2	$ 400
Mar. 6	500	4	2,000
Apr. 9	400	6	2,400
June 7	300	7	2,100
	1,400		$6,900

On June 30, there are 350 units in ending inventory.

What is cost of ending inventory using FIFO?
a. $1,000
b. $1,726
c. $2,400
d. $5,175

(SO 6)   *19.   Using the data for Czepanski Company in question 18, what is cost of goods sold using average cost?
a. $1,000
b. $1,726
c. $2,400
d. $5,175

Problems

(SO 1)   1.   Jensen Corporation has just completed a physical inventory count at its year end, December 31, 2012. Only the items on the shelves, in storage, and in the receiving area were counted and included in inventory cost (using the FIFO cost formula). Ending inventory amounted to $88,000. During the audit of inventory, the following additional information was discovered:

a.   Some office supplies in the amount of $400 were included in the inventory count. These supplies will be used in the office and are not be available for sale.

b.   On December 27, 2012, Jensen shipped goods to a customer. The goods (purchased by Jensen for $900) were sold for $1,200. The goods were shipped FOB destination and were received by the customer on January 3, 2013. Because the goods were not on the shelves, Jensen excluded them from its physical inventory count.

c.   On the date of the inventory count, Jensen received notice from a supplier that goods ordered earlier, at a cost of $3,500, had been delivered to the transportation company on December 28, 2012. The terms were FOB shipping point. Because the shipment had not arrived on December 31, 2012, it was excluded from the physical inventory count.

d.   On December 31, 2012, there were goods in transit to customers, with terms FOB shipping point, amounting to $750 (expected delivery on January 8, 2013). Because the goods had been shipped, they were excluded from the physical inventory count.

CHAPTER 6   Reporting and Analyzing Inventory   107

e.   On December 31, 2012, Jensen shipped $1,200 worth of goods to a cus-
tomer, FOB destination, on January 5, 2013. Because the goods were not on
hand, they were not included in the physical inventory count.

f.   Jensen, as the consignee, had goods (costing $3,700) on consignment.
Because these goods were on hand as at December 31, 2012, they were
included in the physical inventory count.

Analyze the information above and calculate a corrected amount of ending
inventory. Explain the basis for your treatment of each item.

2.   A company has the following transactions for the month of May: (SO 2)

Date	Explanation	Units	Unit Cost	Total Cost
May 1	Beginning inventory	3,000	$4	$12,000
12	Purchase	7,000	5	35,000
20	Sale	8,000		
25	Purchase	3,200	6	19,200
30	Sale	4,300		
				$66,200

Determine cost of goods sold and ending inventory under a perpetual inventory
system using (a) FIFO and (b) average cost.

3.   A company, in its first year of operations, has the following inventory   (SO 2, 6)
transactions for the year:

Date	Units Purchased	Unit Cost	Units Sold
Jan. 5	500	$5.00	
Feb. 10	800	6.75	
Mar. 6			1,000
June 15	700	7.00	
July 16			400
Aug. 12	500	8.00	
Sep. 11	300	10.00	
Oct. 25			500
Nov. 25	200	12.00	
Dec. 20			500

a.   Assume the company uses a perpetual inventory system and average cost
formula. What is the cost of goods sold for the March 6 sale?

b.   Assume the company uses a perpetual inventory system and FIFO cost
formula. What is the cost of goods sold for the March 6 sale?

*c.   Assume the company uses a periodic inventory system and FIFO cost
formula. What is the cost of goods sold for the year?

*d.   Assume the company uses a periodic inventory system and average cost
formula. What is the cost of goods sold for the year?

108   Study Guide to Accompany Financial Accounting: Tools for Business Decision-Making, Fifth Canadian Edition

(SO 4)   4.   A company has the following income statements:

	2012	2013
Sales	$50,000	$70,000
Cost of goods sold	30,000	45,000
Gross profit	20,000	25,000
Operating expenses	14,000	15,000
Profit before income tax	6,000	10,000
Income tax expense (25%)	1,500	2,500
Profit	$ 4,500	$ 7,500

After the preparation of the above income statements, it was discovered that ending inventory on December 31, 2012, was understated by $3,000. Ending inventory on December 31, 2013, was correct. The company uses a perpetual inventory system, and ending inventory, before the understatement was discovered, was $8,000 for 2012 and $10,000 for 2013.
a.   Prepare corrected income statements for 2012 and 2013.
b.   Calculate the effect of the inventory correction on gross profit margin.
c.   Calculate the effect of the inventory correction on profit margin.

(SO 3, 5)   5.   Please refer to the HMV and WHSmith financial statements found in the appendices at the end of this study guide for information in answering the following questions. Do not forget to use the **Decision Toolkit** approach for help in answering the questions.

a.   HMV uses FIFO cost formula and WHSmith uses average cost formula. Why might HMV use a different cost formula than WHSmith?
b.   For both HMV and WHSmith, calculate inventory turnover and days in inventory for 2010.
c.   Assume that industry ratios are as follows for 2010:

Inventory turnover   5.5
Days in inventory   67

Compare the 2010 performance of HMV and WHSmith in terms of inventory management.

Solutions to Self-Test

Multiple Choice

1.   a   A company that uses a periodic inventory system takes a physical inventory count at year end to determine the amount of inventory on hand, and to determine cost of goods sold. Answer d is incorrect—counting inventory will not determine which party owns the goods.

2.   a   Under a consignment arrangement, the holder of the goods (the *consignee*) does not have legal title or ownership of the goods, and therefore would not include the consigned goods in its inventory.

CHAPTER 6 Reporting and Analyzing Inventory 109

3. c   When goods are shipped FOB destination, the seller retains legal title to the goods until they reach the buyer's place of business. Since the seller has legal title to the goods during transit, the seller would include the goods in its inventory even while they are in transit.

4. a   Consigned goods are always the property of the consignor (the shipper of the goods).

5. d   FIFO and average cost both assume a flow of costs that may not be the same as the actual physical flow of goods, unlike the specific identification method. NRV is not a method of cost determination.

6. a   Answers b and d are correct under a periodic inventory system. Under a perpetual inventory system, the specific identification, FIFO, or average cost method may be used.

7. b   Although the calculation format may differ, the results under FIFO in a perpetual inventory system are the same as under a periodic inventory system.

8. c $14,000 + $19,000 = $33,000.

9. b $8,000 + $10,000 = $18,000.

10. a   The following objectives should be considered:

   1. Choose a method that corresponds as closely as possible to the physical flow of goods.
   2. Report an inventory cost on the statement of financial position that is close to the inventory's recent cost.
   3. Use the same method for all inventories having a similar nature and usage in the company.

11. b   The specific identification method flows actual costs of goods sold to the income statement.

12. c $30,000 ÷ $20,000 = 1.5 times.

13. a   Assuming that ending inventory is calculated correctly at the end of the year, an error in beginning inventory does not have an effect on ending inventory of the same year.

14. a   2012: $50,000 + $10,000 = $60,000.
        2013: $75,000 − $10,000 − $5,000 = $60,000.

15. c   ($12 × 170) + ($5 × 155) + ($15 × 135) = $4,840.

16. c   Cost of goods sold % = 100% − 30% = 70%.
        Cost of goods sold = 70% × $400,000 = $280,000.

$$\text{Inventory turnover} = \frac{\text{Cost of goods sold}}{\text{Average inventory}}$$

$$= \frac{\$280,000}{(\$14,000 + \$18,000) \div 2} = 17.5 \text{ times}$$

17. b   365 days ÷ 17.5 times = 21 days.

*18. c

June 7	300 ×	$7 =	$2,100
Apr. 9	50 ×	6 =	300
	350		$2,400 ending inventory

*19. d $6,900.00 ÷ 1,400 = $4.93/unit; $4.93/unit × 1,050 units = $5,175.00.

110   Study Guide to Accompany Financial Accounting: Tools for Business Decision-Making, Fifth Canadian Edition

Problems

1.

$88,000 Unadjusted ending inventory amount

a. −$400. The office supplies are not for sale and should be excluded from ending merchandise inventory.

b. +$900. The goods should be included Jensen's ending inventory because they were shipped FOB destination, meaning Jensen owns the goods until they are received by the customer on January 3.

c. +$3,500. The goods should be included in Jensen's ending inventory because they were shipped by the supplier with terms FOB shipping point, meaning Jensen owns the goods from the date of shipment.

d. $0. Because the goods were shipped FOB shipping point, Jensen no longer has legal title to the goods as at December 31, 2012. The items were properly excluded from Jensen's ending inventory.

e. +$1,200. The goods were shipped FOB destination, meaning Jensen retains legal title to the goods until they are received by the customer.

f. −$3,700. These consigned goods are owned by the consignor, not the consignee (Jensen), and should not be included in Jensen's inventory.

$89,500 corrected ending inventory amount ($88,000 − $400 + $900 + $3,500 + $1,200 − $3,700)

2.

a. FIFO—Perpetual

Date	Purchases			Cost of Goods Sold			Balance		
	Units	Cost	Total	Units	Cost	Total	Units	Cost	Total
May 1							3,000	$4	$12,000
12	7,000	$5	$35,000				3,000 7,000	4 5 }	47,000
20				3,000 5,000	$4 5 }	$37,000	2,000	5	10,000
25	3,200	6	19,200				2,000 3,200	5 6 }	29,200
30				2,000 2,300	5 6 }	$23,800	900	6	5,400
	10,200		$54,200	12,300		$60,800			

Hint: Check that cost of goods sold plus ending inventory equals cost of goods available for sale: $60,800 + $5,400 = $66,200 ($12,000 + $54,200).

CHAPTER 6   Reporting and Analyzing Inventory   111

b. Average—Perpetual

	Purchases			Cost of Goods Sold			Balance		
Date	Units	Cost	Total	Units	Cost	Total	Units	Cost	Total
May 1							3,000	$4.00	$12,000
12	7,000	$5	35,000				10,000	4.70	47,000
20				8,000	$4.70	$37,600	2,000	4.70	9,400
25	3,200	6	19,200				5,200	5.50	28,600
30				4,300	5.50	23,650	900	5.50	4,950
	10,200		$54,200	12,300		$61,250			

Hint: Check that the cost of goods sold and ending inventory equals the cost of goods available for sale: $61,250 + $4,950 = $66,200 ($12,000 + $54,200).

3.

a. Cost of goods sold for the March 6 sale is $6,076.92. The full perpetual inventory schedule is shown below for average cost formula.

	Purchases			Cost of Goods Sold			Balance		
Date	Units	Cost	Total	Units	Cost	Total	Units	Cost	Total
Jan. 5	500	$5.00	$2,500.00				500	$5.00	$2,500.00
Feb. 10	800	6.75	5,400.00				1,300	6.08	7,900.00
Mar. 6				1,000	$6.08	$6,076.92	300	6.08	1,823.08
June 15	700	7.00	4,900.00				1,000	6.72	6,723.08
July 16				400	6.72	2,689.23	600	6.72	4,033.85
Aug. 12	500	8.00	4,000.00				1,100	7.30	8,033.85
Sep. 11	300	10.00	3,000.00				1,400	7.88	11,033.85
Oct. 25				500	7.88	3,940.66	900	7.88	7,093.19
Nov. 25	200	12.00	2,400.00				1,100	8.63	9,493.19
Dec. 20				500	8.63	4,315.09	600	8.63	5,178.10

Cost of goods sold, under a perpetual inventory system using average cost, is shown in the above table. Under a perpetual inventory system, cost of goods sold is calculated each time a sale is made. Total cost of goods sold is $17,021.90 ($6,076.92 + $2,689.23 + $3,940.66 + $4,315.09).

b. Under a perpetual inventory system, cost of goods sold is calculated each time a sale is made. Cost of goods sold, under a perpetual inventory system using FIFO, for the 1,000 units sold on March 6 is:

Jan. 5	500	units	×	$5.00	=	$2,500
Feb. 10	500	units	×	$6.75	=	3,375
	1,000					$5,875

112   Study Guide to Accompany Financial Accounting: Tools for Business Decision-Making, Fifth Canadian Edition

*c. Under a periodic inventory system, at the end of the accounting period, we allocate the entire pool of cost of goods available for sale between cost of goods sold and ending inventory for the period. Calculation of the cost of goods available for sale is shown in the following table:

Date	Units Purchased	Unit Cost	Total Cost
Jan. 5	500	$5.00	$ 2,500
Feb. 10	800	6.75	5,400
June 15	700	7.00	4,900
Aug. 12	500	8.00	4,000
Sep. 11	300	10.00	3,000
Nov. 25	200	12.00	2,400
Total goods available for sale	3,000		$22,200

Total units sold = 1,000 + 400 + 500 + 500 = 2,400 units.

Ending inventory = 3,000 − 2,400 units = 600 units.

Ending inventory, under FIFO, consists of inventory purchased in the most recent purchase transactions as follows:

Nov. 25	200	×	$12	=	$2,400
Sep. 11	300	×	10	=	3,000
Aug. 12	100	×	8	=	800
	600				$6,200

Cost of goods sold is calculated by subtracting ending inventory from cost of goods available for sale as follows:

Cost of goods available for sale	$22,200
Less: ending inventory	6,200
Cost of goods sold	$16,000

*d. Ending inventory, under average cost, equals number of units in ending inventory times weighted average unit cost of the units purchased, as follows:

Weighted average unit cost is:

$$\frac{\$22,200}{3,000 \text{ units}} = \$7.40 \text{ per unit}$$

Ending inventory is: 600 units × $7.40 = $4,440.

Cost of goods sold is calculated by subtracting ending inventory from cost of goods available for sale as follows:

Cost of goods available for sale	$22,200
Less: ending inventory	4,440
Cost of goods sold	$17,760

4.

a. If ending inventory is understated by $3,000 in 2012, then cost of goods sold is overstated in 2012 because there is an inverse relationship between cost of goods sold and ending inventory. Furthermore, beginning inventory for 2013 is also understated because ending inventory in 2012 is assumed to have been carried forward to 2013. As a result, cost of goods sold for 2013 is understated by $3,000. Assuming ending inventory is calculated correctly at the end of 2013, the error will affect only 2012 and 2013. The corrected income statements for 2012 and 2013 are as follows:

	2012		2013	
	Incorrect	Correct	Incorrect	Correct
Sales	$50,000	$50,000	$70,000	$70,000
Cost of goods sold	30,000	27,000	45,000	48,000
Gross profit	20,000	23,000	25,000	22,000
Operating expenses	14,000	14,000	15,000	15,000
Profit before income tax	6,000	9,000	10,000	7,000
Income tax expense (25%)	1,500	2,250	2,500	1,750
Profit	$ 4,500	$ 6,750	$ 7,500	$ 5,250

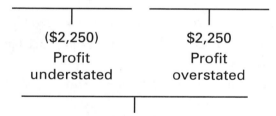

($2,250) Profit understated

$2,250 Profit overstated

The combined profit for 2 years is correct because the errors cancel each other out.

In this illustration, the 2012 understatement of ending inventory results in an overstatement of cost of goods sold, and an understatement of gross profit, profit before income tax, and profit, in the same year. The 2012 understatement of ending inventory also results in an understatement of cost of goods sold in 2013, and an overstatement of gross profit, profit before income tax, and profit in the same year.

b.

Gross profit margin = Gross profit ÷ Net sales

	2012	2013
Before inventory correction:		
$20,000 ÷ $50,000	40.0%	
$25,000 ÷ $70,000		35.7%
After inventory correction:		
$23,000 ÷ $50,000	46.0%	
$22,000 ÷ $70,000		31.4%

114 Study Guide to Accompany Financial Accounting: Tools for Business Decision-Making, Fifth Canadian Edition

c.

Profit margin = Profit ÷ Net sales

	2012	2013
Before inventory correction:		
$4,500 ÷ $50,000	9.0%	
$7,500 ÷ $70,000		10.7%
After inventory correction:		
$6,750 ÷ $50,000	13.5%	
$5,250 ÷ $70,000		7.5%

5.

a. HMV may use the FIFO cost formula because it results in an inventory cost on the statement of financial position that is closest to the inventory's recent cost. WHSmith may use the weighted average cost formula because it corresponds more closely to its actual physical flow of goods or because, due to volatility of costs, the weighted average cost formula may report an inventory cost on the statement of financial position that is closer to the inventory's recent cost. Choice of cost determination method may vary, even between competitors in the same industry; however, companies are required to consider the same guidelines in making the choice between FIFO and average cost formulas:

- Choose a method that corresponds as closely as possible to the physical flow of goods.

- Report an inventory cost on the statement of financial position that is close to the inventory's recent cost.

- Use the same method for all inventories having a similar nature and usage in the company.

b. HMV: average inventory = (£213.9 million + £247.8 million) ÷ 2 = £230.9 million.

Inventory turnover = cost of goods sold ÷ average inventory

£1,855.6 million ÷ £230.9 million = 8.0 times.

Days in inventory = 365 days ÷ inventory turnover

365 days ÷ 8.0 times = 46 days.

WHSmith: average inventory = (£151 million + £151 million) ÷ 2 = £151 million.

Inventory turnover = cost of goods sold ÷ average inventory

£650 million ÷ £151 million = 4.3 times.

Days in inventory = 365 days ÷ inventory turnover

365 days ÷ 4.3 times = 85 days.

c. HMV's inventory ratios are better than the industry averages of 5.5 times for inventory turnover and 67 for days in inventory. WHSmith's inventory ratios are below the industry averages. It appears that HMV managed its inventory more effectively in 2010, and achieved higher inventory turnover and fewer days in inventory compared with WHSmith and the industry. However, some of the difference in inventory ratio results can be explained by each company's nature of inventory. HMV's product mix includes packaged music, visual products, and games; live music and entertainment; and books. WHSmith's product mix includes newspapers, magazines, books, stationery, and entertainment products.

chapter 7

Internal Control and Cash

Chapter Overview

Chapter 7 discusses the importance of managing cash and ways of controlling it effectively. Essential features of an internal control system are discussed, along with ways of applying internal controls to cash receipts and disbursements. You will learn how to prepare a bank reconciliation and how to report cash on the statement of financial position. You will also learn the basic principles of cash management.

Review of Specific Study Objectives

Fraud and Internal Control

study objective 1
Explain the activities that help achieve internal control and prevent fraud.

- **Fraud** is an intentional act to misappropriate (steal) assets or misstate financial statements. In response to recent high-profile corporate failures and scandals, regulation has increased to emphasize the importance of internal controls within public companies.

- Good **internal control systems** have five primary components, listed below:

  1. **Control environment:** It is management's responsibility to make it clear that the organization values integrity and that unethical activity will not be tolerated (often referred to as "setting the tone at the top").

116   **Study Guide to Accompany Financial Accounting: Tools for Business Decision-Making, Fifth Canadian Edition**

2. **Risk assessment**: Companies must identify and analyze the various factors that create risk for the business and determine how to manage these risks.
3. **Control activities**: To reduce the occurrence of fraud, management must design policies and procedures to address the specific risks faced by the company.
4. **Information and communication**: The system must capture and communicate all pertinent information both down and up the organization and communicate it to appropriate external parties.
5. **Monitoring**: Internal control systems must be monitored periodically for their adequacy. Significant deficiencies need to be reported to management and the board of directors.

- We will focus on **control activities** because these activities form the backbone of a company's plan to address the risks it faces. Control activities include the following:

    1. **Authorization of transactions and activities**: Responsibilities should be assigned to specific employees. This control activity is most effective when only one person is authorized to perform a specific task.
    2. **Segregation of duties**: Responsibility for related activities should be assigned to different individuals, to decrease the potential for errors and irregularities. In general, authorization of transactions and activities, recording of transactions, and custody of assets should be delegated to different employees to decrease the potential for errors. For example, purchasing activities—including ordering merchandise, recording invoices and payments, and receiving goods—should be delegated to different employees. Sales activities—including making sales, billing customers, and delivering goods—should also be delegated to different employees.
    3. **Documentation**: Procedures should be established for documents even if they are in electronic format. Whenever possible, documents should be prenumbered and all documents should be accounted for. Source documents (original receipts) should be forwarded promptly to the accounting department to ensure accurate and timely recording of transactions.
    4. **Physical controls**: Physical controls can be used to safeguard assets and enhance the reliability of accounting records. Physical controls include mechanical and electronic controls to safeguard assets.
    5. **Independent checks of performance**: The four internal control activities discussed above (authorization of transactions and activities, segregation of duties, documentation, and physical controls) must be reviewed independently and frequently. These reviews should take place internally and externally, as described below.

        a. **Internal reviews**: Independent internal reviews are especially useful in comparing accounting records with existing assets to ensure that nothing has been stolen. For independent internal reviews to be beneficial, three measures are recommended:

            1. The review should be done periodically and sometimes on a surprise basis.
            2. The review should be done by an employee who is independent of the personnel responsible for the information.
            3. Discrepancies and exceptions should be reported to a management-level employee who can take appropriate corrective action.

CHAPTER 7 Internal Control and Cash 117

    b. **External reviews**: An important type of external review is conducted by the external auditors. External auditors, in contrast to internal auditors, are independent of the company. They are professional accountants hired by a company to report on whether or not the company's financial statements fairly present its financial position and results of operations.

  6. **Human resource controls**: Other control measures include the following:

    a. **Conducting thorough background checks**: An inexpensive measure any company can take to reduce employee theft and fraud is for the human resources department to conduct thorough background checks of job applicants.

    b. **Bonding of employees who handle cash**: Bonding involves acquiring insurance protection against theft of assets by dishonest employees.

    c. **Rotating employees' duties, and requiring employees to take vacations**: These measures help to deter employees from attempting theft because the employees know that they will not be able to permanently conceal their improper actions.

- Good internal controls provide **reasonable assurance** that assets are safeguarded and that the accounting records are accurate and reliable. However, internal control systems have limitations, and the costs of establishing an internal control system should not exceed its benefits. It may be prohibitively expensive to design very highly complex internal control systems. As well, the human element is an important factor in every internal control system. A dishonest or incompetent employee can render an internal control system ineffective if he or she actively finds ways to circumvent the system; as well, two or more employees may collude to circumvent the system. The size of the company is also a factor. A large company may have both human and financial resources necessary to implement a sophisticated system of internal control, including optimal segregation of duties and an internal audit committee. A small company may have limited resources, and must do the best it can with what it has.

Cash Controls

- **Cash** consists of coins, currency (paper money), cheques, money orders, and money on hand or on deposit in a bank or similar depository. In general, if a bank will accept an item at face value as a deposit, then it is considered cash. Debit card transactions and bank credit card transactions, such as VISA, MasterCard, and American Express transactions, are considered cash, but nonbank credit card receipts are not. As well, cash does not include postdated cheques, stale-dated cheques (cheques more than six months old), or returned cheques (due to insufficient funds in the payer's account). Postage stamps and IOUs from employees are also not cash. Because cash is readily convertible into other assets, and easily concealed and transported, strong internal controls over cash are absolutely necessary.

> **study objective 2**
>
> Apply control activities to cash receipts and payments.

- A retailer may allow its customers to use credit cards to pay for purchases. Sales paid for by bank credit cards are considered cash sales by the retailer and recorded as cash rather than as receivables. In return for cash payments on behalf of credit card customers, issuing banks charge retailers credit card fees (usually a percentage of credit card sales). Therefore, acceptance of bank credit cards is another form of sale of receivables. Accepting payment by bank credit card translates to increased sales with zero bad debts for the retailer. For example, if a jewellery store sells $5,000 of

118   **Study Guide to Accompany Financial Accounting: Tools for Business Decision-Making, Fifth Canadian Edition**

jewellery to customers who pay using bank credit cards, and the issuing bank charges a 4% fee, then the jewellery store records the following entry:

Cash	4,800	
Credit Card Expense ($5,000 × 4%)	200	
Sales		5,000
(To record credit card sales)		

- A retailer may also allow its customers to use debit cards to pay for purchases. Debit cards allow customers to pay only up to the amount that is in their bank account. Credit cards, on the other hand, give customers access to money made available by a bank or other financial institution, similar to a loan. The journal entry to record debit card sales is identical to the journal entry shown to record bank credit card sales.

- Generally, internal control over cash receipts is more effective when cash receipts are deposited intact into the bank account on a daily basis or are made by **electronic funds transfer**. Electronic funds transfer (EFT) is a way of transferring money electronically from one bank account directly to another without any paper money changing hands. Debit and credit card transactions, mentioned above, are examples of EFTs.

- A company must have effective control over cash receipts. The control activities discussed earlier apply to cash receipts as follows:

  1. **Authorization of transactions and activities**: Only designated personnel should be authorized to handle cash receipts.
  2. **Segregation of duties**: Assign different individuals to record cash receipts and handle cash or cheques.
  3. **Documentation**: Remittance advices, cash register tapes, and deposit slips should be used to document transactions.
  4. **Physical controls**: Cash should be stored in safes and bank vaults with limited access; cash registers should be used.
  5. **Independent checks of performance**: Supervisors should count cash receipts daily; an accountant should compare total receipts with bank deposits on a daily basis.
  6. **Human resource controls**: Background checks should be conducted; personnel who handle cash should be bonded; employees should be required to take vacations.

- In general, internal control over cash payments is more effective when payments are made by cheque or by EFT. The control activities discussed earlier apply to cash payments as follows:

  1. **Authorization of transactions and activities**: Only authorized personnel should sign cheques or issue electronic payments.
  2. **Segregation of duties**: Have different individuals approve and make payments; ensure that cheque signers do not record cash payments.
  3. **Documentation**: Cheques should be prenumbered and used in sequence; each cheque should be matched with an approved invoice.
  4. **Physical controls**: Cash should be stored in safes and bank vaults with limited access; access to blank cheques and signing machines should be restricted; payments should be electronic whenever possible.
  5. **Independent checks of performance**: Cheques should be compared with invoices; the bank statement should be reconciled on a monthly basis.

CHAPTER 7   Internal Control and Cash   119

6. **Human resource controls**: Background checks should be conducted; personnel who handle cash should be bonded; employees should be required to take vacations.

Control Features: Use of a Bank

- **Use of a bank contributes significantly to good internal control over cash.** A company can safeguard its cash by using a bank as a depository and clearing house for its cash, cheques received and written, and electronic funds received and paid. Use of a bank minimizes the amount of currency that must be kept on hand, and internal control is stronger because a second record of all transactions is kept and sent to the company in the form of a monthly bank statement.

> **study objective 3**
>
> Prepare a bank reconciliation.

- A company receives bank statements monthly, and as an independent check of performance, the company should reconcile (explain the difference between) the ending balance on the bank statement and the ending balance in its general ledger account "Cash." The ending balance on the bank statement and the ending balance in the company's "Cash" account are often different because of time lags (for example, if the bank has recorded a transaction that has affected the company's bank account, which the company has not yet recorded in its general ledger "Cash" account, there will be a difference between the two amounts due to a time lag).

- In reconciling a bank account, it is customary to reconcile the balance per books (the balance per the general ledger "Cash" account) and the balance per bank (the balance per the bank statement) to their adjusted (correct) cash balances. The bank reconciliation should be prepared by someone who has no other responsibilities related to cash.

- The following are typical adjustments made to "Balance per bank":

  1. **Deposits in transit**: deposits that the company has recorded but the bank has not recorded (because it does not know about them yet) are always added to the balance per bank column.
  2. **Outstanding cheques**: cheques recorded by the company that have not yet cleared (or been paid by the bank) are always subtracted from the balance per bank column.
  3. **Bank errors**: may either be added to or subtracted from the balance per bank column, depending on the nature of the error.

- The following are adjustments made to "Balance per books":

  1. **Credit memoranda and other deposits**: any electronic funds transfers from customers paying their accounts on-line (that have not been recorded by the company in its books yet) should be added to the balance per books.
  2. **Debit memoranda and other payments**: any bank service charges or unrecorded payments (that have not been recorded by the company in its books yet) should be deducted from the balance per books.
  3. **Company errors**: may either be added to or subtracted from the balance per books column, depending on the nature of the error.

- The **key** question to ask when preparing a bank reconciliation is: *"Who knows about the transaction and has already recorded it, and who does not yet know about it and therefore has yet to record it?"* For example, with respect to bank service charges, the bank knows about these and has already subtracted them from the company's bank

120   **Study Guide to Accompany Financial Accounting: Tools for Business Decision-Making, Fifth Canadian Edition**

account (per the company's bank statement). However, the company may not know the exact amount of the bank service charges until it receives the bank statement, so the company may have yet to record them in its own books.

- After the bank reconciliation is prepared, each reconciling item in the balance per books column must be recorded by the company in its books in the form of a journal entry. (Bank personnel correct bank errors identified in the balance per bank column, by adjusting the company's bank account and bank statement; note that deposits in transit and outstanding cheques are not recorded as adjusting journal entries by either party.) After the journal entries are journalized and posted by the company, the balance in the general ledger "Cash" account should equal the adjusted (correct) cash balance shown on the bank reconciliation.

Reporting and Managing Cash

---

study objective 4

Explain the reporting and management of cash.

- **Cash** is reported on the statement of financial position and the statement of cash flows. Cash on hand and cash in banks are combined and reported simply as Cash on the statement of financial position. If assets are listed in order of liquidity, Cash is listed first in the current assets section because it is the most liquid asset. (If assets are listed in order of reverse liquidity, Cash is listed last in the current assets section.) The sources and uses of cash are shown on the statement of cash flows and reconciled to the ending cash balance reported on the statement of financial position.

- Many companies combine cash with cash equivalents. A **cash equivalent** is a short-term, highly liquid (easily sold) investment that is readily convertible to cash and subject to an insignificant risk of change in value. Examples include treasury bills and short-term notes that have maturities of three months or less when purchased.

- If use of cash is restricted for a special purpose, it should be reported separately as **"restricted cash."** If the restricted cash is to be used within the next year, the amount should be reported as a current asset; if the restricted cash is to be used beyond the next year, the amount should be reported as a non-current asset.

- In making loans to depositors, banks commonly require borrowers to maintain minimum cash balances. These minimum balances, called **compensating balances**, provide the bank with support for the loans. They are a form of restriction on the use of cash. Similar to other restricted cash, compensating balances should be reported as a non-current asset.

- Effective management of cash is critical to a company's success. It can be difficult to effectively manage cash so that a company has sufficient cash on hand to make payments as they come due and to meet operational objectives.

- There are six basic principles of cash management:

  1. **Increase the speed of collection of receivables**. A company should aim to receive cash from its customers as quickly as possible so that it can increase cash on hand sooner.
  2. **Keep inventory levels low**. Minimizing inventory levels also minimizes the costs associated with carrying inventory.
  3. **Delay payment of liabilities**. A company should aim to pay its bills on time but not too early, and to take advantage of all cash discounts offered.
  4. **Plan the timing of major expenditures**. A company should aim to make major expenditures when it has excess cash, usually during the off-season.

CHAPTER 7   Internal Control and Cash   121

5. **Invest idle cash.** A company should aim to invest idle cash in highly liquid (easily sold) and risk-free (low risk of default) investments.
6. **Prepare a cash budget.** A company should prepare a cash budget, showing anticipated cash flows over a one- or two-year period.

comparing
IFRS and ASPE

Key Differences	International Financial Reporting Standards (IFRS)	Accounting Standards for Private Enterprises (ASPE)
No significant differences		

Chapter Self-Test

As you work through the questions and problems, remember to use the **Decision Toolkit** discussed and used in the text:

1. *Decision Checkpoints:* Ask a question relevant to the decision being made.
2. *Info Needed for Decision:* Make a choice regarding the information needed to answer the question.
3. *Tools to Use for Decision:* Review what the information identified in step 2 does for the decision-making process.
4. *How to Evaluate Results:* Identify specifically how the information identified in step 2 should be evaluated to answer the question relevant to the decision being made.

Note: The notation "(SO 1)" means that the question relates to study objective 1.

Multiple Choice

Please circle the correct answer.

1. Which of the following statements is correct? (SO 1)
   a. Internal control is most effective when two or three people are authorized to perform a specific task.
   b. The person who has custody of assets should not record the related transactions.
   c. The person who has custody of assets should also record the related transactions.
   d. Having an employee perform an independent internal review is an inefficient use of company resources.

2. Which of the following statements is incorrect? (SO 1)
   a. Related purchasing activities should be assigned to different individuals.
   b. Use of physical controls enhances safeguarding of assets.
   c. Independent checks of performance should be done by an employee independent of the personnel responsible for the information.
   d. Use of prenumbered documents is not an important control activity.

122 Study Guide to Accompany Financial Accounting: Tools for Business Decision-Making, Fifth Canadian Edition

(SO 1)   3. The custodian of a company asset should
- a.   have access to the accounting records for that asset.
- b.   be someone outside the company.
- c.   not have access to the accounting records for that asset.
- d.   be an accountant.

(SO 1)   4. The *Sarbanes-Oxley Act* (SOX)
- a.   requires public companies to maintain adequate systems of internal controls and to have senior company officers sign certifications to that effect.
- b.   was enacted in reaction to recent high-profile corporate failures and accounting scandals.
- c.   was enacted in the United States, and soon after, provisions similar to SOX were adopted in Canada.
- d.   All of the above.

(SO 1)   5. Which of the following is one of the primary components of a good internal control system?
- a.   Risk assessment
- b.   Documentation
- c.   Human resource controls
- d.   Segregation of duties

(SO 2)   6. Having one person responsible for the related activities of making sales, billing customers, and delivering goods
- a.   is a good way to ensure that transactions are recorded properly.
- b.   decreases the potential for errors and fraud.
- c.   is an example of good internal control.
- d.   increases the potential for errors and fraud.

(SO 2)   7. An employee authorized to sign cheques should *not*
- a.   record cash deposits.
- b.   receive company mail.
- c.   record cash payment transactions.
- d.   approve sales transactions.

(SO 2)   8. Which of the following is not considered cash?
- a.   Coins
- b.   Money orders
- c.   Short-term investment in another company's shares
- d.   Chequing account

(SO 2, 4)   9. A company has the following items: cash on hand, $1,000; cash in a chequing account, $3,000; cash in a savings account, $5,000; postage stamps, $50; and 120-day treasury bills, $10,000. How much should the company report as cash on its statement of financial position?
- a. $9,000
- b. $9,050
- c. $19,000
- d. $19,050

(SO 2)   10. Effective internal control over cash payments includes
- a.   use of prenumbered cheques.
- b.   storage of blank cheques in a secure place.

CHAPTER 7 Internal Control and Cash 123

c. separation of payment authorization and actual writing of cheques.
d. All of the above.

11. Fiddler Corporation gathered the following information in preparing its June (SO 3)
bank reconciliation:

Cash balance per books, June 30	$3,500
Deposits in transit	150
Electronic deposit	850
Bank charge for cheque printing	20
Outstanding cheques	2,000
NSF cheque	170

What is the adjusted cash balance per books on July 30?
a. $4,160
b. $4,010
c. $2,310
d. $2,460

12. Which of the following is added to the "Balance per books" on a bank reconciliation? (SO 3)
a. An outstanding cheque for $300
b. An electronic deposit of $500 made by a customer
c. A deposit in transit of $150
d. A bank service charge for $50 for cheque printing

13. Cooper Corporation showed a balance in its general ledger "Cash" account of (SO 3)
$1,250 when it received its monthly bank statement. Cooper found the following
reconciling items in preparing for its monthly bank reconciliation: deposits in
transit, $256; outstanding cheques, $375; NSF cheque, $102; bank service charges,
$27; and an EFT into the bank account, $850. What is the adjusted (correct) cash
balance Cooper will show on its bank reconciliation?
a. $1,131
b. $1,852
c. $1,971
d. $1,981

14. Which of the following items should be added to "Balance per bank" on a bank (SO 3)
reconciliation?
a. A $200 cheque returned from the bank, due to insufficient funds
b. A $600 deposit incorrectly recorded by the bank as a $60 deposit
c. A $991 deposit incorrectly recorded in the company's books as a
$919 deposit
d. An $87 cheque recorded as a $78 cheque in the company's books

15. Which of the following bank reconciliation items would *not* result in an adjusting (SO 3)
entry?
a. An error made by the company in recording a cheque
b. An outstanding cheque
c. Interest revenue earned on a bank account
d. Collection of a note by the bank, on behalf of the company

124   Study Guide to Accompany Financial Accounting: Tools for Business Decision-Making, Fifth Canadian Edition

(SO 4)   16.   Cash equivalents include
- a.   short-term, highly liquid investments.
- b.   notes receivable, due within three months.
- c.   guaranteed investment certificates, due within the next year.
- d.   investment securities, such as investments in shares of other companies.

(SO 4)   17.   Cash is reported on the
- a.   statement of financial position and the statement of cash flows.
- b.   statement of financial position and the income statement.
- c.   statement of financial position and the statement of changes in equity.
- d.   income statement and the statement of cash flows.

(SO 4)   18.   If use of a portion of cash is restricted, but will be used within the next year, the portion of cash that is restricted should be
- a.   included with Cash on the statement of financial position.
- b.   reported as a current liability on the statement of financial position.
- c.   reported as a non-current asset on the statement of financial position.
- d.   reported as a current asset separate from Cash and Cash Equivalents on the statement of financial position.

(SO 4)   19.   Keeping inventory levels low and planning the timing of major expenditures are two basic principles of
- a.   internal control.
- b.   cash management.
- c.   inventory management.
- d.   share capital management.

(SO 4)   20.   With respect to cash management, most companies try to
- a.   keep as much spare cash on hand as possible in case of emergency.
- b.   keep a lot of cash in a non–interest-bearing chequing account because that type of account has the lowest fees.
- c.   invest idle cash, even if only overnight.
- d.   invest idle cash in illiquid investments in order to earn the greatest returns.

(SO 4)   21.   A minimum cash balance that a borrower is required to maintain, in order to provide its bank with support for the loan, is called a
- a.   compensating balance.
- b.   cash equivalent.
- c.   liability.
- d.   financing balance.

Problems

(SO 1, 2)   1.   You have been asked to help Basil Corporation with its internal control problems. Basil has 12 employees. There has not been any staff rotation among employee positions for at least six years because management believes that the training costs associated with implementing staff rotation would be too high. In addition to its main store, Basil has a small showroom store staffed by one person who also works in Basil's accounting department. This person orders and receives goods and pays invoices. A different person in the accounting department records all sales and makes deposits to the bank when the deposit is large enough to make it worthwhile to go to the bank. This person also opens the mail and holds all cash and cheques in a desk drawer until a deposit is made.

CHAPTER 7 Internal Control and Cash 125

Identify four weaknesses in Basil's internal control system and make recommendations to correct them.

2. The following information is available for the Jay Corporation as at June 30, 2012, to assist you in preparing its bank reconciliation.

(SO 3)

- Balance per bank, June 30, $1,617.
- Balance per books, June 30, $2,151.
- Outstanding cheques as at June 30 totalled $559.
- Deposits in transit as at June 30 totalled $802.
- An NSF cheque for $67 was returned by the bank. The cheque was originally received by Jay from a customer who made a payment on account.
- The bank statement showed bank service charges totalling $35 plus a $40 charge for processing the NSF cheque.
- An electronic deposit of $760 was made by a customer in payment of her account.
- On June 15, Jay issued a cheque for $1,587 to a supplier on account. The cheque, which cleared the bank in June, was incorrectly journalized by Jay for $1,578.
- Included with the cancelled cheques was a cheque issued by Gee Corporation for $100, which was incorrectly charged to Jay by the bank.
- A pre-authorized electronic payment of $800 was made for insurance for the month of June. This payment was not recorded in Jay's books.

a. Prepare a bank reconciliation for Jay Corporation as at June 30, 2012, using the above data.

b. Prepare any journal entries required by the bank reconciliation.

3. The bank reconciliation prepared by Star Corporation at July 31 showed the following outstanding cheques:

(SO 3)

#101	$245
#113	560
#114	465
#117	657

A list of cheques paid and other debits recorded by the bank during August is as follows:

Bank Statement
Cheques Paid and Other Debits
August 31

Date	Cheque Number	Amount
August 1	101	$245
2	121	352
5	122	678
11	114	465
13	123	560
15	Returned cheque—NSF	440
15	NSF fee	40
17	124	137

126 **Study Guide to Accompany Financial Accounting: Tools for Business Decision-Making, Fifth Canadian Edition**

19	126	267
21	127	432
30	130	765
31	EFT, payment of insurance	568
31	Service charge	20

A list of cash payments recorded by Star during August is as follows:

Cash Payments Journal
August 31

Date	Cheque Number	Amount
August 1	121	$352
3	122	687
6	123	560
9	124	137
13	125	287
14	126	267
16	127	432
20	128	206
22	129	925
24	130	765
29	131	429

Additional information:
The bank did not make any errors and the company did not record the EFT payment of insurance or the NSF cheque in its books.

a.   List and total the outstanding cheques at August 31.
b.   List any other items that must be included in the August bank reconciliation.

(SO 4)   4.   Refer to the HMV and WHSmith financial statements found in the appendices at the end of this study guide for information in answering the following questions. Do not forget to use the **Decision Toolkit** approach for help in answering the questions.

a.   What is the most liquid asset on each company's statement of financial position? Explain the two components.
b.   For each company, did Cash increase or decrease from 2009 to 2010?
c.   How did HMV and WHSmith use their cash in 2010?

Solutions to Self-Test

Multiple Choice

1.   b   To achieve segregation of duties, the person who has custody of assets should be different from the person who records the related transactions. Internal reviews are important independent checks of performance.

CHAPTER 7　Internal Control and Cash　127

2. **d** Use of prenumbered documents is an important control activity.

3. **c** To achieve segregation of duties, the custodian of a company asset should not be responsible for recording the related transactions and should not have access to the accounting records for that asset.

4. **d** SOX was enacted in response to recent high-profile corporate failures and scandals. It emphasizes the importance of internal controls within public companies and requires that senior company officers sign certifications to that effect. Provisions similar to SOX have been enacted in Canada.

5. **a** Answers b, c, and d are control activities.

6. **d** When the same individual is responsible for related activities, the potential for errors and irregularities is increased.

7. **c** To achieve segregation of duties, an employee authorized to sign cheques should not record the related transactions.

8. **c** A short-term investment in another company's shares is not considered cash.

9. **a** $1,000 + $3,000 + $5,000 = $9,000. Postage stamps are office supplies and are expensed when purchased. Treasury bills, due in four months, are short-term investments.

10. **d** Use of prenumbered cheques is a "documentation" control activity; storage of blank cheques in a secure place is a "physical" control activity; and separation of payment authorization and actual writing of cheques is a "segregation of duties" control activity.

11. **a** $3,500 + $850 − $20 − $170 = $4,160.

12. **b** An outstanding cheque is subtracted from the "Balance per bank," a deposit in transit is added to the "Balance per bank," and a service charge is subtracted from the "Balance per books."

13. **c** $1,250 − $102 − $27 + $850 = $1,971.

14. **b** All of the other items would be recorded as adjustments to the "Balance per books."

15. **b** Outstanding cheques are deducted from the "Balance per bank" and thus would not result in an adjusting entry.

16. **a** Cash equivalents are short-term, highly liquid (easily sold) investments that are subject to an insignificant risk of changes in value. Short-term notes receivable, one-year GICs, and investments in shares of other companies are not considered cash equivalents.

17. **a** Cash does not appear on the income statement or the statement of changes in equity.

18. **d** Restricted cash that is expected to be used within the next year is reported as a current asset. Cash (and Cash Equivalents) should include only unrestricted cash.

19. **b** There are six basic principles of cash management, including keeping inventories low and planning the timing of major expenditures.

20. **c** Keeping spare cash on hand or in a non–interest-bearing account does not take advantage of the interest-earning ability of cash. Investing in illiquid investments may be risky, because they cannot be easily converted into cash if the need arises.

128 **Study Guide to Accompany Financial Accounting: Tools for Business Decision-Making, Fifth Canadian Edition**

21. a In making loans to depositors, banks commonly require borrowers to maintain minimum cash balances. These minimum balances are called compensating balances.

Problems

1. a. There is no rotation of employees, which means that Basil is more susceptible to employee fraud. Rotating employees' duties is a human resource control, which is a key control activity. Basil should institute an employee duty rotation system and have a few employees change jobs at a time. This would deter employee fraud as it would be more difficult to permanently conceal fraudulent activity.

   b. Having one person order and receive goods and pay invoices does not provide adequate segregation of duties. These three activities are referred to as "related activities." Having inadequate segregation of duties increases the potential for errors and irregularities. To remedy this weakness, Basil should assign these different functions to different employees. If Basil cannot afford to hire the required number of additional employees, it should reorganize to at least separate the invoice paying function from the ordering and receiving functions. The invoice paying function could be assigned to the employee who handles the sales and cash deposit functions, and perhaps the mail handling function could be assigned to an employee in the main store.

   c. Not depositing cash to a bank daily and keeping cash in an unlocked desk drawer does not provide adequate physical controls over cash receipts. Cash should be deposited to a bank daily unless the amount of cash on hand is insignificant. In any event, cash should be stored in a locked safe or locked filing cabinet. Basil should also consider the possibility of having its customers pay their accounts through EFT, as this would limit the amount of cash on hand.

   d. Mail containing cash receipts should be opened with two people present. This would prevent the possibility of an employee keeping a cash receipt. A supervisor or another person should be present when mail is opened.

2.
   a.

JAY CORPORATION
Bank Reconciliation
June 30, 2012

Balance per bank		$1,617
Add: Deposits in transit	$802	
Cheque error	100	902
		2,519
Less: Outstanding cheques		559
Adjusted balance per bank		$1,960
Balance per books		$2,151
Add: Electronic deposit		760
		2,911

CHAPTER 7 Internal Control and Cash 129

Less: NSF cheque	$ 67	
Bank service charges ($35 + $40)	75	
Electronic payment—insurance	800	
Cheque recording error ($1,587 − $1,578)	9	
		951
Adjusted balance per books		$1,960

b. Journal entries are recorded only for the "Balance per books" side of the bank reconciliation. (Bank personnel would record an adjustment to Jay's bank account, only for the cheque error; deposits in transit and outstanding cheques are not adjusting journal entries recorded by either party.)

June 30	Cash	760	
	Accounts Receivable		760
	(To record electronic deposit)		
30	Accounts Receivable ($67 + $40)	107	
	Cash		107
	(To record NSF cheque and related service charge)		
30	Bank Charges Expense	35	
	Cash		35
	(To record bank service charges)		
30	Accounts Payable	9	
	Cash		9
	(To record cheque error)		
30	Insurance Expense	800	
	Cash		800
	(To record electronic payment for insurance)		

3.

a. The outstanding cheques at August 31 are:

Cheque Number	Amount
113	$ 560
117	657
125	287
128	206
129	925
131	429
	$3,064

b. Adjustments that must be included on the "Balance per books" side of the August bank reconciliation are as follows:

1. Star recorded Cheque #122 for $687. The cheque should have been recorded for $678. Star therefore over-deducted from its general ledger "Cash" account by $9, which must be added to the "Balance per books" on the bank reconciliation.

2. The following items were not recorded in Star's books and must therefore be shown as deductions from "Balance per books" on the bank reconciliation:

– NSF cheque	440
– NSF fee	40
– EFT payment	568
– Service charge	20

4.

a. For HMV, the most liquid asset is cash and short-term deposits, where short-term deposits include deposits made for varying periods of between one day and three months. For WHSmith, the most liquid asset is cash and cash equivalents, where cash equivalents include short-term deposits with an original maturity of three months or less. Cash represents all coins, currency, and amounts in bank accounts as at the statement of financial position date.

b. HMV: Cash and short-term deposits decreased by £23 million (£29.7 million − £52.7 million).

WHSmith: Cash and cash equivalents increased by £9 million (£56 million − £47 million).

c. HMV's statement of cash flows shows that in 2010, three major uses of its cash were purchase of property, plant, and equipment; business acquisition of a subsidiary; and payment of dividends to its shareholders.

WHSmith's statement of cash flows shows that in 2010, three major uses of its cash were purchase of property, plant, and equipment; payment of dividends to its shareholders; and repurchase of shares for cancellation.

A summary for 2010 follows:

	HMV (£ millions)	WHSmith (£ millions)
Net cash flows from operating activities	£65.9	£104
Net cash flows from investing activities	(81.2)	(28)
Net cash flows from financing activities	(2.7)	(67)
Net increase in cash and cash equivalents before adjustments	(18.0)	9
Adjustments	(0.2)	–
Opening net cash and cash equivalents	45.5	47
Closing net cash and cash equivalents	£27.3[1]	£ 56

[1] Note that on HMV's statement of cash flows, net cash and cash equivalents includes bank overdrafts of £2.4 million. (A bank overdraft is cash owed to a bank related to a chequing account in which cash payments have exceeded cash receipts.) However, on its statement of financial position, HMV's bank overdrafts are classified with interest-bearing loans and borrowings in the current liabilities section. Therefore, cash and cash equivalents on the statement of financial position can be reconciled to net cash and cash equivalents on the statement of cash flows as follows: £29.7 million cash and cash equivalents on the statement of financial position − £2.4 million bank overdrafts = £27.3 million closing net cash and cash equivalents on the statement of cash flows.

chapter 8

Reporting and Analyzing Receivables

Chapter Overview

In this chapter, you will learn how to recognize and value accounts receivable, and how to record both estimated and actual bad debts (uncollectible receivables). You will also learn how receivables are reported in financial statements, and how they are managed in order to minimize losses due to uncollectible accounts.

- The term "receivables" refers to amounts that are due to a business from its customers or other entities. Receivables are claims that are expected to be collected in cash and are typically classified as accounts receivable, notes receivable, and other receivables.

- **Accounts receivable** are amounts owed by customers on account, resulting from sales of goods and services.

- **Notes receivable** are claims where formal instruments of credit (written promises to repay) are issued as evidence of the debt.

- **Trade receivables** are accounts receivable and notes receivable that result from sales transactions.

- **Other receivables** include credit card receivables from company-sponsored credit cards, interest receivable, loans to company officers, advances to employees, and recoverable sales tax and income tax. Other receivables are generally classified and reported as separate items in the current or non-current assets section of the statement of financial position, according to their due dates.

132 **Study Guide to Accompany Financial Accounting: Tools for Business Decision-Making, Fifth Canadian Edition**

Review of Specific Study Objectives

Recognizing Accounts Receivable

---

study objective 1

Explain how accounts receivable are recognized and valued in the accounts.

- A company that earns revenue by providing services will record a receivable when a service is provided on account.

- A merchandising company will record a receivable at the point of sale of merchandise on account.

- Receivables are created by providing services or selling goods on account, and are reduced when cash is collected or when the customer takes advantage of a sales discount or returns the product (sales returns).

- An **accounts receivable subsidiary ledger** provides a record of all accounts receivable transactions, grouped by customer account, and helps to organize and track individual customer balances. The total of all customer account balances in the accounts receivable subsidiary ledger agrees with the overall accounts receivable balance in the general ledger. Thus, the general ledger contains only one Accounts Receivable account, which acts as a control account to the total of all accounts in the accounts receivable subsidiary ledger.

Valuing Accounts Receivable

- Receivables are reported on the statement of financial position as a current asset; however, determining the amount that they should be reported at is sometimes difficult because inevitably some accounts receivable become uncollectible. For example, even though customers must satisfy the seller's credit requirements before credit is extended, a particular credit customer may not be able to pay its account due to unforeseen circumstances (such as a decline in its sales due to an economic downturn). In this case, the credit loss (or uncollectible account) is debited to Bad Debts Expense (an income statement account).

- The key issue in valuing accounts receivable is determining when to record bad debts expense. If a company does not record bad debts expense until it knows for certain that a specific account will not be collected, it may end up recording bad debts expense in periods after the related revenues are earned and recorded. This would cause mismatching of expenses and revenues.

- To avoid mismatching of expenses and revenues, the allowance method of accounting for bad debts is used to record estimated uncollectible accounts. Under the allowance method of accounting for bad debts, uncollectible accounts receivable are estimated and Allowance for Doubtful Accounts is adjusted to equal the estimate of uncollectible accounts receivable. (Allowance for Doubtful Accounts is a contra asset account with a credit balance that is shown below Accounts Receivable on the statement of financial position.) The adjustment or increase in Allowance for Doubtful Accounts is also recorded as a debit to bad debts expense. Therefore, the allowance method of accounting for bad debts ensures that receivables are shown on the statement of financial position at their net realizable value (the difference between Accounts Receivable and Allowance for Doubtful Accounts, or the amount that the company actually expects to collect).

CHAPTER 8   Reporting and Analyzing Receivables   133

- The allowance method of accounting for bad debts has three essential features:

1. **Recording estimated uncollectible accounts.** Allowance for Doubtful Accounts is adjusted to equal estimated uncollectible accounts, and the offsetting debit is recorded as Bad Debts Expense. This results in recording the estimated bad debts expense in the same period in which the related revenues are earned and recorded. Therefore, the adjusting journal entry to record estimated uncollectible accounts is as follows:

Bad Debts Expense	XXX	
Allowance for Doubtful Accounts		XXX
(To record estimate of uncollectible accounts)		

Bad Debts Expense is reported on the income statement as an operating expense. Allowance for Doubtful Accounts is reported on the statement of financial position as a contra asset deducted from Accounts Receivable. The difference between Accounts Receivable and Allowance for Doubtful Accounts represents the net realizable value of accounts receivable at the statement of financial position date.

Note that the amount in the journal entry to record estimated uncollectible accounts is an estimate. The amount is an estimate because at this point, the company does not know exactly which customers will default. While there are several acceptable ways to estimate uncollectible accounts, most companies use the percentage of receivables basis to determine the appropriate Allowance for Doubtful Accounts account balance.

Under the percentage of receivables basis, management estimates the percentage of receivables that is likely to be uncollectible. An overall percentage of uncollectible receivables can be applied to total receivables, or different percentages can be applied to receivables stratified (divided further) by their age. Receivables by age are normally shown on an **aging schedule**, which shows customer balances broken down by the length of time they have been outstanding. Because of its emphasis on number of days outstanding, stratification of receivables by age is called **aging the accounts receivable**. In general, larger percentage estimates of uncollectible receivables are applied to older receivables categories.

Consider the following example. Edison Inc. ages its receivables, applies age-stratified percentage estimates of uncollectible accounts, and calculates that total estimated allowance for doubtful accounts is $2,500. Prior to recording the adjusting entry, the Allowance for Doubtful Accounts account (a statement of financial position account) has a credit balance of $300. The required adjusting entry is:

Bad Debts Expense	2,200	
Allowance for Doubtful Accounts		2,200
(To record estimate of uncollectible accounts)		

The Allowance for Doubtful Accounts account must have a $2,500 balance after the adjusting journal entry is recorded, because this amount is the total estimated allowance for doubtful accounts. Since Allowance for Doubtful Accounts already contains a balance of $300, only $2,200 should be added to the account to bring it up to date.

134 Study Guide to Accompany Financial Accounting: Tools for Business Decision-Making, Fifth Canadian Edition

If the Allowance for Doubtful Accounts account had a $400 debit balance before adjustment, the adjusting journal entry would have been:

Bad Debts Expense	2,900	
Allowance for Doubtful Accounts		2,900
(To record estimate of uncollectible accounts)		

If Allowance for Doubtful Accounts has an unadjusted debit balance of $400, and the account must have a credit balance of $2,500 after adjustment, the account must be credited for $2,900 in order to have an overall credit balance of $2,500.

2. **Recording the write-off of an uncollectible account.** Actual uncollectibles are written off at the time the specific account is determined to be uncollectible. The journal entry to record the write-off of an uncollectible account is as follows:

Allowance for Doubtful Accounts	XXX	
Accounts Receivable		XXX
(To write off an uncollectible account)		

Bad Debts Expense is not affected in this journal entry because the related bad debts expense was already estimated and recorded in the period when the related revenue was earned and recorded. The amount recorded in this journal entry is an actual amount (not an estimate) because at this point the company knows exactly which amount is uncollectible and can remove the uncollectible amount from the specific customer account in default.

Proper authorization of a write-off of an uncollectible account is critical. Note that the journal entry to record collection of an amount outstanding requires a debit to Cash and a credit to Accounts Receivable. If a company does not require proper authorization to record this journal entry, a dishonest employee might steal cash from a customer paying its account, and attempt to hide the theft by fictitiously recording a write-off of the customer's account as uncollectible.

Net realizable value of accounts receivable does not change after the write-off of an uncollectible account. This is because the write-off of an uncollectible account reduces both Accounts Receivable and Allowance for Doubtful Accounts by the same amount.

3. **Recording the recovery of an uncollectible account.** If an account previously written off is subsequently collected in cash, the original journal entry recording the write-off of the uncollectible account is reversed to reinstate the customer's account, and collection of the account is recorded as normal:

Accounts Receivable	XXX	
Allowance for Doubtful Accounts		XXX
(To reverse the write-off of an account)		
Cash	XXX	
Accounts Receivable		XXX
(To record collection on account)		

While the net effect of the two journal entries is a debit to Cash and a credit to Allowance for Doubtful Accounts, it is important to reinstate the receivable and

CHAPTER 8 Reporting and Analyzing Receivables 135

show its subsequent collection, in order to provide an information trail in the customer's account. Note that neither the write-off nor the subsequent recovery of an uncollectible account has an impact on the income statement.

Notes Receivable

- Credit may also be granted in exchange for a formal credit instrument known as a promissory note. A promissory note is a written promise to pay a specified amount of money on demand or at a definite time. The maker of a note is the party making the promise to pay; the payee of a note is the party who will be paid.

- Often notes receivable arise from lending transactions. Because accounts receivable are less formal than notes receivable, notes receivable tend to have a stronger legal claim. However, both accounts receivable and notes receivable can readily be sold to another party.

- The formula for calculating interest is as follows:

Interest = Principal or Face Value of Note × Annual Interest Rate × Time in Terms of One Year

Interest on a $12,000, 4% interest rate, three-month note is $120, calculated as follows:

$120 = \$12,000 \times 4\% \times {}^{3}/_{12}$ months

- A note receivable is initially recorded at its principal or face value, and no interest revenue is recorded at the time the note is initially recorded, because the revenue recognition principle requires that revenue must be earned before it is recorded.

- If a note receivable is accepted in settlement of an account receivable, the initial journal entry to record the note receivable is a debit to Notes Receivable and a credit to Accounts Receivable. If a note receivable is received in exchange for cash, the initial journal entry to record the note receivable is a debit to Notes Receivable and a credit to Cash.

- Notes are normally held to their maturity date, at which time the principal value plus accrued interest is due.

- A note is honoured when it is paid in full at its maturity date. For the $12,000, 4% three-month note, with $120 of interest due at maturity, at the maturity date, the payee would record the following journal entry:

Cash	12,120	
Notes Receivable		12,000
Interest Revenue		120
(To record collection of note)		

If the note had been issued on December 1 and the payee had a December 31 year end, then the payee would have accrued interest on December 31 with the following journal entry:

Interest Receivable	40	
Interest Revenue		40
(To record accrued interest: $12,000 \times 4\% \times {}^{1}/_{12}$)		

> **study objective 2**
>
> Explain how notes receivable are recognized and valued in the accounts.

136   Study Guide to Accompany Financial Accounting: Tools for Business Decision-Making, Fifth Canadian Edition

At the maturity date (March 1), the payee would record the following journal entry:

Cash	12,120	
Notes Receivable		12,000
Interest Receivable		40
Interest Revenue		80

- A note is dishonoured if it is not paid in full at maturity. If the $12,000, 4% three-month note was not collected on March 1, then the following journal entry would have been required:

Accounts Receivable	12,120	
Notes Receivable		12,000
Interest Revenue		120

- A dishonoured note receivable is no longer negotiable. However, the payee still has a claim against the maker of the note for both the principal and any unpaid interest. If the payee later determines that the account receivable is not collectible, the payee will write off the account receivable by debiting Allowance for Doubtful Accounts and crediting Accounts Receivable.

- Like accounts receivable, notes receivable are reported at their net realizable value. The difference between Notes Receivable and Allowance for Doubtful Accounts (Notes) represents the net realizable value of notes receivable at the statement of financial position date.

Statement Presentation of Receivables

study objective 3
Explain the statement presentation of receivables.

- Short-term receivables are reported in the current assets section of the statement of financial position, following cash and short-term investments, if items are presented from most to least liquid. Although only the net realizable value of receivables must be disclosed, it is helpful to report both the gross amount of receivables and the allowance for doubtful accounts either on the statement of financial position or in the notes to the financial statements.

- Bad Debts Expense is reported in the operating expense section of the income statement. Interest Revenue is reported in the non-operating income section of the income statement.

- A company must also disclose any particular problem with receivables, such as significant risk of uncollectible accounts.

Managing Receivables

study objective 4
Apply the principles of sound accounts receivable management.

- Managing accounts receivable involves five steps:

  1. Determine who to extend credit to.
  2. Establish a payment period.
  3. Monitor collections.
  4. Evaluate the liquidity of receivables.
  5. Accelerate cash receipts from receivables when necessary.

- A critical part of managing receivables is determining who should receive credit and who should not. If a company's credit policy is too generous it may have higher sales but may end up extending credit to risky customers who may pay either very late

CHAPTER 8 Reporting and Analyzing Receivables 137

or not at all. On the other hand, if a company's credit policy is too tight, it may lose sales. Before extending credit, a company should ask a potential customer for references, and the company should check with these references to determine the potential customer's payment history. If credit is extended, the company should continue to monitor the customer's financial health.

- Companies that extend credit should determine a required payment period and inform their customers about it. Normally, this period would be similar to the payment period offered by competitors.

- A company must monitor collections by preparing and reviewing an accounts receivable aging schedule. An accounts receivable aging schedule helps to establish the allowance for doubtful accounts, aids in estimating the timing of future cash inflows, provides information about the company's collection experience, and identifies problem accounts. If a company sells services or products to only a few customers, it has a concentration of credit risk and the company is required to disclose this risk in the notes to its financial statements. Concentration of credit risk is risk of nonpayment by a single customer or class of customers that could adversely affect the company's financial health.

- **Receivables turnover** is a ratio that helps evaluate the liquidity of receivables. Receivables turnover is calculated by dividing net credit sales by average gross accounts receivable. (Average receivables are calculated by adding together the beginning and ending balances of receivables and dividing the sum by two.) This ratio measures the number of times receivables are collected during the period. If net credit sales total $25,000 and average receivables total $5,000, then the receivables turnover is five times, meaning that the company collected its receivables five times during the period. A decreasing receivables turnover ratio should be of concern to a company, particularly if its competitors' receivables turnover ratios are holding steady or increasing.

- **Average collection period** is another ratio that helps evaluate the liquidity of receivables. Average collection period is calculated by dividing 365 days by receivables turnover. Using the numbers in the calculation of receivables turnover above, the average collection period would be 73 days ($365 \div 5$). In general, the average collection period should not greatly exceed the credit-term period.

- As credit sales grow, collection of receivables may slow down, causing a company increased costs due to delayed payments to its suppliers. There are two ways that a company can accelerate the receipt of cash from receivables: (1) use the receivables to secure a loan or (2) sell the receivables.

- A company can speed up cash flow from receivables by going to a bank and borrowing money using its receivables as collateral. Quite often, these arrangements occur through a credit facility or an operating line of credit.

- A company can also speed up cash flow from receivables by selling its receivables to another company for cash. There are three reasons for the sale of receivables: (1) due to the company's size, it may make sense to establish a financing subsidiary that buys the receivables from the company; (2) selling receivables provides a source of immediate cash flow for the company; and (3) selling receivables allows the company to save costs related to monitoring and collection of receivables.

- Two types of sales of receivables are securitization and factoring. Securitization is a transfer of receivables to investors in return for cash. This topic is normally covered in detail in an intermediate financial accounting course. Factoring is the sale of receivables to a finance company or bank that buys receivables from companies for

138   Study Guide to Accompany Financial Accounting: Tools for Business Decision-Making, Fifth Canadian Edition

a fee (the finance company or bank then collects payments directly from the company's credit customers).

- Sales paid for by nonbank credit cards are treated as credit sales by the retailer and recorded as credit card receivables.

comparing
IFRS and ASPE

Key Differences	International Financial Reporting Standards (IFRS)	Accounting Standards for Private Enterprises (ASPE)
No significant differences.		

Chapter Self-Test

As you work through the questions and problems, remember to use the **Decision Toolkit** discussed and used in the text:

1. *Decision Checkpoints:* Ask a question relevant to the decision being made.
2. *Info Needed for Decision:* Make a choice regarding the information needed to answer the question.
3. *Tools to Use for Decision:* Review what the information identified in step 2 does for the decision-making process.
4. *How to Evaluate Results:* Identify specifically how the information identified in step 2 should be evaluated to answer the question relevant to the decision being made.

Note: The notation "(SO1)" means that the question relates to study objective 1.

Multiple Choice

Please circle the correct answer.

(SO 1)   1. Accounts and notes receivable that result from sales transactions are called
   a.   other receivables.
   b.   non-trade receivables.
   c.   trade receivables.
   d.   non-current receivables.

(SO 1)   2. Interest receivable and loans to company officers are included in
   a.   other receivables.
   b.   trade receivables.
   c.   notes receivable.
   d.   accounts receivable.

(SO 1)   3. For a service company, a receivable is recorded
   a.   when a customer pays its bill.
   b.   when a service is provided on account.

CHAPTER 8   Reporting and Analyzing Receivables   139

c.   30 days after a service is provided.
d.   when an invoice is sent to a customer (one week after a service is provided).

4.   An accounts receivable subsidiary ledger   (SO 1)
    a.   is used by corporations that have subsidiary companies.
    b.   provides supporting detail to the general ledger.
    c.   replaces the main general ledger accounts receivable account.
    d.   is used by all companies.

5.   The journal entry to record estimated uncollectibles is   (SO 1)

    a.   Bad Debts Expense
            Accounts Receivable
    b.   Allowance for Doubtful Accounts
            Accounts Receivable
    c.   Accounts Receivable
            Allowance for Doubtful Accounts
    d.   Bad Debts Expense
            Allowance for Doubtful Accounts

6.   The journal entry to record the write-off of an uncollectible account is   (SO 1)

    a.   Bad Debts Expense
            Accounts Receivable
    b.   Allowance for Doubtful Accounts
            Accounts Receivable
    c.   Accounts Receivable
            Allowance for Doubtful Accounts
    d.   Bad Debts Expense
            Allowance for Doubtful Accounts

7.   Before the write-off of an uncollectible account, Accounts Receivable had a   (SO 1)
    $10,000 debit balance, and Allowance for Doubtful Accounts had a $500 credit
    balance. After a write-off of $100, the net realizable value of accounts receivable is
    a. $10,000.
    b. $9,500.
    c. $9,400.
    d. $9,300.

8.   Allowance for Doubtful Accounts has a $400 credit balance. An aging schedule   (SO 1)
    shows that the total estimated allowance for doubtful accounts is $3,600.
    The adjusting journal entry will require a debit and a credit for
    a. $4,000.
    b. $3,600.
    c. $3,200.
    d.   some other amount.

140 Study Guide to Accompany Financial Accounting: Tools for Business Decision-Making, Fifth Canadian Edition

(SO 1)   9. Allowance for Doubtful Accounts has a $400 debit balance. An aging schedule shows that the total estimated allowance for doubtful accounts is $3,600. The adjusting journal entry will require a debit and a credit for
- a. $4,000.
- b. $3,600.
- c. $3,200.
- d. some other amount.

(SO 1)   10. When an account is written off using the allowance method of accounting for bad debts,
- a. the net realizable value of total accounts receivable will increase.
- b. net accounts receivable will decrease.
- c. Allowance for Doubtful Accounts account will increase.
- d. the net realizable value of accounts receivable will remain the same.

(SO 1)   11. ABC Company's Allowance for Doubtful Accounts account had an opening unadjusted balance of $3,000 on December 1, and a closing adjusted balance of $3,500 on December 31. A $3,200 adjustment was recorded in December to bring Allowance for Doubtful Accounts to the total estimated allowance for doubtful accounts. The amount of uncollectible accounts written off in December is
- a. $2,700.
- b. $3,000.
- c. $3,300.
- d. not determinable from the information given.

(SO 2)   12. The journal entry recorded by the payee at the maturity date of a three-month, 4%, $15,000 note, with interest due at maturity, will include a
- a. debit to Cash for $15,150.
- b. credit to Notes Receivable for $15,150.
- c. debit to Interest Revenue for $150.
- d. credit to Cash for $15,150.

(SO 2)   13. A company holds a four-month, 5%, $21,000 note that was dishonoured at the maturity date. Interest was also due at the maturity date. If eventual collection is expected, the journal entry at the maturity date will include a
- a. debit to Accounts Receivable for $21,350.
- b. credit to Notes Receivable for $21,350.
- c. debit to Cash for $21,350.
- d. debit to Notes Receivable for $21,000.

(SO 2)   14. The two key parties to a promissory note are:
- a. the debtor and a bank.
- b. the debtor and the sender.
- c. the receiver and the sender.
- d. the payee and the maker.

CHAPTER 8   Reporting and Analyzing Receivables   141

15. Total interest on a $5,000, 5%, three-month note receivable is   (SO 2)
   a. $62.50.
   b. $83.33.
   c. $250.00.
   d. $125.00.

16. Accounts receivable are valued and reported on the statement of financial   (SO 3)
   position
   a. at the gross amount.
   b. when a customer makes a payment.
   c. at net realizable value.
   d. in the Other Assets category.

17. Bad Debts Expense is reported on the income statement as   (SO 3)
   a. an operating expense.
   b. part of net sales.
   c. part of cost of goods sold.
   d. a contra-revenue account.

18. Which of the following is a step involved in the management of accounts   (SO 4)
   receivable?
   a. Write off an uncollectible account.
   b. Establish a payment period.
   c. Calculate bad debts expense.
   d. Recognize an account receivable when work has been done on account.

19. Risk of nonpayment by a single customer or class of customers that could   (SO 4)
   adversely affect a company's financial health is called
   a. accounts receivable concentration risk.
   b. notes receivable concentration risk.
   c. credit risk.
   d. concentration of credit risk.

20. Net credit sales are $800,000, average gross receivables is $150,000, average   (SO 4)
   inventory is $200,000, and allowance for doubtful accounts is $8,000. Receivables
   turnover is
   a. 100 times.
   b. 5.3 times.
   c. 4.0 times.
   d. 1.3 times.

21. Referring to the information in question 20 (above), the average collection   (SO 4)
   period is
   a. 100 days.
   b. 75 days.
   c. 69 days.
   d. 5.3 days.

142 Study Guide to Accompany Financial Accounting: Tools for Business Decision-Making, Fifth Canadian Edition

(SO 4)   22. Kerrison Corporation sold $6,000 of merchandise to customers who paid for their purchases with nonbank credit cards. The journal entry to record the credit card sales will include a
a.   debit to Cash for $6,000.
b.   debit to Notes Receivable for $6,000.
c.   debit to Credit Card Receivables for $6,000.
d.   debit to Accounts Receivable for $6,000.

(SO 4)   23. The receivables turnover ratio is used to analyze
a.   creditworthiness.
b.   profitability.
c.   solvency.
d.   liquidity.

Problems

(SO 1)   1.   Record journal entries for the following items for Morrison Corporation.

a.   At the end of the accounting period on June 30, Morrison prepares an aging schedule of accounts receivable that shows a total estimated allowance for doubtful accounts of $5,200. On this date, Allowance for Doubtful Accounts has a debit balance of $300, and Accounts Receivable has a balance of $85,000.

b.   On July 5, Morrison receives word that Sperry Ltd. has declared bankruptcy. Morrison writes off its $800 account receivable from Sperry.

c.   On September 12, Sperry notifies Morrison that it can pay its $800 debt and delivers a cheque for the entire amount.

d.   What is the net realizable value of accounts receivable after the entry in (a) is recorded? What is the net realizable value of accounts receivable after the entry in (b) is recorded?

Date	Account Title	Debit	Credit

CHAPTER 8   Reporting and Analyzing Receivables   143

2. The December 31, 2011, statement of financial position of Master Retailer   (SO 1)
Limited had Accounts Receivable of $650,000 and a $32,500 credit balance in
Allowance for Doubtful Accounts. The accounting manager estimates that 5% of
total receivables will be uncollectible.

During 2012, the following transactions occurred:

1.	Sales on account	$1,150,000
2.	Sales returns and allowances	20,000
3.	Collections from customers	900,000
4.	Accounts written off	10,000
5.	Accounts previously written off and subsequently collected	2,500

a. Record the 2012 summary transactions.

b. Record any required adjusting journal entry(ies) at December 31, 2012.

Date	Account Title	Debit	Credit

3. A company's partial statement of financial position, as at December 31, appears   (SO 1, 2, 4)
as follows (adjusting journal entries for 2012 have not been recorded yet):

	2012	2011
Current Assets		
Cash	$ 50,000	$ 60,000

144 Study Guide to Accompany Financial Accounting: Tools for Business Decision-Making, Fifth Canadian Edition

Short-term investments		40,000		30,000
Accounts receivable	$90,000		$80,000	
Less: Allowance for doubtful accounts	15,000	75,000	10,000	70,000
Notes receivable		80,000		75,000
Other current assets		90,000		95,000
Total current assets		$335,000		$330,000

a. An aging of accounts receivable prepared on December 31, 2012, indicates that the total estimated allowance for doubtful accounts is $17,000. Prepare any required adjusting journal entry.

b. The $80,000 note shown above for 2012 represents a three-month, 4.5% interest-bearing note issued on November 1, 2012. Interest is due at maturity. Prepare any required adjusting journal entry.

c. Journalize the entry that would be required when the note is collected at maturity in 2013, assuming that the adjusting journal entry in (a) was recorded.

d. Calculate the receivables turnover and the average collection period for 2012, assuming net credit sales for 2012 are $501,500.

(SO 4) 4. The following accounts appear in the general ledger of Majestic Corporation at December 31, 2012, with the following balances:

Accounts Receivable	$125,000
Accumulated Depreciation	60,000
Allowance for Doubtful Accounts	18,000
Depreciation Expense	10,000
Cash	$90,000
Dividends	8,000
Equipment	200,000
Merchandise Inventory	100,000
Notes Payable	50,000
Office Supplies	1,000
Prepaid Expenses	12,000
Sales	250,000
Sales Returns and Allowances	10,000
Short-Term Notes Receivable	75,000
Short-Term Investments	80,000

Prepare a partial statement of financial position for current assets of Majestic Corporation.

(SO 1, 4) 5. Refer to the HMV and WHSmith financial statements found in the appendices at the end of this study guide for information in answering the following questions. Do not forget to use the **Decision Toolkit** approach for help in answering the questions.

a. What is the percentage increase or decrease in net trade receivables from 2009 to 2010?

b. For both HMV and WHSmith, calculate receivables turnover and average collection period for 2010. Assume revenues are net credit sales, and use net trade receivables rather than gross receivables in your calculations.

c. Compare the results calculated in (b).

CHAPTER 8 Reporting and Analyzing Receivables 145

Solutions to Self-Test

Multiple Choice

1. c   Other and non-trade receivables are very similar and arise from such items as interest receivable and loans to company officers. Accounts receivable are always current assets.

2. a   Trade receivables arise from sales transactions, notes receivable are written promises to pay a specified amount of money on demand or at a definite time, and accounts receivable are amounts owed by customers on account.

3. b   A receivable is recorded before a customer pays its bill. A receivable should be recorded when a service is performed, not at some other specific date.

4. b   An accounts receivable subsidiary ledger provides supporting detail to the accounts receivable control account in the general ledger, freeing the general ledger from excessive detail.

5. d   The Allowance for Doubtful Accounts account is used to record estimated uncollectibles.

6. b   Under the allowance method of accounting for bad debts, the journal entry to record the write-off of an uncollectible account requires a debit to Allowance for Doubtful Accounts, not to Bad Debts Expense.

7. b   The net realizable value of accounts receivable is $9,500 ($10,000 − $500) before the write-off and $9,500 ($9,900 − $400) after the write-off.

8. c $3,600 is the amount that must be in Allowance for Doubtful Accounts after adjustment. Since the account already has a credit balance of $400, a $3,200 credit is required to increase the account balance to $3,600.

9. a $3,600 is the amount that must be in Allowance for Doubtful Accounts after adjustment. Since the account has a debit balance of $400, a $4,000 credit is required to increase the account balance to $3,600.

10. d   Both Accounts Receivable and Allowance for Doubtful Accounts decrease by the same amount, resulting in no net change to the net realizable value of accounts receivable.

11. a   (Opening) unadjusted Allowance for Doubtful Accounts − uncollectible accounts written off in the period + adjustment to bring Allowance for Doubtful Accounts to the total estimated allowance for doubtful accounts = (closing) adjusted Allowance for Doubtful Accounts.

12. a   The journal entry is:

Cash	15,150	
Notes Receivable		15,000
Interest Revenue		150

$(\$15,000 \times 4\% \times {}^{3}/_{12} = \$150)$

13. a   The journal entry is:

Accounts Receivable	21,350	
Notes Receivable		21,000
Interest Revenue		350

$(\$21,000 \times 5\% \times {}^{4}/_{12} = \$350)$

146 **Study Guide to Accompany Financial Accounting: Tools for Business Decision-Making, Fifth Canadian Edition**

14. d   The two key parties to a promissory note are the payee (the party who will be paid) and the maker (the party making the promise to pay).

15. a $\$5,000 \times 5\% \times {}^{3}/_{12} = \$62.50$

16. c   Although only the net realizable value of receivables must be disclosed, it is helpful to report both the gross amount of receivables and the allowance for doubtful accounts either in the statement or in the notes to the financial statements.

17. a   Bad debts expense is an operating expense.

18. b   There are five steps in managing accounts receivable:
1. Determine who to extend credit to.
2. Establish a payment period.
3. Monitor collections.
4. Evaluate the liquidity of receivables.
5. Accelerate cash receipts from receivables when necessary.

19. d   If a company sells services or products to only a few customers, it has a concentration of credit risk.

20. b   Net credit sales ÷ Average gross receivables = $\$800,000 \div \$150,000$ = 5.3 times.

21. c   365 ÷ Receivables turnover = 365 ÷ 5.3 = 69 days.

22. c   The journal entry is:

Credit Card Receivables	6,000	
Sales		6,000

23. d   Receivables turnover is an important measure of a company's overall liquidity.

Problems

1.

a.   June 30

Bad Debts Expense	5,500	
Allowance for Doubtful Accounts		5,500
(To record the estimate of uncollectible accounts: $300 + $5,200)		

b.   July 5

Allowance for Doubtful Accounts	800	
Accounts Receivable—Sperry		800
(To write off the Sperry account)		

c.   Sept. 12

Accounts Receivable—Sperry	800	
Allowance for Doubtful Accounts		800
(To reverse write-off of the Sperry account)		
Cash	800	
Accounts Receivable—Sperry		800
(To record collection from Sperry)		

CHAPTER 8   Reporting and Analyzing Receivables   147

d.

	Before Write-Off	After Write-Off
Accounts receivable	$85,000	$84,200
Less: Allowance for doubtful accounts	5,200	4,400
Net realizable value	$79,800	$79,800

Net realizable value does not change because both Accounts receivable and Allowance for doubtful accounts are reduced by the same amount.

2.

a.

1.	Accounts Receivable	1,150,000	
	Sales		1,150,000
	(To record credit sales)		
2.	Sales Returns and Allowances	20,000	
	Accounts Receivable		20,000
	(To record credits to customers)		
3.	Cash	900,000	
	Accounts Receivable		900,000
	(To record collection of receivables)		
4.	Allowance for Doubtful Accounts	10,000	
	Accounts Receivable		10,000
	(To write off specific uncollectible accounts)		
5.	Accounts Receivable	2,500	
	Allowance for Doubtful Accounts		2,500
	(To reverse write-off of accounts)		
	Cash	2,500	
	Accounts Receivable		2,500
	(To record collection of accounts)		

b.   Percentage of receivables basis:

Accounts Receivable		Allowance for Doubtful Accounts	
650,000	20,000	10,000	32,500
1,150,000	900,000		2,500
2,500	10,000		Bal. 25,000
	2,500		
Bal. 870,000			

Required balance ($870,000 × 5%)	$43,500
Balance before adjustment	25,000
Adjustment required	$18,500

Dec. 31	Bad Debts Expense	18,500	
	Allowance for Doubtful Accounts		18,500
	(To record estimate of uncollectible accounts)		

148 **Study Guide to Accompany Financial Accounting: Tools for Business Decision-Making, Fifth Canadian Edition**

3.

a. Dec. 31, 2012	Bad Debts Expense	2,000	
	Allowance for Doubtful Accounts		2,000

$17,000 - $15,000 = $2,000

b. Dec. 31, 2012	Interest Receivable	600	
	Interest Revenue		600

$80,000 \times 4.5\% \times {}^2/_{12} = \$600$

c. Feb. 1, 2013	Cash	80,900	
	Interest Receivable		600
	Interest Revenue		300
	Notes Receivable		80,000
	Interest Revenue		

$80,000 \times 4.5\% \times {}^1/_{12} = \$300$

d.

Receivables turnover $\dfrac{\$501,500}{(\$90,000 + \$80,000) \div 2}$ = 5.9 times

Average collection period $\dfrac{365}{5.9}$ = 62 days

4.

MAJESTIC CORPORATION
Statement of Financial Position (Partial)
December 31, 2012

Current assets		
Cash		$ 90,000
Short-term investments		80,000
Accounts receivable	$125,000	
Less: Allowance for doubtful accounts	18,000	107,000
Short-term notes receivable		75,000
Merchandise inventory		100,000
Office supplies		1,000
Prepaid expenses		12,000
Total current assets		$465,000

5. Please note that the amounts shown for HMV and WH Smith are stated in pounds (£) millions.

a. HMV: Net trade receivables increased by 33.3%.

£13.2 − £9.9 = £3.3 (referring to note 18 of the financial statements)

£3.3 ÷ £9.9 = 33.3%

WHSmith: Net trade receivables decreased by 4.5%.

£21 − £22 = (£1) (referring to note 17 of the financial statements)

(£1) ÷ £22 = (4.5%)

CHAPTER 8   Reporting and Analyzing Receivables   149

b.   HMV:

Average receivables = (£13.2 + £9.9) ÷ 2 = £11.6

Receivables turnover = net credit sales ÷ average receivables

£2,016.6 ÷ £11.6 = 173.8 times

Average collection period = 365 ÷ receivables turnover

365 ÷ 173.8 = 2 days

WHSmith:

Average receivables = (£21 + £22) ÷ 2 = £21.5

Receivables turnover = net credit sales ÷ average receivables

£1,312 ÷ £21.5 = 61.0 times

Average collection period = 365 ÷ receivables turnover

365 ÷ 61.0 = 6 days

c.   The average collection period for WHSmith is slightly longer than for HMV. However, both companies generally have limited trade receivables due to the nature of their business as retailers, receiving cash as the predominant method of customer payment.

chapter 9

Reporting and Analyzing Long-Lived Assets

Chapter Overview

This chapter discusses accounting for long-lived assets, including recording the initial purchase of long-lived assets and allocating their cost to expense based on different depreciation methods. You will also learn how to account for the disposition of long-lived assets, how to report long-lived assets in the financial statements, and how to evaluate a company's use of long-lived assets.

Review of Specific Study Objectives

Property, Plant, and Equipment

- Most companies record property, plant, and equipment at cost, which includes the following:

  1. the purchase price, including certain kinds of taxes and duties, less any discounts or rebates, and
  2. the expenditures necessary to bring the asset to its required location and to make it ready for its intended use.

> study objective 1
>
> Determine the cost of property, plant, and equipment.

152 Study Guide to Accompany Financial Accounting: Tools for Business Decision-Making, Fifth Canadian Edition

All of these costs are **capitalized** (recorded as property, plant, and equipment), rather than expensed, if it is probable that the company will receive an economic benefit in the future from the asset and this benefit can be measured.

- **Operating expenditures** are costs that benefit only the current period and are expensed in the period incurred.

- **Capital expenditures** are costs that benefit future periods and are included in a long-lived asset account.

- Property, plant, and equipment are often subdivided into four classes:

  1. **Land**, such as a building site
  2. **Land improvements**, such as driveways, parking lots, fences, and underground sprinkler systems
  3. **Buildings**, such as stores, offices, factories, and warehouses
  4. **Equipment**, such as store checkout counters, cash registers, computers, office furniture, factory machinery, and delivery equipment.

The cost of land includes all costs related to the purchase of land, including the cash purchase price and closing costs, such as survey and legal fees. All costs incurred in preparing land for its intended use are also included in the cost of land, including the cost of clearing, draining, filling, and grading the land. If the land has a building on it that must be removed to make the site suitable for construction of a new building, all demolition and removal costs, less any proceeds from salvaged materials, are added to the Land account. Once the land is prepared for its intended use, recurring costs such as annual property taxes are expensed. The cost of land is not depreciated over life of the land because land has an unlimited useful life.

The cost of land improvements includes all costs related to structural additions made to land, including driveways, sidewalks, fences, lighting, and parking lots. Land improvements decline in service potential over time and require maintenance and replacement. Because of this, the cost of land improvements is recorded separately from land and depreciated over their limited useful lives.

The cost of a building includes all costs that are directly related to the purchase or construction of the building. If a building is purchased, the cost of the building includes the purchase price, closing costs, and all costs necessary to make the building ready for its intended use. For example, costs of remodelling rooms and offices and replacing or repairing the roof, floors, electrical wiring, and plumbing are all costs necessary to make the building ready for its intended use, and are therefore included in the cost of the building. If a building is constructed, the cost of the building includes the contract price, plus payments made for architects' fees, building permits, and excavation costs. In addition, interest costs relating to a loan obtained to finance the construction project are also included in the cost of the asset, but only up to the date that the asset is ready for use. Specific rules for determining the amount of interest costs to capitalize are normally taught in an intermediate accounting course.

The cost of equipment includes all costs that are necessary to get the equipment ready for its intended use, including purchase price, freight charges, costs of insurance during transit (if paid by the purchaser), assembly charges, installation charges, and costs of testing the equipment. Fees incurred after the equipment is operational, such as vehicle licence fees and accident insurance premiums, are debited to an expense account or recorded as a prepaid expense before consumption.

CHAPTER 9 Reporting and Analyzing Long-Lived Assets 153

The cost of property, plant, and equipment must also include an estimate of the cost of any obligation to dismantle, remove, or restore the long-lived asset when it is retired. These **asset retirement costs** must be estimated (using present-value concepts), added to the cost of the related asset when it is acquired, and therefore depreciated over the life of the related asset. Because these costs will not be paid for some time, the offsetting credit is to a long-term liability account called Asset Retirement Obligation. These costs, and the related long-term liability, are recorded in the period in which the related asset is acquired, because in acquiring the asset, the company also takes on an obligation to pay the related asset retirement costs at some time in the future. If the use of the asset causes further liabilities to arise, the Asset Retirement Obligation account is increased, as is the related asset account. Under IFRS, asset retirement is often referred to as asset decommissioning. A more detailed discussion of asset retirement costs and their related liabilities will be covered in a future accounting course. In this chapter, we will assume that asset retirement costs are zero in all examples.

- Companies often **lease** assets. In a lease, the party that owns the asset (the lessor) agrees to allow another party (the lessee) to rent the asset for an agreed period of time at an agreed price. Some advantages of leasing an asset rather than purchasing it include reduced risk of the negative impact of asset obsolescence, 100% financing with no down payment required, income tax advantages, and off–balance sheet financing (which means the company does not have to show any related liability on its statement of financial position). In an **operating lease**, the lessee uses the asset but accounts for the lease as a rental and does not record a related asset or a liability. Instead, the lessee records its periodic lease payments as rent expense (or prepaid rent). In a **finance lease**, the lessee uses the asset and actually records a related asset and liability. In a finance lease, the lessee controls the asset and therefore must account for the lease as a purchase financed with a loan provided by the seller of the asset.

- Companies reporting under IFRS may soon be required to treat most leases as finance leases.

- Under IFRS, companies have two models to choose from when accounting for property, plant, and equipment: the cost model and the revaluation model. The cost model is more commonly used under IFRS, and is the only model allowed for use under ASPE. We will cover the cost model in the following sections of the chapter, and refer briefly to the revaluation model later in the chapter.

- The **cost model** records property, plant, and equipment at cost at acquisition. Subsequent to acquisition, depreciation is recorded each period and the assets are carried at cost less accumulated depreciation.

Depreciation

- **Depreciation** is the systematic allocation of the cost of property, plant, and equipment (and certain other long-lived assets) over the asset's useful life. The asset's cost is allocated to expense over the asset's useful life, so that expenses are recorded according to expected use of the asset's future economic benefits.

- The journal entry to record depreciation is:

    Depreciation Expense
        Accumulated Depreciation

> study objective 2
>
> Explain and calculate depreciation.

154 Study Guide to Accompany Financial Accounting: Tools for Business Decision-Making, Fifth Canadian Edition

Depreciation Expense appears on the income statement. Accumulated Depreciation is a contra asset account to the relevant property, plant, or equipment account. The difference between cost in the relevant property, plant, or equipment asset account and its accumulated depreciation is the asset's carrying amount (or carrying value) on the statement of financial position.

- Accumulated depreciation of an asset does not represent an accumulation of cash for replacement of the asset. Depreciation is simply a process of cost allocation. Also, depreciation is not a process of asset valuation. An asset's carrying amount may differ significantly from its fair value.

- Land improvements, buildings, and equipment are depreciable assets because they decrease in utility, due to wear and tear and obsolescence. However, land is not a depreciable asset. Land has an indefinite useful life and often appreciates in value.

- Three factors affect the calculation of depreciation: cost, useful life (an estimate of the asset's productive or service life, expressed in terms of time, units of production, or units of output), and residual value (an estimate of the amount that a company would obtain from disposal of the asset at the end of its useful life).

- Depreciation is generally calculated using one of three methods:

  1. Straight-line
  2. Diminishing-balance
  3. Units-of-production

  Company management must choose the depreciation method that it believes will best reflect the estimated pattern in which the asset's benefits are expected to be consumed. The depreciation method must be reviewed at least once a year. If the expected pattern of consumption of the asset's future economic benefits has changed, the depreciation method must be changed, and the change must be disclosed in the notes to the financial statements.

  Under the **straight-line method**, an equal amount of depreciation is expensed in each year of the asset's useful life. Depreciable amount, which is the asset's cost less its residual value, is divided by the useful life of the asset in years, to arrive at annual depreciation expense. A straight-line rate can also be calculated (100% ÷ useful life in years) and multiplied by depreciable amount, to arrive at annual depreciation expense.

  Consider the following example. A company purchased a truck on January 2 for $58,000. The truck has a useful life of five years and a residual value of $8,000. The depreciable amount is $50,000 ($58,000 − $8,000), and annual depreciation expense is $10,000 (50,000 ÷ 5 years). The straight-line rate is 20% (100% ÷ 5 years); multiplying $50,000 by 20% also yields $10,000 depreciation expense per year. After five years, total accumulated depreciation is $50,000, and the asset's carrying amount is $8,000 ($58,000 − $50,000). Note that the asset's carrying amount after five years equals the originally estimated residual value. If the asset was purchased on July 1, depreciation expense recorded in the first year ended December 31 would have been $5,000 ($10,000 × $^6/_{12}$).

  The **diminishing-balance method** produces a decreasing annual depreciation expense over the asset's useful life. It is called the "diminishing-balance" method because periodic depreciation is calculated using the asset's carrying amount, which diminishes

CHAPTER 9   Reporting and Analyzing Long-Lived Assets   155

each year as accumulated depreciation increases. Annual depreciation expense is calculated by multiplying the asset's carrying amount at the beginning of the year by the depreciation rate. The depreciation rate remains constant from year to year, but the asset's carrying amount (to which the depreciation rate is applied) declines each year. In the early years of the asset's useful life, depreciation expense under the diminishing-balance method will be higher than depreciation expense under the straight-line method. In the later years of the asset's useful life, depreciation expense under the diminishing-balance method will be lower than depreciation expense under the straight-line method. However, total depreciation expense recorded over an asset's useful life (its depreciable amount) is the same, regardless of the method of depreciation used. A common way to apply the diminishing-balance method is to use a rate that is double the straight-line rate, referred to as the double diminishing-balance method.

Under the **units-of-production method**, useful life is expressed using a measure of output such as units produced, or a measure of use such as machine hours worked, rather than the number of years that the asset is expected to be used. Examples of measures of output include units of output, machine hours, kilometres driven, and hours flown. The units-of-production method is well suited for depreciation of factory machinery, vehicles, and airplanes.

● Below is an example of a calculation of depreciation expense using the diminishing-balance method and the units-of-production method.

Under the **diminishing-balance method**, depreciation expense is calculated by multiplying the asset's carrying amount by its straight-line rate (residual value does not affect the calculation of depreciation under the diminishing-balance method). Later in the asset's useful life, depreciation expense is no longer recorded when the asset's carrying amount reaches its residual value. Double diminishing-balance is a version of the diminishing-balance method, which calculates the asset's depreciation rate as its straight-line rate multiplied by two. If an asset has a useful life of four years, its straight-line rate is 25% (100% ÷ 4 years). The asset's double diminishing-balance depreciation rate would be 25% multiplied by 2 (50%).

Assume that an asset purchased for $50,000 has a four-year useful life and a residual value of $5,000. Depreciation expense under the double diminishing-balance method for the four years is calculated as follows:

| | | | | | End of Year | |
Year	Carrying Amount, Beginning of Year	Depreciation Rate	=	Depreciation Expense	Accumulated Depreciation	Carrying Amount
1	$50,000	50%		$25,000	$25,000	$25,000
2	25,000	50%		12,500	37,500	12,500
3	12,500	50%		6,250	43,750	6,250
4	6,250	50%		1,250	45,000	5,000
	Total depreciation expense:			$45,000		

Note that in year 4 only $1,250 of depreciation would be recorded, even though the carrying amount of $6,250 multiplied by the 50% depreciation rate would yield

156 **Study Guide to Accompany Financial Accounting: Tools for Business Decision-Making, Fifth Canadian Edition**

$3,125. Recall that the asset's carrying amount must equal its residual value at the end of the four years, and that recording $3,125 depreciation expense would have caused the asset's carrying amount to be too low relative to its residual value. In the final year, only $1,250 of depreciation expense should be recorded, in order to arrive at accumulated depreciation of $45,000 ($50,000 − $5,000).

Depreciation under the diminishing-balance method is a function of time. Therefore, an asset purchased during the year must have its depreciation expense prorated. If the asset above had been purchased on April 1, depreciation expense for year 1 would have been $18,750 ($50,000 × 50% × $^{9}/_{12}$). The carrying amount at the end of year 1 would have been $31,250 ($50,000 − $18,750).

Under the **units-of-production method**, the depreciable amount per unit is calculated and applied to units of activity during the year, to arrive at depreciation expense.

Assume that an asset purchased for $30,000 has an estimated useful life of five years, estimated units of output of 50,000, and residual value of $5,000. In year 1, the asset produces 12,000 units. Depreciation expense is calculated as follows:

$30,000 − $5,000 = $25,000 depreciable amount

$25,000 ÷ 50,000 units = $0.50 per unit

$0.50 per unit × 12,000 actual units of activity during year 1 = $6,000

Note that estimated useful life in years does not affect the calculation of depreciation expense under the units-of-production method. Note, too, that this method begins with the calculation of the depreciable amount, just as the straight-line method does. Since the units-of-production method is a function of usage and not time, it is not necessary to prorate depreciation expense if the asset is purchased during the year.

All three methods produce the same amount of accumulated depreciation at the end of the asset's useful life. The timing and amount of depreciation expense is what differs in each method.

Other Depreciation Issues

---

study objective 3

Describe other accounting issues related to depreciation.

- When an item of property, plant, and equipment includes individual components for which different depreciation methods or rates are appropriate, the cost should be allocated to the asset's significant components and each component should be depreciated separately.

Further discussion of calculating depreciation for the different parts of an asset will be left to a later accounting course. For simplicity, we will assume in this text that all of the components of the depreciable asset have the same useful life and we will therefore depreciate each asset as a whole.

- The Canada Revenue Agency (CRA) allows companies to deduct specified amounts of depreciation expense from taxable income. However, companies must deduct depreciation expense calculated based on the CRA version of depreciation, which is known as capital cost allowance (CCA). In calculating CCA, assets are grouped into various classes, and companies can apply at most the maximum depreciation rates for each asset class, as specified by the CRA. In contrast, for accounting purposes, a company should choose the depreciation method that best reflects the pattern in which the asset's future economic benefits are expected to be consumed.

CHAPTER 9   Reporting and Analyzing Long-Lived Assets   157

- Recall that an asset's carrying amount is its cost less accumulated depreciation to date. On a regular basis, companies are required to determine if there are signs of impairment of their property, plant, and equipment assets, which may indicate that certain assets are overvalued (in terms of carrying amount). If there are indicators of impairment, companies are required to conduct an asset impairment test, which provides that if a property, plant, or equipment asset's carrying amount exceeds its recoverable amount (determined by observing the asset's fair value less selling costs of similar assets in an active market), the asset is impaired. If an asset is impaired according to the asset impairment test, an **impairment loss** is recorded, equal to the amount by which the asset's carrying amount exceeds its recoverable amount.

  The journal entry to record an impairment loss is:

  Impairment Loss

  Accumulated Depreciation

  The impairment loss is recorded on the income statement as part of continuing operations, and not under "other expenses and losses."

- Under ASPE, asset impairment tests are conducted using a two-step approach. The first step requires comparing the undiscounted cash flows expected to be received from the asset with the asset's carrying amount. If the undiscounted cash flows expected to be received from the asset are less than the asset's carrying amunt, an impairment loss would be calculated and recorded as discussed above.

- Under IFRS, reversal of a previously recorded impairment loss is allowed, but only to the extent that the reversal returns the asset's carrying amount to what it would have been, net of depreciation, if the original impairment loss was never recorded. Under ASPE, reversal of impairment losses is not permitted.

- As mentioned earlier, under IFRS, companies can choose to account for property, plant, and equipment under either the cost model or the **revaluation model**. Under the revaluation model, the carrying amount of property, plant, and equipment is adjusted to reflect its fair value. This model can be applied only to assets with a reliably measurable fair value, and revaluations must be carried out often enough that the asset's carrying amount is not materially different from its fair value at the statement of financial position date.

- Under the revaluation model, **revaluation losses** (or asset writedowns to fair value) are recorded on the income statement, and reversals of revaluation losses are recorded on the income statement to the extent that losses due to revaluation of the same asset were previously recorded on the income statement. Any remaining reversals of revaluation losses are recorded in Revaluation Surplus (an equity account). However, **revaluation gains** (or asset write-ups to fair value) are recorded in Other Comprehensive Income, and reversals of revaluation gains are recorded in Other Comprehensive Income to the extent that gains due to revaluation of the same asset were previously recorded in Other Comprehensive Income. Any remaining reversals of revaluation gains are recorded on the income statement.

- Under IFRS, **investment properties** are properties that are not occupied by the owner and are held for the purpose of earning rental income or capital appreciation. Under IFRS, companies can choose to apply the cost model or the **valuation model**

158 Study Guide to Accompany Financial Accounting: Tools for Business Decision-Making, Fifth Canadian Edition

in accounting for investment properties. The valuation model requires that the carrying amount of an investment property be adjusted to fair value, with all fair value adjustments (gains and losses) recorded on the income statement. As well, under the valuation model, investment properties are not depreciated.

- Under ASPE, neither the revaluation model nor the valuation model is used.

- There are several reasons why **periodic depreciation** may need to be revised during an asset's useful life, including:

  1. **Capital expenditures during the asset's useful life.** After purchasing an asset, the company may incur additional costs related to the asset, which will benefit future periods. If the additional cost relates to an item that meets the definition of an asset, then the cost is a capital expenditure and should be added to the asset's cost.

     If a cost, such as ordinary repairs and maintenance, benefits the company only in the current period, the cost is an operating expenditure and is recorded as an expense on the income statement. However, if a cost, such as a replacement of a major part or an addition to a building, will benefit future periods, then it is a capital expenditure and is added to the asset's cost on the statement of financial position. As capital expenditures during the asset's useful life increase the cost of a long-lived asset, the asset's depreciation calculations will have to be revised from that point onward.

  2. **Impairment losses.** As described in the previous section, an impairment loss will result in a reduction of the asset's carrying amount. Since the carrying amount is reduced, the depreciation calculations will also have to be revised.

  3. **Changes in estimated useful life or residual value.** Management should regularly review its estimates of useful life and residual value. For example, wear and tear or obsolescence might indicate that annual depreciation is either not enough or too much. Capital expenditures may increase the asset's useful life and/or its residual value. Impairment losses might signal a reduction in useful life and/or residual value. Regardless of the reason for the change, a change in estimated useful life or residual value will require the revision of depreciation calculations.

  4. **Changes in the pattern in which the asset's economic benefits are consumed.** As discussed earlier, management must review its choice of depreciation method at least annually. If the pattern in which the future benefits will be consumed is expected to change, the depreciation method must change as well. A change in method will also require revision of depreciation calculations.

- Revising depreciation is known as a change in estimate. Changes in estimates are reflected in current and future years' financial statements, but not in prior years' financial statement periods (which means that prior years' financial statements do not have to be restated). A significant change in estimate must be disclosed in the notes to the financial statements.

- Regardless of the method of asset disposal, a company must perform four steps to record sale, retirement, or exchange of property, plant, or equipment: (1) update depreciation; (2) calculate the asset's carrying amount at the time of disposal; (3) calculate the gain or loss on disposal, if any; and (4) record the disposal (credit the asset account for the asset's cost, and debit accumulated depreciation for the asset's accumulated depreciation to date).

CHAPTER 9   Reporting and Analyzing Long-Lived Assets   159

Disposal of Property, Plant, and Equipment

study objective 4

Account for the disposal of property, plant, and equipment.

If the disposal is a sale, the asset's carrying amount is compared with the proceeds of the sale. If the proceeds of the sale exceed the carrying amount of the asset, there is a gain on disposal. If the proceeds are less than the carrying amount, there is a loss on disposal.

Consider the following example. A company sells a piece of machinery for $5,000. The machinery's original cost was $10,000. Accumulated depreciation to date is $6,000. The journal entry to record the sale is as follows:

Cash	5,000	
Accumulated Depreciation	6,000	
Machinery		10,000
Gain on Disposal		1,000
(To record sale of machinery at a gain)		

The carrying amount of the asset just prior to disposal was $4,000 ($10,000 − $6,000). Since the company received $5,000 for the asset, the asset was sold for a $1,000 gain. The gain appears in the "Other Revenues and Gains" section of the income statement.

If the company had sold the asset for $2,000, it would have incurred a loss of $2,000 ($4,000 carrying amount − $2,000 cash proceeds). The journal entry to record the sale would be as follows:

Cash	2,000	
Accumulated Depreciation	6,000	
Loss on Disposal	2,000	
Machinery		10,000
(To record sale of machinery at a loss)		

Loss on Disposal appears in the "Other Expenses and Losses" section of the income statement.

- If the disposal is a retirement rather than a sale, it is recorded similar to a sale with zero cash proceeds. Therefore, asset retirement will never result in a gain on disposal. The journal entry to record retirement of the asset in the two journal entries above is as follows:

Accumulated Depreciation	6,000	
Loss on Disposal	4,000	
Machinery		10,000
(To record retirement of machinery)		

- In an exchange of assets, a new asset is typically purchased by trading in an old asset, and a trade-in allowance is given toward the purchase price of the new asset. An additional cash payment is usually also required for the difference between the trade-in allowance and the purchase price of the new asset.

study objective 5

Identify the basic accounting issues for intangible assets and goodwill.

Intangible Assets and Goodwill

- **Intangible assets** involve rights, privileges, and/or competitive advantages that result from ownership of long-lived assets that do not have physical substance.

An intangible asset must be identifiable, which means it must meet one of the two following criteria:

1. it can be separated from the company and sold, whether or not the company intends to do so, or
2. it is based on contractual or legal rights, regardless of whether or not it can be separated from the company.

Since goodwill cannot be separated from a company and sold, there are differences in the accounting for goodwill compared with other intangible assets.

- Intangible assets are recorded at cost. If an intangible asset has a finite or limited life, its amortizable amount (cost less residual value) should be allocated over the shorter of its (1) estimated useful life and (2) legal life. Similar to depreciation, the company must use the amortization method that best matches the pattern in which the asset's future economic benefits are expected to be consumed. If that pattern cannot be reliably determined, the straight-line method should be used. The journal entry to record amortization expense includes a debit to amortization expense and a credit to accumulated amortization. If an intangible asset has an indefinite (unlimited) life, it is not amortized.

- On a regular basis, companies are required to determine if there are signs of impairment of their intangible assets, which may indicate that certain intangible assets are overvalued (in terms of carrying amount). If there are indicators of impairment, companies are required to conduct an impairment test, which provides that if an intangible asset's carrying amount exceeds its recoverable amount (determined by observing the asset's fair value less selling costs of similar assets in an active market), the intangible asset is impaired. If an intangible asset is impaired according to the impairment test, an **impairment loss** is recorded, equal to the amount by which the intangible asset's carrying amount exceeds its recoverable amount. The impairment test must be applied annually to all intangible assets with indefinite lives, even if there are no indicators of impairment. Under ASPE, the impairment test is not required for intangible assets unless there are indicators of impairment. Similar to the reversal of impairment losses for property, plant, and equipment, under IFRS, the reversal of previously recorded impairment losses is allowed (except for previously recorded impairment losses related to goodwill). However, reversals of impairment losses are not allowed under ASPE.

As mentioned above, intangible assets are segregated into two categories: those with finite (limited) lives and those with indefinite (unlimited) lives. Below are some examples of intangible assets with finite lives.

- A **patent** is an exclusive right issued by the Canadian Intellectual Property Office of Industry Canada that allows the patent holder to manufacture, sell, or otherwise control an invention for a period of 20 years from the date of the application. The initial cost of a patent is the price paid to acquire it. The cost of the patent should be amortized over its 20-year legal life or its useful life, whichever is shorter.

- A **copyright** is granted by the Canadian Intellectual Property Office, giving the owner the exclusive right to reproduce and sell an artistic or published work. Copyrights are valid for the life of the creator plus 50 years, and the cost of the copyright consists of the cost of acquiring and defending it. Generally, a copyright's useful life is significantly shorter than its legal life, and the copyright is therefore amortized over its useful life.

- **Research and development** (R&D) costs present two accounting problems: (1) it is sometimes difficult to determine the costs related to a specific project, and (2) it is hard to know the extent and timing of future benefits. As a result, we consider three phases a company goes through in developing its own intangibles: research, development, and post-development.

  Research is original planned investigation that is done to gain new knowledge and understanding. All research costs should be expensed as incurred.

  Development is the application of research to a plan or design for a new or improved product or process for commercial use. **Development costs with reasonably certain future benefits can be capitalized**. Specifically, all of the following criteria must be met, in order for the project's future development expenditures to be capitalized: (1) the project is technically feasible, (2) the company has a desire to complete development, (3) the company is able to complete development, and (4) a market exists for the product. All of these conditions must be met in order to capitalize project development costs now and in the future; otherwise the related costs must be expensed.

  Post-development begins when commercial production of the developed product or process begins. During this stage, development costs should be amortized over the useful life of the product or process developed.

- An intangible asset is considered to have an indefinite life when there is no foreseeable limit to the length of time over which the asset is expected to generate net cash inflows for the company. Below are some examples of intangible assets with indefinite lives.

- A **trademark** or trade name is a word, phrase, jingle, or symbol that distinguishes or identifies a particular business or product. Trademarks and trade names have tremendous value to companies and are typically vigorously defended. The creator or original user may obtain the exclusive legal right to a trademark or trade name by registering it with the Canadian Intellectual Property Office. This registration provides continuous protection and may be renewed every 15 years as long as the trademark or trade name is in use. If a trademark is developed internally rather than purchased, it cannot be recognized as an intangible asset on the statement of financial position. Expenditures on internally developed trademarks or brands cannot be distinguished from the cost of developing the business as a whole and consequently cannot be measured.

- A **franchise** is a contractual agreement under which the franchisor grants the franchisee the right to sell certain products, to provide specific services, or to use certain trademarks or trade names, normally within a designated geographic area. Another type of franchise is granted by a government body and permits a company to use public property in performing its services. When costs can be identified with the acquisition of the franchise or licence, an intangible asset should be recognized. These rights have indefinite lives and are not amortized.

  Annual payments, often in proportion to the franchise's total sales, are sometimes required under a franchise agreement. These are called royalties and are recorded as **operating expenses** in the period in which they are incurred.

- **Goodwill** represents the future economic benefits arising from the purchase of a business that are not individually identified and separately recognized. Goodwill represents the excess amount paid for a business above the fair market value of its identifiable assets, less the fair market value of its liabilities. Goodwill is the extra value relating to a business due to, for example, excellent management, desirable

162   **Study Guide to Accompany Financial Accounting: Tools for Business Decision-Making, Fifth Canadian Edition**

location, skilled employees, good customer relations, high-quality products, fair pricing policies, and harmonious relations with labour unions. Unlike other assets, such as investments or property, plant, and equipment, which can be sold individually in the marketplace, goodwill can be identified only with the business as a whole.

Goodwill is recorded only when there is a purchase of an entire business, at which time an independent valuation can be determined. The cost of the goodwill is measured by comparing the cost paid to acquire the business with the fair value of its net identifiable assets (assets less liabilities). If the cost is greater than the net identifiable assets, then the purchaser has paid for something that is not identifiable. The purchaser has paid for something that cannot be separated and sold—goodwill. Because a transaction has occurred, the cost of the goodwill purchased can be measured and therefore recorded as an asset.

Because goodwill has an indefinite life, it is not amortized. Since goodwill is measured using a company's fair value, a subjective value that can easily change, IFRS requires goodwill to be tested annually for impairment even if there are no indicators of impairment. Under ASPE, impairment tests on goodwill are only conducted if indicators of impairment exist. Under both IFRS and ASPE, impairment losses on goodwill are never reversed, even if the company's value increases after the impairment loss has been recorded.

Statement Presentation of Long-Lived Assets

study objective 6
Illustrate how long-lived assets are reported in the financial statements.

- Long-lived assets are normally reported under the headings "Property, Plant, and Equipment," "Intangible Assets," and "Goodwill." Sometimes intangible assets are listed separately, following Property, Plant, and Equipment, with no separate caption. Goodwill must be separately disclosed; other intangibles can be grouped together for reporting purposes.

- Either on the statement of financial position or in the notes, the cost of each of the major classes of assets should be disclosed, as well as the accumulated depreciation for assets that are depreciated and accumulated amortization for intangible assets that are amortized. In addition, the depreciation and amortization methods used and the useful lives or rates applied must be specified in the notes to the financial statements.

- Under IFRS, companies also have to disclose if they are using the cost or the revaluation model for each class of assets, and include a reconciliation of the carrying amount at the beginning and end of the period for each class of long-lived assets in the notes to financial statements. This means they must show all of the following for each class of long-lived assets: (1) additions; (2) disposals; (3) depreciation or amortization; (4) impairment losses; and (5) reversals of impairment losses. If a company uses the revaluation model, it must also disclose any increases or decreases from revaluations as well as other information about the revaluation.

- The depreciation expense, gains and losses on disposal, and impairment losses are reported in the operating section of the income statement. The cash flows resulting from the purchase or sale of long-lived assets are reported in the investing activities section of the statement of cash flows.

CHAPTER 9 Reporting and Analyzing Long-Lived Assets 163

Analyzing Assets

- Two ratios are used to analyze assets: return on assets and asset turnover.

> **study objective 7**
>
> Describe the methods for evaluating the use of assets.

1. The **return on assets ratio** measures a company's overall profitability. It is calculated by dividing profit by average total assets. The return on assets ratio indicates the amount of profit generated by each dollar invested in assets. The higher the return on assets, the more profitable the company is.

2. The **asset turnover ratio** indicates how efficiently a company uses its assets to generate sales. It is calculated by dividing net sales by average total assets. A higher asset turnover ratio implies better efficiency in using assets to generate sales. If the ratio is 1.25 times, for each dollar invested in assets, the company is generating sales of $1.25. Asset turnover ratios vary considerably among industries.

- To complete an analysis of the sales-generating ability of a company's assets, profit margin, discussed in Chapter 5, can be used in conjunction with an asset turnover ratio to explain the return on assets ratio. The relationship is as follows:

$$\text{Profit Margin} \quad \times \quad \text{Asset Turnover} \quad = \quad \text{Return on Assets}$$

$$\frac{\text{Profit}}{\text{Net Sales}} \quad \times \quad \frac{\text{Net Sales}}{\text{Average Total Assets}} \quad = \quad \frac{\text{Profit}}{\text{Average Total Assets}}$$

This relationship has important implications for management. If a company wants to increase its return on assets, it can do so either by increasing the margin it generates from each dollar of goods that it sells (profit margin) or by trying to increase the volume of goods that it sells (asset turnover).

comparing
IFRS and ASPE

Key Differences	International Financial Reporting Standards (IFRS)	Accounting Standards for Private Enterprises (ASPE)
Models for valuing property, plant, and equipment	Choice of cost model or revaluation model	Only cost model allowed
Models for valuing investment properties	Choice of cost model or valuation model for investment properties	No separate recognition of investment properties—considered to be property, plant, and equipment—so only cost model allowed
Impairment requirements for property, plant, and equipment and intangible assets with finite lives	Must determine each year if indicators of impairment are present and if so perform an impairment test. Reversals of impairment losses are allowed.	No annual requirement to determine if indicators of impairment exist, but when it is apparent they exist, an impairment test must be done. An impairment test occurs in two steps: (1) determine that the cash flows from the asset do not exceed its carrying value, and (2) calculate the impairment loss. Impairment losses cannot be reversed.

164 Study Guide to Accompany Financial Accounting: Tools for Business Decision-Making, Fifth Canadian Edition

Goodwill and intangible assets with indefinite lives	Must perform impairment test annually. Impairment losses can be reversed on intangible assets but not on goodwill.	Same approach used as above.
Terminology	*Depreciation* is used to describe cost allocation for property, plant, and equipment. Long-term leases that are essentially the purchase of an asset are called *finance leases*.	*Amortization* may be used instead of *depreciation* for property, plant, and equipment. Long-term leases that are essentially the purchase of an asset are known as *capital leases*.

Chapter Self-Test

As you work through the questions and problems, remember to use the **Decision Toolkit** discussed and used in the text:

1. *Decision Checkpoints:* Ask a question relevant to the decision being made.
2. *Info Needed for Decision:* Make a choice regarding the information needed to answer the question.
3. *Tools to Use for Decision:* Review what the information identified in step 2 does for the decision-making process.
4. *How to Evaluate Results:* Identify specifically how the information identified in step 2 should be evaluated to answer the question relevant to the decision being made.

Note: The notation "(SO 1)" means that the question relates to study objective 1.

Multiple Choice

Please circle the correct answer.

(SO 1)   1.   A company purchases a used delivery van for $20,000. The company logo is painted on the side of the van at a cost of $600. The van licence is $60, and a one-time safety test for the van costs $110. What does the company record as the cost of the new van?
a. $20,600
b. $20,660
c. $20,710
d. $20,770

(SO 1)   2.   Nazemi Corporation purchased a piece of land for $50,000. Nazemi paid legal fees of $9,000 and demolition costs of $2,000 (to tear down an old building on the land). Proceeds from the scrap were $500. The total to be debited to the Land account is
a. $61,000.
b. $60,500.
c. $59,000.
d. $50,000.

CHAPTER 9   Reporting and Analyzing Long-Lived Assets   165

3. Newcomb Corporation installed a new parking lot for its employees at a cost of   (SO 1)
   $10,000. The $10,000 should be debited to
   a. Repairs and Maintenance Expense.
   b. Land.
   c. Land Improvements.
   d. Parking Lot.

4. Aliabadi Corporation purchased a piece of equipment for $20,000. It paid shipping   (SO 1)
   charges of $500 and insurance during transit of $200. Installation and testing of the
   equipment cost $1,000. The total to be debited to the Equipment account is
   a. $20,000.
   b. $20,500.
   c. $20,700.
   d. $21,700.

5. Which of the following is a way of expressing the estimated useful life of a depre-   (SO 2)
   ciable asset?
   a. 5 years
   b. 10,000 machine hours
   c. 30,000 units
   d. All of the above are ways of expressing the estimated useful life of a depre-
      ciable asset.

6. Which of the following statements is correct?   (SO 2)
   a. Straight-line depreciation is an accelerated method of depreciation.
   b. The total amount of depreciation for an asset is the same, regardless of the
      method used.
   c. The total amount of depreciation for an asset differs depending on the
      method used.
   d. In the later years of an asset's useful life, the straight-line method results in
      lower depreciation expense than the diminishing-balance method.

7. At the beginning of the year, Powers Corporation purchased a piece of machin-   (SO 2)
   ery for $50,000. It has a residual value of $5,000; an estimated useful life of nine
   years; and estimated units of output of 90,000 units. Actual units produced during the first year were 11,000. Depreciation expense for the first year under the
   straight-line method is
   a. $5,556.
   b. $5,500.
   c. $5,300.
   d. $5,000.

8. On January 3, 2012, Boulay Corporation purchased a piece of machinery for $50,000.   (SO 2)
   The machinery has a residual value of $5,000, an estimated useful life of nine years,
   and an estimated 90,000 units of output. During the first year, 11,000 units were produced. Depreciation expense for 2012 under the units-of-production method is
   a. $5,556.
   b. $5,500.
   c. $5,300.
   d. $5,000.

166   **Study Guide to Accompany Financial Accounting: Tools for Business Decision-Making, Fifth Canadian Edition**

(SO 2)   9.   On January 4, 2012, Sacks Corporation purchased a piece of equipment for
$20,000. The equipment has a residual value of $4,000 and an estimated useful
life of eight years. Depreciation expense for 2012 under the double diminishing-
balance method is
a. $5,000.
b. $4,000.
c. $2,000.
d.   None of the above is the correct amount.

(SO 2)   10.   Under the cost model, a building's carrying amount is calculated as follows:
a.   original cost of the building less residual value.
b.   fair value of the building less accumulated depreciation.
c.   original cost of the building less accumulated depreciation.
d.   fair value of the building less residual value.

(SO 3)   11.   Which of the following statements is correct?
a.   Under IFRS, for property, plant, and equipment, and intangible assets with
finite lives, there is no annual requirement to determine if indicators of
impairment exist.
b.   Under IFRS, for property, plant, and equipment, and intangible assets
with finite useful lives, the impairment test occurs in two steps: the first
step requires a comparison of expected cash flows from the asset with
its carrying value and the second step requires calculation of the
impairment loss.
c.   Under IFRS, reversals of impairment losses are allowed, except for
impairment losses related to goodwill.
d.   Under ASPE, reversals of impairment losses are allowed, except for
impairment losses related to goodwill.

(SO 3)   12.   Which of the following statements is correct?
a.   Periodic depreciation is never revised during an asset's useful life.
b.   A change in depreciation estimate only affects prior periods.
c.   A change in depreciation estimate affects current and future periods, but
not prior periods.
d.   A change in depreciation estimate affects current and future periods, as well
as prior periods.

(SO 3)   13.   When the carrying amount of a long-lived asset exceeds its recoverable amount,
the required journal entry records
a.   an impairment loss.
b.   asset disposal.
c.   earnings management.
d.   a capital expenditure.

(SO 3)   14.   Under IFRS, property, plant, and equipment must be accounted for using
a.   the cost model.
b.   the revaluation model.
c.   either the cost model or the valuation model.
d.   either the cost model or the revaluation model.

CHAPTER 9 Reporting and Analyzing Long-Lived Assets 167

15. A company sold for $3,000 a machine that had a cost of $10,000 and accumu-   (SO 4)
    lated depreciation of $7,500. The company had a
    a. loss of $500.
    b. gain of $500.
    c. gain of $3,000.
    d. loss of $7,000.

16. A company sold for $2,000 a machine that had a cost of $10,000 and accumu-   (SO 4)
    lated depreciation of $7,500. The company had a
    a. loss of $500.
    b. gain of $500.
    c. gain of $2,000.
    d. loss of $8,000.

17. Quick Corporation retired a piece of equipment that had a cost of $8,000 and   (SO 4)
    accumulated depreciation of $7,000. The journal entry to record the retirement
    will include a
    a. debit to Gain on Disposal for $1,000.
    b. credit to Gain on Disposal for $1,000.
    c. credit to Loss on Disposal for $1,000.
    d. debit to Loss on Disposal for $1,000.

18. Which of the following gives the recipient the right to manufacture, sell, or   (SO 5)
    otherwise control an invention for a period of 20 years?
    a. Patent
    b. Copyright
    c. Trademark
    d. Licence

19. A company spent $75,000 to successfully defend its copyright on a piece of   (SO 5)
    literature. The journal entry to record the cost includes a debit to
    a. Legal Fees Expense for $75,000.
    b. Intangible Assets for $75,000.
    c. Copyright for $75,000.
    d. Research and Development Expense for $75,000.

20. At the beginning of the year, Righter Corporation purchased for $10,000 a patent   (SO 5)
    with a legal life of eight years. Righter estimates that the patent's useful life will be
    four years. Amortization expense on the patent for the year is:
    a. $2,500.
    b. $1,250.
    c. $588.
    d. $250.

21. With respect to long-lived assets, which of the following must be disclosed in the   (SO 6)
    financial statements or in the notes to financial statements?
    a. The balances of major classes of assets
    b. Accumulated depreciation by major classes of assets
    c. Depreciation methods used
    d. All of the above must be disclosed.

168   Study Guide to Accompany Financial Accounting: Tools for Business Decision-Making, Fifth Canadian Edition

(SO 6)   22.   An impairment loss is reported
  a.   in a note to the financial statements.
  b.   in the operating activities section in the statement of cash flows.
  c.   as a special item in the statement of changes in equity.
  d.   in the operating expenses section on the income statement.

(SO 7)   23.   A company's average total assets is $200,000; depreciation expense is $10,000; and accumulated depreciation is $60,000. Net sales total $250,000. Asset turnover is
  a.   0.8 times.
  b.   1.25 times.
  c.   3.33 times.
  d.   4.17 times.

(SO 7)   24.   The return on assets ratio
  a.   indicates how efficiently a company uses its assets.
  b.   measures a company's overall profitability.
  c.   indicates whether assets should be replaced.
  d.   measures a company's liquidity.

(SO 7)   25.   A company can increase its return on assets by
  a.   decreasing its average assets and holding its net sales and profit constant.
  b.   increasing its average assets and holding its net sales and profit constant.
  c.   increasing its net sales and holding its profit and average total assets constant.
  d.   decreasing its profit and holding its net sales and average total assets constant.

Problems

(SO 2, 4)   1.   Townsend Corporation owns a piece of machinery that it had purchased three years ago for $40,000, at which time the machinery had an estimated residual value of $5,000 and an estimated useful life of 10 years. At the end of 2011, the Accumulated Depreciation account had a balance of $10,500. On April 1, 2013, the corporation sold the machinery for $27,000.

Record the following journal entries:
  a.   The depreciation entry on December 31, 2012.
  b.   The entry or entries to record the sale on April 1, 2013.
  c.   If Townsend had simply retired the machinery on April 1, 2013, what would the journal entry or entries have been?

Date	Account Title	Debit	Credit

CHAPTER 9   Reporting and Analyzing Long-Lived Assets   169

2. The Sligo Corporation uses the straight-line method of depreciation for all of   (SO 1, 2, 4)
    its machinery. On January 2, 2010, machinery was purchased for cash at a cost
    of $45,000. The machinery has an estimated useful life of 10 years and a residual
    value of $8,000.

    On June 29, 2013, Sligo decided to lease new, more efficient machinery;
    consequently, the machinery described above was sold on this date for
    $33,350 cash.

    Prepare the journal entries to:
    a.   record the purchase of the machinery.
    b.   record depreciation expense for 2010, 2011, and 2012.
    c.   record the disposal of the machinery on June 29, 2013.

Date	Account Title	Debit	Credit

170 Study Guide to Accompany Financial Accounting: Tools for Business Decision-Making, Fifth Canadian Edition

(SO 2)   3. Assume that a company purchases machinery at a cost of $100,000 on April 1, 2012. The machinery has a five-year useful life and a residual value of $8,000. The company uses the diminishing-balance method of depreciation at twice the straight-line rate. The company's year ends on December 31.
   a.   Prepare a five-year depreciation schedule.
   b.   Prepare a journal entry to record depreciation for 2013.
   c.   Prepare a journal entry to record depreciation for 2017.

(SO 6)   4. The following account balances are provided for Vic Corporation as at December 31, 2012:

Cash	$200,000
Accounts receivable	260,000
Accumulated depreciation—equipment	300,000
Accumulated depreciation—building	370,000
Accumulated amortization—patents	10,000
Allowance for doubtful accounts	70,000
Building	900,000
Equipment	800,000
Goodwill	150,000
Inventories	180,000
Land	700,000
Patents	40,000
Prepaid expenses	30,000
Short-term investments	90,000

Prepare the assets section of the statement of financial position for Vic Corporation as at December 31, 2012.

(SO 1, 2, 6, 7)   5. Please refer to the HMV and WHSmith financial statements found in the appendices at the end of this study guide for information in answering the following questions. Do not forget to use the **Decision Toolkit** approach for help in answering the questions.
   a.   What line items concerning property, plant, and equipment and intangible assets can be found on HMV's and WHSmith's statement of financial position and statement of cash flows for 2010?
   b.   Calculate the profitability of both companies for 2010, breaking down each company's return on assets ratio into its profit margin and asset turnover components.
   c.   Compare the performance of HMV and WHSmith for 2010 using the information calculated in question 5b. In 2010, return on assets for the industry was 4.3%.

Solutions to Self-Test

Multiple Choice

1. c $20,000 + $600 + $110 = $20,710. The cost of the licence would be recorded as an expense.

2. b $50,000 + $9,000 + $2,000 − $500 = $60,500.

CHAPTER 9 Reporting and Analyzing Long-Lived Assets 171

3. c Recording the cost as an expense is incorrect because the parking lot will provide a benefit in future periods. Land has an indefinite life; however, a parking lot will decline in service potential over time and require maintenance and replacement. Typically, a company will not have an account called "Parking Lot" but will use an account called "Land Improvements."

4. d $20,000 + $500 + $200 + $1,000 = $21,700.

5. d Answer a applies to the straight-line method of depreciation and answers b and c apply to the units-of-production method of depreciation.

6. b The straight-line method results in an even amount of depreciation expense for each year of an asset's useful life. In the later years of an asset's useful life, the straight-line method results in higher depreciation expense than the diminishing-balance method.

7. d ($50,000 − $5,000) ÷ 9 years = $5,000.

8. b $50,000 − $5,000 = $45,000; $45,000 ÷ 90,000 units = $0.50/unit; $0.50/unit 11,000 actual units = $5,500 depreciation expense.

9. a The double diminishing-balance rate is 25% [(100% ÷ 8 years) × 2], and $20,000 × 25% = $5,000.

10. c Under the cost model, the carrying amount of a depreciable asset is cost less accumulated depreciation.

11. c Answers a and b are true for impairment testing of property, plant, and equipment, and intangible assets with finite lives, under ASPE. Also under ASPE, reversals of impairment losses are not allowed.

12. c There are several reasons why periodic depreciation may need to be revised during an asset's useful life, including additional capital expenditures during the asset's useful life, changes in estimated useful life or residual value, and changes in the pattern in which the asset's economic benefits are consumed. A change in depreciation estimate only affects current and future periods, not prior periods.

13. a Assuming the company has not sold, retired, or exchanged the long-lived asset, it has not been disposed of. Earnings management involves timing the recognition of gains and losses to achieve certain results. A capital expenditure is an expenditure that benefits future periods and is recorded as a long-lived asset.

14. d Under IFRS, investment properties may be accounted for under either the cost model or the valuation model. Under IFRS, property, plant, and equipment must be accounted for using either the cost model (which requires that an asset be carried at cost less accumulated depreciation) or the revaluation model (which requires that an asset's carrying amount be adjusted to fair value).

15. b The carrying amount is $2,500 ($10,000 − $7,500). Since the proceeds exceed the carrying amount by $500, there is a gain of $500.

16. a The carrying amount is $2,500 ($10,000 − $7,500). Since the carrying amount exceeds the proceeds by $500, there is a loss of $500.

17. d Since the carrying amount is $1,000 ($8,000 − $7,000), there is a loss on disposal, and losses are always debited.

172   **Study Guide to Accompany Financial Accounting: Tools for Business Decision-Making, Fifth Canadian Edition**

18. a   A copyright protects literary and artistic works. A trademark is a word, phrase, jingle, or symbol that distinguishes or identifies a particular business or product. A licence is an operating right.

19. c   The amount spent to successfully defend an intangible asset is debited to the related asset's account.

20. a $10,000 ÷ 4 years. For an intangible asset with a finite life, its amortizable amount is amortized over the shorter of its estimated useful life and its legal life.

21. d   Either on the statement of financial position or in the notes to the financial statements, the cost of each of the major classes is disclosed, as well as the accumulated depreciation pertaining to tangible assets and accumulated amortization relating to intangible assets. In addition, the depreciation and amortization methods used, the useful lives or rates used, and whether the company is following the cost model or the revaluation model should be specified in the notes to the financial statements.

22. d   Depreciation expense and impairment losses are presented in the operating expenses section of the income statement.

23. b   Asset turnover = net sales ÷ average total assets; $250,000 ÷ $200,000 = 1.25 times.

24. b   The return on assets ratio measures overall profitability.

25. a   Return on assets = profit margin × asset turnover. Decreasing average assets increases asset turnover and therefore increases return on assets.

Problems

1.

a.

Dec. 31, 2012	Depreciation Expense	3,500	
	Accumulated Depreciation—Machinery		3,500
	(To record annual depreciation)		
	40,000 − $5,000 = $35,000 ÷ 10 years = $3,500		

Note: The company must be using straight-line depreciation because the Accumulated Depreciation account at the end of three years after the asset was purchased is $10,500. On a straight-line basis, 3 years × $3,500 = $10,500.

b.

Apr. 1, 2013	Depreciation Expense	875	
	Accumulated Depreciation—Machinery		875
	(To bring depreciation up to date)		
	$3,500 annual depreciation × $3/_{12}$ = $875		
Apr. 1, 2013	Cash	27,000	
	Accumulated Depreciation—Machinery	14,875	
	Machinery		40,000
	Gain on Disposal		1,875
	(To record disposal at a gain)		

CHAPTER 9   Reporting and Analyzing Long-Lived Assets   173

Accumulated depreciation = $10,500 + $3,500 + $875 = $14,875

Carrying amount = $40,000 − $14,875 = $25,125

Gain = $27,000 − $25,125 = $1,875

c.

Apr. 1, 2013	Depreciation Expense	875	
	Accumulated Depreciation—Machinery		875
	(To bring depreciation up to date)		

$3,500 annual depreciation $\times \, ^{3}/_{12}$ = $875

	Loss on Disposal	25,125	
	Accumulated Depreciation—Machinery	14,875	
	Machinery		40,000
	(To record retirement of asset)		

Accumulated depreciation = $10,500 + $3,500 + $875 = $14,875

Carrying amount = $40,000 − $14,875 = $25,125

Loss on disposal equals carrying amount of the machinery.

2.

a.

Jan. 2, 2010	Machinery	45,000	
	Cash		45,000
	(To record purchase of machinery)		

b.

Dec. 31, 2010	Depreciation Expense	3,700	
	Accumulated Depreciation—Machinery		3,700
	(To record depreciation for 2010)		

$45,000 − $8,000 = $37,000 ÷ 10 years = $3,700

Dec. 31, 2011	Depreciation Expense	3,700	
	Accumulated Depreciation—Machinery		3,700
	(To record depreciation for 2011)		
Dec. 31, 2012	Depreciation Expense	3,700	
	Accumulated Depreciation—Machinery		3,700
	(To record depreciation for 2012)		

c.

June 29, 2013	Depreciation Expense	1,850	
	Accumulated Depreciation—Machinery		1,850
	(To bring depreciation up to date prior to		
	disposal of machinery: $3,700 ÷ 2 = $1,850)		

174 Study Guide to Accompany Financial Accounting: Tools for Business Decision-Making, Fifth Canadian Edition

Cash	33,350	
Accumulated Depreciation—Machinery	12,950	
Machinery		45,000
Gain on Disposal		1,300

(To record disposal at a gain)

Accumulated depreciation = \$3,700 + \$3,700 + \$3,700 + \$1,850 = \$12,950

Carrying amount = \$45,000 − \$12,950 = \$32,050

Gain = \$33,350 − \$32,050 = \$1,300

3. a.

					End of Year	
Year	Carrying Amount, Beginning of Year	Depreciation Rate	=	Depreciation Expense	Accumulated Depreciation	Carrying Amount
						\$100,000
2012	\$100,000	40%[1]		\$30,000[2]	\$30,000	70,000
2013	70,000	40%		28,000	58,000	42,000
2014	42,000	40%		16,800	74,800	25,200
2015	25,200	40%		10,080	84,880	15,120
2016	15,120	40%		6,048	90,928	9,072
2017	9,072	40%		1,072[3]	92,000	8,000
	Total depreciation expense:			\$92,000		

Note 1: 100% ÷ 5 = 20% × 2 = 40%.

2: The machinery was purchased on April 1, 2012; therefore, only nine months of depreciation apply in 2012: ($100,000 × 40% × $\frac{9}{12}$ = $30,000).

3: Calculation of \$3,628.80 (\$9,072 × 40%) is adjusted to \$1,072 so that the carrying amount will equal the residual value.

b.

Dec. 31, 2013	Depreciation Expense	28,000	
	Accumulated Depreciation—Machinery		28,000
	(To record depreciation for 2013)		

c.

Dec. 31, 2017	Depreciation Expense	1,072	
	Accumulated Depreciation—Machinery		1,072
	(To record depreciation for 2017)		

CHAPTER 9   Reporting and Analyzing Long-Lived Assets   175

4.

VIC CORPORATION
Statement of Financial Position (Partial)
December 31, 2012

Current assets

Cash		$ 200,000
Accounts receivable	$260,000	
Less: Allowance for doubtful accounts	70,000	190,000
Short-term investments		90,000
Inventories		180,000
Prepaid expenses		30,000
Total current assets		690,000

Property, plant, and equipment

Land		700,000
Building	$900,000	
Less: Accumulated depreciation	370,000	530,000
Equipment	$800,000	
Less: Accumulated depreciation	300,000	500,000
Total property, plant, and equipment		1,730,000

Intangible assets

Patents	$ 40,000	
Less: Accumulated amortization	10,000	30,000

Goodwill		150,000
Total assets		$2,600,000

5. Please note that the amounts shown for HMV and WH Smith are stated in pounds (£) millions.

a. HMV:

On the statement of financial position: property, plant, and equipment of £167.3 and intangible assets of £122.2.

On the statement of cash flows: depreciation of £43.4; purchases of property, plant, and equipment of £39.9; and proceeds from sale of property, plant, and equipment of £1.1.

WHSmith:

On the statement of financial position: property, plant, and equipment of £158; other intangible assets of £24; and goodwill of £32.

On the statement of cash flows: purchase of property, plant, and equipment of £24 and purchase of intangible assets of £5; depreciation of property, plant, and equipment of £31; impairment of property, plant, and equipment of £3; and amortization of intangible assets of £5 (referring to note 24 of the financial statements).

b.

Profit Margin	×	Asset Turnover	=	Return on Assets
$\dfrac{\text{Profit}}{\text{Net Sales}}$	×	$\dfrac{\text{Net Sales}}{\text{Average Total Assets}}$	=	Return on Assets

HMV: $\dfrac{£49.2}{£2,016.6}$ × $\dfrac{£2,016.6}{(£705.4 + £616.5) \div 2}$

  2.4% × 3.1 times = 7.4%

WHSmith: $\dfrac{£69}{£1,312}$ × $\dfrac{£1,312}{(£513 + £494) \div 2}$

  5.3% × 2.6 times = 13.8%*

* *Note:* Some rounding discrepancies may exist.

c. WHSmith's profit margin of 5.3% was significantly better than HMV's profit margin of 2.4%; however, HMV's asset turnover of 3.1 times was better than WHSmith's asset turnover of 2.6 times. Overall, WHSmith had a higher return on assets (13.8%) than HMV (7.4%), and both companies performed better than the industry average return on assets of 4.3%.

chapter 10

Reporting and Analyzing Liabilities

Chapter Overview

Chapter 10 discusses two basic types of liabilities: current and non-current. Current liabilities include operating lines of credit, sales taxes payable, property taxes payable, salaries payable, short-term notes or loans payable, and current maturities of non-current debt. Non-current liabilities include instalment notes payable and bonds payable. In this chapter, you will also learn about the effective-interest method of amortizing a bond premium or discount, and financial statement presentation and analysis of liabilities.

Review of Specific Study Objectives

Current Liabilities

- A **current liability** is a debt that will be paid within one year and from existing current assets or through the creation of other current liabilities. A debt that does not meet both criteria is classified as a non-current or long-term liability.

study objective 1

Account for current liabilities.

- An **operating line of credit** is a credit facility set up at a company's bank to help the company manage temporary cash shortfalls. A company with an operating line of credit is effectively pre-authorized by its bank to borrow money on an

178 Study Guide to Accompany Financial Accounting: Tools for Business Decision-Making, Fifth Canadian Edition

as-needed basis, up to a pre-set limit. Security, called collateral, is often required by the bank as protection against a possible default on the loan by the borrower (the company). Collateral for an operating line of credit normally includes some, or all, of the company's current assets. Operating line of credit borrowings are normally on a short-term basis, repayable immediately upon request by the bank (on demand).

- Many companies show a negative or overdrawn cash balance at year end, as a result of using an operating line of credit. However, no special journal entry is required to record the overdrawn amount. Credits to the cash account are simply accumulated, and the net negative cash account balance is reported as **bank indebtedness** in the current liabilities section of the statement of financial position, with a suitable note disclosure.

- When a company sells goods, the company usually collects **sales taxes** from the customer, and periodically (normally monthly) remits (sends) total sales taxes collected to the designated federal and/or provincial government taxing authorities. Sales tax may take the form of Goods and Services Tax (GST), Provincial Sales Tax (PST), or Harmonized Sales Tax (HST). In Quebec, the PST is known as the Quebec Sales Tax (QST).

- In collecting and remitting sales taxes, the company serves as a collection agent for the designated federal and/or provincial government taxing authorities. When an item is sold, the amount of the sale and the amount of each sales tax collected are usually rung up separately on the cash register. For example, if $500 of merchandise is sold, and the applicable HST percentage is 13%, the following journal entry would record the sale:

Cash	565	
Sales		500
Sales Tax Payable		65
(To record sale and sales tax)		

- When the sales tax recorded above is remitted to the government, the following journal entry would record the remittance:

Sales Tax Payable	65	
Cash		65
(To remit sales tax)		

- Businesses that own property pay **property taxes** annually. However, property tax bills are not usually issued until the spring of each year. Therefore, until the property tax bill is received, a company typically does not know exactly how much property tax expense it has incurred so far in the year.

To illustrate, assume that a company's year end is December 31 and that the company records adjusting journal entries annually. If the company receives its property tax bill of $8,400 on March 1, and pays the bill on May 31, on March 1, the company would record the following property tax expense and liability for the two months that have already passed:

CHAPTER 10 Reporting and Analyzing Liabilities 179

Mar. 1	Property Tax Expense ($8,400 \times ^2/_{12}$)	1,400	
	Property Tax Payable		1,400
	(To record property tax expense for January and February)		

In May, when the company records the payment of the liability recorded on March 1, it also records property tax expense incurred to date for March, April, and May. As at the May 31 payment date, five months have passed and therefore five months of property tax expense should be recorded. Since the company is paying the entire $8,400 property tax bill on May 31, the portion that is prepaid for the remaining seven months of the year is recorded as a prepayment, as shown in the following journal entry:

May 31	Property Tax Payable	1,400	
	Property Tax Expense ($8,400 \times ^3/_{12}$)	2,100	
	Prepaid Property Tax ($8,400 \times ^7/_{12}$)	4,900	
	Cash		8,400
	(To record payment of property tax expense for March through May, and prepayment of property tax expense for June through December)		

After payment of the property tax bill, the company has a zero balance in its Property Tax Payable account, and a $4,900 balance in its Prepaid Property Tax account. Since the company makes adjusting entries annually, it would not adjust the Prepaid Property Tax account until year end, December 31. At that time, it would make the following journal entry:

Dec. 31	Property Tax Expense	4,900	
	Prepaid Property Tax		4,900
	(To record property tax expense for June through December)		

- Every employer incurs three types of liabilities related to employees' salaries or wages: (1) net pay owed to employees, (2) employee payroll deductions, and (3) employer payroll obligations.

- Employee payroll deductions are amounts withheld from employees' paycheques, which must be remitted to the appropriate government authorities by the employer. Mandatory payroll deductions include amounts withheld for federal and provincial income taxes, Canada Pension Plan (CPP) contributions, and Employment Insurance (EI) premiums. Voluntary payroll deductions include health plan premiums, union dues, and charitable contributions.

- Employer payroll obligations are various employer payroll costs that are charged on certain payroll deductions, such as the employer's share of CPP and EI. In addition, provincial governments mandate employer funding of a workers' compensation plan. All of these contributions, plus items such as employer-sponsored health plans and pensions and compensated absences, are collectively referred to as employee benefits.

180 **Study Guide to Accompany Financial Accounting: Tools for Business Decision-Making, Fifth Canadian Edition**

- Payroll and payroll tax liability accounts are classified as current liabilities because they must either be paid to employees or remitted to government authorities or other third parties in the near term.

- A **note (or loan) payable** is a promise to repay a specified amount of money, either at a fixed future date or on demand. Notes payable give the lender written documentation of the borrower's obligation, which helps if legal action is needed to collect the debt. Most notes require the borrower to pay interest. If a note is due for payment within one year of the statement of financial position date, then it is classified as a current liability.

- Consider the following example. Robinson Ltd. borrows $20,000 and issues a three-month, 6% note on May 1. Interest plus principal are repayable at maturity. The entry on May 1 is:

Cash	20,000	
Notes Payable		20,000
(To record issue of three-month, 6% note)		

If Robinson prepares financial statements as at June 30, prior to the preparation of financial statements, Robinson would record an adjusting journal entry for accrued interest:

Interest Expense	200	
Interest Payable		200
(To record accrued interest for May and June: $\$20,000 \times 6\% \times {}^2/_{12}$)		

On the maturity date, August 1, the following journal entry is recorded:

Notes Payable	20,000	
Interest Payable	200	
Interest Expense	100	
Cash		20,300
(To record payment of note plus interest)		

Total interest expense on the note is $300, and the note's maturity value is $20,300. On August 1, interest payable of $200 must be removed from the books since it is being paid, and August interest expense ($\$20,000 \times 6\% \times {}^1/_{12}$) must be recorded since it is also being paid but was not previously accrued. Recall from Chapter 4 that interest is calculated for short-term notes by multiplying the principal amount of the note by the annual interest rate, and prorating this amount by the fraction of the year for which interest expense has been incurred. In this example, 6% is the annual interest rate; therefore, the product of the principal amount and the annual interest rate must be prorated by the fraction of the year for which interest expense has been incurred. Interest rates are always expressed as an annual (one-year) rate, regardless of the term of the note.

- Companies often have non-current (long-term) debt of which a portion is due in the current year. If a company has a 10-year mortgage, the principal amount due in the current period is a current maturity of non-current debt and must be classified as a current liability.

CHAPTER 10   Reporting and Analyzing Liabilities   181

Non-Current Liabilities: Instalment Notes Payable

- A **non-current liability** is an obligation that is expected to be paid after one year or longer. These obligations are often in the form of instalment notes or bonds.

- A **long-term note payable** is similar to a short-term note payable, except that the term of the note is for more than one year.

- A long-term note may be secured or unsecured. A **secured** note pledges title to specific assets of the issuer as collateral or security for the loan, and is also known as a mortgage. A **mortgage payable** may be signed by an individual to purchase a home or by a company to acquire property, plant, and equipment. An **unsecured** note is issued against the borrower's general credit. An unsecured note is also known as a debenture, and is issued by corporations with good credit ratings.

- Most long-term notes are repayable in a series of periodic payments. These payments are known as **instalments** and are paid monthly, quarterly, semi-annually, or at another defined period. Each payment consists of (1) interest on the unpaid balance of the loan, and (2) a reduction of the loan principal. Payments generally take one of two forms: fixed principal payment plus interest or blended principal and interest payments.

- Instalment notes with **fixed principal** payments **are repayable in equal periodic amounts, plus interest**. Interest may either be at a fixed or floating rate. A fixed interest rate note will have a constant interest rate over the term of the note. A floating (or variable) interest rate note will have a fluctuating interest rate over the term of the note. Changes in floating rate are generally tied to changes in the prime rate.

  Assume that on January 1, 2012, a company issues a five-year, 6%, $114,000 note payable, and that the interest rate is fixed. The journal entry to record the note is:

> study objective 2
>
> Account for instalment notes payable.

Jan. 1	Cash	114,000	
	Notes Payable		114,000
	(To record issue of five-year, 6% note)		

The terms of the note provide for fixed monthly principal payments of $1,900 ($114,000 ÷ 60 monthly periods) due on the first of each month, plus 6% interest on the outstanding principal balance.

On the first payment date, February 1, interest expense is $570 ($114,000 $\times$ 6% $\times$ $^1/_{12}$). Similar to interest on short-term notes payable, the 6% is an annual interest rate and must be prorated by the fraction of the year for which interest expense has been incurred. The cash payment of $2,470 for the month of February is the total of the instalment payment of $1,900, which is applied against the principal, plus interest of $570.

The entry to record the first instalment payment on February 1 is as follows:

Feb. 1	Interest Expense ($114,000 $\times$ 6% $\times$ $^1/_{12}$)	570	
	Note Payable	1,900	
	Cash ($1,900 + $570)		2,470
	(To record instalment payment on note)		

182   Study Guide to Accompany Financial Accounting: Tools for Business Decision-Making, Fifth Canadian Edition

An instalment payment schedule is a useful tool to help organize the information that is required to prepare journal entries for instalment notes payable. A partial instalment payment schedule for the first few months of the above note payable is as follows, with amounts rounded to the nearest dollar:

| | | | (C) | |
Interest Period	(A) Cash Payment (B + C)	(B) Interest Expense (D × 6% × $^1/_{12}$)	Reduction of Principal ($114,000 ÷ 60)	(D) Principal Balance (D − C)
Instalment Payment Schedule—Fixed Principal Payments				
Jan. 1				$114,000
Feb. 1	$2,470	$570	$1,900	112,100
Mar. 1	2,461	561	1,900	110,200
Apr. 1	2,451	551	1,900	108,300

- Instalment notes with **blended principal and interest payments are repayable in equal periodic amounts, including interest**. Blended principal and interest payments result in changing amounts of interest and principal applied to the loan. As with fixed principal payments, the interest decreases each period (as the principal decreases). In contrast to fixed principal payments, with blended principal and interest payments, the portion applied to the loan principal increases each period.

To illustrate this option, assume that instead of making fixed principal payments, the company repays its note in equal monthly instalments of $2,213. (The cash payment of $2,213 can be calculated mathematically or determined using present value techniques, which are discussed later in the chapter.) As with the fixed principal payments illustrated above, the monthly interest expense is calculated by multiplying the outstanding principal balance by the interest rate, and prorating by the fraction of the year for which interest expense has been incurred. On the first payment date, February 1, interest expense is $570 ($114,000 × 6% × $^1/_{12}$). The instalment payment of $2,213 is fixed for each month, and includes interest and principal portions that will vary each month. On February 1, the principal balance will be reduced by $1,643, which is the difference between the instalment payment of $2,213 and interest expense of $570.

The journal entry to record issue of the note payable is the same as that shown on the previous page for the issue of a fixed principal payment note.

However, the journal entry to record the instalment payment uses the same accounts but different amounts. The first instalment payment on February 1 is recorded as follows:

Feb. 1	Interest Expense ($114,000 × 6% × $^1/_{12}$)	570	
	Note Payable ($2,213 − $570)	1,643	
	Cash ($1,643 + $570)		2,213
	(To record instalment payment on note)		

A partial instalment payment schedule for the first few months of the note payable is as follows, with amounts rounded to the nearest dollar:

CHAPTER 10 Reporting and Analyzing Liabilities 183

Instalment Payment Schedule—Blended Payments			
Interest Period	(A) Cash Payment (B + C)	(B) Interest Expense (D × 6% × $^1/_{12}$)	(C) Reduction of Principal (A − B)	(D) Principal Balance (D − C)
Jan. 1				$114,000
Feb. 1	$2,213	$570	$1,643	112,357
Mar. 1	2,213	562	1,651	110,706
Apr. 1	2,213	554	1,659	109,047

- With both fixed principal plus interest and blended principal and interest instalment loans, principal payments for the next year must be reported as a current liability, with the remaining unpaid principal classified as a non-current liability (unless it is expected to be refinanced).

Non-Current Liabilities: Bonds Payable

- **A bond** is a form of interest-bearing note payable. Bonds are issued in small denominations (usually $1,000 or multiples of $1,000) and attract many investors.

study objective 3
Account for bonds payable.

- Like notes, bonds may be unsecured or secured. **Unsecured bonds** are also known as **debentures**. Bonds that mature on a single specified date are known as **term bonds**. Bonds that mature in instalments are known as **serial bonds**. **Redeemable (callable) bonds** can be retired by the company before they mature. **Convertible bonds** can be exchanged (converted) into common shares at an agreed-upon price.

- A bond certificate is issued to bondholders to provide evidence of a bondholder's credit claim against the issuing company. A bond certificate provides information such as the name of the issuing company, face value of the bond, coupon (contractual) interest rate, and maturity date of the bond. The maturity date is the date when final payment is due to the bondholder from the issuing company. The coupon interest rate is the rate used to determine the amount of cash interest the issuing company pays to the bondholder.

- Bonds may be issued at **face value**, at a **discount** (below face value), or at a **premium** (above face value), where face value is usually the amount of principal due at maturity.

- Bond prices are quoted as a percentage of the bonds' face value, such as 97 or 101. If a $1,000 bond sells at 97, the issuing corporation receives 97% of face value, or $970. If the bond sells at 101, the issuing corporation receives 101% of face value, or $1,010. These percentages multiplied by the bonds' face value represent the bonds' present value.

- If the bonds' coupon interest rate equals the market interest rate at the time of bond issuance, the bonds are issued (or sold) at **face value**, and the journal entry to record the issue is a debit to Cash and a credit to Bonds Payable. When bond interest is paid, the debit is to Bond Interest Expense, and the credit is to Cash. If bond interest is accrued, the debit is to Bond Interest Expense, and the credit is to Bond Interest Payable. Bonds Payable is usually reported as a non-current (long-term) liability, and Bond Interest Payable is reported as a current liability.

184 **Study Guide to Accompany Financial Accounting: Tools for Business Decision-Making, Fifth Canadian Edition**

- If the bonds' coupon interest rate exceeds the market interest rate at the time of bond issuance, the bonds are issued (or sold) at a **premium**. For example, if the market interest rate is 4%, and the bonds' coupon interest rate is 5%, bondholders (investors) would be willing to purchase the bonds for an amount higher than their face value, in order to arrive at a total effective yield of 4% interest on the bonds. Therefore, the issuing corporation would issue the bonds at a **premium**.

- If the bonds' coupon interest rate is less than the market interest rate at the time of bond issuance, the bonds are issued (or sold) at a **discount**. For example, if the market interest rate is 6%, and the bonds' coupon interest rate is 5%, bondholders (investors) would only be willing to purchase the bonds for an amount less than the bonds' face value, in order to arrive at a total effective yield of 6% interest on the bonds. Therefore, the issuing corporation would issue the bonds at a **discount**.

- Consider the following example. Jays Corporation issued $500,000, five-year, 5% bonds at 96 on January 1, 2012, with interest payable each July 1 and January 1. The journal entry on January 1, 2012, is as follows:

Cash ($500,000 × 96%)	480,000	
Bonds Payable		480,000
(To record issue of five-year, 5% bonds at 96)		

Note that Bonds Payable is always credited for the bonds' issue price, which is also their carrying amount at the time of bond issuance. The credit to the Bonds Payable account is net of the bond discount ($500,000 − $20,000).

- Rather than crediting the Bonds Payable account for the issue price of $480,000, some companies use a separate contra liability account to keep track of the unamortized bond discount ($20,000 in the example above). However, both IFRS and ASPE require presentation of bonds net of any discounts or premiums. Consequently, many companies record their journal entries on a net basis as shown in the example above and in all other examples in this chapter.

- Let us now assume that Jays Corporation issued $500,000, five-year, 5% bonds at 102 on January 1, 2012, with interest payable each July 1 and January 1. The journal entry on January 1, 2012, is as follows:

Cash ($500,000 × 102%)	510,000	
Bonds Payable		510,000
(To record issue of five-year, 5% bonds at 102)		

Note that again, Bonds Payable is credited for the bonds' issue price, which is also their carrying amount at the time of bond issuance. The credit to the Bonds Payable account is net of the bond premium ($500,000 + $10,000).

In the above examples, the bonds' issue price or fair value was determined by applying a percentage factor to the bonds' face value. This percentage factor represents the value at which the bonds will be sold in the marketplace. Multiplying this percentage factor by the bonds' face value arrives at the amount at which the bonds are sold to bondholders (investors), which is also the bonds' present value. Present value of the bonds depends on three factors: (1) the dollar amounts (the bonds' face

CHAPTER 10   Reporting and Analyzing Liabilities   185

value and interest payments) to be received by bondholders; (2) the length of time until the dollar amounts are received by bondholders; and (3) the market (effective) interest rate.

● The face value of the bonds and the coupon interest rate are used to calculate bond interest payments; however, market (effective) interest rate is used to determine the bonds' present value.

● To find the correct present value factor to use in calculating the present value of the bonds' face value, using the present value table for **Present Value of $1** (present value tables are included in Appendix C of the textbook), locate the factor at the intersection of the number of periods until bond maturity and the market interest rate. To calculate the present value of the bonds' face value using a financial calculator or spreadsheet program, input the future value (FV), the market interest rate per period (i), and the number of interested periods (n). If interest is paid semi-annually, the number of periods until bond maturity must be doubled, and the market interest rate must be halved, in locating the correct factor.

● To find the correct present value factor to use in calculating the present value of the bonds' interest payments, using the present value table for **Present Value of an Annuity of $1**, locate the factor at the intersection of the number of periods until bond maturity and the market interest rate. To calculate the present value of the bonds' interest payments using a financial calculator or spreadsheet program, input the interest payment (PMT), the market interest rate per period (i), and the number of interest periods (n). Again, if interest is paid semi-annually, the number of periods until bond maturity must be doubled, and the market interest rate must be halved, in locating the correct factor.

For example, assume Jays Corporation issues a $500,000, five-year, 5% bond on January 1, 2012, with interest payable each July 1 and January 1. If the market (effective) interest rate is 6%, the bond will be sold at a discount, and there will be 10 semi-annual interest periods, at a market (effective) interest rate of 3%.

Present value of $500,000 received in 10 periods

$500,000 × 0.74409 ($n = 10, i = 3$) (from Present Value of $1 table) $372,045

Present value of $12,500 received for each of 10 periods ($500,000 × 5% × $^{6}/_{12}$)

$12,500 × 8.53020 ($n = 10, i = 3$) (from Present Value of an Annuity of $1 table)   106,628

Present value (issue price) of bonds $478,673

Note that the percentage applied to the bond's face value to determine its selling price is:

Issue price = $478,673 ÷ $500,000 = 95.73%.

The following journal entry records the January 1, 2012, transaction:

Cash	478,673	
Bonds Payable		478,673
(To record issue of bonds)		

186 Study Guide to Accompany Financial Accounting: Tools for Business Decision-Making, Fifth Canadian Edition

Once the bond has been issued, Jays Corporation is obligated to pay interest to the bondholders on a semi-annual basis. The discount on the bonds payable will also need to be amortized throughout the life of the bond. The following steps are required to calculate amortization of the bond discount.

1. Calculate **bond interest expense**: Multiply the bonds' carrying amount at the beginning of the interest period by the market (effective) interest rate.
2. Calculate **bond interest paid** (or accrued): Multiply the bonds' face value by the coupon interest rate (contractual interest rate).
3. Calculate **amortization amount**: Calculated as the difference between the amounts calculated in steps (1) and (2).

The bond discount amortization schedule is shown below for the amortization of the $21,327 discount on bonds payable using the **effective-interest method**. All figures have been rounded to the nearest dollar for simplicity.

		JAYS CORPORATION			
		Bond Discount Amortization Schedule			
		Effective-Interest Method			
Semi-Annual Interest Period	(A) Interest Payment ($500,000 × 5% × $^6/_{12}$)	(B) Interest Expense (Preceding Bond Carrying Amount × 6% × $^6/_{12}$)	(C) Discount Amortization (B − A)	(D) Unamortized Discount (D − C)	(E) Bond Carrying Amount ($500,000 − D)
Issue Date				$21,327	$478,673
1	$12,500	$14,360	$1,860	19,467	480,533
2	12,500	14,416	1,916	17,551	482,449
3	12,500	14,473	1,973	15,578	484,422
4	12,500	14,533	2,033	13,545	486,455
5	12,500	14,594	2,094	11,451	488,549
6	12,500	14,656	2,156	9,295	490,705
7	12,500	14,721	2,221	7,074	492,926
8	12,500	14,788	2,288	4,786	495,214
9	12,500	14,856	2,356	2,430	497,570
10	12,500	14,927	2,430[1]	0	500,000

[1]$3 difference due to cumulative rounding.

The journal entry for the first interest payment on July 1, 2012, is as follows:

Bond Interest Expense	14,360	
Bonds Payable		1,860
Cash		12,500

(To record payment of interest and amortization of bond discount)

Amortization of the bond discount is an additional cost of borrowing and should be included in bond interest expense over the life of the bonds. Amortization of the bond

CHAPTER 10   Reporting and Analyzing Liabilities   187

discount results in an increase in bond interest expense and an increase in carrying amount of the bonds payable.

The journal entry for the second interest payment on December 31, 2012, is as follows:

Bond Interest Expense	14,416	
Bonds Payable		1,916
Cash		12,500
(To record payment of interest and amortization of bond discount)		

Note that when bonds are issued at a discount, the amount of periodic bond interest expense increases over the life of the bond. This is because a constant (market interest rate) percentage is applied to an increasing bond carrying amount in calculating bond interest expense. The bond carrying amount increases over the life of the bond due to amortization of the bond discount.

A bond amortization schedule would be constructed in the same manner for a bond issued at a premium. The only difference would be that the amount of periodic bond interest expense would decrease over the life of the bond. This is because a constant (market interest rate) percentage would be applied to a decreasing bond carrying amount in calculating bond interest expense. Amortization of the bond premium would be considered a reduction in the cost of borrowing. The bond carrying amount would decrease over the life of the bond due to amortization of the bond premium.

- At maturity, the bonds' carrying amount equals their face value, and the journal entry to redeem the bonds requires a debit to Bonds Payable and a credit to Cash.

- If bonds are redeemed before maturity, it is necessary to (1) update any unrecorded interest, including amortization; (2) eliminate the bonds' carrying amount at the redemption date; (3) record the cash paid; and (4) recognize the gain or loss on redemption. If $500,000 of bonds with a carrying amount of $496,000 are redeemed at 101, the following journal entry is required:

Bonds Payable	496,000	
Loss on Redemption ($505,000 − $496,000)	9,000	
Cash ($500,000 × 101%)		505,000
(To record redemption of bonds)		

Losses or gains on bond redemption are reported on the income statement as "other expenses and losses" or "other revenues and gains."

Statement Presentation and Analysis

- **Current liabilities** are generally reported as the first category in the liabilities section of the statement of financial position. Each of the primary types of current liabilities is listed separately within the category or detailed in notes to the financial statements. Similar to current assets, current liabilities are generally listed in order of liquidity (by due date).

- **Non-current liabilities** are usually reported separately, immediately following current liabilities if companies follow the traditional North American order, or preceding current liabilities if companies use a reverse-liquidity order. Summary information regarding debts is usually presented on the statement of financial

study objective 4

Identify the requirements for the financial statement presentation and analysis of liabilities.

188 Study Guide to Accompany Financial Accounting: Tools for Business Decision-Making, Fifth Canadian Edition

position, while detailed information (such as interest rates, maturity dates, conversion privileges, assets pledged as collateral, and fair values if available) are shown in notes to the financial statements.

- Information regarding cash inflows and outflows during the year from the proceeds of debt issues and debt repayments, respectively, is provided in the financing activities section of the **statement of cash flows**.

- A concern for analysts when they evaluate a company's liquidity and solvency is whether the company has properly recorded all of its liabilities and obligations.

- **Provisions** are liabilities of uncertain timing or amount, where there is no uncertainty about the fact that a charge will result. Provisions are recorded in the accounts using reliable estimates based on past experience and future expectations. An example of a provision is a provision for product warranty costs.

- **Contingent liabilities** are existing or possible obligations arising from past events, where the liability is contingent (dependent) on whether or not some uncertain future event will occur that will confirm either its existence or the amount payable, or both. An example of a contingency is an unsettled lawsuit. Accounting rules require that uncertain liabilities either be recorded (accrued) or disclosed (in notes to the financial statements), unless the possibility of occurrence is remote. Whether a liability should be recorded or disclosed depends on the probability of the future event occurring that will confirm whether there is a liability and a related loss. **Under IFRS, if the loss is probable or "more likely than not," the company should record the liability as a provision. Under ASPE, if the loss is "likely," the company should record the liability as a provision.** Under both IFRS and ASPE, the amount must be reasonably estimable before any liability can be recorded (accrued), regardless of the likelihood of occurrence. Uncertain liabilities that are not recorded (accrued) as provisions are treated as contingent liabilities and disclosed in notes to the financial statements, unless their probability of occurrence is remote.

- **Liquidity ratios** measure a company's short-term ability to pay its maturing obligations and to meet unexpected needs for cash. A commonly used measure of liquidity is the **current ratio** (current assets divided by current liabilities). The current ratio can be misleading because some current asset items, such as receivables and inventory, may not be very liquid but are included in the numerator. Consequently, analysis of the current ratio should be supplemented by analysis of other ratios, such as receivables turnover and inventory turnover.

- **Solvency ratios** measure a company's ability to repay its non-current debt and survive over a long period of time. A commonly used measure of solvency is **debt to total assets** (total liabilities divided by total assets). This ratio indicates the extent to which a company's assets are financed by debt. To supplement analysis of the debt to total assets ratio, the **times interest earned ratio** may be analyzed (profit before interest expense and income tax expense [EBIT] divided by interest expense). This ratio provides an indication of a company's ability to meet interest payments as they come due.

- **Off–balance sheet financing** refers to a situation where liabilities are not recorded on the statement of financial position. One common type of off–balance sheet financing is financing from operating lease transactions, which was discussed in Chapter 9.

CHAPTER 10   Reporting and Analyzing Liabilities   189

comparing
IFRS and ASPE

Key Differences	International Financial Reporting Standards (IFRS)	Accounting Standards for Private Enterprises (ASPE)
Bonds	Must use the effective-interest method to amortize any bond premium or discount.	Normally will use the effective-interest method to amortize any bond premium or discount but permitted to use alternative methods if the results do not differ materially from the effective-interest method.
Contingent liability	The definition of probability used to record a contingent liability (called a provision when recorded) is "more likely than not."	The definition of probability used to record a contingent liability is "likely," which is a higher level of probability than under IFRS.

Chapter Self-Test

As you work through the questions and problems, remember to use the **Decision Toolkit** discussed and used in the text:

1. *Decision Checkpoints:* Ask a question relevant to the decision being made.
2. *Info Needed for Decision:* Make a choice regarding the information needed to answer the question.
3. *Tools to Use for Decision:* Review what the information identified in step 2 does for the decision-making process.
4. *How to Evaluate Results:* Identify specifically how the information identified in step 2 should be evaluated to answer the question relevant to the decision being made.

Note: The notation "SO 1" means that the question relates to study objective 1.

Multiple Choice

Please circle the correct answer.

1. The journal entry to record accrual of the employer's share of Canada Pension   (SO 1)
   Plan (CPP) contributions would include a
   a.   credit to CPP Payable.
   b.   debit to Salaries Expense.
   c.   credit to Employee Benefits Expense.
   d.   debit to CPP Payable.

2. A retailer that collects HST from its customers would   (SO 1)
   a.   debit Sales Tax Payable.
   b.   debit Sales Tax Expense.
   c.   credit Sales Tax Payable.
   d.   credit Sales Tax Revenue.

190   Study Guide to Accompany Financial Accounting: Tools for Business Decision-Making, Fifth Canadian Edition

(SO 1)   3. Which of the following is a criterion for classification of a liability as current?
  a.   The liability is a debt that can be paid from existing current assets.
  b.   The liability is a debt that can be paid through the creation of other current liabilities.
  c.   The liability must be paid within one year.
  d.   All of the above are criteria for classification of a liability as current.

(SO 1)   4. The total interest charged on an $80,000, six-month, 5% note payable would be
  a. $4,000.
  b. $2,000.
  c. $3,000.
  d. $1,000.

(SO 1)   5. On July 1, a corporation issued a $50,000, four-month, 6% note payable. Interest is payable at maturity. If the corporation's year end is September 30, the adjusting journal entry to record on that date is:

a.	Interest Expense	750	
	Notes Payable		750
b.	Interest Expense	750	
	Interest Payable		750
c.	Interest Expense	1,000	
	Notes Payable		1,000
d.	Interest Expense	1,000	
	Interest Payable		1,000

(SO 1)   6. When the corporation in question 5 (above) pays the amount due on the maturity date, the journal entry will include a
  a.   debit to Notes Payable for $51,000.
  b.   credit to Cash for $50,000.
  c.   debit to Interest Expense for $1,000.
  d.   debit to Interest Payable for $750.

(SO 2)   7. Monthly instalment note payable payments consist of
  a.   interest expense only.
  b.   principal repayment only.
  c.   interest expense and principal repayment.
  d.   neither interest expense nor principal repayment.

(SO 2)   8. On November 1, 2012, a company issued a note payable of $50,000, of which $10,000 is repaid each year for the next five years. What is the proper classification of this note on the December 31, 2012, statement of financial position?
  a. $10,000 current liability; $40,000 non-current liability
  b. $50,000 current liability
  c. $50,000 non-current liability
  d. $10,000 non-current liability; $40,000 current liability

CHAPTER 10   Reporting and Analyzing Liabilities   191

9. Notes that are issued against the general credit of the borrower are called   (SO 2)
    a.   unsecured notes.
    b.   secured notes.
    c.   mortgages.
    d.   convertible notes.

10. Instalment notes payable requiring blended principal and interest payments   (SO 2)
    a.   result in reduction of principal by equal amounts each period.
    b.   result in increasing reduction of principal each period.
    c.   result in increasing interest expense each period.
    d.   result in decreasing cash payments each period.

11. A corporation issues $1 million of five-year, 4% bonds. The 4% interest rate is   (SO 3)
    called the _____ rate.
    a.   yield
    b.   effective
    c.   market
    d.   coupon

12. The issue price of a bond is equal to the   (SO 3)
    a.   present value of the bond's face value.
    b.   present value of the bond's face value and interest payments.
    c.   present value of the bond's interest payments.
    d.   face value of the bond.

13. When the coupon interest rate exceeds market interest rate, the bond   (SO 3)
    sells at
    a.   face value.
    b.   a discount.
    c.   a premium.
    d.   an amount other than those listed above.

14. When calculating the carrying amount of bonds payable,   (SO 3)
    a.   a bond premium is subtracted from, and a bond discount is added to, bonds
         payable.
    b.   a bond discount is subtracted from, and a bond premium is added to, bonds
         payable.
    c.   both a bond discount and a bond premium are subtracted from bonds
         payable.
    d.   both a bond discount and a bond premium are added to bonds payable.

15. Bonds payable with a face value of $200,000 and a carrying amount of $196,000   (SO 3)
    are redeemed prior to maturity at 102. There is a
    a.   loss on redemption of $4,000.
    b.   gain on redemption of $4,000.
    c.   loss on redemption of $8,000.
    d.   gain on redemption of $8,000.

192   **Study Guide to Accompany Financial Accounting: Tools for Business Decision-Making, Fifth Canadian Edition**

(SO 3)   16.   A gain or loss on early redemption of bonds payable is classified as a(n)
- a.   operating expense on the income statement.
- b.   addition to or subtraction from bonds payable on the statement of financial position.
- c.   other revenues and gains or other expenses and losses on the income statement.
- d.   non-current liability on the statement of financial position.

(SO 3)   17.   On January 1, a company issued $600,000 of 10-year, 6% bonds at 102, which reflects a 5% market interest rate. Interest is payable on July 1 and January 1. On July 1 of the first year of the bond, the journal entry to record interest will include a
- a.   credit to Cash for $15,000.
- b.   debit to Bonds Payable for $2,700.
- c.   credit to Bonds Payable for $2,700.
- d.   debit to Bond Interest Expense for $18,000.

(SO 3)   18.   Companies that prepare financial statements in accordance with ASPE must amortize a bond premium or discount using
- a.   the simple interest method.
- b.   the contractual interest method.
- c.   the effective-interest method.
- d.   any method, as long as the results do not differ materially from the effective-interest method.

(SO 4)   19.   A company's total debt is $250,000, while its total assets are $500,000. Profit before interest expense and income tax is $300,000, and interest expense is $30,000. The company's times interest earned ratio is
- a.   10 times.
- b.   2 times.
- c.   50%.
- d.   10%.

(SO 4)   20.   Rouse Corporation is being sued by a customer. At the statement of financial position date, Rouse's lawyers feel that it is "more likely than not" that the company will lose the lawsuit and that a reasonable estimate of the loss is $50,000. If Rouse prepares financial statements in accordance with IFRS, on the statement of financial position date, Rouse should:
- a.   not disclose the lawsuit because the jury has not yet ruled.
- b.   disclose the lawsuit in notes to the financial statements.
- c.   record (accrue) the loss by debiting an expense and crediting a liability.
- d.   ask for a second opinion from another law firm.

(SO 4)   21.   Some companies finance assets without showing a liability on the statement of financial position. This procedure is called
- a.   fraud.
- b.   finance leasing.
- c.   off–balance sheet financing.
- d.   capitalizing.

CHAPTER 10   Reporting and Analyzing Liabilities   193

22. In 2012, Caron Corporation introduced an extended warranty program to   (SO 4)
all of its customers. However, Caron does not know exactly when it will incur
the related program charges or how much it will cost to honour the program.
Charges related to Caron's extended warranty program should be
   a.   estimated based on reasonable and probable estimates, and disclosed in
        Caron's 2012 notes to financial statements.
   b.   estimated based on reasonable and probable estimates, and recorded
        (accrued) in Caron's 2012 financial statements.
   c.   monitored by management but not disclosed or recorded in Caron's 2012
        financial statements, due to uncertainty of timing and amount of program
        charges.
   d.   recorded in the future years in which the extended warranty program is
        honoured.

23. Which is a very common way to present current liabilities on the statement of   (SO 4)
    financial position?
   a.   Notes payable are listed first.
   b.   Current maturities of non-current debt are listed first.
   c.   They are listed in alphabetical order.
   d.   They are listed by order of liquidity.

Problems

1.   Dhalwala Corporation incurred the following transactions in the month of June: (SO 1)

     June 1: Dhalwala borrowed $100,000 on a one-year, 6% note. Interest is payable
     at maturity.
     June 20: Monthly payroll showed total salaries of $10,000 and the following
     employee payroll deductions: CPP $495, EI $178, income tax $1,195, and health
     insurance premiums $200. The employer's payroll obligations were CPP $495
     and EI $249.
     June 30: Pre-tax sales for June totalled $125,000. The HST rate is 13%.
     June 30: The payroll deductions and health insurance premiums for June
     were remitted to the Receiver General and the health insurance organization,
     respectively.

     Record all June transactions.

2.   Jansen Corporation incurred the following transactions: (SO 1, 2)
   a.   On May 1, Jansen issued a $20,000, six-month, 6% note. Interest is payable
        at maturity. Record the adjusting journal entry for interest on June 30 (no
        adjusting entry for interest was recorded in May).
   b.   On March 1, Jansen received its $10,020 property tax invoice for the calen-
        dar year due to be paid on May 31. Record the
        1.   journal entry on March 1 to record the receipt of the property tax bill.
        2.   payment of the property tax bill on May 31.
        3.   adjusting journal entry required on December 31, assuming Jansen
             makes adjusting entries annually.

194 Study Guide to Accompany Financial Accounting: Tools for Business Decision-Making, Fifth Canadian Edition

c. On July 1, Jansen borrowed $300,000 from the bank for a five-year period at a 6% interest rate. The terms of the loan provide for equal monthly installment payments of $5,000 ($300,000 ÷ 60 monthly periods), plus interest of 6% on the outstanding principal balance. Record the journal entry for the first installment payment on August 1.

Date	Account Titles	Debit	Credit

(SO 3) 3. Dove Corporation issues $100,000 of 10-year, 7% bonds for proceeds of $107,473, which reflects a 6% market interest rate. The bonds pay interest semi-annually.

a. Prepare the journal entry to record the issue of the bond.
b. Prepare the journal entry to record payment of interest and amortization of any bond premium or discount for the first interest period.

Date	Account Titles	Debit	Credit

CHAPTER 10   Reporting and Analyzing Liabilities   195

4. The following selected general ledger account balances are provided for Rebus   (SO 4)
   Corporation as at December 31, 2012.

Accounts payable	$ 15,000
Accounts receivable	70,000
Accumulated depreciation—building	10,000
Advertising expense	1,000
Allowance for doubtful accounts	20,000
Bad debt expense	2,000
Bonds payable	98,000
Building	350,000
Cash	140,000
Common shares	234,000
Depreciation expense	5,000
Dividends	10,000
Employee benefits expense	1,000
Income tax expense	13,000
Interest expense	8,000
Interest payable	13,000
Land	100,000
Mortgage payable	175,000
Notes payable, due in six months	40,000
Retained earnings, January 1	15,000
Sales tax payable	13,000
Service revenue	75,000
Salaries expense	10,000
Salaries payable	2,000

   a. Prepare an income statement, a statement of changes in equity, and a
      statement of financial position for Rebus Corporation for 2012, assuming
      $30,000 of the mortgage is payable next year and that no common shares
      were issued in 2012.
   b. Using appropriate ratios, comment on Rebus Corporation's liquidity and
      solvency.

5. Please refer to the HMV and WHSmith financial statements found in the appen-   (SO 1, 2, 4)
   dices at the end of this study guide for information for answering the following questions. Do not forget to use the **Decision Toolkit** approach for help in
   answering the questions.

   a. What is HMV's non-current debt in 2010, and how much did it increase or
      decrease from 2009?
   b. What is current liabilities as a percentage of total liabilities in 2010 for (1)
      HMV and (2) WHSmith?
   c. Assess HMV's and WHSmith's solvency using the debt to total assets ratio
      and times interest earned ratios for 2010 and 2009.

196 **Study Guide to Accompany Financial Accounting: Tools for Business Decision-Making, Fifth Canadian Edition**

Solutions to Self-Test

Multiple Choice

1. a The employer owes its share of CPP contributions to the government. Therefore, a liability account, CPP Payable, is credited.

2. c A retailer that collects HST from its customers owes those amounts to the federal government. Therefore, a liability account, Sales Tax Payable, is credited.

3. d A current liability is a debt that will be paid within one year and from existing current assets or through the creation of other current liabilities.

4. b $\$80,000 \times 5\% \times {}^{6}/_{12} = \$2,000$.

5. b Interest expense = interest payable = $\$50,000 \times 6\% \times {}^{3}/_{12} = \$750$.

6. d The journal entry on the maturity date would be:

Notes Payable	50,000	
Interest Payable	750	
Interest Expense	250	
Cash		51,000

7. c Instalment note payable payments consist of a mix of interest expense on the unpaid balance of the loan and repayment of the loan principal.

8. a $10,000 of the note payable is a current maturity of non-current debt.

9. a Secured notes pledge title (give ownership) to specific assets as collateral or security for the loan, and are also known as mortgages.

10. b Installment notes payable requiring blended principal and interest payments result in increasing reduction of principal each period.

11. d Yield and effective interest rate are different terms for market interest rate.

12. b Bonds involve two streams of cash flow: repayment of principal and payment of interest. Bond principal is another term for the face value of the bond.

13. c If the coupon interest rate and market interest rate are the same, the bond sells at face value. If the coupon interest rate is lower than the market interest rate, the bond sells at a discount.

14. b A bond discount is subtracted from bonds payable, and a bond premium is added to bonds payable.

15. c The company had to pay ($\$200,000 \times 1.02 =$) $204,000 for bonds with a carrying amount of $196,000. The difference between these two amounts is a loss on redemption.

16. c A gain or loss on early redemption of bonds payable is classified as a revenue and gain or other expense and loss.

17. b The journal entry is:

Bond Interest Expense ($\$612,000 \times 5\% \times {}^{6}/_{12}$)	15,300	
Bonds Payable ($\$18,000 - \$15,300$)	2,700	
Cash ($\$600,000 \times 6\% \times {}^{6}/_{12}$)		18,000

18. d Companies that prepare financial statements in accordance with IFRS must use the effective-interest method to amortize bond premium or discount. Companies that prepare financial statements in accordance with ASPE

CHAPTER 10   Reporting and Analyzing Liabilities   197

normally use the effective-interest method to amortize any bond premium or discount, but are permitted to use alternative methods if the results do not differ materially from the effective-interest method.

19. a   The times interest earned ratio is calculated by dividing profit before interest expense and income tax by interest expense. In this question, $300,000 ÷ $30,000 = 10 times.

20. c   Under IFRS, an uncertain liability should be recorded (or accrued) in the financial statements if a loss is probable or "more likely than not," and if the amount is reasonably estimable. However, note that under ASPE, an uncertain liability is recorded (accrued) in the financial statements if a loss is "likely" (which is a higher level of probability than "more likely than not").

21. c   Off–balance sheet financing refers to situations where liabilities are not recorded on the statement of financial position, and should be carefully considered in analyzing a company's solvency.

22. b   A provision should be recorded (accrued) in 2012 because although an extended warranty program is a liability of uncertain timing and amount, there is no uncertainty about the fact that a charge will result. The provision should be recorded using reasonable and probable estimates.

23. d   Current liabilities are generally listed in order of liquidity (maturity), although other orders are also possible.

Problems

1.

Date	Account Titles	Debit	Credit
June 1	Cash	100,000	
	Notes Payable		100,000
	(To record issue of note)		
20	Salaries Expense	10,000	
	CPP Payable		495
	EI Payable		178
	Income Tax Payable		1,195
	Health Insurance Payable		200
	Cash		7,932
	(To record payroll and employee deductions)		
20	Employee Benefits Expense	744	
	CPP Payable		495
	EI Payable		249
	(To record employee benefits)		
30	Cash ($125,000 + $16,250)	141,250	
	Sales		125,000
	Sales Tax Payable ($125,000 × 13%)		16,250
	(To record sales and sales taxes)		

30	CPP Payable ($495 + $495)	990	
	EI Payable ($178 + $249)	427	
	Income Tax Payable	1,195	
	Cash		2,612
	(To record remittance to Receiver General)		
30	Health Insurance Payable	200	
	Cash		200
	(To record remittance to health insurance organization)		
30	Interest Expense ($100,000 × 6% × $1/_{12}$)	500	
	Interest Payable		500
	(To accrue interest for the month of June on note payable)		

2. a.

June 30	Interest Expense	200	
	Interest Payable		200
	(To record interest on note: $20,000 × 6% × $2/_{12}$)		

b.

1.	Mar. 1	Property Tax Expense ($10,020 × $2/_{12}$)	1,670	
		Property Tax Payable		1,670
		(To record property tax expense for January and February)		
2.	May 31	Property Tax Payable	1,670	
		Property Tax Expense ($10,020 × $3/_{12}$)	2,505	
		Prepaid Property Tax ($10,020 × $7/_{12}$)	5,845	
		Cash		10,020
		(To record payment of property tax for January through May, and prepaid property tax for June through December)		
3.	Dec. 31	Property Tax Expense	5,845	
		Prepaid Property Tax		5,845
		(To record property tax expense for June through December)		

c.

July 1	Interest Expense ($300,000 × 6% × $1/_{12}$)	1,500	
	Bank Loan Payable	5,000	
	Cash ($1,500 + $5,000)		6,500
	(To record the first installment payment on August 1)		

3. a.

Cash	107,473	
Bonds Payable		107,473
(To record issue of bonds at a premium)		

b.

Bond Interest Expense	3,224	
Bonds Payable	276	
Cash		3,500

Bond interest expense = $107,473 × 6% × $6/_{12}$

Bonds payable = $3,500 − $3,224

Cash = $100,000 × 7% × $6/_{12}$

CHAPTER 10   Reporting and Analyzing Liabilities   199

4. a.

REBUS CORPORATION
Income Statement
Year Ended December 31, 2012

Service revenue		$75,000
Operating expenses		
Salaries expense	$10,000	
Interest expense	8,000	
Depreciation expense	5,000	
Bad debt expense	2,000	
Employee benefits expense	1,000	
Advertising expense	1,000	
Total operating expenses		27,000
Profit before income tax		48,000
Income tax expense		13,000
Profit		$35,000

REBUS CORPORATION
Statement of Changes in Equity
Year Ended December 31, 2012

	Common Shares	Retained Earnings	Total Equity
Balance, January 1	$234,000	$15,000	$249,000
Add: profit		35,000	35,000
Less: dividends		10,000	10,000
Balance, December 31	$234,000	$40,000	$274,000

REBUS CORPORATION
Statement of Financial Position
December 31, 2012

Assets

Current assets		
Cash		$140,000
Accounts receivable	$ 70,000	
Less: allowance for doubtful accounts	20,000	50,000
Total current assets		190,000
Property, plant, and equipment		
Land		100,000
Building	$350,000	
Less: accumulated depreciation—building	10,000	340,000
Total property, plant, and equipment		440,000
Total assets		$630,000

200 Study Guide to Accompany Financial Accounting: Tools for Business Decision-Making, Fifth Canadian Edition

Liabilities and Shareholders' Equity

Current liabilities

Accounts payable	$ 15,000	
Salaries payable	2,000	
Interest payable	13,000	
Sales tax payable	13,000	
Notes payable, due in six months	40,000	
Current portion of mortgage payable	30,000	
Total current liabilities		$113,000

Non-current liabilities

Bonds payable	$ 98,000	
Mortgage payable	145,000	
Total non-current liabilities		243,000
Total liabilities		356,000

Shareholders' equity

Common shares	$234,000	
Retained earnings	40,000	
Total shareholders' equity		274,000
Total liabilities and shareholders' equity		$630,000

b. Rebus's current ratio is $190,000 \div \$113,000 = 1.7:1$, which means that for every dollar of current liabilities, Rebus has $1.70 of current assets. At first glance, it would appear as though the company's liquidity is strong; however, we would want to analyze additional ratios, such as receivables turnover and inventory turnover, before arriving at a conclusion regarding the company's liquidity.

Rebus's debt to total assets is $356,000 \div \$630,000 = 56.5\%$, which means that 56.5% of total assets are financed by debt. The debt to total assets ratio can be analyzed along with the times interest earned ratio, which provides an indication of the company's ability to meet interest payments as they come due. Rebus's times interest earned ratio, calculated as profit before interest expense and income tax expense (EBIT) divided by interest expense, is 7 times $[(\$35,000 + \$13,000 + \$8,000) \div \$8,000]$. Thus, the company's current profit before interest expense and income tax expense is more than sufficient to cover its interest expense. Overall, Rebus's solvency looks favourable.

5. Please note that the amounts shown for HMV and WHSmith are stated in pounds (£) millions.

a. HMV's non-current debt is £53.5 in 2010 and £26.3 in 2009, an increase of £27.2.

b. Current liabilities as a percentage of total liabilities in 2010 is as follows:

1. HMV: £551.5 ÷ £605.0 = 91.2%
2. WHSmith: £300 ÷ £327 = 91.7%

c. **HMV:**

Debt to total assets:
2009: £516.9 ÷ £616.5 = 83.8%
2010: £605.0 ÷ £705.4 = 85.8%

CHAPTER 10   Reporting and Analyzing Liabilities   201

Times interest earned:
2009: (£44.2 + £8.5 + £17.1) ÷ £8.5 = 8.2 times
2010: (£49.2 + £6.6 + £19.7) ÷ £6.6 = 11.4 times

WHSmith:

Debt to total assets:
2009: £306 ÷ £494 = 61.9%
2010: £327 ÷ £513 = 63.7%

Times interest earned:
2009: (£63 + £2 + £18) ÷ £2 = 41.5 times
2010: (£69 + £1 + £20) ÷ £1 = 90.0 times

HMV's debt to total assets ratio is high in 2009 and 2010, compared with WHSmith's debt to total assets ratio for the same years. This means that a higher proportion of HMV's assets are financed by debt, compared with WHSmith. In general, a lower proportion of assets financed by debt is considered favourable and less risky. Referring to the analysis in the solution to problem 5 b, a high proportion of HMV's debt (in the debt to total assets ratio) is current, meaning that a significant portion of HMV's debt will be due within one year and paid from existing current assets or through the creation of other current liabilities.

Both WHSmith's and HMV's times interest earned ratios increased between 2009 and 2010. This means that between 2009 and 2010, both companies improved their ability to meet interest payments as they come due. However, WHSmith's times interest earned ratio is higher than HMV's in both years, meaning that WHSmith's current profit before interest expense and income tax expense covers its interest expense by a larger margin.

Considering debt to total assets and times interest earned ratios for both HMV and WHSmith in 2009 and 2010, WHSmith appears to be more solvent than HMV.

chapter 11

Reporting and Analyzing Shareholders' Equity

Chapter Overview

In this chapter, you will learn about the essential features of a corporation and how to account for transactions involving common shares, preferred shares, and dividends. You will also learn about the presentation of shareholders' equity in the financial statements, and how to measure earnings performance using various ratios.

Review of Specific Study Objectives

The Corporate Form of Organization

- A **corporation** is a legal entity that is separate and distinct from its owners, who are known as shareholders.

- **Corporations** may be classified in a variety of ways. Two common classifications are by purpose (for example, for-profit or not-for-profit), and by ownership (for example, public or private). A **public corporation** may have thousands of shareholders, and its shares are actively traded on a securities market, such as the Toronto Stock Exchange. A **private corporation** usually has only a few shareholders and does not offer its shares for sale to the general public.

study objective 1

Identify and discuss the major characteristics of a corporation.

204   **Study Guide to Accompany Financial Accounting: Tools for Business Decision-Making, Fifth Canadian Edition**

The following are **characteristics of a corporation:**

1. **Separate legal existence**, which means that a corporation acts under its own name and is a separate legal entity that is distinct from its owners. A corporation may buy, own, or sell property; borrow money; and enter into legally binding contracts in its own name. A corporation may also sue or be sued, and a corporation pays its own taxes.

2. **Limited liability of shareholders**, which means that the liability of shareholders is limited to their investment in the shares of the corporation.

3. **Transferable ownership rights**, which means that ownership of a corporation is held in shares of capital, which are transferable units. A shareholder may buy or sell shares in the corporation and does not require approval of the corporation or of other shareholders to do so.

4. **Ability to acquire capital**, through issue of shares.

5. **Continuous life**, which means that corporations have an unlimited life. A corporation's continuance as a going concern is not affected by withdrawal, death, or incapacity of a shareholder, employee, or officer of the corporation.

6. **Corporation management**, meaning that shareholders can invest in a corporation without having to manage it personally. Shareholders manage the corporation indirectly through a board of directors they elect.

7. **Government regulation**, and compliance with federal and provincial laws and securities regulations in multiple jurisdictions, increase the cost and complexity of the corporate form of organization.

8. **Income tax** must be paid by corporations because they are separate legal entities. Some argue that corporate profit is taxed twice (double taxation): once at the corporate level and again at the individual level when dividends are received. This is not completely true, however, as individuals receive a dividend tax credit to reduce some of the tax burden.

- A **corporation may sell ownership rights** in the form of shares. A corporation's shares are divided into different classes, such as Class A, Class B, and so on. The different classes are usually identified by the generic terms **common shares** and **preferred shares**. If a corporation has only one class of shares, that class of shares is identified as common shares. Each common shareholder has the following rights:

1. The **right to vote** in the election of the board of directors, and to vote on matters requiring shareholder approval.

2. The **right to share in corporate profit** through receipt of dividends, if a dividend is declared by the board of directors.

3. The **right to share in the distribution of assets upon liquidation of the corporation** in proportion to the shareholders' holdings.

- **Authorized share capital** is the amount of share capital that a corporation is authorized to sell, according to its articles of incorporation. This may be specified as an unlimited amount or a specific amount. If an amount is specified, the specific amount of authorized shares normally anticipates the corporation's initial and future share capital needs. **Issued shares** are authorized shares that have been sold. No formal journal entry is required to record authorized shares; however, the number of shares authorized and issued must be disclosed in the shareholders' equity section of the statement of financial position.

- A **corporation may sell its share capital** either directly to investors or indirectly through an investment banking firm. The first time a corporation's shares are

CHAPTER 11 Reporting and Analyzing Shareholders' Equity 205

offered for sale to the public, the offer is called an **initial public offering (IPO)**. The company receives the cash (less any financing or issue fees) from the sale of the IPO shares.

Once a public corporation's shares are sold and issued to the public, the shares continue trading on the secondary market. That is, investors buy and sell shares from and to each other, rather than from and to the corporation. When shares are sold between investors, there is no impact on the company's financial position.

- For a public corporation, the **fair value of its shares** is established by the interaction between buyers and sellers trading the corporation's shares on the secondary market. In general, a corporation's share price follows the trend of its profit and dividends. Factors beyond a corporation's control (such as wars, trade embargoes, elections, recessions, and changes in interest rates) can also influence the fair value of a corporation's shares.

One commonly reported measure of the fair value of a company's total equity is its market capitalization. A company's **market capitalization** is calculated by multiplying the number of shares issued by the share price at any given date.

Common Shares

- Share capital is **legal capital** that cannot be distributed to shareholders. Share capital must remain invested in the corporation for the protection of corporate creditors. In some countries, notably in the United States, a specific par or stated value may be assigned to shares to predetermine the amount of legal capital. Use of par or stated values for shares is rare in Canada. In fact, corporations that are incorporated federally, or that are incorporated in certain provinces, are not allowed to issue shares with par value.

> **study objective 2**
>
> Record common share transactions.

- **No par value shares** are shares that have not been assigned a predetermined legal capital. When no par value shares are issued, all of the proceeds received are considered to be legal capital.

- **Contributed capital** is the amount shareholders paid, or contributed, to the corporation in exchange for share ownership. Contributed capital includes **share capital**, in addition to other sources of capital affected by share transactions.

  When **no par value common shares** are issued, all proceeds of share issues are considered legal capital of the no par value common shares. If 100 common shares are sold for $5 per share, the journal entry to record the issue is:

Cash	500	
Common Shares		500
(To record sale of 100 common shares for $5 per share)		

  If another 100 common shares are sold for $7 per share, the journal entry to record the issuance is:

Cash	700	
Common Shares		700
(To record sale of 100 common shares for $7 per share)		

206 Study Guide to Accompany Financial Accounting: Tools for Business Decision-Making, Fifth Canadian Edition

Note that in each case the Common Shares account is credited for the entire proceeds of the sale.

- When shares are issued for **noncash consideration**, the shares should be recorded at the **fair value of the consideration (for example, goods or services) received**. If the fair value of the consideration received cannot be reliably determined, the shares should be recorded at the fair value of the consideration given up.

- Under ASPE, when shares are issued for noncash consideration, the shares should be recorded at the fair value of the consideration received or the fair value of the consideration given up, whichever is more reliably determinable. For a private corporation, the fair value of consideration received is usually more reliably determinable, because a private corporation's shares are seldom traded and typically do not have a readily determinable market value.

- **Reacquisition of shares** occurs when a company purchases its own shares on the open market. A company may purchase its own shares in order to:

  1. increase trading of the company's shares in the securities market in the hope of enhancing the company's value;
  2. reduce the number of shares issued, and cause earnings per share and return on equity to increase;
  3. eliminate hostile shareholders by buying them out; or
  4. have additional shares available for issue to employees under bonus and stock compensation plans, or for use in acquiring other companies.

Shares repurchased by federally incorporated companies, and most provincially incorporated companies, must be retired (cancelled), which effectively restores the shares to the status of authorized but unissued shares. In some Canadian provinces, in the United States, and internationally, reacquired shares can be held in "treasury" for subsequent reissue.

Three steps are required to record the reacquisition and retirement of common shares (or preferred shares):

1. remove the cost of the shares from the relevant share capital account, based on average cost per share;
2. record the cash paid to reacquire the shares; and
3. record the gain or loss on reacquisition, which is the difference between the price paid to reacquire the shares and their original (or average) cost. However, because companies cannot realize a gain or suffer a loss from share transactions with their own shareholders, these amounts are not reported on the income statement. Instead, the gain or loss on reacquisition is considered an excess or deficiency belonging to the original shareholders and is reported as an increase or decrease in shareholders' equity.

Assume that a company has 100,000 shares issued, $400,000 in its Common Shares account, and $20,000 in contributed capital. The company decides to reacquire and retire 60,000 of its common shares on the open market. The following journal entry would be recorded if the company repurchases its shares at $3.50 each.

Common Shares ($400,000 ÷ 100,000 = $4; $4 × 60,000)	240,000	
Contributed Capital—Reacquisition of Common Shares		30,000
Cash (60,000 × $3.50)		210,000

The average cost of each common share is $4 ($400,000 ÷ 100,000), and the average cost of the common shares retired must be removed from the Common Shares account. Contributed Capital is increased by the difference between cash paid ($3.50 per share) and average cost of each share ($4 per share).

If the company had repurchased its shares at $4.50 each (instead of $3.50 each), the following journal entry would be recorded:

Common Shares ($400,000 ÷ 100,000 = $4; $4 × 60,000)	240,000	
Contributed Capital—Reacquisition of Shares	20,000	
Retained Earnings ($30,000 − $20,000)	10,000	
Cash (60,000 × $4.50)		270,000

If a company repurchases its shares at a price greater than the average cost of each common share, the difference between repurchase price and average cost is debited to Contributed Capital first (if any exists), and any excess difference is debited to Retained Earnings. In this example, Contributed Capital has an existing account balance of $20,000, which is debited first. The excess difference ($10,000) is recorded as a debit to Retained Earnings.

Preferred Shares

- **Preferred shares** have contractual provisions that give them a preference, or priority, over common shares in certain areas. Typically, preferred shareholders have priority in terms of dividend payments and in terms of distribution of assets in the event of liquidation. However, preferred shareholders usually have no voting rights. If a company issues 500 preferred shares for $30 per share, the journal entry to record the transaction is:

> **study objective 3**
>
> Record preferred share transactions.

Cash	15,000	
Preferred Shares		15,000
(To record sale of 500 shares at $30 per share)		

- **Preferred shares** are listed before common shares on the statement of financial position, because they have dividend and liquidation preferences.

- **Preferred shareholders have the right to share in the distribution of dividends before common shareholders do.** However, there is no requirement for the company to pay an annual dividend. The dividend amount is stated as an annual amount per share; for example, $5 preferred shares means that common shareholders will not receive any dividends in the current year until preferred shareholders have received $5 per share. Normally, dividends are paid quarterly, so shareholders would receive $1.25 ($5 ÷ 4) each quarter.

Preferred shares may contain a **cumulative** dividend feature. This right means that when dividends are declared, preferred shareholders must be paid both current-year dividends and any unpaid prior-year dividends before common shareholders receive dividends. When preferred shares are cumulative, preferred dividends not declared in a period are called **dividends in arrears**, and no distribution can be made to common shareholders until the entire cumulative preferred dividend is paid.

208   **Study Guide to Accompany Financial Accounting: Tools for Business Decision-Making, Fifth Canadian Edition**

Dividends in arrears are not a liability. No obligation exists until a dividend is declared by the board of directors. If preferred shares are **non-cumulative**, any dividend not declared and paid is lost forever.

- Relative to common shareholders, **preferred shareholders** also have a priority claim over corporate assets in the event of liquidation of the corporation. However, creditors still rank above (and must be paid before) all shareholders in the event of liquidation.

- **Convertible preferred shares** allow the preferred shareholder to exchange preferred shares for common shares at a specified ratio.

- **Redeemable (callable) preferred shares** give the issuing corporation the option to purchase the preferred shares from shareholders at specified future dates and prices. **Retractable preferred shares** give the shareholder the option to sell the preferred shares to the issuing corporation at specified future dates and prices.

- A **dividend** is a pro rata (equal) distribution of a portion of a corporation's retained earnings to its shareholders.

Retained Earnings

study objective 4
Prepare the entries for cash dividends, stock dividends, and stock splits, and understand their financial impact.

- For a corporation to pay a **cash dividend**, its board of directors must declare (officially state) that a dividend is a payable. While many companies pay a quarterly dividend, there are companies (for example, growth companies) that pay no dividends but instead reinvest cash in the company for future growth.

- In declaring and paying dividends, there are **three important dates:** (1) declaration date, (2) record date, and (3) payment date. Journal entries are required to record the events on the first and third dates. For a **cash dividend**, the declaration date journal entry is as follows if a corporation declares a $0.25-per-share cash dividend on 100,000 shares:

Cash Dividends	25,000	
Dividends Payable		25,000
(To declare a cash dividend of $0.25 per share)		

Dividends Payable is a current liability, because it is normally paid within the next month.

On the **record date**, ownership of the shares is determined for dividend payment purposes. No journal entry is required on this date.

On the **payment date**, the following journal entry is required:

Dividends Payable	25,000	
Cash		25,000
(To record payment of cash dividend)		

The declaration and payment of a cash dividend reduces both shareholders' equity and total assets.

- A **stock dividend** is a distribution of the corporation's own shares to shareholders. A stock dividend results in a decrease in retained earnings and an increase in

CHAPTER 11   Reporting and Analyzing Shareholders' Equity   209

share capital. Therefore, total shareholders' equity remains the same because dollar amounts are simply transferred from retained earnings to share capital accounts. An investor who receives a stock dividend does not receive cash or an increase in ownership percentage on the day he or she receives the stock dividend.

- **Corporations issue stock dividends to:**

1. satisfy shareholders' dividend expectations while conserving cash;
2. increase the shares' marketability by reducing the market price per share (when the number of shares issued increases, the share price decreases on the stock market, making it easier for investors to purchase the shares); and
3. emphasize that a portion of equity has been permanently reinvested in the business and is unavailable for cash dividends.

Consider the following example of a stock dividend. If a corporation has 500,000 common shares issued on the day its board of directors declares a 10% stock dividend, 50,000 new shares (500,000 × 10%) will be issued on the distribution date. If the fair value of the shares is $30 per share, the declaration date journal entry would be:

Stock Dividends (50,000 shares × $30)	1,500,000	
Common Stock Dividends Distributable		1,500,000
(To record declaration of 10% stock dividend)		

Common Stock Dividends Distributable is a shareholders' equity account. If a statement of financial position is prepared after the dividend declaration, the account would appear directly under Common Shares in the share capital section of shareholders' equity.

On the **distribution (payment) date**, the journal entry would be:

Common Stock Dividends Distributable	1,500,000	
Common Shares		1,500,000
(To record distribution of 10% stock dividend)		

- Like a stock dividend, a **stock split** involves the issue of additional shares to shareholders according to their percentage ownership. However, a stock split is usually much larger than a stock dividend. The **main purpose of a stock split** is to increase the marketability of the shares by lowering the price per share. If a corporation has 200,000 common shares issued, with a current price per share of $100, and the corporation declares a 2-for-1 stock split, the number of shares will double to 400,000 and the price per share will be reduced by half, to $50 per share. Note that the Common Shares account does not change. A stock split has no effect on total share capital, retained earnings, or total shareholders' equity. No journal entry is required to record a stock split.

- The **balance in retained earnings** is generally available for dividend declarations. However, in some instances, there may be **retained earnings restrictions**, which make a portion of the retained earnings balance unavailable for dividends. Retained earnings restrictions may be legal or contractual in nature, or they may be voluntary. No journal entry is required to record a retained earnings restriction, it would be disclosed in the notes to the financial statements.

210   Study Guide to Accompany Financial Accounting: Tools for Business Decision-Making, Fifth Canadian Edition

Presentation of Shareholders' Equity

> **study objective 5**
>
> Indicate how share-holders' equity is presented in the financial statements.

- Shareholders' equity transactions are reported in the statement of financial position and the statement of changes in equity. Contributed capital, retained earnings, and accumulated other comprehensive income are reported in the shareholders' equity section of the statement of financial position. **Contributed capital** includes share capital and additional contributed capital. **Share capital** consists of preferred shares and common shares; preferred shares are shown before common shares because of their additional preferential rights. Stock dividends distributable that exist at year end are also reported under share capital. **Additional contributed capital** includes amounts contributed from reacquiring and retiring shares.

- **Retained earnings** are the cumulative profits (or losses) that have been retained in the company (i.e., not distributed to shareholders) since incorporation. Just as profit is credited to Retained Earnings, a loss is debited to Retained Earnings, even if there is an overall debit balance in the account. A debit balance in Retained Earnings is called a deficit and is reported as a deduction in the shareholders' equity section of the statement of financial position.

- **Other comprehensive income (or loss)** includes certain gains and losses that bypass profit, which are recorded as direct adjustments to shareholders' equity.

- **Comprehensive income (or loss)** includes both profit and other comprehensive income. This means that it includes:

  1. the revenues, expenses, gains, and losses included in profit; and
  2. the gains and losses that bypass profit but affect shareholders' equity.

- **Accumulated other comprehensive income** is the *cumulative* change in shareholders' equity that results from the gains and losses that bypass profit but affect shareholders' equity. Similar to retained earnings, which is the cumulative total of profit retained in the business, accumulated other comprehensive income is the cumulative total of all past credits and charges to other comprehensive income. In other words, accumulated other comprehensive income starts with the beginning balance, and is increased by other comprehensive income and decreased by other comprehensive losses during the period, to arrive at the ending balance of accumulated other comprehensive income. It is this ending balance that is reported in the shareholders' equity section of the statement of financial position.

Only companies reporting under IFRS will report other comprehensive income (if they have other comprehensive income). These companies must report other comprehensive income on the statement of comprehensive income and accumulated other comprehensive income on the statement of changes in equity and on the statement of financial position.

Companies reporting under ASPE do not report other comprehensive income. These companies typically have simpler capital structures and fewer share transactions, and are not required to prepare a statement of changes in equity. Instead, these companies prepare a statement of retained earnings. Any changes in share capital and other accounts are presented in notes to the financial statements.

CHAPTER 11 Reporting and Analyzing Shareholders' Equity 211

Measuring Corporate Performance

- The **payout ratio** measures the percentage of profit distributed in the form of cash dividends to common shareholders. It is calculated by dividing total cash dividends to common shareholders by profit. A company with a high growth rate typically has a low payout ratio because it will normally reinvest excess cash in the business.

- **Dividend yield** measures the profit generated for each shareholder by each share, based on the shares' market price. It is calculated by dividing dividend per share by market price per share.

- As discussed in Chapter 2, **earnings per share** is calculated by dividing profit available to common shareholders by weighted average number of common shares during the year. The numerator (profit available to common shareholders) is calculated by subtracting any preferred dividends from profit. The denominator (weighted average number of common shares) is calculated by weighting the shares issued or purchased during the current period by the fraction of the year (or period) that they were issued or reacquired. If there is no change in the number of common shares during the year, the weighted average number of common shares will be the same as the ending balance. If new common shares are issued during the year, these shares are adjusted for the fraction of the year they were issued, to determine the weighted average number of common shares.

  Disclosure of earnings per share is required for companies reporting under IFRS; however, companies reporting under ASPE do not have to report earnings per share.

- A company's profit performance is also measured by its **return on common shareholders' equity**, which shows how many dollars were earned for each dollar invested by common shareholders. It is calculated by dividing profit available to common shareholders (profit minus preferred share dividends) by average common shareholders' equity. Common shareholders' equity is total shareholders' equity, less the legal capital of any preferred shares.

> **study objective 6**
>
> Evaluate dividend and earnings performance.

comparing
IFRS and ASPE

Key Differences	International Financial Reporting Standards (IFRS)	Accounting Standards for Private Enterprises (ASPE)
Issue of shares for a noncash consideration	When shares are issued for a noncash consideration, they should be recorded at the fair value of the consideration (e.g., goods or services) received. If the fair value of the consideration received cannot be reliably determined, then the fair value of the consideration given up would be used instead.	When shares are issued for a noncash consideration, they should be recorded at the most reliable of the two values– the fair value of the consideration (e.g., goods or services) received or the fair value of the consideration given up.
Authorized share capital	Must present the number of shares authorized, in addition to the number of shares issued, along with their related rights and privileges in the financial statements.	Not required to disclose the number of shares authorized in the financial statements, only the number issued along with their related rights and privileges.

212   Study Guide to Accompany Financial Accounting: Tools for Business Decision-Making, Fifth Canadian Edition

Key Differences	International Financial Reporting Standards (IFRS)	Accounting Standards for Private Enterprises (ASPE)
Comprehensive income	Must present accumulated other comprehensive income in statement of financial position and detail changes in other comprehensive income in the statement of changes in equity	Disclosure of comprehensive income is not required.
Statement of changes in equity/retained earnings	Changes in all shareholders' equity accounts are presented in a statement of changes in equity.	Changes in retained earnings are presented in a statement of retained earnings. Changes in share capital and other accounts are presented in the notes to the financial statements.
Earnings per share	Required to present in the income statement (or statement of comprehensive income).	Not required to present in the income statement.

Chapter Self-Test

As you work through the questions and problems, remember to use the **Decision Toolkit** discussed and used in the text:

1. *Decision Checkpoints*: Ask a question relevant to the decision being made.
2. *Info Needed for Decision*: Make a choice regarding the information needed to answer the question.
3. *Tools to Use for Decision*: Review what the information identified in step 2 does for the decision-making process.
4. *How to Evaluate Results*: Identify specifically how the information identified in step 2 should be evaluated to answer the question relevant to the decision being made.

Note: The notation "(SO 1)" means that the question relates to study objective 1.

Multiple Choice

Please circle the correct answer.

(SO 1)   1. Which of the following is considered a disadvantage of the corporate form of business organization?
a.   Limited liability of shareholders
b.   Separate legal existence
c.   Continuous life
d.   Federal and provincial government regulation

(SO 1)   2. Shares that have not been assigned a legal value per share in the corporate charter are called:
a.   legal capital shares.
b.   par value shares.
c.   no par value shares.
d.   stated value shares.

(SO 2)   3. Davis Corporation issues 1,000 common shares in exchange for a piece of equipment, on a date when its common shares are trading at $5 per share. The piece of equipment is valued at $6,000 on the date of the acquisition. If Davis prepares

CHAPTER 11   Reporting and Analyzing Shareholders' Equity   213

financial statements in accordance with IFRS, the journal entry to record the
transaction should credit Common Shares for:
a. $1,000
b. $5,000.
c. $6,000.
d. $5,000 or $6,000, whichever is more reliably determinable.

4.   If 3,000 common shares are sold for $6 per share, the journal entry to record the   (SO 2)
transaction would include a:
a.   credit to Investments for $18,000.
b.   credit to Cash for $18,000.
c.   credit to Retained Earnings for $18,000.
d.   credit to Common Shares for $18,000.

5.   Assume that a corporation issued a total of 20,000 common shares for $100,000,   (SO 2)
and that it reacquires and retires 2,000 of those common shares at a price of $4 per
share. The journal entry to record reacquisition of the 2,000 shares would include a:
a.   debit to Contributed Capital—Reacquisition of Common Shares for $2,000.
b.   credit to Contributed Capital—Reacquisition of Common Shares for $2,000.
c.   credit to Common Shares for $10,000.
d.   debit to Common Shares for $8,000.

6.   Which of the following statements is *not* correct?   (SO 2, 3)
a.   Dividends cannot be paid to common shareholders while any dividend on
preferred shares is in arrears.
b.   Dividends in arrears on preferred shares are not considered a liability.
c.   Dividends may be paid on common shares while dividends are in arrears on
preferred shares.
d.   When preferred shares are non-cumulative, any dividend not declared in a
year is lost forever.

7.   On December 1, a corporation declares a $1 cash dividend per share on its   (SO 4)
500,000 common shares. The payment date journal entry, recorded on December
20, includes a debit to:
a.   Dividends Payable for $500,000.
b.   Cash Dividends for $500,000.
c.   Cash for $500,000.
d.   Common Stock Dividends Distributable for $500,000.

8.   A corporation is authorized to sell 1 million common shares and has issued   (SO 4)
500,000 shares. The board of directors declares a 10% stock dividend. How many
new shares will be issued as a result of the stock dividend?
a.   100,000.
b.   50,000.
c.   None. The corporation will pay the dividend in cash.
d.   None of the above is correct.

9.   The board of directors of a corporation declares a 5% stock dividend when there are   (SO 4)
20,000 common shares issued. On the declaration date, the fair value of each share
is $40. The journal entry to record the declaration of the stock dividend includes a:
a.   debit to Stock Dividends for $1,000.
b.   debit to Cash for $40,000.

214   **Study Guide to Accompany Financial Accounting: Tools for Business Decision-Making, Fifth Canadian Edition**

    c.   credit to Common Stock Dividends Distributable for $40,000.

    d.   credit to Common Shares for $40,000.

(SO 4)   10.   A corporation has 100,000 common shares issued with a fair value of $80 per share. If the board of directors declares a 2-for-1 stock split:

    a.   the number of shares doubles and fair value per share decreases to $40.

    b.   both the number of shares and fair value per share remain the same.

    c.   the number of shares reduces by half and fair value per share doubles.

    d.   both the number of shares and fair value per share reduce by half.

(SO 4)   11.   A retained earnings restriction:

    a.   makes a portion of the balance of retained earnings unavailable for dividends.

    b.   may be legal or contractual in nature, or it may be voluntary.

    c.   is generally disclosed in notes to the financial statements.

    d.   All of the above are correct.

(SO 4)   12.   Declaration of a cash dividend has the following effects on the statement of financial position:

	Total Assets	Total Liabilities	Total Shareholders' Equity
a.	Increase	Decrease	No change
b.	No change	Increase	Decrease
c.	Decrease	Increase	Decrease
d.	Decrease	No change	Increase

(SO 5)   13.   Red Corporation prepares financial statements in accordance with IFRS. It has the following accounts and balances: Contributed Capital, $23,000; Retained Earnings, $30,000; and Accumulated Other Comprehensive Income, $10,000. Red's total shareholders' equity is:

    a. $63,000.

    b. $53,000.

    c. $40,000.

    d. $33,000.

(SO 5)   14.   Accumulated other comprehensive income is shown on the:

    a.   income statement.

    b.   statement of comprehensive income.

    c.   shareholders' equity section of the statement of financial position.

    d.   statement of retained earnings.

(SO 5)   15.   A corporation has the following accounts and balances:

Retained Earnings	$(10,000)
Common Stock Dividends Distributable	20,000
Common Shares	255,000
Accumulated Other Comprehensive Income	50,000
Dividends Payable	25,000

CHAPTER 11   Reporting and Analyzing Shareholders' Equity   215

What is total shareholders' equity?
a. $335,000
b. $360,000
c. $340,000
d. $315,000

16. In the shareholders' equity section of the statement of financial position: (SO 5)
a. dividends in arrears appear as a retained earnings restriction.
b. both preferred and common shares appear under Share Capital.
c. Common Stock Dividends Distributable appears in its own subsection of shareholders' equity.
d. Common Stock Dividends Distributable appears as a contra account to Retained Earnings.

17. Which of the following is a complete list of categories that might appear in the   (SO 5)
shareholders' equity section of the statement of financial position of a company using IFRS?
a. Retained Earnings and Common Stock Dividends Distributable
b. Share Capital and Retained Earnings
c. Preferred Shares and Common Shares
d. Contributed Capital, Retained Earnings, and Accumulated Other Comprehensive Income

Use the following information for questions 18–20.

Consider the following data for Blue Corporation:

Gross profit	$900,000
Profit	$800,000
Number of common shares issued	400,000
Common dividends per share	$0.75
Preferred dividends	$50,000
Price per preferred share	$25
Price per common share	$20
Number of preferred shares issued	110,000
Average common shareholders' equity	$3,000,000

18. What is Blue's return on common shareholders' equity?   (SO 6)
a. 25.0%
b. 26.7%
c. 30.0%
d. 29.1%

19. What is Blue's payout ratio?   (SO 6)
a. 37.5%
b. 33.3%
c. 40.0%
d. 35.0%

216   Study Guide to Accompany Financial Accounting: Tools for Business Decision-Making, Fifth Canadian Edition

(SO 6)   20. What is Blue's dividend yield?

    a.   3.0%

    b.   3.8%

    c.   3.2%

    d.   4.0%

(SO 6)   21. During its past fiscal year, a corporation had a profit of $175,000, and paid preferred share dividends of $50,000 and common share dividends of $25,000. The corporation had 80,000 common shares issued at the beginning of the year, and issued an additional 40,000 shares halfway through the year. The corporation's earnings per share is:

    a. $0.83

    b. $1.00

    c. $1.04

    d. $1.25

Problems

(SO 2, 4)   1. Windsor Corporation shows the following information:

Common shares, 500,000 no par value shares authorized, 300,000 shares issued	$1,700,000
Retained earnings	3,200,000

Record the following transactions:

a.   Sold 10,000 common shares for $9 per share.

b.   Declared and distributed a 15% stock dividend. Fair value of the shares on this date was $12 per share.

c.   Sold 8,000 common shares for $15 per share.

d.   Declared a 2-for-1 stock split. Fair value of the shares on this date was $18 per share.

e.   Declared and paid a $0.10-per-share cash dividend.

Account Titles	Debit	Credit

CHAPTER 11 Reporting and Analyzing Shareholders' Equity 217

2. At June 30, 2012, Atlantis Corporation had the following selected account balances: (SO 2)

Common shares, no par value, 100,000 shares issued $500,000

Contributed capital—reacquisition of common shares   20,000

Prepare journal entries to record each of the following two independent situations:

a. On July 1, 2012, Atlantis reacquires and retires 70,000 of its shares for $4 each.
b. On July 1, 2012, Atlantis reacquires and retires 70,000 of its shares for $5.50 each.

Account Titles	Debit	Credit

3. Axwell Corporation had the following shareholders' equity balances at January 1, 2012: (SO 5, 6)

Common shares, no par value, 900,000 shares
     authorized; 700,000 shares issued $6,610,000

Retained earnings   850,000

Accumulated other comprehensive income   188,000

The following information is available for the year ended December 31, 2012:
Issued 20,000 common shares for $200,000.
Reported profit of $360,000.
Declared dividends of $0.10 per share to shareholders of record on December 31, 2012.
Reported an unrealized gain (other comprehensive income) of $45,000.

218 Study Guide to Accompany Financial Accounting: Tools for Business Decision-Making, Fifth Canadian Edition

The price per common share on December 31, 2012, was $10.
a. Prepare the statement of changes in equity for the year ended December 31, 2012.
b. Calculate the payout ratio, dividend yield, and return on common shareholders' equity for 2012.

(SO 6)   4. Nenshi Corporation, a private company, has the following shareholders' equity accounts at January 1, 2012:

$2 non-cumulative preferred shares (20,000 shares issued)	$1,050,000
Common shares (100,000 shares issued)	4,000,000
Retained earnings	3,750,000
Total shareholders' equity	$8,800,000

The following transactions occurred during 2012:

Mar. 1   Reacquired and retired 4,800 common shares for $38 per share.

July 1   Issued 12,000 common shares in exchange for land with a fair value of $525,000.

Sept. 20   Declared a preferred dividend to shareholders of record on October 17, payable on October 31.

Nov. 1   Issued 12,000 common shares for $45 per share.

Dec. 31   Profit for the year ended December 31, 2012, was $549,600.

a. Calculate earnings per share for 2012.
b. Is Nenshi Corporation required to report its 2012 earnings per share on its income statement?
c. Prepare the statement of retained earnings for the year ended December 31, 2012.

(SO 5, 6)   5. Refer to the HMV and WHSmith financial statements found in the appendices at the end of this study guide for information in answering the following questions. Do not forget to use the **Decision Toolkit** approach for help in answering the questions.
a. Which financial statements include information about shares?
b. What is the payout ratio for both HMV and WHSmith for 2010 and 2009?
c. What is the return on common shareholders' equity for both HMV and WHSmith for 2010?

Solutions to Self-Test

Multiple Choice

1. d   The other three choices are considered advantages of the corporate form of business organization.

2. c   There is no such thing as legal capital shares. Par value shares have a specified (legal) value.

CHAPTER 11 Reporting and Analyzing Shareholders' Equity 219

3. c Under IFRS, when shares are issued for noncash consideration, they would be recorded at the fair value of the consideration received (in this case, fair value of the piece of equipment). Under ASPE, the shares would be recorded at the fair value of the consideration received or fair value of the shares, whichever is more reliably determinable.

4. d The journal entry is:

Cash	18,000	
Common Shares		18,000

5. b The average cost per share is: $100,000 ÷ 20,000 = $5 per share. The journal entry to record reacquisition is:

Common Shares (2,000 × $5)	10,000	
Contributed Capital—Reacquisition		
of Common Shares		2,000
Cash (2,000 × $4)		8,000

6. c Dividends may not be paid on common shares as long as preferred dividends are in arrears.

7. a The journal entry is:

Dividends Payable	500,000	
Cash		500,000

8. b 500,000 shares × 10% = 50,000 new shares.

9. c The journal entry to record declaration of the stock dividend is:

Stock Dividends	40,000	
Common Stock Dividends		
Distributable		40,000

20,000 × 5% = 1,000 new shares; 1,000 × $40 fair value per share = $40,000.

10. a In a 2-for-1 stock split, each shareholder receives one additional share for each share they already own. Therefore, the number of shares doubles (to 200,000), and fair value per share is reduced by half (to $40 per share).

11. d Retained earnings restrictions make a portion of the balance of retained earnings unavailable for dividends. Retained earnings restrictions may be legal or contractual in nature, or they may be voluntary. No journal entry is required to record a retained earnings restriction; however, a retained earnings restriction is disclosed in the notes to the financial statements.

12. b The journal entry to record declaration of a cash dividend is:
Cash Dividends
    Dividends Payable

This journal entry results in a decrease in shareholders' equity (because the Cash Dividends account is closed into Retained Earnings) and an increase in a liability account, Dividends Payable.

220 Study Guide to Accompany Financial Accounting: Tools for Business Decision-Making, Fifth Canadian Edition

13. a $23,000 + $30,000 + $10,000 = $63,000.

14. c Accumulated other comprehensive income is the cumulative change in shareholders' equity that results from the gains and losses that bypass profit but affect shareholders' equity. Other comprehensive income, reported on the statement of comprehensive income, is added to the beginning balance of accumulated other comprehensive income to determine the ending balance of accumulated other comprehensive income, which is reported in the shareholders' equity section of the statement of financial position. Private companies preparing a statement of retained earnings do not report accumulated other comprehensive income.

15. d −$10,000 + $20,000 + $255,000 + $50,000 = $315,000.
Dividends Payable would appear under Current Liabilities.

16. b Share capital includes preferred and common shares.

17. d The following are categories reported in the shareholders' equity section of the statement of financial position: (1) contributed capital, (2) retained earnings, and (3) accumulated other comprehensive income.

18. a ($800,000 − $50,000) ÷ $3,000,000 = 25.0%.

19. a 400,000 × $0.75 = $300,000; $300,000 ÷ $800,000 = 37.5%.

20. b $0.75 ÷ $20 = 3.8%.

21. d ($175,000 − $50,000) ÷ [80,000 + (40,000 × $^6/_{12}$)] = $1.25.

Problems

1. a.

Cash	90,000	
Common Shares		90,000

(To record issue of shares—10,000 shares at $9 per share)

b.

Stock Dividends	558,000	
Common Stock Dividends Distributable		558,000

(To record declaration of 15% stock dividend)

Common Stock Dividends Distributable	558,000	
Common Shares		558,000

(To record distribution of 15% stock dividend)

310,000 shares × 15% = 46,500 new shares;

46,500 new shares × $12 fair value per share = $558,000

c.

Cash	120,000	
Common Shares		120,000

(To record issue of shares—8,000 shares at $15 per share)

d. No journal entry required. The number of shares issued at this point, 364,500 (300,000 + 10,000 + 46,500 + 8,000), doubles to 729,000. Fair value per share decreases to $9 per share.

CHAPTER 11 Reporting and Analyzing Shareholders' Equity 221

e. Cash Dividends 72,900
    Dividends Payable 72,900
    (To declare a $0.10-per-share cash dividend)
Dividends Payable 72,900
    Cash 72,900
    (To record payment of cash dividend)
    729,000 shares × $0.10 per share = $72,900

2. a. Common Shares ($500,000 ÷ 100,000 × 70,000) 350,000
    Contributed Capital—Reacquisition of 70,000
      Common Shares
    Cash (70,000 × $4) 280,000

b. Common Shares ($500,000 ÷ 100,000 × 70,000) 350,000
    Contributed Capital—Reacquisition of Shares 20,000
    Retained Earnings 15,000
    Cash (70,000 × $5.50) 385,000

3. a.

AXWELL CORPORATION
Statement of Changes in Equity
Year Ended December 31, 2012

	Common Shares		Retained Earnings	Accumulated Other Comprehensive Income	Total
	Number of Shares	Legal Capital			
Bal., Jan. 1	700,000	$6,610,000	$ 850,000	$188,000	$7,648,000
Common share issue	20,000	200,000			200,000
Dividend declaration			(72,000)		(72,000)
Comprehensive income					
Profit			360,000		360,000
Unrealized gain				45,000	45,000
Bal., Dec. 31	720,000	$6,810,000	$1,138,000	$233,000	$8,181,000

b. Payout ratio = Cash dividends to common shareholders divided by profit = $72,000 ÷ $360,000 = 20.0%.

Dividend yield = Cash dividend per common share divided by market price per share = $0.10 ÷ $10.00 = 1.0%.

222 **Study Guide to Accompany Financial Accounting: Tools for Business Decision-Making, Fifth Canadian Edition**

Return on common shareholders' equity = (Profit − Preferred dividends) divided by average common shareholders' equity, where average common shareholders' equity = ($7,648,000 + $8,181,000) ÷ 2 = $7,914,500; ($360,000 − $0) ÷ $7,914,500 = 4.5% return on common shareholders' equity.

4. a. The formula for earnings per share (EPS) is:

Profit available to common shareholders ÷ Weighted average number of common shares

Profit available to common shareholders is:

$549,600 − $40,000* = $509,600.

*Preferred dividend = 20,000 shares × $2 per share = $40,000.

Weighted average number of common shares for the year is:

Jan. 1	$100,000 \times {}^{12}/_{12} =$	100,000
Mar. 1	$(4,800) \times {}^{10}/_{12} =$	(4,000)
July 1	$12,000 \times {}^{6}/_{12} =$	6,000
Nov. 1	$12,000 \times {}^{2}/_{12} =$	2,000
Weighted average number of common shares		104,000

EPS = $509,600 ÷ 104,000 ÷ $4.90.

b. In contrast to publicly-traded companies, private companies are not required to report earnings per share on their income statements.

c.

NENSHI CORPORATION
Statement of Retained Earnings
Year Ended December 31, 2012

Balance, January 1	$3,750,000
Add: Profit	549,600
	4,299,600
Less: Preferred dividend	40,000
Balance, December 31	$4,259,600

5. Please note that the amounts shown for HMV and WHSmith are stated in pounds (£) millions.

   a. Statement of financial position, statement of changes in equity, and statement of cash flows.
   b. Payout ratio is calculated by dividing total cash dividends by profit. Total cash dividends can be read from the statement of cash flows for each company.

HMV

2009: £29.7 ÷ £44.2 = 67.2%.

2010: £31.2 ÷ £49.2 = 63.4%.

CHAPTER 11 Reporting and Analyzing Shareholders' Equity 223

WHSmith

2009: £23 ÷ £63 = 36.5%.

2010: £26 ÷ £69 = 37.7%.

c. Return on common shareholders' equity is calculated by dividing profit available to common shareholders (profit minus preferred dividends) by average common shareholders' equity.

HMV

Common shareholders' equity for 2009 = £99.6.

Common shareholders' equity for 2010 = £99.4.

Average common shareholders' equity = (£99.6 + £99.4) ÷ 2 = £99.5.

Return on common shareholders' equity for 2010 is:

£49.2 ÷ £99.5 = 49.4%.

WHSmith

Common shareholders' equity for 2009 = £188.

Common shareholders' equity for 2010 = £186.

Average common shareholders' equity = (£188 + £186) ÷ 2 = £187.

Return on common shareholders' equity for 2010 is:

£69 ÷ £187 = 36.9%.

chapter 12

Reporting and Analyzing Investments

Chapter Overview

In this chapter, you will learn about reasons to invest, and the classification of investments into two categories: non-strategic and strategic investments. You will also learn about accounting for non-strategic investments, accounting for strategic investments, and reporting of investments in the financial statements.

Review of Specific Study Objectives

Classifying Investments

- Financial investments may be made for one of two reasons:

  1. as a **non-strategic investment** to generate investment income, or
  2. as a **strategic investment** to influence or control the operations of another company in some way.

> **study objective 1**
>
> Identify reasons to invest, and classify investments.

While either debt or equity securities can be purchased for non-strategic purposes, equity securities (normally common shares) are purchased for strategic purposes. Equity securities purchased for strategic purposes are purchased to influence or control the activities of another company. Therefore, a company making a strategic investment would purchase common shares because only common shareholders have voting rights and therefore have influence or control over another company's major decisions.

226 Study Guide to Accompany Financial Accounting: Tools for Business Decision-Making, Fifth Canadian Edition

- There are several reasons for a company to purchase debt or equity securities of another company as a non-strategic investment:

  1. The company may have **excess cash** that it does not immediately need. Excess cash may arise from seasonal fluctuations in sales. When investing excess cash for short periods of time, corporations generally invest in debt securities that have low risk and high liquidity. Examples include guaranteed investment certificates, bankers' acceptances, term deposits, and treasury bills. It is usually not wise to invest short-term excess cash in equity securities, because if the value of the shares drops just before the company needs the cash again, the company will be forced to sell the shares at a loss.

  2. Excess cash may also be invested for longer periods of time to **generate investment revenue**. The company may generate investment revenue in the form of interest revenue from debt securities and dividend revenue from some equity securities.

  3. The company may also invest in debt and equity securities with the hope of selling them later at a higher price than it originally paid for them. Selling a security for a higher price than the company originally paid results in a capital gain. Non-strategic investments that are held for the purpose of earning capital gains are called **trading investments**.

- Non-strategic investments can be further classified as **short-term investments** or **long-term investments** depending on how liquid the investment is and how long management intends to hold it.

- Strategic investments can only be classified as **long-term investments**.

- Fair value of debt and equity securities can vary greatly in the time that they are held. Therefore an important question arises: how should investments be valued on the statement of financial position? Should they be valued at cost or fair value or some other value?

Accounting for Non-Strategic Investments

study objective 2
Account for non-strategic investments.

- The three major models for valuing investments are the fair value model, amortized cost model, and cost model:

  1. **Fair value model**: Under this model, debt and equity investments are adjusted upwards or downwards to reflect their fair value at year end (fair value is defined as the amount that would be exchanged between knowledgeable parties in an arm's-length [unrelated] transaction). The adjustment to fair value (unrealized gain or loss) is recorded on the income statement along with any interest or dividend revenue. When the investment is sold, the resulting gain or loss (realized gain or loss) is also recorded on the income statement.

  2. **Amortized cost model**: Under this model, the debt investment's carrying amount is not adjusted to reflect fair value (unless the debt investment is impaired); however, if the debt investment is a bond investment purchased at a discount or premium, the bond discount or premium is amortized over the period of time the bond is held, until it matures. Under the amortized cost model, no unrealized gains and losses are recorded over the period of time the debt investment is held, and any interest revenue or realized gains and losses earned on the debt investment are recorded on the income statement.

CHAPTER 12 Reporting and Analyzing Investments 227

3. **Cost model**: Under this model, the equity investment's carrying amount is not adjusted to reflect fair value (unless the equity investment is impaired). Any dividend revenue or realized gains and losses earned on the equity investment are recorded on the income statement.

- The **fair value model** is used for all non-strategic investments unless either of the following two exceptions is present:

1. **The investment is held to earn cash flows (a business model test) with fixed payment dates specified in a contract (a characteristic of asset test).** Investments held to earn cash flows on fixed payment dates are generally not purchased to earn gains through trading activities; therefore, the **amortized cost model** is used to account for these investments.
2. **The investment is not held to earn cash flows and there is no fair value available because the security does not trade in an active market.** In this case, the fair value model cannot be used so the cost model is adopted. However, this exception is rare in practice as most non-strategic investments that are held for trading purposes are made in investments that can be easily sold (investments that are traded in an active market).

Assume that Siraj Corporation has the following **non-strategic investments** on December 31, 2012, and that the current carrying amount equals cost:

Trading Investments	Cost	Fair Value	Unrealized Gain (Loss)
Royal Bank bonds	$100,000	$120,000	$20,000
Fortis shares	48,000	45,000	(3,000)
Total	$148,000	$165,000	$17,000

On December 31, 2012, Siraj has an overall unrealized gain of $17,000, because the total fair value ($165,000) exceeds the total carrying amount ($148,000) by $17,000. The overall unrealized gain of $17,000 would be reported on the income statement as other revenues and gains, and trading investments of $165,000 would be reported in the current assets section on the December 31, 2012, statement of financial position.

Adjustment of the trading investments to fair value and recognition of the unrealized gain is recorded as follows:

Trading Investments—Royal Bank Bonds	20,000	
Trading Investments—Fortis Shares		3,000
Unrealized Gain on Trading Investments		17,000

(To record unrealized gain on trading investments)

If, early in January 2013, Siraj sells its Fortis shares for $45,000, the following journal entry would be recorded:

Cash	45,000	
Trading Investments—Fortis Shares		45,000

(To record sale of Fortis shares)

228 **Study Guide to Accompany Financial Accounting: Tools for Business Decision-Making, Fifth Canadian Edition**

Although the Fortis shares originally cost $48,000, their carrying amount on the date of sale is $45,000, because the shares were written down to fair value of $45,000 on December 31, 2012.

If the shares were sold for $44,000 instead of $45,000, a realized loss of $1,000 ($45,000 – $44,000) would be recorded on the date of sale. In all, a loss of $3,000 ($48,000 – $45,000) would have been recorded on December 31, 2012, and a further loss of $1,000 would be recorded on the date of sale. Losses would be recorded in the period in which they were incurred.

- If a company has a non-strategic equity investment that is not held for trading or cannot be promptly liquidated, the company is allowed to make an irrevocable election to account for the equity investment using the **fair value through other comprehensive income model** (a modified fair value approach). The fair value through other comprehensive income model is the same as the fair value model discussed above, except that unrealized gains and losses are recorded in other comprehensive income instead of profit. When the investment is sold, its cumulative unrealized gains and losses are reversed out of other comprehensive income and recorded either in profit as realized gains or losses or directly in retained earnings. Therefore, to be able to make the necessary reversals upon sale, it is important to keep track of each investment's original cost, as well as subsequent unrealized gains and losses recorded in other comprehensive income. The fair value through other comprehensive income model is currently in use and investments accounted for under this method are known as **available-for-sale investments**. (The term *available-for-sale investments* was expected to be discontinued in the future by most companies, even if the fair value through other comprehensive income model is used.) The fair value through other comprehensive income model is not used under ASPE.

- Reported financial performance is affected by investment valuation models. For example, investments accounted for under the fair value model are adjusted to fair value at each statement of financial position date, with unrealized gains and losses included in profit. Therefore, changing market prices can have a significant impact on the company's financial position and performance.

Accounting for Strategic Investments

study objective 3
Account for strategic investments.

- The **investor** is the company that purchases (owns) the securities of the **investee** company. An investor that owns common shares has the potential to strategically influence the investee. Accounting for equity investments in common shares is based on how much influence the investor has over the investee's operating and financial policies.

Guidelines are as follows:

1. If the investor holds **less than 20%** of the investee's common shares, then the investor is presumed to have **insignificant influence** over the investee, and the investor uses the **fair value model** to account for its investment in the investee. (*Note*: although the fair value model is normally used, an irrevocable election can be made to account for the investment using the fair value through other comprehensive income model, as discussed earlier.)

CHAPTER 12   Reporting and Analyzing Investments   229

2. If the investor holds **20% to 50%** of the investee's common shares, then the investor is presumed to have **significant influence** over the investee, the investee company is the investor company's **associate**, and the investor uses the **equity method** to account for its investment in the investee. Under ASPE, the investor has a choice to use either the equity method or the cost model in accounting for significantly influenced investments.

3. If the investor holds **more than 50%** of the investee's common shares, then the investor is presumed to have **control** over the investee, the investee company is a **subsidiary company** of the investor, and the investor company is referred to as the **parent company**. The investee remains a separate legal entity but is considered part of a group of corporations controlled by the parent. In order to show users of the parent's financial statements the full extent of the group's operations, the financial statements of all entities within the group are combined together, resulting in **consolidated financial statements**. In its own books, the parent company records its investment in the investee using the cost model or the equity method.

- It is important to note that the presumption of insignificant or significant influence may not be valid if other evidence exists to refute it. For example, an investor who holds 15% of the investee's common shares may have significant influence over the investee if the investee's remaining shares are widely held. As another example, an investor who holds 25% of the investee's common shares may not have significant influence over the investee if a majority shareholder of the investee does not allow the investor to have any influence.

- To determine an investor's influence, the following questions should be asked:

    1. Does the investor have representation on the investee's board of directors?
    2. Does the investor participate in the investee's policy-making process?
    3. Are there material transactions between the investor and the investee?
    4. Are the investor and investee exchanging managerial personnel?
    5. Is the investor providing the investee with key technical information?

    Companies are required to use judgement in determining an investor's influence, instead of blindly following the guidelines.

- Under the **equity method**, the investment is initially recorded at cost in an account called Investment in Associates. The Investment in Associates account is adjusted annually to show how the investor's equity in the associate has changed, so that the movement in the Investment in Associates account reflects the changes that are occurring in the associate's retained earnings. For example, the investor debits Investment in Associates for its share of the associate's profit, and the investor credits Investment in Associates for the investor's share of dividends declared by the associate.

- Assume that on January 1, 2012, Reiher Corporation purchased 40% of the common shares of Ott Corporation for $250,000. The journal entry is:

Jan. 1	Investment in Associates	250,000	
	Cash		250,000
	(To record purchase of Ott common shares)		

230 Study Guide to Accompany Financial Accounting: Tools for Business Decision-Making, Fifth Canadian Edition

For the year ended December 31, 2012, Ott reported $200,000 of profit and paid dividends of $50,000. Under the equity method, Reiher would record the following journal entries:

Dec. 31	Investment in Associates	80,000	
	Revenue from Investment in Associates		80,000
	(To record 40% equity in Ott's profit: $200,000 × 40% = $80,000)		

Dec. 31	Cash	20,000	
	Investment in Associates		20,000
	(To record dividend received: $50,000 × 40% = $20,000)		

After these journal entries, the balance in Investment in Associates totals $310,000 ($250,000 + $80,000 − $20,000).

- As discussed earlier, the cost model is used if a non-strategic investment is not held to earn cash flows and there is no fair value available because the security does not trade in an active market. In terms of strategic investments, the cost model may also be used under ASPE to account for significantly influenced investments. Under the cost model, the investment is initially recorded at cost, and dividend revenue is recorded when the investee declares a dividend. Application of the cost model is the same regardless of whether the equity investment is short-term or long-term.

- Assume that on October 1, 2012, Yellow Corporation acquired 2,000 common shares of Gard Corporation at $50 per share, and that Yellow does not plan to trade these shares. Gard is a private corporation with a total of 16,000 common shares, meaning that Yellow has a 12.5% (2,000 ÷ 16,000) ownership interest in Gard. Because Gard is a private corporation and its shares are not actively traded, we will assume the fair value of Gard's shares is not readily obtainable. Yellow's investment in Gard would be accounted for using the cost model as follows:

Oct. 1	Long-Term Investments	100,000	
	Cash		100,000
	(To record purchase of 2,000 common shares of Gard)		

This investment would be reported as a non-current asset on the statement of financial position if it is held for strategic purposes.

On December 1, 2012, a $3-per-share dividend is declared and paid by Gard. The journal entry is:

Dec. 1	Cash	6,000	
	Dividend Revenue		6,000
	(To record dividend received: 2,000 × $3 = $6,000)		

CHAPTER 12 Reporting and Analyzing Investments 231

Dividend Revenue is reported as other revenue on the income statement.

On December 15, 2012, Yellow sells its shares for $105,000. The journal entry is:

Dec. 15	Cash	105,000	
	Long-Term Investments		100,000
	Realized Gain on Long-Term Investments		5,000
	(To record sale of Gard common shares)		

The gain is reported in the other revenues and gains section of the income statement. A loss would be reported in the other expenses and losses section of the income statement.

Reporting Investments

- Realized gains and losses, unrealized gains and losses from trading investments, and interest and dividend revenues are included in the other revenues and gains or other expenses and losses section of the **income statement**.

> **study objective 4**
>
> Indicate how investments are reported in the financial statements.

- The statement of **comprehensive income** includes not only profit reported on the income statement but also "other comprehensive income" transactions. Examples of other comprehensive income include certain translation gains and losses on foreign currency; revaluations of property, plant, and equipment under the revaluation model; and unrealized gains and losses on available-for-sale investments using the fair value through other comprehensive income model; among other items that are covered in more advanced accounting courses. Companies can present the items included in other comprehensive income in a separate statement or at the bottom of the income statement in a combined statement of comprehensive income.

- The **statement of changes in equity** includes changes in share capital, retained earnings, accumulated other comprehensive income (loss), and any other equity items that a company might report.

- The **statement of financial position** includes investments that are classified as short-term or long-term. Trading investments are always classified as **current assets**, whereas available-for-sale investments may be classified as either current or long-term, depending on whether the investment can be liquidated promptly and when management intends to sell it. Regardless of their classification, these investments are carried at fair value. Debt and equity securities are usually combined and reported as one portfolio amount on the statement of financial position.

- Long-term investments include debt securities held to earn interest revenue until they mature and consequently they are reported at amortized cost. Any portion that is expected to mature within the year is classified as a current asset. Long-term investments include equity securities that are purchased to have significant influence or control over the investee. If an investment is not large enough to exercise either significant influence or control but is still being held for long-term purposes, it is typically accounted for using the fair value model unless the investor opts to use the fair value through other comprehensive income model. As discussed earlier, investments recorded using the latter approach are currently called available-for-sale securities.

- If an investor owns 20%–50% of the common shares of an investee, and the investor has significant influence over the investee, the investor accounts for the investment using the equity method (with the option to use the cost model under ASPE), and reports the investment as a long-term investment. If an investor owns more than 50%

232 Study Guide to Accompany Financial Accounting: Tools for Business Decision-Making, Fifth Canadian Edition

of the common shares of an investee, and the investor has control over the investee, **consolidated financial statements** are prepared, which show the combined assets and liabilities of both the parent and subsidiary companies. Most publicly traded companies present consolidated financial statements.

Investments in Bonds with Discounts and Premiums

study objective 5
Compare the accounting for a bond investment and a bond payable (Appendix 12A).

- Short-term investments in bonds are usually accounted for using the fair value model, because they are not held for the purposes of earning interest until the bond matures. Long-term investments in bonds, on the other hand, are usually accounted for using the amortized cost model.

- When a bond is purchased, the investment account is debited for the purchase cost of the bond (i.e., for the face value net of any premium or discount). You will recall from Chapter 10 that premiums or discounts on long-term bonds payable must be amortized using the effective-interest method of amortization. Similarly, premiums or discounts on bond investments must be amortized using the effective-interest method. However, under ASPE, companies have the choice of amortizing premiums and discounts on a straight-line basis over the period to maturity if the results do not differ materially from the effective-interest method. This is true for all bond investments except those that are trading investments. Because these investments are expected to be held only for a short time, there is no requirement to amortize any premium or discount.

- For a long-term bond investment, amortization is recorded in an Interest Revenue account. If there is a bond premium on a long-term bond investment, the Interest Revenue account and carrying amount of the investment are *reduced* by the amortization amount. If there is a bond discount, the Interest Revenue account and carrying amount of the investment are *increased* by the amortization amount.

comparing
IFRS and ASPE

Key Differences	International Financial Reporting Standards (IFRS)	Accounting Standards for Private Enterprises (ASPE)
Fair value through OCI model	Allowed	Not allowed because other comprehensive income is not reported
Accounting for investments in associates	Must use the equity method	Choice of using the equity method or cost model if shares do not have quoted prices. If they are quoted, the equity method or the fair value model can be chosen
Investments in bonds	Must use the effective-interest method to amortize any bond premium or discount	Normally will use the effective-interest method to amortize any bond premium or discount but permitted to use alternative methods if the results do not differ materially from the effective-interest method
Consolidation of financial statements	Consolidation required if investor controls investee	Consolidation is optional. If consolidation is not used, there is a choice of using the equity method or cost model if shares do not have quoted prices. If they are quoted, the equity method or the fair value model can be chosen

CHAPTER 12 Reporting and Analyzing Investments 233

Chapter Self-Test

As you work through the questions and problems, remember to use the **Decision Toolkit** discussed and used in the text:

1. *Decision Checkpoints*: Ask a question relevant to the decision being made.
2. *Info Needed for Decision*: Make a choice regarding the information needed to answer the question.
3. *Tools to Use for Decision*: Review what the information identified in step 2 does for the decision-making process.
4. *How to Evaluate Results*: Identify specifically how the information identified in step 2 should be evaluated to answer the question relevant to the decision being made.

Note: The notation "(SO 1)" means that the question relates to study objective 1.

All questions marked with an asterisk (*) relate to the material in Appendix 12A.

Multiple Choice

Please circle the correct answer.

1. Corporations invest in other companies for all of the following reasons *except* to   (SO 1)
   a. use excess cash that they do not immediately need.
   b. generate investment revenue.
   c. meet strategic goals.
   d. increase the trading volume of other companies' shares.

2. Non-strategic investments can include: (SO 1)
   a. debt investments held to earn interest.
   b. trading investments.
   c. available-for-sale investments.
   d. all of the above.

3. On January 1, 2012, Meyers Corporation acquired, as a trading investment, 20   (SO 2)
   Sayer Corporation five-year, 6%, $1,000 bonds for $22,000. Meyers Corporation's year end is December 31. The journal entry to record acquisition of the bonds includes a debit to:
   a. Trading Investments—Sayer Bonds for $20,000.
   b. Bonds Payable for $22,000.
   c. Trading Investments—Sayer Bonds for $22,000.
   d. Cash for $22,000.

4. Refer to the facts in question 3 above. On December 31, 2012, the fair value of   (SO 2)
   the Sayer bonds is $19,000. Meyers' adjusting journal entry on December 31, 2012, would include a:
   a. debit to Unrealized Loss on Trading Investments for $3,000.
   b. debit to Unrealized Loss on Trading Investments for $1,000.
   c. credit to Cash for $3,000.
   d. credit to Trading Investments—Sayer Bonds for $1,000.

5. Debt investments held to earn interest revenue are valued at: (SO 2)
   a. acquisition cost.
   b. fair value.

234   **Study Guide to Accompany Financial Accounting: Tools for Business Decision-Making, Fifth Canadian Edition**

c.   amortized cost.

d.   equity value.

(SO 2)   6.   An unrealized gain on trading investments would be shown:

a.   in the "other revenues and gains" section in the income statement.

b.   in the statement of cash flows.

c.   as other comprehensive income in the statement of comprehensive income.

d.   as a contra account to the trading investment account on the statement of financial position.

(SO 2)   7.   Caissie Corporation has a portfolio of trading investments with a total carrying amount of $75,000. On the statement of financial position date, the portfolio's fair value is $78,000. The adjusting journal entry is:

a.	Trading Investments	3,000	
	Unrealized Gain on Trading Investments		3,000
b.	Unrealized Gain on Trading Investments	3,000	
	Trading Investments		3,000
c.	Cash	3,000	
	Unrealized Gain on Trading Investments		3,000
d.	No adjusting journal entry is required.		

(SO 3)   8.   Mack Corporation owns 10% of the common shares of Cepollina Corporation. When Mack receives $5,000 in cash dividends from Cepollina, the journal entry on Mack's books is:

a.	Cash	5,000	
	Dividend Revenue		5,000
b.	Cash	5,000	
	Trading Investments—Cepollina Shares		5,000
c.	Cash	5,000	
	Investment in Associates		5,000
d.	Dividend Revenue	5,000	
	Cash		5,000

(SO 3)   9.   Mack Corporation owns 40% of the common shares of Cepollina Corporation. When Mack receives $5,000 in cash dividends from Cepollina, the journal entry on Mack's books is:

a.	Cash	5,000	
	Dividend Revenue		5,000
b.	Cash	5,000	
	Trading Investments—Cepollina Shares		5,000

CHAPTER 12   Reporting and Analyzing Investments   235

c.   Cash   5,000
        Investment in Associates   5,000
d.   Dividend Revenue   5,000
        Cash   5,000

10. Ross Corporation owns 40% of the common shares of Searcy Corporation.   (SO 3)
     When Searcy reports profit of $200,000, the journal entry on Ross's books is:

a.   Cash   80,000
        Revenue from Investment in   80,000
        Associates

b.   Investment in Associates   80,000
        Revenue from Investment in   80,000
        Associates

c.   Investment in Associates   200,000
        Revenue from Investment in   200,000
        Associates

d.   Investment in Associates   200,000
        Cash   200,000

11. Trice Corporation, a publicly-traded company, purchased 80% of the common   (SO 4)
     shares of Waters Corporation. Trice is the _____ company, and Waters is
     the _____ company.
     a.   subsidiary, controlling
     b.   controlling, subsidiary
     c.   subsidiary, parent
     d.   parent, subsidiary

12. With respect to Trice's purchase of Waters Corporation shares in question 11   (SO 4)
     above, which of the following is true?
     a.   Only consolidated financial statements are prepared.
     b.   Trice and Waters each prepare their own financial statements. In its own finan-
          cial statements, Trice uses the equity method to account for its investment in
          Waters. Consolidated financial statements are also prepared.
     c.   Trice and Waters each prepare their own financial statements, and consoli-
          dated financial statements are not prepared.
     d.   Trice prepares its own financial statements, Waters does not prepare its own
          financial statements, and consolidated financial statements are prepared.

13. A portfolio of trading investments that is intended to be sold in two years is   (SO 4)
     reported in the:
     a.   shareholders' equity section of the statement of financial position.
     b.   current assets section of the statement of financial position.
     c.   non-current assets section of the statement of financial position.
     d.   statement of comprehensive income.

14. Shares of another corporation purchased to gain some influence in the investee   (SO 4)
     corporation are reported in the:
     a.   shareholders' equity section of the statement of financial position.
     b.   current assets section of the statement of financial position.

236 Study Guide to Accompany Financial Accounting: Tools for Business Decision-Making, Fifth Canadian Edition

    c.   non-current assets section of the statement of financial position.

    d.   statement of changes in equity.

Use the following information for questions 15–17.

Pujol acquired 100, five-year, 7%, $1,000 bonds issued by Smec on January 1, 2012, for $95,948. The bond price is based on a market interest rate of 8%. The bonds pay interest on July 1 and January 1. Assume that Pujol intends to hold these bonds until maturity.

(SO 2, 5) *15. Pujol's journal entry to record the investment on January 1 is:

    a.   Long-Term Investments   95,948

                Cash   95,948

    b.   Long-Term Investments   95,948

        Unrealized Loss   4,052

                Cash   100,000

    c.   Cash   95,948

                Bonds Payable   95,948

    d.   Long-Term Investments   100,000

                Cash   100,000

(SO 2, 5) *16. On July 1, Pujol receives interest from the Smec bonds. Pujol's journal entry to record receipt of interest is:

    a.   Interest Expense ($95,948 $\times$ 8% $\times$ $^6/_{12}$)   3,838

                Bonds Payable ($3,838 − $3,500)   338

                Cash   3,500

    b.   Cash ($100,000 $\times$ 7% $\times$ $^6/_{12}$)   3,500

        Long-Term Investments ($3,838 − $3,500)   338

             Interest Revenue ($95,948 $\times$ 8% $\times$ $^6/_{12}$)   3,838

    c.   Cash ($100,000 $\times$ 7% $\times$ $^6/_{12}$)   3,500

        Bond Payable ($3,838 − $3,500)   338

            Interest Revenue ($95,948 $\times$ 8% $\times$ $^6/_{12}$)   3,838

    d.   Cash ($100,000 $\times$ 7% $\times$ $^6/_{12}$)   3,500

        Interest Revenue   3,500

(SO 2, 5) *17. Smec's journal entry to record the issue of the bonds on January 1 is:

    a.   Cash   95,948

                Long-Term Investments   95,948

    b.   Cash   95,948

        Unrealized Loss   4,052

             Bonds Payable   100,000

CHAPTER 12   Reporting and Analyzing Investments   237

c.	Cash	95,948	
	Bonds Payable		95,948
d.	Cash	100,000	
	Bonds Payable		100,000

Problems

1. Assume that on December 31, 2012, Turegun Corporation's trading investments   (SO 2)
    have the following carrying amounts and fair values:

Trading Investments	Carrying Amount	Fair Value	Unrealized Gain (Loss)
Royal Bank bonds	$125,000	$128,000	$3,000
Rogers shares	75,000	70,000	(5,000)
Total	$200,000	$198,000	$(2,000)

a. Prepare the required adjusting journal entry on December 31, 2012.

b. Assume that on January 30, 2013, Turegun sells its Rogers shares for
    $72,000. Prepare the journal entry to record the sale.

Date	Account Titles	Debit	Credit

2. On February 1, 2012, Floss Corporation, a publicly-traded company, acquired   (SO 3)
    10% of the common shares of Georgia Corporation for $50,000. Georgia is a
    private corporation and Floss does not plan to trade these securities. On March
    31, 2012, Georgia reported $300,000 of profit and paid cash dividends of $80,000.
    On July 1, 2012, Floss sells the Georgia shares for $55,000.

238   Study Guide to Accompany Financial Accounting: Tools for Business Decision-Making, Fifth Canadian Edition

a.   Record Floss's purchase of the shares and any other necessary journal entries, assuming Floss uses the cost model to account for this investment.

Date	Account Titles	Debit	Credit

b.   Assume the same data as shown above, but that the shares purchased represent 30% of the common shares of Georgia. Record Floss's purchase of the shares and any other necessary journal entries, assuming Floss uses the equity method to account for this investment. Assume that on July 1, 2012, Floss sells the Georgia shares for $115,000.

Date	Account Titles	Debit	Credit

CHAPTER 12   Reporting and Analyzing Investments   239

3.   The following selected general ledger account balances are provided for Rebus   (SO 4)
Corporation as at December 31, 2012.

Accounts payable	$ 15,000
Accounts receivable	64,000
Accumulated depreciation—building	10,000
Accumulated other comprehensive income	14,000
Advertising expense	1,000
Allowance for doubtful accounts	20,000
Bad debts expense	2,000
Bonds payable	98,000
Building	350,000
Cash	140,000
Common shares, no par value, 40,000 shares issued	271,000
Debt investments (long-term)	15,000
Depreciation expense	5,000
Dividends	10,000
Employee benefits expense	1,000
Income tax expense	13,000
Interest expense	8,000
Interest payable	13,000
Investment in associates	30,000
Land	100,000
Mortgage payable	175,000
Notes payable, six-month	40,000
Realized gain on trading investments	15,000
Retained earnings, January 1	15,000
Salaries expense	10,000
Salaries payable	2,000
Sales tax payable	13,000
Service revenue	75,000
Trading investments	27,000

a.   Calculate ending retained earnings, as at December 31.
b.   Prepare a statement of financial position for Rebus Corporation as at
December 31, 2012, assuming $30,000 of the mortgage is payable
next year.

240   Study Guide to Accompany Financial Accounting: Tools for Business Decision-Making, Fifth Canadian Edition

(SO 5) *4.   On January 1, 2012, as a long-term investment, Burber Corporation acquired $650,000 of 7%, five-year bonds of Highlife Corporation for $698,354. The price of the bonds is based on a market interest rate of 6%. The bonds pay interest on July 1 and January 1.

a.   Prepare the journal entry to record the purchase on January 1, 2012.

b.   Prepare the journal entry to record the semi-annual interest received on July 1, 2012.

c.   The bonds are sold on September 1, 2012, at 97. Prepare the journal entry to record the receipt of interest and sale of the bonds.

Date	Account Titles	Debit	Credit

CHAPTER 12   Reporting and Analyzing Investments   241

5.   Refer to the HMV and WHSmith financial statements found in the appendices at   (SO 4)
the end of this study guide for information in answering the following question.
What information is provided regarding investments?

Solutions to Self-Test

Multiple Choice

1.   d   Answers a, b, and c are all reasons why corporations invest in other
companies.

2.   d   Non-strategic investments are made to generate investment income and can
include debt and equity investments.

3.   c   The journal entry is:

Trading Investments—Sayer Bonds	22,000	
Cash		22,000

4.   a   The journal entry is:

Unrealized Loss on Trading Investments	3,000	
Trading Investments—Sayer Bonds		3,000

5.   c   Debt investments held to earn interest revenue are valued at amortized cost,
because any premiums or discounts included in the investment account
must be amortized.

6.   a   An unrealized gain or loss on trading investments is included in profit.

7.   a.   Trading investments are valued using the fair value model, under which
investments are reported at fair value on the statement of financial position.
In recording investments at fair value, the difference between carrying
amount and fair value is called an unrealized gain. In this case, the unrealized gain is $78,000 - $75,000 = $3,000$.

8.   a   Mack's investment in Cepollina is non-strategic. Whether the fair value
model or the cost method is used, dividend revenue is recorded on the
income statement with other revenues and gains.

9.   c   Mack's investment in Cepollina is strategic. With 40% of the common
shares of Cepollina, Mack is presumed to have significant influence over
it; therefore, Mack uses the equity method to account for its investment
in Cepollina.

10. b   Ross's investment in Searcy is strategic. With 40% of the common shares
of Searcy, Ross is presumed to have significant influence over it; therefore, Ross uses the equity method to account for its investment in Searcy
($200,000 \times 40\% = $80,000$).

242 **Study Guide to Accompany Financial Accounting: Tools for Business Decision-Making, Fifth Canadian Edition**

11. d   "Controlling" refers to the type of ownership interest the parent has in the subsidiary.

12. b   Consolidated financial statements are prepared in addition to each company's financial statements.

13. b   Trading investments are reported in the current assets section of the statement of financial position at fair value, regardless of when management intends to sell them.

14. c   Shares of another corporation purchased to gain significant influence or control over the investee corporation are classified as long-term investments in the non-current assets section of the statement of financial position.

15. a   The bonds are recorded at the acquisition cost of $95,948. The $4,052 discount on the bonds is not recorded separately.

16. b   Interest received is calculated by multiplying the face value of the bond investment by the coupon interest rate per semi-annual period. Pujol will collect interest of $3,500 ($100,000 $\times$ 7% $\times$ $^6/_{12}$) semi-annually on July 1 and January 1.

Interest revenue is calculated by multiplying the carrying amount of the bond investment by the market rate of interest per semi-annual interest period. Pujol's interest revenue is $3,838 ($95,948 $\times$ 8% $\times$ $^6/_{12}$) for the first interest period. Interest revenue is then compared with interest received to determine the amount of discount to amortize (i.e., the portion of the $4,052 discount that is amortized this six-month period). Discount amortization is $338 ($3,838 $-$ $3,500), in this case, and is debited to the bond investment account.

17. c   The bond discount is netted against the bonds' face value in the bonds payable account ($100,000 $-$ $4,052).

Problems

1.

a.   Dec. 31, 2012   Unrealized Loss on Trading Investments   2,000

                          Trading Investments—Royal Bank Bonds   3,000

                                 Trading Investments—Rogers Shares   5,000

                          (To record unrealized loss on trading investments)

b.   Jan. 30, 2013   Cash   72,000

                          Realized Gain on Trading Investments   2,000

                          Trading Investments—Rogers Shares   70,000

                          (To record realized gain on trading investments)

2. a.   The cost method is used because Floss's investment in Georgia is non-strategic, and because it is assumed that the fair value of the shares is not readily available (the shares are not traded in an active market since Georgia is a private corporation).

CHAPTER 12 Reporting and Analyzing Investments 243

Feb. 1, 2012   Long-Term Investments   50,000

     Cash   50,000

(To record purchase of 10% of the common shares of Georgia)

Mar. 31, 2012   Cash   8,000

     Dividend Revenue   8,000

(To record receipt of cash dividend: 10% × $80,000 = $8,000)

July 1, 2012   Cash   55,000

     Realized Gain on Long-Term Investments   5,000

     Long-Term Investments   50,000

(To record sale of Georgia common shares)

b. The equity method is used because Floss's investment in 30% of the common shares of Georgia results in significant influence over Georgia.

Feb. 1, 2012   Investment in Associates   50,000

     Cash   50,000

(To record purchase of 30% of the common shares of Georgia)

Mar. 31, 2012   Investment in Associates   90,000

     Revenue from Investment in Associates   90,000

(To record 30% equity in Georgia's profit: $300,000 × 30% = $90,000)

     Cash   24,000

     Investment in Associates   24,000

(To record dividends received: 30% × $80,000 = $24,000)

July 1, 2012   Cash   115,000

Realized Loss on Investment in Associates   1,000

     Investment in Associates   116,000

(To record sale of investment in associate: $50,000 + $90,000 − $24,000 = $116,000)

244 **Study Guide to Accompany Financial Accounting: Tools for Business Decision-Making, Fifth Canadian Edition**

3.

a. Retained Earnings = Opening retained earnings balance + all revenues − all expenses − dividends. ($15,000 + $75,000 + $15,000 − $10,000 − $1,000 − $5,000 − $1,000 − $2,000 − $8,000 − $13,000 − $10,000 = $55,000)

b.

REBUS CORPORATION
Statement of Financial Position
December 31, 2012

Assets

Current assets			
Cash			$140,000
Trading investments			27,000
Accounts receivable		$64,000	
Less: Allowance for doubtful accounts		20,000	44,000
Total current assets			211,000
Long-term investments			
Debt investments		$15,000	
Investment in associates		30,000	
Total long-term investments			45,000
Property, plant, and equipment			
Land		$100,000	
Building	$ 350,000		
Accumulated depreciation—building	10,000	340,000	
Total property, plant, and equipment			440,000
Total assets			$696,000

Liabilities and Shareholders' Equity

Current liabilities			
Accounts payable			$ 15,000
Salaries payable			2,000
Interest payable			13,000
Sales tax payable			13,000
Notes payable, 6-month			40,000
Current portion of mortgage payable			30,000
Total current liabilities			113,000
Non-current liabilities			
Bonds payable		$ 98,000	
Mortgage payable		145,000	
Total long-term liabilities			243,000
Total liabilities			356,000

CHAPTER 12   Reporting and Analyzing Investments   245

Shareholders' equity

Common shares, no par value, 40,000 shares issued	$271,000	
Retained earnings	55,000	
Accumulated other comprehensive income	14,000	
Total shareholders' equity		340,000
Total liabilities and shareholders' equity		$696,000

4.

a. Jan. 1, 2012   Long-Term Investments   698,354

      Cash   698,354

(To record purchase of Highlife bonds)

The bonds are recorded at the acquisition cost of $698,354. These bonds were issued at a premium ($698,354 − $650,000), which is netted against the acquisition cost in the investment account.

b. July 1, 2012   Cash ($650,000 $\times$ 7% $\times$ $^6/_{12}$)   22,750

      Long-Term Investments ($22,750 − $20,951)   1,799

      Interest Revenue

      ($698,354 $\times$ 6% $\times$ $^6/_{12}$)   20,951

(To record receipt of interest on Highlife bonds)

Interest revenue is compared with interest received to determine the amount of premium to amortize this six-month period. This period's premium amortization is $1,799 ($22,750 − $20,951) and is credited to the Long-Term Investments account.

c. Sep. 1, 2012   Cash ($650,000 $\times$ 7% $\times$ $^2/_{12}$)   7,583

      Long-Term Investments ($7,583 − $6,966)   617

      Interest Revenue

      ($696,555 $\times$ 6% $\times$ $^2/_{12}$)   6,966

(To record receipt of interest on Highlife bonds)

The carrying amount of the bonds must be adjusted for the premium amortization on July 1, 2012: $698,354 − $1,799 = $696,555.

Carrying amount of the bonds is now 695,938, as shown here:

Long-Term Investments			
Jan. 1	698,354		
		July 1	1,799
		Sep. 1	617
Bal. Sep. 1	695,938		

Sep. 1, 2012	Cash ($650,000 × 97%)	630,500	
	Realized Loss on Long-Term Investments	65,438	
	Long-Term Investments		695,938
	(To record sale of Highlife bonds)		

5. HMV reports investments accounted for using the equity method on its statement of financial position. WHSmith does not separately report information about debt or equity investments on its statement of financial position.

HMV reports finance revenue on its income statement. WHSmith reports investment income on its income statement.

HMV reports interest received, payments to acquire subsidiary, cash acquired with subsidiary, and dividends received from subsidiaries in the investing activities section of its cash flow statement. WHSmith reports interest received in the investing activities section of its statement of cash flows.

chapter 13

Statement of Cash Flows

Chapter Overview

In this chapter, you will learn about the purpose, content, and format of the statement of cash flows. This chapter will also help you practise preparing the operating activities section (using either the direct or the indirect method), the investing activities section, and the financing activities section of a statement of cash flows. You will also learn how to use the statement of cash flows to evaluate a company's liquidity and solvency.

Review of Specific Study Objectives

Reporting of Cash Flows

- The main purpose of the statement of cash flows is to provide information that enables users to assess a company's ability to generate cash, and the company's needs in using these cash flows. The statement of cash flows provides information about a company's increases and decreases in cash for the period, categorized by activity type (operating, investing, or financing), to help users predict the company's ability to affect the amounts and timing of cash flows.

study objective 1
Describe the purpose and content of the statement of cash flows.

- The information in a statement of cash flows helps users analyze the following aspects of a company's financial position:

1. The difference between profit and cash provided (used) by operating activities during the period.
2. The individual inflows (and outflows) of cash provided (used) by investing and financing activities during the period.
3. The company's ability to generate future cash flows.

- The statement of cash flows is often prepared based on **cash and cash equivalents**, rather than just cash. Cash equivalents are short-term, highly liquid investments that are readily convertible to cash within a very short period of time. Generally, only debt instruments due within three months are included in cash equivalents. Examples include treasury bills, commercial paper, and money market funds.

The International Accounting Standards Board and the Financial Accounting Standards Board are currently working on a joint project to improve the presentation of information in the financial statements, including the statement of cash flows. While this project is still under way, one of the proposed recommendations is to exclude "cash equivalents" from the definition of cash in the statement of cash flows. In other words, the statement of cash flows would present information about the changes in cash only, and not cash and cash equivalents. You will note in this chapter that statements of cash flows have been prepared using cash only.

- The statement of cash flows classifies cash receipts and cash payments into three types of activities:

  - **Operating activities** include transactions that create revenues and expenses. The operating activities section shows cash provided (used) by the company's principal revenue-producing operations. Ultimately, a company must generate positive cash from its operating activities in order to continue as a going concern and expand in the long term.
  - **Investing activities** include purchasing and disposing of long-term investments and long-lived assets and extending loans to debtors and collecting loans owed by debtors.
  - **Financing activities** include borrowing cash by issuing debt and repaying amounts borrowed, and obtaining cash from shareholders and paying them dividends.

- In general:

  - **Operating activities** affect income statement accounts and most current asset and current liability accounts.
  - **Investing activities** affect non-current asset accounts.
  - **Financing activities** affect non-current liability accounts and equity accounts.

- Under IFRS, interest and dividends received may be classified as either operating or investing activities, and interest and dividends paid may be classified as either operating or financing activities. However, once the choice is made, it must be applied consistently. Under ASPE, interest received and paid and dividends received are classified as operating activities, and dividends paid are classified as a financing activity.

- A company may also have significant **noncash activities**, such as issue of debt to purchase assets, issue of shares to purchase assets, conversion of debt into equity, and exchange of property, plant, and equipment. Noncash activities are not reported in the body of the statement of cash flows, but are disclosed in a note to the financial statements.

- With respect to the **format of the statement of cash flows**, the operating activities section always appears first, followed by the investing activities section, and the financing

CHAPTER 13 Statement of Cash Flows 249

activities section. Individual inflows and outflows of cash from investing and financing activities are reported separately (they are not netted). Reported inflows (and outflows) of cash provided (used) by each activity result in net cash provided (used) by operating activities, net cash provided (used) by investing activities, and net cash provided (used) by financing activities. Net cash provided (used) by each activity is totalled to arrive at net increase (decrease) in cash for the period. Net increase (decrease) in cash for the period is then added to the beginning-of-period cash balance, to arrive at the end-of-period cash balance. The end-of-period cash balance should agree with the cash balance reported on the statement of financial position.

Preparing the Statement of Cash Flows

- Because the statement of cash flows is not based on accrual accounting, it is not prepared using the adjusted trial balance.

- Information for the preparation of the statement of cash flows comes from three sources: the comparative statement of financial position, the income statement, and selected additional information (including selected transaction data).

- The four steps for preparation of a statement of cash flows are as follows:

  1. **Prepare operating activities section.** Determine the net cash provided (used) by operating activities by converting profit from the accrual basis to the cash basis.
  2. **Prepare investing activities section.** Determine the net cash provided (used) by investing activities by analyzing changes in non-current asset accounts and certain current asset accounts (that are not related to operating activities or investments held specifically for trading purposes).
  3. **Prepare financing activities section.** Determine the net cash provided (used) by financing activities by analyzing changes in non-current liability and equity accounts.
  4. **Complete the statement of cash flows.** Determine the net increase (decrease) in cash. Compare the net change in cash reported on the statement of cash flows with the change in cash reported on the statement of financial position to make sure the amounts agree.

> study objective 2
>
> Prepare the operating activities section of a statement of cash flows using one of two approaches: (a) the indirect method or (b) the direct method.

Operating Activities

- In order to perform step one (prepare the operating activities section), **profit must be converted from the accrual basis to the cash basis.** This conversion may be done by either **the indirect or the direct method.** Both methods arrive at the same amount of net cash provided (used) by operating activities, but each method calculates net cash provided (used) by operating activities differently. Note that the choice between indirect and direct method affects only the operating activities section of the statement of cash flows.

- While both the indirect and direct methods are acceptable choices in presenting cash flows from operating activities, the direct method is preferred by standard setters. It is considered to be more informative to users and easier to compare with other financial statements. Despite this preference, most companies use the indirect method because it is easier to prepare, and because it reveals less company information to competitors (it focuses on the difference between profit and net cash provided [used] by operating activities, rather than cash receipts and cash payments).

250   **Study Guide to Accompany Financial Accounting: Tools for Business Decision-Making, Fifth Canadian Edition**

---

study objective 2(a)

Prepare the operating activities section of the statement of cash flows using the indirect method.

- **Under the indirect method,** profit is converted from the accrual basis to the cash basis, by adjusting for items that affected accrual basis profit but did not affect cash. There are various expenses and losses that reduce profit but do not affect cash (for example, depreciation or loss on sale of asset), and various revenues and gains that increase profit but do not affect cash (for example, gain on sale of asset). Under the indirect method, these noncash expenses and losses are added back to profit, and the noncash revenues and gains are subtracted from profit, to convert profit to net cash provided (used) by operating activities.

- Under the indirect method, depreciation expense is often the first item added back to profit in the operating activities section. It is important to understand that depreciation expense is not added back to profit because it was a source of cash. Depreciation expense is added back to profit because the indirect method begins with profit, which includes a deduction for depreciation expense. Therefore, adding depreciation expense back to profit cancels the effect of the depreciation expense (a noncash item) that was deducted to arrive at profit.

- The textbook's discussion of the mechanics applied in analyzing increases (or decreases) in noncash current asset and current liability accounts is comprehensive. The following is a summary of adjustments to and from profit, as a result of changes in various working capital accounts, to arrive at net cash provided (used) by operating activities under the indirect method:

Change in	Add to Profit	Deduct from Profit
Current assets		
Accounts receivable	Decrease	Increase
Inventory	Decrease	Increase
Prepaid expenses	Decrease	Increase
Current liabilities		
Accounts payable	Increase	Decrease
Accrued expenses payable	Increase	Decrease

For example, if the balance in the Accounts Receivable account decreased during the period, the decrease is added to accrual-based profit in calculating cash provided (used) by operating activities. If the balance in the Accounts Receivable account increased during the period, the increase is deducted from accrual-based profit in calculating cash provided (used) by operating activities.

---

study objective 2(b)

Prepare the operating activities section of the statement of cash flows using the direct method.

- As discussed above, the choice between indirect and direct methods affects only the operating activities section of the statement of cash flows. **Under the direct method,** each item on the income statement is adjusted from the accrual basis to the cash basis, to arrive at net cash provided (used) by operating activities. Only major classes of operating cash receipts and cash payments are reported. An efficient way to apply the direct method is to analyze revenues and expenses in the order in which they are reported on the income statement.

- The textbook's discussion of the mechanics applied in analyzing cash receipts and cash payments is comprehensive. The following is a summary of formulas for calculating cash receipts and cash payments, in arriving at net cash provided (used) by operating activities under the direct method:

CHAPTER 13   Statement of Cash Flows   251

To calculate **Cash receipts from customers:**

Revenue
Add: Decrease in accounts receivable OR
Deduct: Increase in accounts receivable
Equals: Cash receipts from customers

To calculate **Cash payments to suppliers:**

Purchases*
Add: Decrease in accounts payable OR
Deduct: Increase in accounts payable
Equals: Cash payments to suppliers

*To solve for purchases:

Cost of goods sold
Add: Increase in inventory OR
Deduct: Decrease in inventory
Equals: Purchases

To calculate **Cash payments for operating expenses:**

Operating expenses
Add: Increase in prepaid expenses OR
Deduct: Decrease in prepaid expenses AND
Add: Decrease in accrued expenses payable OR
Deduct: Increase in accrued expenses payable
Equals: Cash payments for operating expenses

To calculate **Cash payments to employees:**

Salaries expense
Add: Decrease in salaries payable OR
Deduct: Increase in salaries payable
Equals: Cash payments to employees

To calculate **Cash payments for interest:**

Interest expense
Add: Decrease in interest payable OR
Deduct: Increase in interest payable
Equals: Cash payments for interest

To calculate **Cash payments for income tax:**

Income tax expense
Add: Decrease in income tax payable OR
Deduct: Increase in income tax payable
Equals: Cash payments for income tax

- Profit, depreciation, loss on sale of assets, and gain on sale of assets do not appear on a statement of cash flows under the direct method because they are accrual basis items.

- Under the direct method, cash payments are subtracted from cash receipts to arrive at net cash provided (used) by operating activities.

252 Study Guide to Accompany Financial Accounting: Tools for Business Decision-Making, Fifth Canadian Edition

- Regardless of whether the indirect or direct method is used to calculate operating activities, investing and financing activities are measured and reported in the same way.

Investing Activities

study objective 3
Prepare the investing activities section of a statement of cash flows.

- The **investing activities** section looks at cash inflows and outflows from changes in non-current asset accounts (for example, long-term investments; property, plant, and equipment; and intangible assets), and changes in certain current asset accounts (that are not related to operating activities such as short-term notes receivable issued for lending purposes rather than for trade).

- When analyzing investment accounts in particular, it is important to remove the effect of any noncash items included in the accounts, such as amortization of bond discounts and premiums, and realized and unrealized gains and losses on investments carried at fair value through profit and loss. Cash inflow or outflow reported for an investment on a statement of cash flows should consist only of the amount paid to purchase the investment or amount received upon sale of the investment.

Financing Activities

study objective 4
Prepare the financing activities section of a statement of cash flows.

- The **financing activities** section looks at cash inflows and outflows from changes in non-current liability accounts, equity accounts, and short-term loan payable accounts (including notes payable accounts) incurred for lending purposes rather than for trade.

- Note that other comprehensive income would not affect a company's statement of cash flows, because other comprehensive income items do not affect cash.

Completing the Statement of Cash Flows

study objective 5
Complete the statement of cash flows.

- Major items in the operating, investing, and financing activities sections should be listed separately (not netted against one another). For example, if a company purchases one asset for $80,000 and sells another asset for $20,000, each cash flow should be listed separately (the cash flows should not be combined and reported as a net cash outflow of $60,000).

- Reported inflows (and outflows) of cash provided (used) by each activity result in net cash provided (used) by operating activities, net cash provided (used) by investing activities, and net cash provided (used) by financing activities. Net cash provided (used) by each activity is totalled to arrive at net increase (decrease) in cash for the period. Net increase (decrease) in cash for the period is then added to the beginning-of-period cash balance, to arrive at the end-of-period cash balance. The end-of-period cash balance should agree with the cash balance reported on the statement of financial position.

Using Cash Flows to Evaluate a Company

study objective 6
Use the statement of cash flows to evaluate a company's liquidity and solvency.

- **Liquidity** is the ability of a company to pay obligations expected to become due within the next year. In Chapter 2, you learned that one measure of liquidity is the current ratio (current assets divided by current liabilities). Another measure of liquidity is the **cash current debt coverage ratio** (net cash provided [used] by operating activities divided by average current liabilities).

- **Solvency** is the ability of a company to survive over the long term. Two cash-based measures of solvency are cash total debt coverage ratio and free cash flow. The

CHAPTER 13 Statement of Cash Flows 253

cash total debt coverage ratio (net cash provided [used] by operating activities divided by average total liabilities) indicates a company's ability to repay its liabilities from cash generated by operating activities. **Free cash flow** (net cash provided [used] by operating activities – net capital expenditures – dividends paid) helps users determine how much discretionary cash flow a company has left from its operating activities available to use, for example, to expand operations, reduce debt, pursue new opportunities, or pay additional dividends.

comparing
IFRS and ASPE

Key Differences	International Financial Reporting Standards (IFRS)	Accounting Standards for Private Enterprises (ASPE)
Classification of activities	Interest and dividends received may be classified as operating or investing activities.	Interest and dividends received are classified as operating activities.
	Interest and dividends paid may be classified as operating or financing activities.	Interest paid is classified as an operating activity. Dividends paid are classified as a financing activity.
	Once the choice is made, it must be applied consistently.	

Chapter Self-Test

As you work through the questions and problems, remember to use the **Decision Toolkit** discussed and used in the text:

1. *Decision Checkpoints:* Ask a question relevant to the decision being made.
2. *Info Needed for Decision:* Make a choice regarding the information needed to answer the question.
3. *Tools to Use for Decision:* Review what the information identified in step 2 does for the decision-making process.
4. *How to Evaluate Results:* Identify specifically how the information identified in step 2 should be evaluated to answer the question relevant to the decision being made.

Note: The notation "(SO 1)" means that the question relates to study objective 1.

Multiple Choice

Please circle the correct answer.

1. The purchase of a piece of equipment is a(n)   (SO 1)
   a. operating activity.
   b. investing activity.
   c. financing activity.
   d. statement of financial position activity.

254 **Study Guide to Accompany Financial Accounting: Tools for Business Decision-Making, Fifth Canadian Edition**

(SO 1)   2. Which of the following sections is listed first on the statement of cash flows?
- a. Operating activities
- b. Investing activities
- c. Financing activities
- d. Revenue-producing activities

(SO 1)   3. Which of the following statements is correct?
- a. Significant noncash activities are never reported in a company's financial statements.
- b. Significant noncash activities are reported in the body of the statement of cash flows.
- c. Significant noncash activities are reported in a separate note to the financial statements.
- d. Significant noncash activities are always reported on the company's statement of financial position.

(SO 1)   4. The primary purpose of the statement of cash flows is to:
- a. prove that net cash provided (used) by operating activities equals the amount shown for cash on the statement of financial position.
- b. prove that revenues exceed expenses if there is a profit.
- c. provide information that enables users to assess a company's ability to generate cash, and the company's needs in using these cash flows.
- d. show the relationship between accrual basis profit and net cash provided (used) by operating activities.

(SO 1)   5. Which of the following is a source of information for the preparation of the statement of cash flows?
- a. Comparative statement of financial position
- b. Current period income statement
- c. Selected additional information
- d. All of the above

(SO 2)   6. If a company reports a loss, it:
- a. may still have positive net cash provided by operating activities.
- b. will not be able to pay cash dividends.
- c. will not be able to get a loan from a bank.
- d. will not be able to purchase more assets.

(SO 2)   7. An indirect method statement of cash flows is the same as a direct method statement of cash flows for the same company, except for the
- a. significant noncash activities section.
- b. operating activities section.
- c. investing activities section.
- d. financing activities section.

(SO 2a)   8. If the indirect method is used for preparation of the statement of cash flows, a decrease in accounts receivable is recorded as a(n):
- a. cash inflow in the investing activities section.
- b. cash inflow in the financing activities section.

CHAPTER 13   Statement of Cash Flows   255

   c.   addition to profit in the operating activities section.
   d.   deduction from profit in the operating activities section.

9. If the indirect method is used for preparation of the statement of cash flows, an   (SO 2a)
    increase in accounts payable is recorded as a(n):
    a.   cash inflow in the investing activities section.
    b.   cash inflow in the financing activities section.
    c.   addition to profit in the operating activities section.
    d.   deduction from profit in the operating activities section.

10. A company has $200,000 of profit, $500,000 of revenues, and an increase in   (SO 2b)
    accounts receivable of $50,000. If the company uses the direct method of preparing the statement of cash flows, cash receipts from customers total:
    a. $500,000.
    b. $450,000.
    c. $300,000.
    d. $150,000.

11. A company has a cost of goods sold of $300,000, an increase in inventory of   (SO 2b)
    $100,000, and an increase in accounts payable of $30,000. If the company uses the direct method of preparing the statement of cash flows, purchases total:
    a. $400,000.
    b. $370,000.
    c. $300,000.
    d. $200,000.

12. A company has a cost of goods sold of $300,000, an increase in inventory of   (SO 2b)
    $100,000, and an increase in accounts payable of $30,000. If the company uses the direct method of preparing the statement of cash flows, cash payments to suppliers total:
    a. $400,000.
    b. $370,000.
    c. $300,000.
    d. $200,000.

13. A company's purchase of land paid for with the issue of long-term bonds is   (SO 3, 4)
    reported as a(n):
    a.   operating activity.
    b.   investing activity outflow and financing activity inflow.
    c.   investing activity inflow and financing activity outflow.
    d.   significant noncash investing and financing activity that merits disclosure.

The following information relates to questions 14 and 15:
On December 31, 2011, the balance in ABC Co.'s cash account is $12,500. During 2011, ABC Co. had cash receipts from operating activities of $42,000, cash proceeds from the sale of investment securities (not held specifically for trading purposes) of $3,500, cash payments for operating activities of $21,500, a cash payment for purchase of equipment of $5,000, a purchase of land for $11,000 paid for with a note payable, and total debt repayment of $9,000.

256   Study Guide to Accompany Financial Accounting: Tools for Business Decision-Making, Fifth Canadian Edition

(SO 3)   14.   What is ABC Co.'s net cash provided (used) by investing activities in 2011?
  a. $1,500 net cash used by investing activities
  b. $12,500 net cash used by investing activities
  c. $21,500 net cash used by investing activities
  d. $5,000 net cash used by investing activities

(SO 5)   15.   What was ABC Co.'s cash balance on January 1, 2011?
  a. $28,000
  b. $12,500
  c. $10,000
  d. $2,500

(SO 6)   16.   Firth Corporation shows the following:

Cash provided by operating activities	$500,000
Net capital expenditures	125,000
Dividends paid	40,000

What is Firth's free cash flow?
  a. $335,000
  b. $375,000
  c. $415,000
  d. $500,000

(SO 6)   17.   Which of the following ratios is a measure of liquidity?
  a.   Cash total debt coverage
  b.   Free cash flow
  c.   Cash current debt coverage
  d.   Debt to total assets

(SO 6)   18.   The cash current debt coverage ratio measures:
  a.   the company's ability to repay its total liabilities from cash generated from operating activities.
  b.   the company's ability to repay its current liabilities from cash generated from operating activities.
  c.   how fast the company collects cash.
  d.   the company's ability to survive over the long term.

Problems

(SO 2a, 3, 4)   1.   The following are comparative statement of financial position data for Panther Corporation for the years 2012 and 2011:

PANTHER CORPORATION
Comparative Statement of Financial Position Data
December 31

	2012	2011
Cash	$ 3,600	$ 2,300
Accounts receivable	3,500	2,600

CHAPTER 13   Statement of Cash Flows   257

Merchandise inventory	3,200	3,800
Equipment	3,800	3,400
Accumulated depreciation	(2,400)	(2,340)
Long-term investments	2,600	2,840
	$14,300	$12,600
Accounts payable	$ 2,400	$ 1,800
Accrued liabilities	400	500
Bonds payable	2,800	3,100
Common shares	3,800	3,400
Retained earnings	4,900	3,800
	$14,300	$12,600

The bonds were originally issued at face value. Selected data from the income statement include profit of $2,140 and depreciation expense of $60. Cash dividends paid totalled $1,040.

Using the indirect method, prepare a statement of cash flows for Panther Corporation for the year ended December 31, 2012. Make assumptions as necessary.

2.   The income statement for Warnon Corporation is shown below: (SO 2b)

WARNON CORPORATION
Income Statement
Year Ended December 31, 2012

Sales		$12,300,000
Cost of goods sold		8,100,000
Gross profit		4,200,000
Operating expenses	$1,800,000	
Depreciation expense	180,000	1,980,000
Profit before income tax		2,220,000
Income tax expense		888,000
Profit		$ 1,332,000

Additional information:
1.   Accounts receivable increased $600,000 during the year.
2.   Inventory increased $375,000 during the year.
3.   Prepaid expenses, which relate to operating expenses, increased $300,000 during the year.
4.   Accounts payable to merchandise suppliers increased $150,000 during the year.
5.   Accrued expenses payable, which relate to operating expenses, increased $270,000 during the year.
6.   Income tax payable, which relates to income tax expense, decreased $50,000 during the year.

Using the direct method, prepare the operating activities section of the statement of cash flows for Warnon Corporation for the year ended December 31, 2012.

258 **Study Guide to Accompany Financial Accounting: Tools for Business Decision-Making, Fifth Canadian Edition**

(SO 3) 3.   A company has the following selected account balances related to property, plant, and equipment.

	2012	2011
Equipment	$200,000	$175,000
Accumulated depreciation—equipment	88,000	95,000

Additional information:
1. During 2012, the company sold equipment for cash. The equipment had an original cost of $38,000, a carrying amount of $7,000, and a gain on sale of $2,500.
2. During 2012, the company recorded $24,000 of depreciation expense on the equipment.
3. During 2012, the company purchased equipment for cash.

Calculate cash received from the sale of the equipment and cash paid for equipment for 2012.

(SO 6) 4.   Axel Corporation has the following selected general ledger account balances and other information as at December 31, 2012.

Accounts payable	$ 25,000
Bonds payable, due July 1, 2020	87,500
Common shares	270,000
Retained earnings	15,000
Dividends paid	10,000
Interest payable	11,000
Mortgage payable	150,000
Notes payable, due April 1, 2013	20,000
Sales tax payable	8,000
Salaries payable	2,000

Additional information:
1. $20,000 of the mortgage is payable next year.
2. Cash provided by operating activities for 2012 was $139,750.
3. Current liabilities totalled $90,000 on December 31, 2011.
4. Non-current liabilities totalled $212,500 on December 31, 2011.
5. Net capital expenditures for 2012 were $70,000.

Calculate the following for 2012:
a.   cash current debt coverage ratio
b.   cash total debt coverage ratio
c.   free cash flow

(SO 2, 6) 5.   Refer to the HMV and WHSmith financial statements found in the appendices at the end of this study guide for information in answering the following questions. Do not forget to use the **Decision Toolkit** approach for help in answering the questions:
a.   Do HMV and WHSmith use the direct or indirect method in preparing their statements of cash flows?
b.   In 2010, did HMV have a net increase or decrease in cash?

CHAPTER 13   Statement of Cash Flows   259

c.   In 2010, what was HMV's largest use of cash?

d.   Calculate and compare the cash current debt coverage and cash total debt coverage ratios for 2010 for HMV and WHSmith.

Solutions to Self-Test

Multiple Choice

1.   b   Operating activities affect income statement accounts and most current asset and current liability accounts. Financing activities affect non-current liability accounts and equity accounts.

2.   a   The operating activities section is always listed first on the statement of cash flows.

3.   c   Significant noncash activities are not reported in the body of the statement of cash flows because they are noncash items. However, they are reported in a separate note to the financial statements.

4.   c   The primary purpose of the statement of cash flows is to provide information that enables users to assess a company's ability to generate cash, and the company's needs in using these cash flows. Only an indirect method statement of cash flows would show the relationship between accrual basis profit and net cash provided (used) by operating activities.

5.   d   Information for the preparation of the statement of cash flows usually comes from three sources:
   1.   Comparative statement of financial position.
   2.   Current period income statement.
   3.   Selected additional information.

6.   a   Noncash items, such as depreciation expense, may be greater than a reported loss, possibly resulting in positive net cash provided by operating activities.

7.   b   The choice between indirect and direct methods affects only the operating activities section of the statement of cash flows, and it is important to note that both methods arrive at the same amount for "net cash provided (used) by operating activities." The investing and financing activities sections are prepared in the same way under both methods.

8.   c   A change in accounts receivable is an operating activity, not an investing or a financing activity. In the operating activities section, the decrease in accounts receivable is not a deduction from profit.

9.   c   A change in accounts payable is an operating activity, not an investing or a financing activity. In the operating activities section, the increase in accounts payable is not a deduction from profit.

10.   b $500,000 - $50,000 = $450,000$.

11.   a $300,000 + $100,000 = $400,000$.

12.   b $300,000 + $100,000 - $30,000 = $370,000$.

13.   d   This is a noncash transaction; therefore, it is not reported in the body of the statement of cash flows.

260 Study Guide to Accompany Financial Accounting: Tools for Business Decision-Making, Fifth Canadian Edition

14. a Cash proceeds from sale of investment securities (not held specifically for trading purposes) of $3,500 − cash payment for purchase of equipment of $5,000 = net cash used by investing activities of $1,500. Purchase of land paid for with note payable is a noncash transaction and does not affect net cash provided (used) by investing activities. Repayment of debt is a financing activity.

15. d Net cash provided by operating activities of $20,500 − net cash used by investing activities of $1,500 − net cash used by financing activities of $9,000 = net increase in cash in 2011 of $10,000. Cash balance on December 31, 2011, of $12,500 − net increase in cash in 2011 of $10,000 = cash balance on January 1, 2011 of $2,500.

16. a $500,000 − $125,000 − $40,000 = $335,000.

17. c Measures of liquidity include the current ratio and the cash current debt coverage ratio.

18. b The cash current debt coverage ratio measures a company's ability to repay its current liabilities from cash generated from operating activities.

Problems

1.

PANTHER CORPORATION
Statement of Cash Flows
Year Ended December 31, 2012

Operating activities		
Profit		$2,140
Adjustments to reconcile profit to net cash provided by operating activities:		
Depreciation expense	$ 60	
Increase in accounts receivable	(900)	
Decrease in merchandise inventory	600	
Increase in accounts payable	600	
Decrease in accrued liabilities	(100)	260
Net cash provided by operating activities		2,400
Investing activities		
Sale of long-term investments	$ 240	
Purchase of equipment	(400)	
Net cash used by investing activities		(160)
Financing activities		
Issue of common shares	$ 400	
Retirement of bonds payable	(300)	
Payment of cash dividends*	(1,040)	
Net cash used by financing activities		(940)

CHAPTER 13 Statement of Cash Flows 261

Net increase in cash	1,300
Cash, January 1	2,300
Cash, December 31	$3,600

*Note that under ASPE, dividends paid are classified as a financing activity. However, under IFRS, dividends paid may be classified either as an operating or financing activity.

Without additional information, the assumption is that the increase in Equipment is due to a cash purchase of equipment, the decrease in Long-Term Investments is due to a sale of long-term investments, the decrease in Bonds Payable is due to the partial retirement of bonds payable, and the increase in Common Shares is due to the sale of common shares for cash. The increase of $1,100 in Retained Earnings is due to profit of $2,140 less $1,040 dividends declared and paid.

2.

WARNON CORPORATION
Statement of Cash Flows (partial)
Year Ended December 31, 2012

Operating activities		
Cash receipts from customers		$11,700,000 (1)
Cash payments:		
To suppliers	$8,325,000 (2)	
For operating expenses	1,830,000 (3)	
For income tax	938,000 (4)	11,093,000
Net cash provided by operating activities		607,000
Schedules:		
(1) Sales		$12,300,000
Deduct: Increase in accounts receivable		600,000
Cash receipts from customers		$11,700,000
(2) Cost of goods sold		$8,100,000
Add: Increase in inventory		375,000
Purchases		8,475,000
Deduct: Increase in accounts payable		150,000
Cash payments to suppliers		$8,325,000
(3) Operating expenses		$1,800,000
Add: Increase in prepaid expenses		300,000
		2,100,000
Deduct: Increase in accrued expenses payable		270,000
Cash payments for operating expenses		$1,830,000

262   Study Guide to Accompany Financial Accounting: Tools for Business Decision-Making, Fifth Canadian Edition

(4) Income tax expense	$888,000
Add: Decrease in income tax payable	50,000
Cash payments for income tax	$938,000

3.   Accumulated depreciation of the equipment that was sold is determined as follows: original cost $38,000 − carrying amount $7,000 = $31,000.

Cash received from the sale of the equipment is derived from the following journal entry:

Cash	9,500	
Accumulated Depreciation—Equipment	31,000	
Gain on Sale of Equipment		2,500
Equipment		38,000

Cash paid for the purchase of equipment is derived from analysis of the following T account:

Equipment

Opening bal.	175,000		
Purchase of equipment	63,000	Sale of equipment	38,000
Ending balance	200,000		

The following T account would be balanced as indicated:

Accumulated Depreciation—Equipment

		Opening balance	95,000
Sale of equipment	31,000	Depreciation expense	24,000
		Ending balance	88,000

4.   To calculate the ratios, the following needs to be calculated:

Current liabilities, December 31, 2012:

Accounts payable	$ 25,000
Interest payable	11,000
Notes payable, due April 1, 2013	20,000
Sales tax payable	8,000
Salaries payable	2,000
Current portion of mortgage payable	20,000
Total current liabilities	86,000

Non-current liabilities, December 31, 2012:

Bonds payable due July 1, 2020		87,500
Mortgage payable	$150,000	
Less: current portion	20,000	130,000
Total non-current liabilities		217,500
Total liabilities		$303,500

CHAPTER 13 Statement of Cash Flows 263

a. Cash current debt coverage ratio = cash provided by operating activities divided by average current liabilities.
Cash provided by operating activities = $139,750.
Average current liabilities: ($90,000 + $86,000) ÷ 2 = $88,000.
Cash current debt coverage ratio: $139,750 ÷ $88,000 = 1.6 times.

b. Cash total debt coverage ratio = cash provided by operating activities divided by average total liabilities.
Cash provided by operating activities = $139,750.
Total liabilities, December 31, 2011: $90,000 + $212,500 = $302,500.
Average total liabilities: ($302,500 + $303,500) ÷ 2 = $303,000.
Cash total debt coverage ratio: $139,750 ÷ $303,000 = 0.5 times.

c. Free cash flow = cash provided by operating activities − net capital expenditures − dividends paid = $139,750 − $70,000 − $10,000 = $59,750.

5. Please note that the amounts shown for HMV and WHSmith are stated in pounds (£) millions.

a. Referring to the operating activities section of each company's statement of cash flows, both companies report profit and add back noncash items, and add or deduct changes in working capital items to arrive at net cash flows from operating activities. This indicates use of the indirect method by both companies. The direct method would not include profit (loss) in the operating activities section, and net cash provided (used) by operating activities would be calculated by adjusting each item on the income statement from the accrual basis to the cash basis.

b. In 2010, HMV had a net decrease in cash and cash equivalents of £18.0, as shown near the end of the statement of cash flows. This is the main reason for the change in cash and cash equivalents from £45.5 in 2009 to £27.3 in 2010 (the remaining decrease in cash and cash equivalents was due to the effect of exchange rate changes amounting to (£0.2)).

c. In 2010, HMV's largest use of cash was payments of £47.0 to acquire a subsidiary.

d.
HMV:

Cash current debt coverage ratio:

$$\frac{£65.9}{[(£551.5 + £490.6) \div 2]} = 0.1 \text{ times}$$

Cash total debt coverage ratio:

$$\frac{£65.9}{[(£605.0 + £516.9) \div 2]} = 0.1 \text{ times}$$

WHSmith:

Cash current debt coverage ratio:

$$\frac{£104}{[(£300 + £281) \div 2]} = 0.4 \text{ times}$$

Cash total debt coverage ratio:

$$\frac{£104}{[(£327 + £306) \div 2]} = 0.3 \text{ times}$$

In 2010, WHSmith's cash coverage ratios were stronger than HMV's.

chapter 14

Performance Measurement

Chapter Overview

This chapter explains the importance of performance measurement and related concepts, such as sustainable income. Analysis tools, including horizontal analysis, vertical analysis, and ratio analysis, are also discussed.

Review of Specific Study Objectives

Sustainable Income

- **Sustainable income** is the level of profit that is most likely to be obtained in the future. Sustainable income differs from actual profit by the amount of irregular (i.e., non-typical) revenues, expenses, gains, and losses that are included in profit. Two types of irregular items are discussed in this chapter: discontinued operations and changes in accounting policy.

- **Discontinued operations** refers to the disposal or availability for sale of a component of an entity. A **component of an entity**, for the purpose of discontinued operations, is a major line of business or major geographical area of operations that has been disposed of or is held for sale. It must be clearly distinguishable operationally and financially from the rest of the company.

> **study objective 1**
>
> Understand the concept of sustainable income and indicate how irregular items are presented.

- Assets and liabilities of a discontinued operation that are held for sale are reported separately on the **statement of financial position** as current or non-current assets or liabilities, valued at the lower of carrying amount and fair value less costs to sell. Once assets are classified as held for sale, the company no longer records depreciation related to those assets.

- Discontinued operations are also segregated from continuing operations on the **income statement**; any profits or losses related to discontinued operations are reported separately near the bottom of the income statement, net of tax. Discontinued operations on the income statement can consist of two parts: (1) profit (loss) from the discontinued operations, net of any income tax expense or savings; and (2) gain (loss) on disposal of the component, net of any income tax expense or savings. Of course, if the component has not yet been disposed of and is being held for sale, only profit (loss) from the discontinued operations will be reported on the income statement until actual disposal of the component occurs.

- A type of irregular item that affects profits of prior periods is a change in accounting policy. A **change in accounting policy** occurs when the accounting policy used in the current year is different from the one used in the preceding year. A change in accounting policy may be either voluntary or mandatory. A **voluntary** change in accounting policy is allowed when management can show that the new accounting policy results in a more reliable and relevant presentation of events or transactions in the financial statements. An example of a voluntary change in accounting policy is a change in inventory cost formula, if the new cost formula better corresponds to the physical use and flow of goods, and if the new cost formula is comparable with the cost formulas used by other companies in the same industry. A **mandatory** change in accounting policy is one that is required by **standard setters**, such as the transition to IFRS and ASPE from Canadian GAAP in 2011. We can expect to see more mandatory changes in accounting policy in the next few years as more accounting standards are updated and converged.

  Changes in accounting policy affect financial reporting in four ways:

  1. The cumulative effect of the change in accounting policy relating to prior years should be reported (net of any income tax expense or savings) as an adjustment to opening retained earnings. Since prior periods' profits are affected, a change in accounting policy must be reported in the retained earnings section of the statement of changes in equity (or in the statement of retained earnings under ASPE), rather than on the current period's income statement.
  2. The new policy should be used for reporting the results of operations in the current year.
  3. All prior-period financial statements should be restated to make comparisons easier.
  4. The effects of the change should be detailed and disclosed in a note to the financial statements.

- Financial statement users often perform **financial analysis** in order to evaluate a company's past and current financial performance and position, and to help determine future expectations. Financial analysis may involve:

  1. Intracompany comparisons: comparison of financial results on a year-to-year basis (over time) for the same company, in order to detect significant trends and changes in financial performance.

CHAPTER 14   Performance Measurement   267

2. Intercompany comparisons: comparison of financial results with the financial results of a key competitor, in order to provide insight into the company's relative financial performance.
3. Industry comparisons: comparison of financial results with industry averages, in order to provide insight into the company's relative competitive position within its industry.

Comparative Analysis

- **Three basic tools** used in financial statement analysis are: horizontal analysis, vertical analysis, and ratio analysis.

Horizontal Analysis

- **Horizontal analysis**, also called **trend analysis**, is a technique to determine the change (increase or decrease) in a series of financial statement data over time. This change can be expressed as either an amount or a percentage. Expressed as a percentage, this change can be calculated as a horizontal percentage of a base-period amount or as a horizontal percentage change for the period.

> study objective 2
>
> Explain and apply horizontal analysis.

- A company has net sales of $100,000 in 2010, $110,000 in 2011, and $116,000 in 2012. Assume that 2010 is the base year. The formula for calculating the horizontal percentage of base-period amount is:

$$\frac{\text{Analysis-Period Amount}}{\text{Base-Period Amount}}$$

In our example, for 2011, net sales are 110% of the base year:

$$\frac{\$110,000}{\$100,000} = 110\%$$

For 2012, net sales are 116% of the base year:

$$\frac{\$116,000}{\$100,000} = 116\%$$

Note that the base-period amount is usually the earliest year, or $100,000 in 2010, in this case.

If, instead, we wanted to calculate the horizontal percentage change for each period, compared with the base period, we would apply the formula for calculating horizontal percentage change for the period:

$$\frac{\text{Dollar Amount of Change Since Base Period}}{\text{Base-Period Amount}}$$

If we set each prior year as our base year, in 2011, net sales increased by $10,000, or 10%, over 2010:

$$\frac{\$110,000 - \$100,000}{\$100,000} = 10\%$$

In 2012, net sales increased by $6,000, or 5.5%, over 2011:

$$\frac{\$116,000 - \$110,000}{\$110,000} = 5.5\%$$

268   Study Guide to Accompany Financial Accounting: Tools for Business Decision-Making, Fifth Canadian Edition

- **Horizontal analysis** helps to highlight the significance of a change by expressing it in terms of a percentage. It may otherwise be difficult to see the magnitude of a change if we only see it expressed in terms of its dollar amount.

- **Several complications can arise in applying horizontal analysis.** If a particular account has a zero or negative value in the base year or preceding year, but a positive value in the next year, no percentage change can be calculated.

Vertical Analysis

study objective 3

Explain and apply vertical analysis.

- **Vertical analysis**, also called **common size analysis**, is a technique that expresses each item in a financial statement as a percentage of a base amount in the same financial statement. On the statement of financial position, asset items are usually expressed as percentages of total assets, and liability and shareholders' equity items are usually expressed as percentages of total liabilities and shareholders' equity. On the income statement, revenue and expense items are usually expressed as percentages of net sales.

- When comparative statements of financial position and income statements are presented, vertical analysis shows not only the relative size of each item for each year presented, but also the percentage change for each item on the comparative financial statements.

- If current assets are $2,200 and total assets are $9,000, current assets are 24.4% of total assets ($2,200 ÷ $9,000).

- Just as is true with horizontal analysis, **vertical analysis** helps to highlight the significance of a change by expressing it in terms of a percentage. Vertical analysis also helps when comparing two companies of different sizes.

Ratio Analysis

- Ratios can be classified into three types: (1) **liquidity ratios**, which measure a company's short-term ability to pay its maturing obligations and to meet unexpected needs for cash; (2) **solvency ratios**, which measure a company's ability to survive in the long term; and (3) **profitability ratios**, which measure a company's earnings or operating success for a specific period of time.

Liquidity Ratios

study objective 4

Identify and calculate ratios that are used to analyze liquidity.

- The following ratios are **liquidity ratios**:
  1. **Current ratio** is calculated as current assets divided by current liabilities. If the current ratio is 1.2:1, the company has $1.20 of current assets for every $1 of current liabilities. **Working capital**, the difference between current assets and current liabilities, is a related measure of liquidity using the same two inputs.
  2. **Cash current debt coverage ratio** is calculated as net cash provided (used) by operating activities divided by average current liabilities. Instead of using numerator and denominator amounts that are calculated at one point in time, this ratio uses amounts that cover a period of time and thus may provide a better representation of liquidity. If the cash current debt coverage ratio is 0.5 times, on average, the company has $0.50 of net cash provided by operating activities for every $1 of current liabilities. This is a cash basis ratio, not an accrual basis ratio.

CHAPTER 14 Performance Measurement 269

3. **Receivables turnover** is calculated as net credit sales divided by average gross accounts receivable. However, since companies often do not disclose their net credit sales, total sales are often used as a substitute. This ratio measures the number of times, on average, that receivables are collected during the period. If the receivables turnover is 12.5 times, on average, the company collected its receivables 12.5 times during the period.

4. **Average collection period** is calculated as 365 days divided by receivables turnover. Using the receivables turnover of 12.5 times from the previous example, the average collection period for the company would be 29 days (365 ÷ 12.5). The general rule is that average collection period should not greatly exceed the credit period (the time allowed for payment).

5. **Inventory turnover** is calculated as cost of goods sold divided by average inventory. If the ratio is 8 times, on average, the company sold its inventory eight times during the period. This ratio is very closely monitored by merchandisers, since their business is to sell inventory. If inventory turnover changes significantly in either direction, action is taken. This ratio varies widely among industries.

6. **Days in inventory** is calculated as 365 days divided by inventory turnover. Using the inventory turnover of 8 times from the previous example, average days in inventory is 46 days, which means that on average, the company takes 46 days to sell its inventory.

For current ratio, inventory turnover, receivables turnover, and cash current debt coverage ratio, a higher ratio is generally better. However, in some cases, a high current ratio may not be good, as it may be the result of inflated current assets, such as slow-moving inventory and uncollectible receivables. When analyzing liquidity, it is important to check that inventory turnover and receivables turnover are improving and not deteriorating, in addition to evaluating the current ratio. For days in inventory and average collection period, a lower ratio is generally better (fewer days to sell inventory or fewer days to collect receivables).

Solvency Ratios

- The following ratios are **solvency ratios**:

1. **Debt to total assets** is calculated as total liabilities divided by total assets. Debt to total assets measures the percentage of total assets provided by creditors. A higher debt to total assets ratio indicates higher reliance on debt, and higher risk that the company may be unable to meet its maturing obligations. Therefore, from a creditor's point of view, a lower debt to total assets ratio is better. However, a very low debt to total assets ratio may indicate that management is not trying to grow the business by obtaining financing from lenders. If debt to total assets is 65%, creditors have provided financing to cover 65% of the company's total assets. **Debt to equity** (total liabilities divided by total shareholders' equity), is a similar ratio, and shows the use of borrowed funds relative to investments by shareholders.

2. **Times interest earned** is calculated as profit before interest expense and income tax expense (EBIT), divided by interest expense. EBIT (earnings before interest and tax) is calculated by adding interest expense and income tax expense back to profit (profit + interest expense + income tax expense). Times interest earned indicates the company's ability to meet interest payments as they come due. If times interest earned is 13 times, the company's profit before interest and tax was 13 times the amount needed for interest expense.

> **study objective 5**
>
> Identify and calculate ratios that are used to analyze solvency.

270 Study Guide to Accompany Financial Accounting: Tools for Business Decision-Making, **Fifth Canadian Edition**

3. **Cash total debt coverage** is calculated as net cash provided (used) by operating activities divided by average total liabilities. Cash total debt coverage indicates a company's ability to repay its liabilities from cash generated from operating activities, without having to liquidate the assets used in its operations. If cash total debt coverage is 0.24 times, net cash provided by one year of operating activities is sufficient to cover 20% of the company's total liabilities. This is a cash basis ratio, not an accrual basis ratio.

4. **Free cash flow** is calculated as net cash provided (used) by operating activities, minus net capital expenditures, and minus dividends paid. Free cash flow indicates the amount of excess cash available after investing to maintain current productive capacity and after paying current dividends.

For free cash flow, times interest earned, and cash total debt coverage, a higher ratio is generally better. For debt to total assets, a lower ratio is generally better.

Profitability

study objective 6

Identify and calculate ratios that are used to analyze profitability.

- The following ratios are **profitability ratios**:

1. **Return on common shareholders' equity** is calculated as profit available to common shareholders (profit minus preferred dividends) divided by average common shareholders' equity. The numerator is the difference between profit and preferred dividends declared for the period, if any. The denominator is the average difference between total shareholders' equity and preferred shares (if any). Return on common shareholders' equity shows how many dollars of profit were earned for each dollar invested by the shareholders.

2. **Return on assets** is calculated as profit divided by average total assets. Return on assets measures the overall profitability of assets in terms of how much is earned on each dollar invested in assets.

3. **Profit margin** is calculated as profit divided by net sales. Profit margin measures the percentage of profit that each dollar of sales produces. If the profit margin is 12%, then each dollar of sales produces $0.12 of profit.

4. **Asset turnover** is calculated as net sales divided by average total assets. Asset turnover measures how efficiently a company uses its assets to generate sales. Asset turnover varies widely among industries.

5. **Gross profit margin** is calculated as gross profit divided by net sales. Gross profit indicates a company's ability to maintain an adequate selling price above its cost of goods sold. In general, companies in more competitive industries will have lower gross profit margins. If the gross profit margin is 58%, each dollar of net sales generates gross profit of $0.58. High-volume businesses (grocery stores) generally have low gross profit margins, whereas low-volume enterprises (jewellery stores) usually have high gross profit margins.

6. **Earnings per share** is calculated as profit available to common shareholders (profit minus preferred dividends) divided by the weighted average number of common shares (calculated so that common shares are weighted based on the time they have been outstanding). Earnings per share is a measure of profit realized on each common share. If earnings per share is $2.05, then $2.05 of profit was earned on each common share. Earnings per share is generally not comparable between companies because companies may have very different financing structures. Companies following IFRS are required to present earnings per share on the income statement or statement of comprehensive income. Companies following ASPE are not required to report earnings per share.

CHAPTER 14   Performance Measurement   271

7. **Price-earnings ratio** is calculated as market price per common share divided by earnings per share. The price-earnings ratio is a market measure because it uses a company's share price, which reflects the stock market's (investors') expectations for the company. If the price-earnings ratio is 23, on average, each common share sold for 23 times earnings per share.

8. **Payout ratio** is calculated as cash dividends divided by profit. The payout ratio measures the percentage of profit that is distributed as cash dividends. Growth companies usually have low payout ratios because they reinvest profits in the business in order to grow, rather than distributing profits to shareholders in the form of cash dividends.

9. **Dividend yield** is calculated as dividend per share divided by market price per share. Similar to the price-earnings ratio, dividend yield is also a market measure, because it uses the company's share price in its calculation. Dividend yield measures the rate of return a shareholder earned from dividends during the year.

For profitability ratios, a higher ratio is generally better.

- To perform relevant financial statement analysis, pertinent comparative data must be selected, and appropriate ratios to answer the question asked must be selected.

Limitations of Financial Analysis

- Before relying on the information you have gathered through your horizontal, vertical, and ratio analyses, you must understand the limitations of these tools and of the financial statements they are based on. Some of the factors that can limit the usefulness of your analysis include alternative accounting policies, professional judgement, comprehensive income, diversification, inflation, and economic factors.

> study objective 7
>
> Understand the limitations of financial analysis.

- Variations among companies in their application of **generally accepted accounting principles** (GAAP) may lessen the comparability of their financial statements. Companies may choose from a large number of acceptable accounting policies, such as different inventory cost formulas or depreciation methods. Different choices can result in differing financial positions, which affect comparability of financial statements. Also, in many industries, competition is global, which means that companies applying different accounting standards (for example, one company applying IFRS and another company applying U.S. GAAP) are often compared.

- We must also accept that management has to use **professional judgement** in choosing the most appropriate accounting policy for the circumstances. In addition, many estimates are required in preparing financial information. To the extent that these estimates are inaccurate or biased, ratios and percentages that are based on such information will also be inaccurate or biased. To help ensure that the quality of financial information is as high as possible, CEOs and CFOs of Canadian publicly traded companies are required to certify that the financial statements, together with other financial information, "present fairly" and do not misrepresent in all material respects the company's financial condition, financial performance, and cash flows. As well, audit committees are held responsible for questioning management on the degree of aggressiveness or conservatism that has been applied, and the quality of underlying accounting policies, estimates, and judgements.

- Most financial ratios exclude total comprehensive income or **other comprehensive income**. Profitability ratios, including industry averages, generally use data from the income statement and not from the statement of comprehensive income (which

272 Study Guide to Accompany Financial Accounting: Tools for Business Decision-Making, Fifth Canadian Edition

includes both profit and other comprehensive income). In cases where other comprehensive income is significant, depending on its source, some analysis will adjust profitability ratios to incorporate the effect of total comprehensive income. However, because private companies that follow ASPE do not report comprehensive income, this limitation applies only to private and public companies that follow IFRS.

- **Diversification** in Canadian industry can also limit the usefulness of financial analysis. Many companies today are so diversified that they cannot be classified by industry. Because of this diversification, analysts must be careful in interpreting consolidated financial statements. When companies have significant operations in different lines of business, they are required to report additional disclosures in a segmented information note to their financial statements. Many analysts agree that segmented information is the most important information in the financial statements, especially when comparing diversified companies. Note that because segments are not as common in private companies as they are in large public companies, there are no requirements for disclosure of segments in ASPE.

- Our accounting information system does not adjust data for price-level changes. However, in Canada, **inflation** is not very significant right now.

- Financial analysis should consider the **economic circumstances** in which a company operates. During an economic recession, for example, horizontal analyses and ratios compared across years lose much of their relevance. Vertical analyses become more useful in such times.

comparing
IFRS and ASPE

Key Differences	International Financial Reporting Standards (IFRS)	Accounting Standards for Private Enterprises (ASPE)
Change in accounting policy	The cumulative effect of a change in accounting policy is reported retrospectively as an adjustment to opening retained earnings in the statement of changes of equity.	The cumulative effect of a change in accounting policy is reported retrospectively as an adjustment to opening retained earnings in the statement of retained earnings.
Earnings per share	Must be reported on the face of the income statement or statement of comprehensive income.	Earnings per share is not required to be reported.
Comprehensive income	If other comprehensive income is significant, selected profitability ratios should be recalculated using total comprehensive income rather than profit.	Comprehensive income is not reported.
Segmented reporting	There are specific revenue, profit, and asset tests to determine if information must be reported in the notes to the financial statements for segments.	There are no disclosure requirements for reporting segment information.

CHAPTER 14   Performance Measurement   273

Chapter Self-Test

As you work through the questions and problems, remember to use the **Decision Toolkit** discussed and used in the text:

1. *Decision Checkpoints*: Ask a question relevant to the decision being made.
2. *Info Needed for Decision*: Make a choice regarding the information needed to answer the question.
3. *Tools to Use for Decision*: Review what the information identified in step 2 does for the decision-making process.
4. *How to Evaluate Results*: Identify specifically how the information identified in step 2 should be evaluated to answer the question relevant to the decision being made.

Note: The notation "(SO 1)" means that the question relates to study objective 1.

Multiple Choice

Please circle the correct answer.

1. The discontinued operations section of the income statement refers to   (SO 1)
    a.   discontinued product lines.
    b.   profit or loss on products that have been completed and sold.
    c.   obsolete equipment and discontinued inventory items.
    d.   disposal, or availability for sale, of a component of an entity.

2. Sustainable income   (SO 1)
    a.   refers to income that was obtained in the past.
    b.   would include a once-in-a-lifetime gain.
    c.   is the level of profit that is most likely to be obtained in the future.
    d.   includes irregular items such as discontinued operations and changes in accounting policy.

3. A change in accounting policy appears on the   (SO 1)
    a.   income statement net of income taxs, below Profit from Continuing Operations.
    b.   statement of changes in equity in the retained earnings section.
    c.   statement of comprehensive income.
    d.   statement of cash flows.

4. Comparisons of financial data made within a company are called   (SO 2)
    a.   intracompany comparisons.
    b.   interior comparisons.
    c.   intercompany comparisons.
    d.   intramural comparisons.

5. Which of the following is a category of comparison that provides decision useful- (SO 2)
    ness of financial information?
    a.   Industry comparison
    b.   Intercompany comparison
    c.   Intracompany comparison
    d.   All of the above.

274   **Study Guide to Accompany Financial Accounting: Tools for Business Decision-Making, Fifth Canadian Edition**

(SO 2)   6.   Total current liabilities are $10,000 in 2010, $18,000 in 2011, and $22,000 in 2012. What is the horizontal percentage of the base-period amount in 2012, assuming 2010 is the base year?
   a.   22%
   b.   120%
   c.   122%
   d.   220%

(SO 3)   7.   Consider the following data for Elizabeth Corporation:

Net sales	$100,000
Cost of goods sold	30,000
Gross profit	70,000
Operating expenses	50,000
Profit	$ 20,000

Performing a vertical analysis using net sales as the base amount, what is the vertical percentage of the base amount for cost of goods sold?
   a.   20.0%
   b.   30.0%
   c.   70.0%
   d.   33.3%

(SO 4, 5, 6)   8.   Measures of a company's ability to survive in the long term are called
   a.   liquidity ratios.
   b.   solvency ratios.
   c.   profitability ratios.
   d.   vertical analysis.

(SO 4, 5, 6)   9.   _____ is often used as the ultimate test of management's operating effectiveness.
   a.   Profit
   b.   Liquidity
   c.   Solvency
   d.   Profitability

The following information relates to questions 10 through 12.

Current assets	$150,000
Total assets	500,000
Current liabilities	125,000
Total liabilities	200,000
Net credit sales	600,000
Cost of goods sold	160,000
Average accounts receivable	50,000
Average inventory	40,000

CHAPTER 14 Performance Measurement 275

10. What is the receivables turnover? (SO 4)
    a. 3.2 times
    b. 4.0 times
    c. 12.0 times
    d. 15.0 times

11. What is the inventory turnover? (SO 4)
    a. 3.2 times
    b. 4.0 times
    c. 12.0 times
    d. 15.0 times

12. What is debt to total assets? (SO 5)
    a. 25.0%
    b. 40.0%
    c. 62.5%
    d. 83.3%

13. Which of the following is considered a solvency ratio? (SO 5)
    a. Price-earnings ratio
    b. Times interest earned
    c. Average collection period
    d. Cash current debt coverage

14. Net sales are $6 million, profit is $800,000, profit available to common share- (SO 6)
    holders is $700,000, and weighted average number of common shares is 300,000.
    What is the profit margin?
    a. 13.3%
    b. 11.7%
    c. $2.67
    d. $2.33

15. Net sales are $6 million, profit is $800,000, profit available to common share- (SO 6)
    holders is $700,000, and weighted average number of common shares is 300,000.
    What is the earnings per share?
    a. 13.3%
    b. 11.7%
    c. $2.67
    d. $2.33

16. Which of the following is considered a profitability ratio? (SO 6)
    a. Price-earnings ratio
    b. Times interest earned
    c. Average collection period
    d. Cash current debt coverage

17. A factor that limits the usefulness of financial analysis is (SO 7)
    a. management style of corporate executives.
    b. professional judgement.
    c. consistent application of accounting policies from period to period.
    d. sustainable income.

276 Study Guide to Accompany Financial Accounting: Tools for Business Decision-Making, Fifth Canadian Edition

Problems

(SO 4, 5, 6) 1. Selected information from the comparative financial statements of Fallis Ltd. for the year ended December 31 appears below:

	2012	2011
Accounts receivable (gross)	$ 150,000	$170,000
Inventory	110,000	130,000
Total assets	1,170,000	770,000
Current liabilities	110,000	80,000
Non-current liabilities	370,000	270,000
Total liabilities	480,000	350,000
Average common shareholders' equity	525,000	372,000
Net sales	1,470,000	670,000
Cost of goods sold	570,000	500,000
Depreciation expense	25,000	1,000
Interest expense	20,000	5,000
Income tax expense	30,000	9,000
Profit	120,000	55,000
Net cash provided by operating activities	210,000	105,000
Preferred dividends paid	8,000	7,500
Common dividends paid	12,000	11,000
Net capital expenditures	115,000	108,000
Market price per share	28	25
Weighted average number of common shares	30,000	30,000

Note: Weighted average number of common shares equals total number of common shares at December 31, 2012.

Calculate the following for the year ended December 31, 2012 (for common shares only):
a. Liquidity ratios
b. Solvency ratios
c. Profitability ratios

(SO 4) 2. State the effect of the following transactions on a current ratio of 1.5 to 1 (increase, decrease, or no effect).

a. Collection of an account receivable
b. Declaration of a cash dividend
c. Sale of additional shares for cash
d. Payment of an account payable
e. Purchase of equipment for cash
f. Purchase of inventory for cash
g. Purchase of short-term investments for cash

CHAPTER 14   Performance Measurement   277

(SO 5)   3.   The following selected solvency ratios are available for two companies, Olama Corporation and Yomanda Corporation, and their industry, for a recent fiscal year:

Ratio	Olama	Yomanda	Industry
Debt to total assets	45.5%	37.2%	45.3%
Times interest earned	3.7 times	7.6 times	7.2 times

Which company is more solvent? Explain.

4.   The following selected profitability ratios are available for two companies, Pace   (SO 6)
Corporation and Moly Corporation, and their industry, for a recent fiscal year:

Ratio	Pace	Moly	Industry
Gross profit margin	36.5%	42.2%	35.9%
Profit margin	4.2%	3.9%	3.8%
Return on common shareholders' equity	18.3%	12.4%	12.0%
Return on assets	6.6%	6.2%	5.8%
Asset turnover	1.6 times	1.6 times	1.5 times
Payout ratio	18.9%	57.1%	36.5%
Earnings per share	$1.28	$1.56	$1.19
Price-earnings ratio	14.1 times	15.0 times	N/A

a.   Which company is more profitable? Explain.
b.   Which company do investors favour? Is your answer consistent with your findings in (a)?

5.   Please refer to the HMV and WHSmith financial statements found in the appen-   (SO 1, 2, 3, 7)
dices at the end of this study guide for information in answering the follow-
ing questions. Do not forget to use the **Decision Toolkit** approach for help in
answering the questions.

a.   In Chapter 5, profit margin was calculated as 2.4% of net sales for HMV
and 5.3% for WHSmith in 2010. Using vertical analysis, break down the two
companies' profit margins. Note that finance costs and finance (investment)
revenue should be netted for the purpose of this question.
b.   Comment on your results obtained in (a) above.
c.   Using horizontal analysis with 2009 as the base year, determine the trend in
net sales and cost of sales since 2009 for both companies.
d.   Using your results obtained in (a) and (c) above, what further conclusions
can you make regarding the profitability of the two companies?
e.   Did HMV and/or WHSmith have any discontinued operations in 2010?

Solutions to Self-Test

Multiple Choice

1.   d   When a company disposes of one of its components, or makes one of its
components available for sale, the disposal is reported separately on the
income statement as an irregular item called a discontinued operation.

278   **Study Guide to Accompany Financial Accounting: Tools for Business Decision-Making, Fifth Canadian Edition**

2.   c   Sustainable income is the level of profit that is most likely to be obtained in the future. Sustainable income differs from actual profit by the amount of irregular (i.e., non-typical) revenues, expenses, gains, and losses that are included in profit.

3.   b   The cumulative effect of a change in accounting policy is reported (net of any income tax expense or savings) as an adjustment to opening retained earnings in the statement of changes in equity (or in the statement of retained earnings for private companies following ASPE).

4.   a   Intracompany comparison is comparison of financial results on a year-to-year basis (over time) for the same company.

5.   d   Three categories of comparisons for financial analysis are intracompany comparison, intercompany comparison, and industry comparison.

6.   d $22,000 ÷ $10,000 = 220\%$.

7.   b $30,000 ÷ $100,000 = 30\%$.

8.   b   Liquidity refers to a company's short-term ability to pay its maturing obligations, and to meet unexpected needs for cash. Profitability measures a company's operating success for a specific period of time. Vertical analysis compares data within a specific period of time as well.

9.   d   Profit is simply the difference between revenues and expenses. Liquidity refers to a company's short-term ability to pay its maturing obligations, and to meet unexpected needs for cash. Solvency refers to a company's ability to survive in the long term.

10. c $600,000 ÷ $50,000 = 12$ times.

11. b $160,000 ÷ $40,000 = 4$ times.

12. b $200,000 ÷ $500,000 = 40.0\%$.

13. b   Price-earnings ratio is a profitability ratio. Average collection period and cash current debt coverage are liquidity ratios.

14. a $800,000 ÷ $6,000,000 = 13.3\%$.

15. d $700,000 ÷ 300,000$ shares $= 2.33.

16. a   Times interest earned is a solvency ratio. Average collection period and cash current debt coverage are liquidity ratios.

17. b   Some of the factors that can limit usefulness of financial analysis include alternative accounting policies, professional judgement, comprehensive income, diversification, inflation, and economic factors.

Problems

1.

a.   **Liquidity ratios are:**

Current ratio:

$$\frac{\$150,000 + \$110,000}{\$110,000} = 2.4{:}1$$

CHAPTER 14 Performance Measurement 279

Cash current debt coverage:

$$\frac{\$210,000}{(\$110,000 + \$80,000) \div 2} = 2.2 \text{ times}$$

Receivables turnover:

$$\frac{\$1,470,000}{(\$150,000 + \$170,000) \div 2} = 9.2 \text{ times}$$

Average collection period:

$$\frac{365}{9.2} = 40 \text{ days}$$

Inventory turnover:

$$\frac{\$570,000}{(\$110,000 + \$130,000) \div 2} = 4.8 \text{ times}$$

Days in inventory:

$$\frac{365}{4.8} = 76 \text{ days}$$

b. **Solvency ratios are:**

Debt to total assets:

$$\frac{\$110,000 + \$370,000}{\$1,170,000} = 41.0\%$$

Times interest earned:

$$\frac{\$120,000 + \$30,000 + \$20,000}{\$20,000} = 8.5 \text{ times}$$

Cash total debt coverage:

$$\frac{\$210,000}{(\$480,000 + \$350,000) \div 2} = 0.5 \text{ times}$$

Free cash flow:

$$\$210,000 - \$115,000 - \$8,000 - \$12,000 = \$75,000$$

c. **Profitability ratios are:**

Return on common shareholders' equity:

$$\frac{\$120,000 - \$8,000}{\$525,000} = 21.3\%$$

Return on assets:

$$\frac{\$120,000}{(\$1,170,000 + \$770,000) \div 2} = 12.4\%$$

280 Study Guide to Accompany Financial Accounting: Tools for Business Decision-Making, Fifth Canadian Edition

Profit margin:

$$\frac{\$120,000}{\$1,470,000} = 8.2\%$$

Asset turnover:

$$\frac{\$1,470,000}{(\$1,170,000 + \$770,000) \div 2} = 1.5 \text{ times}$$

Gross profit margin:

$$\frac{\$1,470,000 - \$570,000}{\$1,470,000} = 61.2\%$$

Earnings per share:

$$\frac{\$120,000 - \$8,000}{30,000 \text{ common shares}} = \$3.73 \text{ per share}$$

Price-earnings ratio:

$$\frac{\$28.00}{\$3.73} = 7.5 \text{ times}$$

Payout ratio on common shares:

$$\frac{\$12,000}{\$120,000} = 10.0\%$$

Dividend yield on common shares:

$$\frac{\$12,000 \div 30,000 \text{ shares}}{\$28 \text{ per share}} = 1.4\%$$

2.
a. no effect (no effect on current assets: cash increases and accounts receivable decreases)

b. decrease (current liabilities increase: retained earnings decreases and dividend payable increases)

c. increase (current assets increase: cash increases and share capital increases)

d. increase (current liabilities decrease and current assets decrease by the same amount but the proportionate impact is likely higher on the denominator: accounts payable decreases and cash decreases. Assume current assets were $150 and current liabilities $100 before payment of the account payable, and $125 and $75 after payment of the account payable. The current ratio increases from 1.5:1 to 1.7:1.)

e. decrease (current assets decrease: equipment increases and cash decreases)

f. no effect (no effect on current assets: inventory increases and cash decreases)

g. no effect (no effect on current assets: short-term investments increase and cash decreases)

3.   Yomanda appears to be more solvent than Olama. Yomanda has a lower debt to total assets ratio, indicating that a lower percentage of its total assets is financed

CHAPTER 14 Performance Measurement 281

by creditors. As well, Yomanda has higher times interest earned, indicating that it has a better ability to meet interest payments as they come due. When looking at debt to total assets, Olama appears to be on par with the industry average. However, when assessing Olama's ability to meet interest payments as they come due (as indicated by times interest earned), Olama is not as solvent as the average firm in its industry.

4.

a. Both companies appear to be profitable. Moly Corporation has a higher gross profit margin than Pace Corporation, but both companies have a profit margin that is higher than the industry average. It appears that Moly does not do as good a job as Pace at controlling its operating expenses, because Pace has the higher profit margin.

When comparing return ratios (return on common shareholders' equity and return on assets), Pace also appears to be more profitable than Moly. Pace's profit margin and return ratios are also above the industry average. This analysis would indicate that Pace is more profitable than Moly.

b. Despite the findings in (a) that Pace is more profitable than Moly, investors seem to favour Moly, because Moly has the higher price-earnings ratio. This is not consistent with the findings in (a), as we would expect investors to favour the more profitable company. However, investors may be favouring Moly because it has a larger payout ratio, and/or because they may be anticipating better future profitability from Moly.

5.

a.

	Year 2010			
	HMV (£ millions)	%	**WHSmith** (£ millions)	%
Revenue	£2,017	100.0	£1,312	100.0
Cost of sales	1,856	92.0	650	49.5
Gross profit	161	8.0	662	50.5
Less operating expenses:				
Administrative expenses	86	4.3	80	6.1
Other expenses (income)	–	0.0	493	37.6
Total operating expenses	86	4.3	573	43.7
Profit from operations	75	3.7	89	6.8
Net interest expense	6	0.3	–	–
Profit before income tax	69	3.4	89	6.8
Income tax expense	20	1.0	20	1.5
Profit	£ 49	2.4	£ 69	5.3

b. WHSmith's profit margin of 5.3% is higher than HMV's profit margin of 2.4%, primarily because of WHSmith's significantly higher gross profit margin. WHSmith's higher gross profit margin more than compensated for its higher operating expenses as a percentage of sales (43.7% versus HMV's 4.3%).

282　Study Guide to Accompany Financial Accounting: Tools for Business Decision-Making, Fifth Canadian Edition

c.　With 2009 as the base year, performing horizontal analysis requires calculating the percentage increase or decrease for 2010 as a percentage of 2009:

	2010	2009
(£ millions) HMV:		
Revenue	£2,017	£1,957
	103%	100%
Cost of sales	£1,856	£1,804
	103%	100%
(£ millions) WHSmith:		
Revenue	£1,312	£1,340
	98%	100%
Cost of sales	£650	£685
	95%	100%

Horizontal analysis shows that HMV's revenue increased over the period 2009 to 2010, whereas WHSmith's revenue decreased in the same period. HMV's cost of sales increased at the same rate as its revenue increased, whereas WHSmith's cost of sales decreased at a faster rate than its revenues.

d.　Vertical analysis in (a) shows that cost of sales is a major expense category for both companies (92.0% for HMV and 49.5% for WHSmith). Horizontal analysis in (c) shows that HMV's revenue and cost of sales increased at the same rate from 2009 to 2010, and as a result its gross profit margin remained relatively steady (2009: 7.8%; 2010: 8.0%). WHSmith's revenue and cost of sales decreased during the same period, but its cost of sales decreased faster than its revenues, thereby increasing gross profit margin from 2009 to 2010 (2009: 48.9%; 2010: 50.5%).

e.　Neither HMV nor WHSmith had discontinued operations in 2010.

Appendices

In this appendix and the next, we illustrate current financial reporting using the financial statements for two competitors in the entertainment retail industry headquartered in England: HMV Group and WHSmith. We are grateful for permission to include the actual financial statements from each company's 2010 annual report.

Use the financial statements and selected notes to financial statements given in the appendices to complete the problems about HMV and WHSmith at the end of each chapter. Please note that any notes that do not appear here have been left out intentionally.

284   Appendix A: Financial Statements of HMV Group plc

Appendix A: Financial Statements of HMV Group plc

For the 52 weeks ended 24 April 2010 and 25 April 2009

CONSOLIDATED INCOME STATEMENT				
	Notes	Before exceptional items 2010 £m	Exceptional items 2010 £m	Total 2010 £m
Revenue	3,4	2,016.6	—	2,016.6
Cost of sales		(1,853.6)	(2.0)	(1,855.6)
Gross profit		163.0	(2.0)	161.0
Administrative expenses		(82.9)	(3.3)	(86.2)
Trading profit	3	80.1	(5.3)	74.8
Share of post-tax profits of associates and joint ventures accounted for using the equity method	17	0.3	—	0.3
Operating profit	5	80.4	(5.3)	75.1
Finance revenue	10	0.4	—	0.4
Finance costs	10	(6.6)	—	(6.6)
Profit before taxation		74.2	(5.3)	68.9
Taxation	11	(20.7)	1.0	(19.7)
Profit for the period		53.5	(4.3)	49.2
Attributable to:				
Shareholders of the Parent Company		53.5	(4.3)	49.2
Minority interests		—	—	—
		53.5	(4.3)	49.2
Earnings per share for profit attributable to shareholders:	12			
Basic		12.7p	(1.1)p	11.6p
Diluted		12.7p	(1.1)p	11.6p

Appendix A: Financial Statements of HMV Group plc 285

	Notes	Before exceptional items 2009 £m	Exceptional items 2009 £m	Total 2009 £m
Revenue	3,4	1,956.7	—	1,956.7
Cost of sales		(1,799.5)	(4.5)	(1,804.0)
Gross profit		157.2	(4.5)	152.7
Administrative expenses		(87.1)	2.8	(84.3)
Trading profit	3	70.1	(1.7)	68.4
Share of post-tax profits of associates and joint ventures accounted for using the equity method	17	0.2	—	0.2
Operating profit	5	70.3	(1.7)	68.6
Finance revenue	10	1.2	—	1.2
Finance costs	10	(8.5)	—	(8.5)
Profit before taxation		63.0	(1.7)	61.3
Taxation	11	(17.6)	0.5	(17.1)
Profit for the period		45.4	(1.2)	44.2
Attributable to:				
Shareholders of the Parent Company		45.4	(1.2)	44.2
Minority interests		—	—	—
		45.4	(1.2)	44.2
Earnings per share for profit attributable to shareholders:	12			
Basic		11.1p	(0.3)p	10.8p
Diluted		11.0p	(0.3)p	10.7p

286   Appendix A: Financial Statements of HMV Group plc

STATEMENTS OF COMPREHENSIVE INCOME
FOR THE 52 WEEKS ENDED 24 APRIL 2010 AND 25 APRIL 2009

	Notes	Group 2010 £m	Group 2009 £m	Company 2010 £m	Company 2009 £m
Profit for the period		**49.2**	44.2	**82.0**	51.6
Foreign exchange differences on retranslation of foreign operations		**(1.1)**	6.4	—	0.1
Tax effect		**(0.5)**	1.0	—	—
		(1.6)	7.4	—	0.1
Cash flow hedges:					
Gain on forward foreign exchange contracts		—	0.1	—	—
Transfers to the income statement on cash flow hedges (cost of sales)		—	0.4	—	—
		—	0.5	—	—
Actuarial loss on defined benefit pension schemes	32	**(19.3)**	(11.0)	**(19.3)**	(11.1)
Tax effect		**5.4**	3.1	**5.4**	3.1
		(13.9)	(7.9)	**(13.9)**	(8.0)
Other comprehensive loss for the period, net of tax		**(15.5)**	—	**(13.9)**	(7.9)
Total comprehensive income for the period		**33.7**	44.2	**68.1**	43.7
Attributable to:					
Shareholders of the Parent Company		**33.7**	44.2	**68.1**	43.7
Minority interests		—	—	—	—
		33.7	44.2	**68.1**	43.7

Appendix A: Financial Statements of HMV Group plc 287

Balance sheets

	Notes	Group as at 24 April 2010 £m	Group as at 25 April 2009 £m	Company as at 24 April 2010 £m	Company as at 25 April 2009 £m
Assets					
Non-current assets					
Property, plant and equipment	14	167.3	161.9	0.1	0.2
Intangible assets	16	122.2	73.0	—	—
Investments in subsidiaries and joint ventures	17	—	—	695.6	673.6
Investments accounted for using the equity method	17	13.0	14.7	—	—
Deferred income tax asset	11	30.1	26.1	12.6	9.8
Trade and other receivables	18	12.7	1.2	—	—
		345.3	276.9	708.3	683.6
Current assets					
Inventories	19	247.8	213.9	—	—
Trade and other receivables	18	80.7	71.6	28.3	75.4
Derivative financial instruments	24	0.1	0.1	0.1	—
Current income tax recoverable		1.8	1.3	—	—
Cash and short-term deposits	20	29.7	52.7	48.9	15.8
		360.1	339.6	77.3	91.2
Total assets		705.4	616.5	785.6	774.8
Liabilities					
Non-current liabilities					
Deferred income tax liabilities	11	(1.6)	(0.1)	—	—
Retirement benefit liabilities	32	(39.0)	(21.0)	(39.0)	(20.7)
Interest-bearing loans and borrowings	22	(11.8)	(5.0)	—	—
Provisions	23	(1.1)	(0.2)	—	—
		(53.5)	(26.3)	(39.0)	(20.7)
Current liabilities					
Trade and other payables	21	(442.4)	(415.5)	(7.8)	(8.6)
Current income tax payable		(20.8)	(17.2)	(0.9)	(2.3)
Interest-bearing loans and borrowings	22	(84.5)	(53.3)	(227.5)	(267.5)
Derivative financial instruments	24	(0.8)	—	—	—
Provisions	23	(3.0)	(4.6)	—	—
		(551.5)	(490.6)	(236.2)	(278.4)
Total liabilities		(605.0)	(516.9)	(275.2)	(299.1)
Net assets		100.4	99.6	510.4	475.7

288　Appendix A: Financial Statements of HMV Group plc

Balance sheets continued

	Notes	Group as at 24 April 2010 £m	Group as at 25 April 2009 £m	Company as at 24 April 2010 £m	Company as at 25 April 2009 £m
Equity					
Equity share capital	29	**347.1**	347.1	**347.1**	347.1
Other reserve – own shares	29, 30	**(0.6)**	(2.7)	**(0.6)**	(2.7)
Hedging reserve	29	**0.1**	0.1	—	—
Foreign currency translation reserve	29	**12.9**	14.0	—	—
Capital reserve	29	**0.3**	0.3	**0.3**	0.3
Retained earnings		**(260.4)**	(259.2)	**163.6**	131.0
Equity attributable to shareholders of the Parent Company		**99.4**	99.6	**510.4**	475.7
Minority interests		**1.0**	—	—	—
Total equity		**100.4**	99.6	**510.4**	475.7

The financial statements were approved by the Board of Directors on 29 June 2010 and were signed on its behalf by:

Simon Fox
Chief Executive Officer

Neil Bright
Group Finance Director

Statements of changes in equity

Group	Notes	Equity share capital £m	Own shares £m	Hedging reserve £m	Foreign currency translation reserve £m	Capital reserve £m	Retained earnings £m	Total £m	Minority interests £m	Total equity £m
At 26 April 2008		**323.1**	(2.0)	(0.4)	7.6	0.3	(269.8)	58.8	—	58.8
Profit for the period		—	—	—	—	—	44.2	44.2	—	44.2
Other comprehensive income (loss)		—	—	0.5	6.4	—	(6.9)	—	—	—
Total comprehensive income		—	—	0.5	6.4	—	37.3	44.2	—	44.2
Ordinary dividend	13	—	—	—	—	—	(29.7)	(29.7)	—	(29.7)
Issue of equity shares		**24.7**	—	—	—	—	—	24.7	—	24.7
Share issue costs		**(0.7)**	—	—	—	—	—	(0.7)	—	(0.7)
Purchase of own shares	30	—	(1.0)	—	—	—	—	(1.0)	—	(1.0)
Share-based payment awards		—	0.3	—	—	—	(0.3)	—	—	—
Charge for share-based payments		—	—	—	—	—	1.7	1.7	—	1.7
Deferred tax on share-based payments		—	—	—	—	—	1.6	1.6	—	1.6
At 25 April 2009		**347.1**	(2.7)	0.1	14.0	0.3	(259.2)	99.6	—	99.6
Profit for the period		—	—	—	—	—	49.2	49.2	—	49.2
Other comprehensive loss		—	—	—	(1.1)	—	(14.4)	(15.5)	—	(15.5)
Total comprehensive (loss) income		—	—	—	(1.1)	—	34.8	33.7	—	33.7
Ordinary dividend	13	—	—	—	—	—	(31.2)	(31.2)	—	(31.2)
Purchase of own shares	30	—	(0.3)	—	—	—	—	(0.3)	—	(0.3)
Share-based payment awards		—	2.4	—	—	—	(2.4)	—	—	—
Credit for share-based payments		—	—	—	—	—	(1.5)	(1.5)	—	(1.5)
Deferred tax on share-based payments		—	—	—	—	—	(0.9)	(0.9)	—	(0.9)
Minority interests acquired with subsidiary		—	—	—	—	—	—	—	1.0	1.0
At 24 April 2010		**347.1**	(0.6)	0.1	12.9	0.3	(260.4)	99.4	1.0	100.4

290   Appendix A: Financial Statements of HMV Group plc

Statements of changes in equity continued

Company	Notes	Equity share capital £m	Own shares £m	Capital reserve £m	Retained earnings £m	Total £m
At 26 April 2008		323.1	(2.0)	0.3	114.7	436.1
Profit for the period		—	—	—	51.6	51.6
Other comprehensive loss		—	—	—	(7.9)	(7.9)
Total comprehensive income		—	—	—	43.7	43.7
Ordinary dividend	13	—	—	—	(29.7)	(29.7)
Issue of equity shares		24.7	—	—	—	24.7
Share issue costs		(0.7)	—	—	—	(0.7)
Purchase of own shares	30	—	(1.0)	—	—	(1.0)
Share-based payment awards		—	0.3	—	(0.3)	—
Charge for share-based payments		—	—	—	0.3	0.3
Deferred tax on share-based payments		—	—	—	0.9	0.9
Capital contribution to subsidiaries for share-based payments		—	—	—	1.4	1.4
At 25 April 2009		347.1	(2.7)	0.3	131.0	475.7
Profit for the period		—	—	—	82.0	82.0
Other comprehensive loss		—	—	—	(13.9)	(13.9)
Total comprehensive income		—	—	—	68.1	68.1
Ordinary dividend	13	—	—	—	(31.2)	(31.2)
Purchase of own shares	30	—	(0.3)	—	—	(0.3)
Share-based payment awards		—	2.4	—	(2.4)	—
Credit for share-based payments		—	—	—	(0.6)	(0.6)
Deferred tax on share-based payments		—	—	—	(0.3)	(0.3)
Capital contribution to subsidiaries for share-based payments		—	—	—	(1.0)	(1.0)
At 24 April 2010		347.1	(0.6)	0.3	163.6	510.4

Appendix A: Financial Statements of HMV Group plc 291

Cash flow statements
For the 52 weeks ended 24 April 2010 and 25 April 2009

	Notes	Group 2010 £m	Group 2009 £m	Company 2010 £m	Company 2009 £m
Cash flows from operating activities					
Profit (loss) before tax		68.9	61.3	(32.9)	(21.5)
Net finance costs		6.2	7.3	6.7	16.1
Share of post-tax profits of associates and joint ventures		(0.3)	(0.2)	—	—
Depreciation	14	43.4	42.5	—	0.1
Amortisation	16	0.1	—	—	—
Net impairment charges	14, 17	2.0	3.4	25.0	—
Profit on disposal of property, plant and equipment		(0.9)	(0.5)	—	—
Equity-settled share-based payment (credit) charge	28	(1.5)	1.7	(0.6)	0.3
Pension contributions less income statement charge		(2.4)	(6.8)	(2.0)	(6.8)
		115.5	108.7	(3.8)	(11.8)
Movement in inventories		(29.6)	(3.6)	—	—
Movement in trade and other receivables		(6.0)	(6.5)	(0.1)	(0.1)
Movement in trade and other payables		3.4	(5.4)	1.4	(5.5)
Movement in provisions		(1.8)	1.1	—	—
Cash generated from operations		81.5	94.3	(2.5)	(17.4)
Income tax (paid) received		(15.6)	(19.3)	5.6	6.8
Net cash flows from operating activities		65.9	75.0	3.1	(10.6)
Cash flows from investing activities					
Purchase of property, plant and equipment		(39.9)	(51.5)	—	—
Proceeds from sale of property, plant and equipment		1.1	1.5	—	—
Interest received		0.4	1.2	7.8	13.3
Repayment of loan by joint venture	17	4.5	—	4.5	—
Payments to acquire investments in joint ventures	17	(8.1)	(20.0)	—	(20.0)
Payments to acquire subsidiary	15	(47.0)	—	(47.0)	—
Cash acquired with subsidiary	15	7.8	—	—	—
Dividends received from subsidiaries		—	—	112.2	67.1
Net cash flows from investing activities		(81.2)	(68.8)	77.5	60.4
Cash flows from financing activities					
Movements in funding		35.0	11.0	34.8	11.0
Movement in intercompany funding		—	—	(12.5)	44.0
Costs of raising debt		(0.2)	(1.1)	—	(1.1)
Proceeds of issue of equity shares, net of costs	27	—	24.0	—	24.0
Purchase of own shares	30	(0.3)	(1.0)	(0.3)	(1.0)
Interest paid		(5.1)	(7.8)	(15.2)	(26.4)
Equity dividends paid to shareholders	13	(31.2)	(29.7)	(31.2)	(29.7)
Repayment of capital element of finance leases		(0.9)	(0.8)	—	—
Net cash flows from financing activities		(2.7)	(5.4)	(24.4)	20.8
Net (decrease) increase in cash and cash equivalents		(18.0)	0.8	56.2	70.6
Opening cash and cash equivalents	26	45.5	35.5	(14.2)	(84.8)
Effect of exchange rate changes	26	(0.2)	9.2	—	—
Closing cash and cash equivalents	20, 26	27.3	45.5	42.0	(14.2)

292   Appendix A: Financial Statements of HMV Group plc

Notes to the financial statements

1. Authorisation of financial statements and statement of compliance with IFRS

The Group and Company financial statements of HMV Group plc for the period ended 24 April 2010 were authorised for issue by the Board of Directors on 29 June 2010, and the balance sheets were signed on the Board's behalf by Simon Fox and Neil Bright. HMV Group plc is a public limited company incorporated and domiciled in England and Wales. The Company's Ordinary Shares are traded on the London Stock Exchange.

The financial statements of the Group and the Company have been prepared in accordance with International Financial Reporting Standards (IFRS) as adopted by the European Union and as applied in accordance with the provisions of the Companies Act 2006. The principal accounting policies adopted by the Group and the Company are set out below.

The Company has taken advantage of the exemption permitted by Section 408 of the Companies Act 2006 not to publish its individual income statement and related notes.

2. Accounting policies

Basis of preparation

The consolidated financial statements of the Company and its subsidiaries are made up to the Saturday on or immediately preceding 30 April each year. Consequently, the financial statements for the current period cover the 52 weeks ended 24 April 2010, whilst the comparative period covered the 52 weeks ended 25 April 2009. The financial statements are prepared in accordance with applicable accounting standards and specifically in accordance with the accounting policies set out below.

The financial statements are presented in Pounds Sterling and are rounded to the nearest tenth of a million except where otherwise indicated. They are prepared on the historical cost basis, except for certain financial instruments, share-based payments and pensions that have been measured at fair value.

The preparation of financial statements requires management to make estimates and assumptions that affect the amounts reported for assets and liabilities as at the balance sheet date and the amounts reported for revenues and expenses during the year. The nature of estimation means that actual outcomes could differ from those estimates.

Judgements and key sources of estimation uncertainty

The judgements and key sources of estimation uncertainty that have a significant risk of causing material adjustment to the carrying amounts of assets and liabilities within the next financial year are as follows.

Impairment of goodwill and other assets – The Group is required to test goodwill for impairment on at least an annual basis. As part of this testing, the value in use of the cash-generating units to which the goodwill is allocated is assessed, which requires the estimation of future cash flows and choosing a suitable discount rate (see Note 16). Property, plant and equipment are reviewed for impairment if events or changes in circumstances indicate that the carrying amount may not be recoverable. When a review for impairment is conducted, the recoverable amount of an asset or a cash generating unit is determined based on value-in-use calculations prepared on the basis of management's assumptions and estimates (see Note 14).

Measurement of defined benefit pension obligations – This requires estimation of future changes in salaries and inflation, as well as mortality rates, the expected return on assets and the selection of a suitable discount rate (see Note 32).

For the Company, key areas of estimation uncertainty are those listed above for the Group and the measurement and impairment of investments in subsidiaries and joint ventures (see Note 17).

Basis of consolidation

The consolidated financial statements comprise the accounts of the Company and its subsidiaries. All intra-group transactions, balances, income and expenses are eliminated on consolidation. The results of subsidiaries acquired or disposed of during a period are included from the date that effective control passed or up to the effective date of disposal, as appropriate. Where the end of the reporting period of a subsidiary, joint venture or associate is different to that of the Group, the entity prepares additional financial statements, for consolidation purposes, as of the same date as the financial statements of HMV Group plc.

Appendix A: Financial Statements of HMV Group plc 293

Interests in joint ventures and associates

A joint venture is a contractual arrangement with other parties to undertake an economic activity that is subject to joint control. An associate is an entity in which the Company holds a long-term non-controlling interest and has the power to exercise significant influence, being the power to participate in the financial and operating policies of the entity.

The Group recognises its interest in joint ventures and associates using the equity method of accounting. Under the equity method, the interest in the joint venture or associate is carried in the balance sheet at cost plus post-acquisition changes in the Group's share of its net assets, less distributions received and less any impairment in value. The Group income statement reflects the share of the jointly controlled or associated entity's results after tax. The Group statement of comprehensive income reflects the Group's share of any income and expense recognised by the jointly controlled entity or associate outside profit and loss.

Any goodwill arising on the acquisition of a jointly controlled entity, representing the excess of the cost of the investment compared to the Group's share of the net fair value of the entity's identifiable assets, liabilities and contingent liabilities, is included in the carrying value of the jointly controlled entity and is not amortised.

Where necessary, adjustments are made to bring the accounting policies used into line with those of the Group. The Group ceases to use the equity method on the date from which it no longer has joint control over, or significant influence on, the joint venture or associate.

Investments in subsidiaries

In its separate financial statements, the Company recognises its investments in subsidiaries at cost less impairments booked. Income is recognised from these investments when the right to receive the distribution is established.

Revenue

Revenue represents the value of goods supplied, less discounts given, and is recognised when goods are delivered and title has passed. It also includes commission earned on ticket sales and similar activities. Revenue in the HMV Live division is recognised at the point that an event occurs or, in the case of services provided, over a period of time in accordance with the relevant contract in place. Revenue excludes value added tax ('VAT') and similar sales-related taxes.

Interest income is accrued on a time basis, by reference to the principal outstanding and the applicable effective interest rate. Dividend income is recognised when the right to receive payment is established. Rental income from sublet properties is recognised on a straight-line basis over the period of the sublease.

Foreign currencies

Transactions denominated in foreign currencies are recorded at the rates of exchange ruling at the date of the transactions. Monetary assets and liabilities denominated in foreign currencies are retranslated into Sterling at period end rates. The resulting foreign exchange differences are dealt with in the determination of profit (loss) for the period.

On consolidation, average exchange rates are used to translate the results of overseas companies and businesses, and the assets and liabilities of overseas companies and businesses are translated into Sterling at period-end rates. Differences on translation are recognised in other comprehensive income in a separate equity reserve, which was set to zero on transition to IFRS. On disposal of an overseas company or business, the cumulative exchange differences for that entity are recognised in the income statement as part of the profit or loss on disposal.

Exceptional items

The Group presents as exceptional items on the face of the income statement those material items of income and expense which, because of the nature or expected infrequency of the events giving rise to them, merit separate presentation to allow shareholders to better understand the elements of financial performance in the year, so as to facilitate comparison with prior periods and to better assess trends in financial performance. Exceptional items recognised in arriving at operating profit include (but are not limited to) those costs associated with integrating a newly acquired business,

294 Appendix A: Financial Statements of HMV Group plc

impairment losses, reversal of impairments and costs associated with restructuring the business.

Goodwill

On transition to IFRS, the Group utilised the exemption available in IFRS 1 whereby IFRS 3 Business Combinations has not been applied retrospectively to past business combinations. Goodwill arising on acquisitions prior to 25 April 1998 was set off directly against reserves. This goodwill has not been reinstated on the balance sheet on the transition to IFRS. Furthermore, it will not be transferred to the income statement if the subsidiary is disposed of or if the investment in the subsidiary becomes impaired. On transition to IFRS, this goodwill was frozen at its carrying value on the date of transition, 25 April 2004, subject to impairment testing at that date. Positive goodwill arising on acquisitions since the Group's transition to IFRS is also capitalised, classified as an asset on the balance sheet and is not amortised. Goodwill is calculated as the excess of the cost of the business combination over the Group's interest in the net fair value of the identifiable assets, liabilities and contingent liabilities. All capitalised goodwill is reviewed for impairment annually or more frequently if events or changes in circumstances indicate that the carrying value may be impaired.

Property, plant and equipment

The capitalised cost of property, plant and equipment includes only those costs that are directly attributable to bringing an asset to its working condition for its intended use.

Depreciation of property, plant and equipment is calculated on cost, at rates estimated to write off the cost, less the estimated residual value, of the relevant assets by equal annual amounts over their estimated useful lives.

The annual rates used are:

Freehold property	Over 50 years
Leasehold improvements	Shorter of useful life and period of the lease
Plant, equipment and vehicles	10 to $33^{1}/_{3}$%

The carrying values of property, plant and equipment are reviewed for material impairment in periods if events or changes in circumstances indicate the carrying

value may not be recoverable. Useful lives and residual values are reviewed annually and where adjustments are required these are made prospectively.

Leased assets

In respect of property operating leases, benefits received and receivable as an incentive to sign a lease, such as rent-free periods, premiums payable and capital contributions, are spread on a straight-line basis over the lease term. All other operating lease payments are charged directly to the income statement on a straight-line basis over the lease term. The Group has a number of lease agreements in which the rent payable is contingent on revenue, which is expensed in the period in which it is incurred.

Assets held under finance leases, which transfer to the Group substantially all the risks and benefits of ownership of the leased assets, are capitalised at the inception of the lease, with a corresponding liability being recognised for the lower of the fair value of the leased asset and the present value of the minimum lease payments. Lease payments are apportioned between the reduction of the lease liability and finance charges in the income statement so as to achieve a constant rate of interest on the remaining balance of the liability. Assets held under finance leases are depreciated over the shorter of the estimated useful life of the asset and the lease term.

Intangible assets

Intangible assets are valued at cost less amortisation and impairment losses. Intangible assets with finite lives are amortised on a straight-line basis over their useful lives of between three and 20 years and are reviewed for impairment if there is any indication that the carrying value may not be recoverable. Intangible assets with an indefinite useful life are not amortised but are tested for impairment annually or more frequently if events indicate that the carrying value may be impaired.

Impairment of assets

The Group assesses at each reporting date whether there are indicators that an asset may be impaired. Assets are grouped for impairment assessment purposes at the lowest level at which there are identifiable cash inflows that are largely independent of the cash inflows of other groups of assets (cash-generating units). If any indicator of impairment exists, or when annual impairment testing is required, the Group makes an estimate of the asset's recoverable amount, being the higher of its fair value less costs to sell and its value in use. Value in use is the present value of the future cash inflows expected to be derived from the asset. Where the asset does not generate cash inflows that are independent from other assets, the recoverable amount of the cash-generating unit to which the asset belongs is estimated. Where the carrying amount of an asset or cash-generating unit exceeds its recoverable amount, an impairment loss is recognised in the income statement.

If there is an indication at the reporting date that previously recognised impairment losses no longer exist or may have decreased, the recoverable amount is again estimated. To the extent that the recoverable amount has increased, the previously recognised impairment loss is reversed. An impairment loss in respect of goodwill is not reversed.

Inventories

Inventories are stated at the lower of cost and net realisable value on a first-in, first-out basis. Net realisable value is based on estimated selling prices less further costs to be incurred to disposal.

Taxation

Current tax   Current tax assets and liabilities for the current and prior periods are measured at the amount expected to be recovered from, or paid to, the taxation authorities, based on tax rates and laws that are enacted or substantively enacted by the balance sheet date.

Deferred tax   Deferred income tax is recognised on all temporary differences at the balance sheet date between the tax bases of assets and liabilities and their carrying amounts for financial reporting purposes.

Deferred tax liabilities are generally recognised for all temporary differences and deferred income tax assets are recognised to the extent that it is probable that taxable profit will be available against which the deductible temporary differences can be utilised. The carrying amount of deferred income tax assets is reviewed at each balance sheet date and reduced to the extent that it is no longer probable that sufficient taxable profit will

be available to allow all or part of the deferred income tax asset to be utilised.

Such assets and liabilities are not recognised if the temporary difference arises from goodwill or from the initial recognition (other than in a business combination) of other assets and liabilities in a transaction that affects neither the taxable profit nor the accounting profit.

Deferred tax liabilities are not recognised for temporary differences associated with investments in subsidiaries, branches, and joint ventures as the Group has determined that undistributed profits will not be distributed in the foreseeable future.

Deferred income tax assets and liabilities are measured at the tax rates that are expected to apply to the year when the asset is realised or the liability settled, based on tax rates and laws that have been enacted or substantively enacted at the balance sheet date, and are not discounted.

Taxation is charged or credited to other comprehensive income if it relates to items that are themselves charged or credited to other comprehensive income, otherwise it is recognised in the income statement. Taxation relating to items taken directly to equity is also charged or credited directly to equity.

Deferred tax assets and deferred tax liabilities are offset, if a legally enforceable right exists to set off current tax assets against current tax liabilities and the deferred taxes relate to the same taxable entity and the same taxation authority.

Cash and cash equivalents

Cash and short-term deposits comprise cash at bank and in hand and short-term deposits with an original maturity of three months or less. For the purposes of the cash flow statement, cash and cash equivalents consist of cash and short-term deposits less bank overdrafts that are payable on demand.

Interest-bearing loans and borrowings

Interest-bearing loans and borrowings are initially recognised at fair value less directly attributable transaction costs and are subsequently measured at amortised cost using the effective interest rate method.

Provisions

A provision is recognised when the Group has a legal or constructive obligation as a result of a past

296   Appendix A: Financial Statements of HMV Group plc

event and it is probable that an outflow of economic benefits will be required to settle the obligation. If the effect is material, expected future cash flows are discounted using a current pre-tax rate that reflects the risks specific to the liability.

Pension costs

The Group operates both defined benefit and defined contribution pension schemes, the funds of which are held in separate, trustee administered funds.

The cost of providing benefits under the defined benefit scheme is determined using the projected unit credit method, with actuarial valuations being carried out at each balance sheet date. The net retirement benefit obligation recognised in the balance sheet represents the present value of the liabilities of the defined benefit scheme as reduced by the market value of the defined benefit scheme assets.

Actuarial gains and losses are recognised in other comprehensive income in full in the period in which they occur. Other income and expenses associated with the defined benefit scheme are recognised in the income statement.

The defined benefit scheme provides benefits to a number of Group companies. There is no agreement or policy for allocating a share of the defined benefit obligation to each participating entity. Consequently, the Company, as sponsoring employer of the defined benefit scheme, recognises the net pension obligation for the scheme. The other participating members of the scheme account for their relevant pension costs on a defined contribution basis.

Contributions to the defined contribution scheme are charged in the income statement as they become payable in accordance with the rules of the scheme.

Share-based payments

The cost of equity-settled transactions with employees granted on or after 7 November 2002, which had not vested by 1 January 2005, is measured by reference to the fair value at the date at which they are granted and is recognised as an expense over the vesting period, which ends on the date on which the relevant employees become fully entitled to the award. Fair value is determined by using an appropriate pricing model.

Except for awards subject to market related conditions, the cumulative expense is calculated at each balance sheet date before vesting, representing the extent to which the vesting period has expired and management's best estimate of the achievement or otherwise of non-market performance conditions, and hence the number of equity instruments that will ultimately vest. The movement in cumulative expense since the previous balance sheet date is recognised in the income statement, with a corresponding entry in equity. No expense is recognised for awards that do not ultimately vest. If options are subject to market related conditions awards are not cumulatively adjusted for the likelihood of these targets being met. Instead these conditions are included in the calculation of the fair value of the awards.

Treasury shares

HMV Group plc shares held by the Group's Employee Benefit Trust are classified in shareholders' equity as 'other reserve – own shares' and are recognised at cost. No gain or loss is recognised in the financial statements on the purchase, sale, issue or cancellation of equity shares.

Derivative financial instruments

The Group may from time to time use derivative financial instruments for hedging purposes, including forward foreign exchange contracts. The Group does not enter into derivative financial instruments for speculative purposes.

Derivative financial instruments are stated at their fair value. The fair value of forward foreign exchange contracts is their quoted market value at the balance sheet date, being the present value of the quoted forward price.

Hedge accounting

Changes in the fair value of derivative financial instruments that are designated and effective as hedges of future cash flows are recognised in other comprehensive income and any ineffective portion is recognised immediately in the income statement. Amounts taken to other comprehensive income are transferred to the income statement when hedged transactions affect profit or loss, such as when a forecast sale or purchase occurs.

Hedge accounting is discontinued when the hedging instrument expires or is sold, terminated or exercised, or no longer qualifies for hedge accounting. At that time any cumulative gain or loss on the hedging instrument previously recognised in other comprehensive income is retained in equity until the hedged transaction occurs. If the hedged transaction is no longer expected to occur, the net cumulative gain or loss recognised in other comprehensive income is then transferred to the income statement.

Changes in the fair value of derivative financial instruments that do not qualify for hedge accounting are recognised in the income statement as they arise.

Customer loyalty schemes

The fair value of loyalty points awarded is deferred until the awards are redeemed, after adjustment for the number of points expected never to be redeemed. Fair value is determined by reference to the value for which the points can be redeemed.

New accounting standards

The Group and the Company have adopted the following new accounting standards, amendments to accounting standards and interpretations, which are either mandatory for the first time for the financial year ending 24 April 2010 or have been adopted early as appropriate.

- IAS 1 Presentation of Financial Statements (revised 2007), effective for periods beginning on or after 1 January 2009. This is a presentational change only, affecting the naming and positioning of items within the financial statements. It has no impact on reported income or total equity.

The following have been adopted but have no material impact on the Group or Company:

- Amendments to IFRS 1 and IAS 27 Cost of an investment in a subsidiary, joint-controlled entity or associate (effective 1 January 2009)

- Amendment to IFRS 2 Share-based Payment vesting conditions and cancellations (1 January 2009)

- Amendment to IFRS 7 Improving disclosures about financial instruments (1 January 2009)

- IAS 23 Borrowing Costs (1 January 2009)

- IAS 32 Financial Instruments: Presentation and IAS 1 Financial Instruments – Puttable Financial Instruments and Obligations Arising on Liquidation (Amendments) (1 January 2009)

- IFRIC 9 Reassessment of Embedded Derivatives, IAS 39 Financial Instruments: Recognition and Measurement (periods ending on or after 30 June 2009)

- IFRIC 15 Agreements for the Construction of Real Estate (1 January 2009)

- IFRIC 16 Hedges of a Net Investment in a Foreign Operation (1 October 2008)

- IFRIC 18 Transfer of Assets from Customers (1 July 2009)

- Annual improvements to IFRS (1 January 2009)

The Group has not adopted early the requirements of the following accounting standards and interpretations, which have an effective date after the start date of these financial statements:

- IFRS 3 (R) Business Combinations (revised 2008) (1 July 2009)

- IAS 27 Consolidated and Separate Financial Statements (revised 2008) (1 July 2009)

- IFRIC 17 Distribution of Non-cash Assets to Owners (1 July 2009)

- IAS 39 Eligible Hedged Items (1 July 2009)

- Annual improvements to IFRS (various effective dates)

The Directors do not anticipate that the adoption of these standards and interpretations in the year ended 30 April 2011 will have a material impact on the Group's financial statements.

The effective dates stated are those given in the original IASB/IFRIC standards and interpretations. As the Group prepares its financial statements in accordance with IFRS as adopted by the European Union, the application of new standards and interpretations will be subject to their having been endorsed for use in the EU via the EU endorsement mechanism.

298 Appendix A: Financial Statements of HMV Group plc

18. Trade and other receivables

	Group 2010 £m	Group 2009 £m	Company 2010 £m	Company 2009 £m
Non-current				
Lease premiums paid	11.9	—	—	—
Other receivables	0.8	1.2	—	—
	12.7	1.2	—	—
Current				
Trade receivables	13.2	9.9	—	—
Amounts owed by subsidiary undertakings	—	—	27.7	69.0
Amounts owed by joint venture	—	5.5	—	5.5
Other receivables	16.9	10.1	—	—
Prepayments and accrued income	50.6	46.1	0.6	0.9
	80.7	71.6	28.3	75.4

The carrying value of trade and other receivables approximates to fair value. The terms and conditions of amounts owed by subsidiary undertakings are given in Note 35.

Trade receivables are denominated in the following currencies:

	Group 2010 £m	Group 2009 £m
Sterling	12.7	9.4
Euro	0.2	0.3
Canadian dollar	0.3	0.1
Singapore dollar	—	0.1
	13.2	9.9

The Group's credit risk is limited due to the nature of its retailing business. As at 24 April 2010 £0.8m of Group trade receivables was overdue (2009: £0.7m), of which £0.4m (2009: £0.6m) was provided for. See Note 25 for further discussion of credit risk. Trade and other receivables are non-interest bearing and are generally on 30 day terms.

The Company has no trade receivables and no provisions for impairment of any financial assets.

19. Inventories

Inventories primarily comprise finished goods and goods for resale. The replacement cost of inventories is considered to be not materially different from the balance sheet value.

20. Cash and short-term deposits

	Group 2010 £m	Group 2009 £m	Company 2010 £m	Company 2009 £m
Cash at bank and in hand	27.8	52.1	48.9	15.8
Short-term deposits	1.9	0.6	—	—
	29.7	52.7	48.9	15.8

Cash at bank earns interest at floating rates based on daily bank deposit rates. Short-term deposits are made for varying periods of between one day and three months depending on the cash requirements of the Group, and earn interest at the respective short-term deposit rates.

Cash balances are deposited through the year with counter parties that have a strong credit rating, with an agreed limit for each counterparty, so as to limit the risk of loss arising from a failure. Counterparties include AAA-rated liquidity funds, as well as banks.

For the purpose of the cash flow statement, cash and cash equivalents comprise the following:

	Group 2010 £m	Group 2009 £m	Company 2010 £m	Company 2009 £m
Cash at bank and in hand	27.8	52.1	48.9	15.8
Short-term deposits	1.9	0.6	—	—
Bank overdrafts	(2.4)	(7.2)	(6.9)	(30.0)
	27.3	45.5	42.0	(14.2)

300   Appendix B: Financial Statements of WHSmith PLC

Appendix B: Financial Statements of WHSmith PLC

GROUP INCOME STATEMENT

FOR THE YEAR ENDED 31 AUGUST 2010

£m	Note	2010 Before exceptional items	2010 Exceptional items	2010 Total	2009 Before exceptional items	2009 Exceptional items	2009 Total
Continuing operations							
Revenue	2	**1,312**	—	**1,312**	1,340	—	1,340
Operating profit	2, 3	**89**	—	**89**	83	—	83
Investment income	9	**1**	—	**1**	1	—	1
Finance costs	10	**(1)**	—	**(1)**	(2)	—	(2)
Profit before tax		**89**	—	**89**	82	—	82
Income tax expense	11	**(20)**	—	**(20)**	(18)	—	(18)
Profit after tax from continuing operations		**69**	—	**69**	64	—	64
Loss for the year from discontinued operations	4	—	—	—	—	(1)	(1)
Profit for the year		**69**	—	**69**	64	(1)	63
Earnings per share[1]							
Basic – continuing operations	13			**47.6p**			42.7p
Diluted – continuing operations	13			**45.7p**			41.3p
Basic	13			**47.6p**			42.0p
Diluted	13			**45.7p**			40.6p
Non GAAP measures **Underlying earnings per share[2]**							
Basic – continuing operations	13			**47.6p**			42.7p
Diluted – continuing operations	13			**45.7p**			41.3p
Basic	13			**47.6p**			42.7p
Diluted	13			**45.7p**			41.3p
Equity dividends per share[3]				**19.4p**			16.7p
Fixed charges cover	8			**1.5×**			1.5×

[1] Earnings per share is calculated in accordance with IAS 33 'Earnings per share'

[2] Underlying earnings per share excludes exceptional items

[3] Dividend per share is the final proposed dividend of 13.3p (2009: 11.3p) and the interim dividend of 6.1 p (2009: 5.4p)

Appendix B: Financial Statements of WHSmith PLC   301

GROUP STATEMENT OF COMPREHENSIVE INCOME

FOR THE YEAR ENDED 31 AUGUST 2010

£m	Note	2010	2009
Profit for the period		**69**	63
Other comprehensive income:			
Actuarial losses on defined pension schemes	5	(12)	(11)
Mark to market valuation of derivative financial asset		(1)	(1)
Other comprehensive loss for the period, net of tax		(13)	(12)
Total comprehensive income for the period		**56**	51

302   Appendix B: Financial Statements of WHSmith PLC

GROUP BALANCE SHEET

AS AT 31 AUGUST 2010

£m	Note	2010	2009	2008
Non-current assets				
Goodwill	14	32	32	32
Other intangible assets	15	24	24	23
Property, plant and equipment	16	158	163	177
Deferred tax assets	21	10	9	11
Trade and other receivables	17	4	4	4
		228	232	247
Current assets				
Inventories		151	151	147
Trade and other receivables	17	57	56	66
Current tax asset		21	7	4
Derivative financial assets	25	—	1	2
Cash and cash equivalents	22	56	47	22
		285	262	241
Total assets		513	494	488
Current liabilities				
Trade and other payables	18	(246)	(242)	(239)
Current tax liabilities		(51)	(34)	(31)
Obligations under finance leases	19, 22	—	(2)	(4)
Bank overdrafts and other borrowings	22	—	—	(25)
Short-term provisions	20	(3)	(3)	(4)
		(300)	(281)	(303)
Non-current liabilities				
Retirement benefit obligation	5	(1)	(2)	—
Deferred tax liabilities	21	(6)	(8)	(10)
Long-term provisions	20	(5)	(5)	(4)
Obligations under finance leases	19, 22	—	—	(2)
Other non-current liabilities		(15)	(10)	(8)
		(27)	(25)	(24)
Total liabilities		(327)	(306)	(327)
Total net assets		186	188	161
Total equity		186	188	161

GROUP BALANCE SHEET (CONTINUED)

£m	Note	2010	2009	2008
Shareholders' equity				
Called up share capital	26	33	35	35
Share premium		1	—	—
Capital redemption reserve		4	2	2
Revaluation reserve		2	2	2
ESOP reserve		(29)	(28)	(28)
Hedging reserve		—	1	2
Translation reserve		(2)	(2)	(2)
Other reserve		(191)	(187)	(179)
Retained earnings		368	365	329
Total equity		**186**	188	161

The consolidated financial statements of WH Smith PLC, registered number 5202036, were approved by the Board of Directors and authorised for issue on 14 October 2010 and were signed on its behalf by:

Kate Swann   **Robert Moorhead**

Group Chief Executive   **Group Finance Director**

304   Appendix B: Financial Statements of WHSmith PLC

GROUP CASH FLOW STATEMENT

FOR THE YEAR ENDED 31 AUGUST 2010

£m	Note	2010	2009
Net cash inflow from operating activities	24	**104**	113
Investing activities			
Interest received		**1**	1
Purchase of property, plant and equipment		**(24)**	(23)
Purchase of intangible assets		**(5)**	(5)
Net cash outflow from investing activities		**(28)**	(27)
Financing activities			
Interest paid		**—**	(1)
Dividend paid		**(26)**	(23)
Purchase of own shares for cancellation		**(35)**	—
Purchase of own shares for employee share schemes		**(4)**	(8)
Repayments of borrowings		**—**	(25)
Repayments of obligations under finance leases		**(2)**	(4)
Net cash used in financing activities		**(67)**	(61)
Net increase in cash and cash equivalents in year		**9**	25
Opening net cash and cash equivalents		**47**	22
Closing net cash and cash equivalents		**56**	47

RECONCILIATION OF NET CASH FLOW TO MOVEMENT IN NET FUNDS / (DEBT)

£m	Note	2010	2009
Net funds / (debt) at beginning of the year		**45**	(9)
Increase in cash and cash equivalents		**9**	25
Decrease in debt		**—**	25
Net movement in finance leases		**2**	4
Net funds at end of the year	22	**56**	45

Appendix B: Financial Statements of WHSmith PLC   305

GROUP STATEMENT OF CHANGES IN EQUITY

FOR THE YEAR ENDED 31 AUGUST 2010

£m	Share capital and share premium	Capital redemption reserve	Revaluation reserve	ESOP reserve	Hedging and translation reserves	Other reserve[1]	Retained earnings	Total
Balance at 1 September 2009	35	2	2	(28)	(1)	(187)	365	188
Total comprehensive (loss) /income or the period	—	—	—	—	(1)	—	57	56
Recognition of share-based payments	—	—	—	—	—	—	7	7
Deferred tax on share-based payments	—	—	—	—	—	—	—	—
Premium on issue of shares	1	—	—	—	—	—	—	1
Dividends paid	—	—	—	—	—	—	(26)	(26)
Employee share schemes	—	—	—	(1)	—	(4)	—	(5)
Purchase of own shares for cancellation	(2)	2	—	—	—	—	(35)	(35)
Balance at 31 August 2010	34	4	2	(29)	(2)	(191)	368	186
Balance at 1 September 2008	35	2	2	(28)	—	(179)	329	161
Total comprehensive (loss) /income or the period	—	—	—	—	(1)	—	52	51
Recognition of share-based payments	—	—	—	—	—	—	6	6
Current tax on share-based payments	—	—	—	—	—	—	1	1
Dividends paid	—	—	—	—	—	—	(23)	(23)
Employee share schemes	—	—	—	—	—	(8)	—	(8)
Balance at 31 August 2009	35	2	2	(28)	(1)	(187)	365	188

[1]The 'Other' reserve includes reserves created in relation to the historical capital reorganisation, proforma restatement and the demerger from Smith News PLC in 2006, as well as movements relating to employee share schemes of £4m (2009: £8m)

306   Appendix B: Financial Statements of WHSmith PLC

NOTES TO ACCOUNTS

1. ACCOUNTING POLICIES

a) Basis of preparation

The consolidated Group financial statements have been prepared in accordance with International Financial Reporting Standards ('IFRS') as adopted by the European Union and with those parts of the Companies Act 2006 applicable to companies reporting under IFRS. These are the standards, subsequent amendments and related interpretations issued and adopted by the International Accounting Standards Board ('IASB') that have been endorsed by the European Union at the year end.

The consolidated Group financial statements have also been prepared in accordance with IFRS adopted for use in the European Union and therefore comply with Article 4 of the EU IAS Regulation. The consolidated financial statements have been prepared on a going concern basis as explained on pages 23 and 24 of the Directors' Report and Business Review.

New Standards

The Group has adopted the following standards which became mandatory during the current financial year:

IAS 1 (revised 2007), Presentation of financial statements, has introduced a number of changes in the format and content of the financial statements, including the renaming of the "Statement of Recognised Income and Expenditure" to the "Group Statement of Comprehensive Income". The revised standard requires the presentation of a third balance sheet whenever previously reported information is restated or an accounting policy is applied retrospectively. IFRS 2 (amended) and IFRS 8 were adopted in the period, and applied retrospectively. While the adoption of both of these standards resulted in no change to the 2008 balance sheet as previously presented, a balance sheet as at 31 August 2008 has been included in accordance with IAS 1. A full explanation of the impact of IFRS 8 is provided in Note 2.

During the period the Group adopted IFRS 2 (amended). This amendment clarifies the treatment of vesting conditions and cancellations of share-based payments. The amendment has been applied retrospectively and has not resulted in any change to previously reported profits or total equity.

Other new accounting standards from the IASB and interpretations from IFRIC which become mandatory for the first time during the current financial year but which have no material impact on the Group's financial statements are:

IFRS 3 (Revised)	Business combinations
Amendments to IFRS 7	Improving disclosures about financial instruments
Amendments to IAS 23	Borrowing costs
Amendments to IAS 27	Consolidated and separate financial statements
Amendments to IAS 38	Intangible assets
Amendments to IAS 39	Eligible hedged items

At the date of authorisation of these consolidated Group financial statements, the following Standards and Interpretations, which have not been applied in these financial statements, were in issue but not yet effective:

Amendments to IFRS 2	Group cash-settled share-based payment transactions
IAS 24 (Revised)	Related party disclosures
Amendments to IAS 32	Classification of rights issues
Amendment to IFRIC 14	Prepayments of a minimum funding requirement
IFRIC 17	Distributions of non-cash assets to owners
IFRIC 18	Transfers of assets from customers
IFRIC 19	Extinguishing financial liabilities with equity instruments
IFRS 9	Financial instruments

The directors anticipate that the adoption of these Standards and Interpretations in future years will have no material impact on the Group's financial statements.

Accounting convention

The financial statements are drawn up on the historical cost basis of accounting. The financial information is rounded to the nearest million, except where otherwise indicated. The principal accounting policies, which have been applied consistently throughout both years, are set out below.

Basis of consolidation

The consolidated Group financial statements incorporate the financial statements of WH Smith PLC and all its subsidiaries up to the year end date.

Subsidiary undertakings are all entities over which the Group has the power to govern the financial and operating policies generally accompanying a shareholding of more than one half of the voting rights so to obtain benefits from its activities.

Goodwill arising on acquisition is recognised as an asset and initially measured at cost, being the excess of the cost of the business combination over the Group's interest in the net fair value of the identifiable assets, liabilities and contingent liabilities recognised. If, after reassessment, the Group's interest in the net fair value of the acquiree's identifiable assets, liabilities and contingent liabilities exceeds the cost of the business combination, after taking into account recognised goodwill, the excess is immediately recognised in the income statement.

The separable net assets, both tangible and intangible, of the newly acquired subsidiary undertakings are incorporated into the financial statements on the basis of the fair value as at the effective date of control, if appropriate.

Results of subsidiary undertakings disposed of during the financial year are included in the financial statements up to the effective date of disposal. Where a business component representing a separate major line of business is disposed of, or classified as held for sale, it is classified as a discontinued operation. The post-tax profit or loss of the discontinued operations is shown as a single amount on the face of the income statement, separate from the other results of the Group.

All intercompany transactions, balances and unrealised gains on transactions between Group companies are eliminated.

b) Revenue

Revenue is measured at the fair value of the consideration received or receivable and represents amounts receivable for goods and services to customers, together with commission and fee income on concession and franchise arrangements. Revenue excludes discounts, estimated returns, VAT and other sales-related taxes.

Revenue on store sales of goods and concession sales is recognised when goods are sold to the customer. Internet sales are recognised when the goods are delivered to the customer and title has passed. Revenue from gift vouchers and gift cards sold by the Group is recognised on the redemption of the gift voucher or gift card. Franchise and concession fees are recognised in revenue based on the terms of the contracts.

c) Retirement benefit costs

Payments to the WH Smith Group defined contribution pension schemes are recognised as an expense in the income statement as they fall due.

The cost of providing benefits for the main defined benefit scheme, WHSmith Pension Trust, and the acquired United News Shops Retirement Benefits Scheme are determined by the Projected Unit Credit Method, with actuarial calculations being carried out at the balance sheet date. Actuarial gains and losses are recognised in full in the period in which they occur. They are recognised outside the income statement in the Group Statement of Comprehensive Income.

The retirement benefit obligation recognised in the balance sheet represents the present value of the defined benefit obligation, as adjusted for unrecognised past service cost, and as reduced by the fair value of scheme assets. Any asset resulting from the calculation is limited to past service cost, plus the present value of available refunds and reductions in future contributions to the plan.

d) Leasing

Leases are classified as finance leases whenever the terms of the lease transfer substantially all the risks and rewards of ownership to the lessee. All other leases are classified as operating leases.

Assets held under finance leases are recognised as assets of the Group at their fair value determined at the inception of the lease or, if lower, at the present value of the minimum lease payments. The corresponding liability to the lessor is included in the balance sheet as a finance lease obligation. Lease payments are apportioned between finance charges and a reduction of the lease obligations so as to achieve a constant rate of interest on the remaining balance of the liability. Finance charges are recognised directly in the income statement.

Rentals payable and receivable under operating leases are charged to the income statement on a straight-line basis over the term of the relevant lease. Benefits received and receivable as an incentive to enter into an operating lease are also spread on a straight-line basis over the lease term. The Group has a number of lease arrangements in which the rent payable is contingent on revenue. Contingent rentals payable, based on store revenues, are accrued in line with revenues generated.

e) Intangible assets

Business combinations

The acquisition of subsidiaries is accounted for using the purchase method. The cost of acquisition is measured at the aggregate of the fair values, at the date of exchange, of assets given, liabilities incurred or assumed, and equity instruments issued by the Group in exchange for control, of the acquiree. Costs directly attributable to the business combination are recognised in the income statement in the period they are incurred. The cost of a business combination is allocated at the acquisition date by recognising the acquiree's identifiable assets, liabilities and contingent liabilities that satisfy the recognition criteria at their fair values at that date. The acquisition date is the date on which the acquirer effectively obtains control of the acquiree. Intangible assets are recognised if they meet the definition of an intangible asset contained in IAS 38 and its fair value can be measured reliably. The excess of the cost of acquisition over the fair value of the Group's share of identifiable net assets acquired is recognised as goodwill.

Goodwill

Goodwill represents the excess of the fair value of purchase consideration over the net fair value of identifiable assets and liabilities acquired.

Goodwill is recognised as an asset at cost and subsequently measured at cost less accumulated impairment. For the purposes of impairment testing, goodwill is allocated to those cash generating units that have benefited from the acquisition. The carrying value of goodwill is reviewed for impairment at least annually or where there is an indication that goodwill may be impaired. If the recoverable amount of the cash generating unit is less than its carrying amount, then the impairment loss is allocated first to reduce the carrying amount of the goodwill allocated to the unit and then to the other assets of the unit on a pro rata basis. Any impairment is recognised immediately in the income statement and is not subsequently reversed.

On disposal of a subsidiary, the attributable amount of goodwill is included in the determination of the profit and loss on disposal.

Other intangible assets

The costs of acquiring and developing software that is not integral to the related hardware is capitalised separately as an intangible asset. These intangibles are stated at cost less accumulated amortisation and impairment losses.

Amortisation is charged so as to write off the costs of assets over their estimated useful lives, using the straight-line method. The estimated lives are usually a period of up to five years. Software assets held under finance leases are depreciated over their expected useful lives on the same basis as owned assets or where shorter, over the term of the relevant lease.

Other intangible assets are valued at cost and amortised over their useful life unless the asset can be demonstrated to have an indefinite life.

All intangible assets are reviewed for impairment in accordance with IAS 36, Impairment of Assets, when there are indications that the carrying value may not be recoverable.

f) Property, plant and equipment

Property, plant and equipment assets are carried at cost less accumulated depreciation and any recognised impairment in value. The carrying values of tangible fixed assets previously revalued have been retained at their book amount. Depreciation is charged so as to write off the costs of assets, other than land, over their estimated useful lives, using the straight-line method, with the annual rates applicable to the principal categories being:

Freehold properties	- over 20 years
Short-leasehold properties	- shorter of the lease period and the estimated remaining economic life
In-store fixtures and fittings	- up to ten years
Equipment and vehicles	- eight to ten years
Computer equipment	- up to five years

The residual values of property, plant and equipment are re-assessed on an annual basis.

Assets held under finance leases are depreciated over their expected useful lives on the same basis as owned assets or, where shorter, over the term of the relevant lease.

At each balance sheet date, property, plant and equipment is reviewed for impairment if events or changes in circumstances indicate that the carrying amount may not be recoverable. When a review for impairment is conducted, the recoverable amount is assessed by reference to the net present value of expected future pre-tax cash flows of the relevant cash-generating unit or fair value, less costs to sell, if higher. Any impairment in value is charged to the income statement in the period in which it occurs.

g) Inventories

Inventories comprise goods held for resale and are stated at the lower of cost or net realisable value. Concession stocks are not included within stocks held by the Group. Inventories are valued using a weighted average cost method.

Cost is calculated to include, where applicable, duties, handling, transport and directly attributable costs in bringing the inventories to their present location and condition. Net realisable value is based on estimated normal selling prices less further costs expected to be incurred in selling and distribution. Cost of inventories includes the transfer from equity of any gains or losses on qualifying cash flow hedges relating to purchases.

Provisions are made for obsolescence, markdown and shrinkage.

h) Provisions

Provisions are recognised in the balance sheet when the Group has a present legal or constructive obligation as a result of a past event and it is probable that an outflow of economic benefits will be required to settle the obligation. Provisions are measured at the directors' best estimate of the expenditure required to settle the obligation at the balance sheet date. Where the effect is material, the provision is determined by discounting the expected future cash flows at the Group's weighted average cost of capital.

Onerous contracts – property provisions

The Group's property provisions represent the present value of future net lease obligations and related costs of leasehold property (net of estimated sublease income and adjusted for certain risk factors) where the space is vacant or currently not planned to be used for ongoing operations. The periodic unwinding of the discount is treated as an imputed interest charge and is disclosed in the income statement as 'unwinding of discount on provisions'.

i) Foreign currencies

Transactions denominated in foreign currencies are recorded at the rates of exchange prevailing on the dates of the transactions. At each balance sheet date, monetary items denominated in foreign currencies are retranslated at the rates prevailing on the balance sheet date. Exchange differences arising on the settlement of monetary items, and on the retranslation of monetary items, are included in the income statement for the period.

In order to hedge its exposure to certain foreign exchange risks, the Group enters into forward contracts and options (see opposite for details of the Group's accounting policies in respect of such derivative financial instruments).

On consolidation the assets and liabilities of the Group's overseas operations are translated into sterling at exchange rates prevailing on the balance sheet date. Income and expense items are translated into sterling at the average exchange rates for the period. Exchange differences arising, if any, are classified as equity and transferred to the Group's translation reserve.

j) Taxation

The tax expense included in the income statement comprises current and deferred tax.

Current tax is the expected tax payable based on the taxable profit for the period, using tax rates that have been enacted or substantively enacted by the balance sheet date.

Deferred tax is recognised on differences between the carrying amounts of assets and liabilities in the accounts and the corresponding tax bases used in the computation of taxable profit, and is accounted for using the balance sheet liability method. Deferred tax liabilities are generally recognised for all taxable temporary differences and

310   Appendix B: Financial Statements of WHSmith PLC

deferred tax assets are recognised to the extent that it is probable that taxable profits will be available against which deductible temporary differences can be utilised. Such assets and liabilities are not recognised if the temporary difference arises from goodwill or from the initial recognition (other than in business combination) of other assets and liabilities in a transaction that affects neither the tax profit nor the accounting profit.

The carrying amount of deferred tax assets is reviewed at each balance sheet date and reduced to the extent that it is no longer probable that sufficient taxable profits will be available to allow all or part of the asset to be recovered. Deferred tax is calculated at the tax rates that are expected to apply in the period when the liability is settled or the asset is realised.

Current and deferred tax is charged or credited in the income statement, except when it relates to items charged or credited directly to equity, in which case the current or deferred tax is also recognised directly in equity.

k) Financial instruments

Trade receivables

Trade receivables are measured at initial recognition, do not carry any interest and are stated at their fair value and are subsequently measured at amortised cost using the effective interest rate method. Appropriate allowances for estimated irrecoverable amounts are recognised in the income statement when there is evidence that the asset is impaired.

Cash and cash equivalents

Cash and cash equivalents in the balance sheet comprise cash at bank and in hand and short-term deposits with an original maturity of three months or less.

Financial liabilities and equity

Financial liabilities and equity instruments are classified according to the substance of the contractual arrangements entered into. An equity instrument is any contract that evidences a residual interest in the assets of the Group after deducting all of its liabilities.

Bank borrowings

Interest-bearing bank loans and overdrafts are initially measured at fair value (being proceeds received, net of direct issue costs), and are subsequently measured at

amortised cost, using the effective interest rate method recorded as the proceeds received, net of direct issue costs. Finance charges, including premiums payable on settlement or redemptions and direct issue costs are accounted for on an accruals basis and taken to the income statement using the effective interest rate method and are added to the carrying value of the instrument to the extent that they are not settled in the period in which they arise.

Trade payables

Trade payables are initially measured at fair value, and are subsequently measured at amortised cost, using the effective interest rate method.

Equity instruments

Equity instruments issued are recorded at the proceeds received, net of direct issue costs.

Derivative financial instruments and hedge accounting

The Group uses certain derivative financial instruments to reduce its exposure to foreign exchange and interest rate movements. The Group does not hold or use derivative financial instruments for speculative purposes.

Changes in the fair value of derivative financial instruments that are designated and effective as hedges of future cash flows are recognised directly in equity and any ineffective portion is recognised immediately in the income statement. If the cash flow hedge of a firm commitment or forecasted transaction results in the recognition of an asset or liability, then, at the time the asset or liability is recognised, the associated gains or losses on the derivative that had previously been recognised in equity are included in the initial measurement of the asset or liability. For hedges that do not result in the recognition of an asset or a liability, amounts deferred in equity are recognised in the income statement in the same period in which the hedged item affects net income.

For an effective hedge of an exposure to changes in the fair value of a recognised asset or liability, changes in fair value of the hedging instrument are recognised in profit or loss at the same time that the recognised asset or liability that is being hedged is adjusted for movements in the hedged risk and that adjustment is also recognised in profit or loss in the same period.

Changes in the fair value of derivative financial instruments that do not qualify for hedge accounting are recognised in the income statement as they arise.

Hedge accounting is discontinued when the hedging instrument expires or is sold, terminated, or exercised, or no longer qualifies for hedge accounting. At that time, any cumulative gain or loss on the hedging instrument recognised in equity is retained in equity until the forecasted transaction occurs. If a hedged transaction is no longer expected to occur, the net cumulative gain or loss recognised in equity is transferred to the net profit or loss for the period.

Derivatives embedded in other financial instruments or other host contracts are treated as separate derivatives when their risks and characteristics are not closely related to those of host contracts and the host contracts are not carried at fair value with unrealised gains or losses reported in the income statement.

l) Share schemes

WH Smith Employee Benefit Trust

The shares held by the WH Smith Employee Benefit Trust are valued at the historical cost of the shares acquired. They are deducted in arriving at shareholders' funds and are presented as an other reserve.

Share-based payments

Employees of the Group receive part of their remuneration in the form of share-based payment transactions, whereby employees render services in exchange for shares or rights over shares (equity settled transactions).

Equity settled share-based payments are measured at fair value at the date of grant. The fair value is calculated using an appropriate option pricing model. The fair value is expensed to the income statement on a straight-line basis over the vesting period, based on the Group's estimate of shares that will eventually vest.

m) Dividends

Final dividends are recorded in the financial statements in the period in which they are approved by the Company's shareholders. Interim dividends are recorded in the period in which they are approved and paid.

n) Critical accounting judgements and key sources of estimation uncertainty

The preparation of financial statements in conformity with general accepted accounting principles requires management to make estimates and assumptions that affect the reported amounts of assets and liabilities and the disclosure of contingent assets and liabilities. Significant items subject to such assumption and estimate include the useful economic life of assets; the measurement and recognition of provisions; the recognition of deferred tax assets; and the liabilities for potential corporation tax. Actual results could differ from these estimates and any subsequent changes are accounted for with an effect on income at the time such updated information becomes available. The most critical accounting policies in determining the financial condition and results of the Group are those requiring the greatest degree of subjective or complex judgement. These relate to retirement benefit obligations, valuation of goodwill and acquired intangible assets, onerous lease costs, inventory valuation and taxation.

Retirement benefit obligation

The Group recognises and discloses its retirement benefit obligation in accordance with the measurement and presentational requirement of IAS 19, 'Retirement Benefit Obligations'. The calculations include a number of judgements and estimations in respect of the expected rate of return on assets, the discount rate, inflation assumptions, the rate of increase in salaries, and life expectancy, amongst others. Changes in these assumptions can have a significant effect on the value of the retirement benefit obligation.

In order to reduce the volatility in the underlying investment performance substantially and reduce the risk of a significant increase in the obligation, a new investment policy in respect of the assets of the WHSmith Pension Trust was adopted in September 2005. This is discussed in more detail in Note 5.

Goodwill, intangible assets and property plant and equipment impairment reviews

The Group is required to review goodwill annually to determine if any impairment has occurred. Value-in-use calculations require the use of estimates in relation to future cash flows and suitable discount rates.

Property, plant and equipment and intangible assets are reviewed for impairment if events or changes in circumstances indicate that the carrying amount may not be recoverable. When a review for impairment is conducted the recoverable amount of an asset or a cash generating unit is determined based on value-in-use calculations prepared on the basis of management's assumptions and estimates.

Inventory valuation

Inventory is carried at the lower of cost and net realisable value which requires the estimation of the eventual sales price of goods to customers in the future. Any difference between the expected and the actual sales price achieved will be accounted for in the period in which the sale is made.

Provisions

Provisions have been estimated for onerous leases and discontinued operation exit costs. These provisions represent the best estimate of the liability at the time of the balance sheet date, the actual liability being dependent on future events such as economic environment and marketplace demand. Expectations will be revised each period until the actual liability arises, with any difference accounted for in the period in which the revision is made.

Appendix B: Financial Statements of WHSmith PLC 313

3. GROUP OPERATING PROFIT

£m	2010	2009
Turnover	**1,312**	1,340
Cost of sales	**(650)**	(685)
Gross profit	**662**	655
Distribution costs[1]	**(495)**	(496)
Administrative expenses	**(80)**	(81)
Other income[1]	**2**	5
Group operating profit	**89**	83

[1]Other income is profit attributable to property and the sale of plant and equipment. During the period there was a £3m impairment charge for property, plant and equipment and other intangible assets included in distribution costs (2009: £3m)

£m	2010	2009
Cost of inventories recognised as an expense	**650**	685
Write-down of inventories in the period	**6**	8
Depreciation and amounts written off property, plant and equipment	**34**	37
Amortisation and amounts written off intangible assets	**5**	4
Net operating lease charges		
– land and buildings	**181**	180
– equipment and vehicles	**1**	—
Other occupancy costs	**62**	58
Staff costs (Note 6)	**203**	202
Auditors' remuneration (see below)	**—**	—
Fees payable to Deloitte LLP, the Group's auditors, included in the income statement relate to:		
Fees payable to the Group's auditors for the audit of the Group's annual accounts	**0.1**	0.1
Fees payable to the Group's auditors for other services to the Group including the audit of the Company's subsidiaries	**0.1**	0.1
Total audit fees	**0.2**	0.2
Non-audit fees including taxation and other services	**0.1**	0.1
	0.3	0.3

A description of the work performed by the Audit Committee is set out in the Corporate Governance section of the Directors' Report and Business Review and includes an explanation of how auditor objectivity and independence are safeguarded when non-audit services are provided by auditors. Non-audit fees relate to taxation and turnover rent certification.

314 Appendix B: Financial Statements of WHSmith PLC

16. PROPERTY, PLANT AND EQUIPMENT

£m	Freehold properties	Short-term leasehold	Fixtures & fittings	Equipment & vehicles	Total
Cost or valuation:					
At 1 September 2009	19	145	130	73	367
Additions	—	11	9	9	29
Reclassification	2	(2)	—	—	—
Disposals	—	(2)	(2)	(2)	(6)
At 31 August 2010	**21**	**152**	**137**	**80**	**390**
Accumulated depreciation:					
At 1 September 2009	7	76	78	43	204
Depreciation charge	1	10	10	10	31
Impairment charge	—	1	1	1	3
Reclassification	1	(1)	—	—	—
Disposals	—	(2)	(2)	(2)	(6)
At 31 August 2010	**9**	**84**	**87**	**52**	**232**
Net book value at 31 August 2010	**12**	**68**	**50**	**28**	**158**
Cost or valuation:					
At 1 September 2008	19	141	136	72	368
Additions	—	9	9	5	23
Disposals	—	(5)	(15)	(4)	(24)
At 31 August 2009	**19**	**145**	**130**	**73**	**367**
Accumulated depreciation:					
At 1 September 2008	6	70	79	36	191
Depreciation charge	1	10	12	11	34
Impairment charge	—	1	2	—	3
Disposals	—	(5)	(15)	(4)	(24)
At 31 August 2009	**7**	**76**	**78**	**43**	**204**
Net book value at 31 August 2009	**12**	**69**	**52**	**30**	**163**

The net book value of finance leases contained within these balances is £3m at 31 August 2010 (31 August 2009: £5m).

17. TRADE AND OTHER RECEIVABLES

£m	2010	2009
Current debtors		
Trade debtors	21	22
Other debtors	12	12
Prepayments and accrued income	24	22
	57	56
Non-current debtors		
Prepayments and accrued income	4	4
Total trade and other receivables	61	60

The ageing of the Group's current trade and other receivables is as follows:

£m	2010	2009
Trade and other receivables gross	35	36
Allowance for doubtful debts	(2)	(2)
Trade and other receivables net	33	34
Of which:		
Amounts neither impaired nor past due on the reporting date	29	30
Amounts past due but not impaired		
Less than one month old	3	3
Between one and three months old	1	1
Between three and six months old	—	—
Between six months and one year old	—	—
Trade and other receivables net carrying amount	33	34

An allowance has been made for estimated irrecoverable amounts from the sale of goods at 31 August 2010 of £2m (31 August 2009: £2m). This allowance reflects the application of the Group's provisioning policy in respect of bad and doubtful debts and is based upon the difference between the receivable value and the estimated net collectible amount. The Group establishes its provision for bad and doubtful debts by reference to past default experience. No collateral is held for amounts past due but not impaired.

No trade and other receivables that would have been past due or impaired were renegotiated during the year. No interest is charged on the receivables balance. The other classes within trade and other receivables do not include impaired assets. The Group does not hold collateral over these balances. The directors consider that the carrying amount of trade and other receivables approximates to their fair value.

At 31 August 2010, trade and other receivables of £2m (2009: £2m) were either partially or fully impaired. The ageing analysis of these receivables is as follows:

£m	2010	2009
Less than one month old	—	—
Between one and three months old	—	—
Between three and six months old	1	1
Between six months and one year old	1	1
	2	2

316   Appendix B: Financial Statements of WHSmith PLC

24. NET CASH INFLOW FROM OPERATING ACTIVITIES

£m	2010	2009
Operating profit from continuing operations	89	83
Depreciation of property, plant and equipment	31	34
Impairment of property, plant and equipment	3	3
Amortisation of intangible assets	5	4
Share-based payments	7	6
Increase in inventories	—	(4)
(Increase) / decrease in receivables	(1)	10
Increase in payables	4	5
Pension funding	(13)	(10)
Income taxes paid	(20)	(17)
Charge to provisions	1	—
Cash spend against provisions	(2)	(1)
Net cash inflow from operating activities	104	113